The State and Development in the Third World

Written under the auspices of the Center of International Studies, Princeton University. A list of other Center publications appears at the back of this book.

A *WORLD*
         POLITICS READER

The State and Development in the Third World

EDITED BY
ATUL KOHLI

PRINCETON UNIVERSITY PRESS

Published by
Princeton University Press,
41 William Street,
Princeton, New Jersey 08540
In the United Kingdom:
Princeton University Press,
Guildford, Surrey
Copyright © 1986 by
Princeton University Press
Library of Congress Cataloging
in Publication Data will be
found on the last printed page
of this book
First Princeton Paperback
printing, 1986
First hardcover printing, 1986
LCC 86-5045
ISBN 0-691-07699-5
ISBN 0-691-02245-3 (pbk.)

Clothbound editions of
Princeton University Press books
are printed on acid-free paper,
and binding materials are chosen
for strength and durability.
Paperbacks, while
satisfactory for personal
collections, are not usually
suitable for library rebinding.

Printed in
the United States of America
by Princeton University Press,
Princeton, New Jersey

CONTENTS

THE CONTRIBUTORS

ATUL KOHLI, Assistant Professor of Politics and International Affairs at Princeton University, has been an Associate Editor of *World Politics* and is at present the Review Article Editor of the journal.

TONY SMITH is Professor of Political Science at Tufts University.

ROBERT H. BATES is Henry R. Luce Professor of Political Science at Duke University.

NELSON KASFIR is Professor of Government at Dartmouth College.

DENNIS A. RONDINELLI is Senior Policy Analyst, Office of International Programs, at the Research Triangle Institute, Research Triangle Park, North Carolina.

FRANCINE R. FRANKEL is Professor of Political Science at the University of Pennsylvania.

HENRY A. LANDSBERGER is Professor of Sociology at the University of North Carolina at Chapel Hill.

TIM MCDANIEL is Associate Professor of Sociology at the University of California, San Diego.

DOUGLAS C. BENNETT is Associate Professor of Political Science at Temple University.

KENNETH E. SHARPE is Professor of Political Science at Swarthmore College.

HAROLD CROUCH is Senior Research Fellow, Department of Political and Social Change, at the Research School of Pacific Studies, Australian National University.

ROBERT H. JACKSON is Professor of Political Science at the University of British Columbia.

CARL G. ROSBERG is Professor of Political Science and Director of the Institute of International Studies at the University of California, Berkeley.

The State and Development
in the Third World

INTRODUCTION

By ATUL KOHLI*

THE articles in this volume represent "third generation" concerns in the study of politics of developing countries. In the United States, the systematic study of developing countries began only after World War II. The "first generation" research questions were inspired by ideas about development and modernization: How does one distinguish "traditional" societies from "modern" ones? What does "political development" mean? And what are the probable political consequences of socioeconomic development, especially of industrialization? In the 1960s and 1970s, a number of scholars in both the U.S. and the developing countries reacted to these early questions. They sought to focus attention on colonialism's history of fostering "underdevelopment" and on the continuing negative consequences of neocolonialism and economic dependency. Some of these scholarly concerns, as well as some of the debates among the advocates of the modernization and the dependency approaches, continue to this day. Other scholars have, however, attempted to move beyond this old debate, or simply away from it.

The essays collected in this volume were published in *World Politics* between 1976 and 1984. Within the study of development politics, they share three characteristics: they tend to treat political structures and processes as significant independent forces; they eschew grand theory for middle-level theory and for greater historical specificity; and they are not consumed by the cold-war passion of liberalism versus Marxism.

The common concern with the autonomy of the political gives this volume a degree of analytical unity. The dependent variables explored in these essays are diverse, and they are similar to those that were explored by modernization and dependency scholars: they touch on issues of political stability and of socioeconomic development. In contrast with the earlier approaches, however, emphasis here is on political forces as significant independent variables. Political stability, for example, is more likely to be treated as a function of intra-elite relations or of choices made by state authorities than as a function of excessive social mobilization or imperialist manipulation alone. Similarly, patterns of socioeconomic change are more likely to be explained with reference to the nature and the role of the state than by placing primary emphasis on domestic cultural or external economic forces.

* I would like to acknowledge the helpful comments of Henry Bienen and Lynn White on an earlier draft.

The essays in the present volume emphasize the state and the political process as forces molding third-world development. As a background to contemporary concerns, this introduction furnishes a brief intellectual history of the politics of development, stressing the tendency in both the modernization and the dependency approaches to reduce politics to social and economic forces.

I. The Intellectual Background

The way in which we think about the political problems of contemporary developing countries has been profoundly influenced by the intellectual debates concerning Europe's modernization. The great transformation of the countries of Western Europe from agrarian to industrial political economies engendered conflicting scholarly interpretations of the process. Marx, Durkheim, and Weber stand out as the three social analysts who sought to conceptualize the nature of Europe's transformation, to explain its dynamics, to predict its future, and to identify the heroes and the villains of historical change. The intellectual influence of these thinkers has both enriched and, on occasion, misled the study of contemporary developing countries.

Karl Marx's materialist interpretation of history led him to view capitalism as the motor force that propelled Western Europe's great transformation.[1] Indeed, capitalism as a system of economic production was responsible both for great increases in economic productivity and the relative immiserization of the working class.

Marx argued that, in order to compete with each other, capitalists continuously stimulated technological innovations. This competition improved productivity, but it also tended to shift investment toward machinery, to the detriment of employment and the wages of the working class. Since Marx considered all profits of capitalists to be a function of surplus value, and since surplus value was created only when workers were employed, a shift of investments toward machinery implied an overall tendency toward declining profits. What may have appeared profitable to the individual entrepreneur—continuous technological in-

[1] For a summary review of Marx's political-sociological writings, see Anthony Giddens, *Capitalism and Modern Social Theory* (Cambridge: Cambridge University Press, 1971), Part 1, and Raymond Aron, *Main Currents in Sociological Thought,* 2 Vols. (New York: Anchor Books, Doubleday, 1965), I, pp. 145-236. A good book-length study of Marx's writings is Shlomo Avineri, *Social and Political Thought of Karl Marx* (Cambridge and New York: Cambridge University Press, 1971). For a sampling of Marx's own writings, see the following selections in Robert C. Tucker, ed., *The Marx-Engels Reader* (New York: W. W. Norton, 1972): "German Ideology, Part I," 110-66; "Wage Labor and Capital," 167-90; and "The Eighteenth Brumaire of Louis Bonaparte," 436-525.

novation—thus turned out to be irrational for the capitalist economy as a whole. Observation of this contradiction led Marx to argue that the inner logic of capitalism generated a tendency for rates of profit to fall.

For Marx, a number of characteristics of 19th-century European capitalism, especially English capitalism, were explicable through this inner logic. Capitalists, along with the state and social institutions that supported capitalism, were continuously seeking new strategies for countering the tendency toward declining rates of profit. Pauperization of the working class, overproduction and underconsumption, and the search for overseas markets and cheap raw materials were some manifestations of the larger problem. Marx focused on the process of relative immiserization experienced by the working class; he expected that it would eventually help to precipitate socialist revolutions. When such revolutions did not materialize, some followers of Marx—such as, for instance, Lenin and contemporary dependency theorists—shifted the analytical emphasis away from the working class and toward the capitalist countries' search for overseas markets and products in their attempts to counter declining rates of profit.

What looked like the drama of capitalism to Marx appeared to be the march of industrialization to Emile Durkheim.[2] Remembering the history of revolutionary France, Durkheim was concerned about the stability—"social solidarity"—of industrial Europe. Industrialization involved the specialization of tasks and led to increasingly greater division of labor. Differentiation of roles undermined the cultural unity of preindustrial society—"mechanical solidarity"—because this unity was based on persons performing similar roles and possessing similar world views. Specialization engendered individualism; it led to different life experiences and different values and attitudes toward society. Diversity and the lack of integration in a society's value system could, in turn, threaten social solidarity.

Durkheim considered the breakdown of social order and the emergence of "anomie" as likely only during the transitional stages toward an industrial society. Specialization and increases in the division of labor would give rise to new forms of social solidarity—"organic solidarity." Social cohesion that was based on organic solidarity would be more durable than that based on mechanical solidarity because organic soli-

[2] A review of Durkheim's political-sociological concerns is available in Giddens (fn. 1), Part 2, and Aron (fn. 1), II, pp. 11-118. A good book-length study of Durkheim is Robert Nisbet, *Sociology of Emile Durkheim* (New York: Oxford University Press, 1973). For a sampling of Durkheim's own writings relevant to the present discussion, see Emile Durkheim, *The Division of Labor in Society* (New York: Free Press, 1969), esp. Book 1, chaps. 1-3, sec. 7.4, and the Conclusion.

darity relied on the mutual dependence that division of labor engendered among the members of an industrial society. A modern society may seem to consist of individuals pursuing their individual interests, but, for Durkheim, the pursuit of such interests presupposed the development of norms that govern contractual relations. Shared norms as a framework of individualism suggested that—contrary to the liberal world view— industrialization and division of labor in 20th-century Europe would give rise, not to an atomized society—that could only lead to persistent anomie—but to new forms of shared values and social solidarity.

Durkheim's analysis of the great transformation of Western European societies focused attention on the process of industrialization, the accompanying increases in division of labor, and the resulting changes in a society's value system. The image of this transformation in Durkheim's writings was one of a process with a beginning and an end: the mechanical solidarity of pre-industrial society was slowly supplanted by and moving toward organic solidarity of industrial society; the in-between, transitional periods were characterized by anomie and breakdown. In the writings of later theorists, this image was to inspire the formulation of the well-known dichotomy of tradition and modernity, and of the troubled process of modernization that characterized the transition from one to the other.

The diverse concerns of Marx and Durkheim can be compared and contrasted on many dimensions. They share, however, two characteristic approaches to the analyses of European transformation that are especially relevant to the subject of this volume. First, both considered their respective analyses of capitalism and industrialization to be of general significance; as other societies underwent such changes—and in due course they would—the social dynamics within them would be similar to those observed in a handful of Western European countries. Second, both tended to focus analytical attention on a society's socioeconomic, rather than its political, structure.

Marx held that social and political change was propelled by capitalism as a mode of production and the dynamics of surplus accumulation. Durkheim considered the increasing division of labor and the resulting changes in the value system to be a partial explanation of the vicissitudes of an industrializing society. For both, the drama of the great transformation was located, not in the state, but in the society. The state and politics were peripheral to the major processes of change. Although both Marx and Durkheim paid some attention to the state, they considered a state's actions and a society's politics to be largely a reflection of the more fundamental dynamics of socioeconomic change. Whatever the merits of such perspectives for the study of industrializing Western Europe, their general significance has turned out to be limited. The importance of the state in late-industrializing countries has been considerably greater than in the cases observed by Marx and Durkheim. The perception of the contemporary third world through these 19th-century glasses has therefore often caused the less important to be taken for the more important.

By contrast to Marx and Durkheim, Max Weber was both less general in his theoretical ambitions and more sensitive politically.[3] One of Weber's central concerns was to explain why capitalism and industrialization took root in Western Europe rather than elsewhere. He explored a number of world religions in the belief that religious teachings had a profound influence on "this-worldly," or secular behavior. His argument tracing the "elective affinity" between the Protestant ethic and capitalism left a number of important methodological legacies for future comparativists: pre-modern culture and social structure have a significant influence on whether a society will "naturally" evolve into a developed capitalist one; since there is often a gap between the motivations of the social actors and the unanticipated consequences of their actions, social change may proceed in a manner not understood by the participants; and the best way to theorize about significant social transformations is to ask historically and spatially limited questions.

Weber's political-sociological concerns spanned the issues of the rise of the modern state, the patterns of authority and legitimacy, the role of leadership, and the nature of bureaucracy as the quintessential "rational" organization. With the unification of Germany as historical background, Weber was concerned about Germany "catching up" with the politically and economically more advanced England.[4] Such "modern" issues naturally focused attention on the problems of carving out cohesive and centralized states, and on the creative role of political leaders. The continuing relevance of Weber for comparative studies is in part caused by the pervasiveness of similar political problems in the second half of the 20th century.

[3] A summary review of Weber's concerns is in Giddens (fn. 1), Part 3, and Aron (fn. 1), II, pp. 219-318. For useful book-length studies of Weber's political and sociological writings, see David Beetham, *Max Weber and the Theory of Modern Politics* (London: George Allen & Unwin, 1974), and Reinhard Bendix, *Max Weber: An Intellectual Portrait* (New York: Anchor Books, Doubleday, 1962). For a sampling of Weber's political-sociological writings, see H. H. Gerth and C. Wright Mills, eds., *From Max Weber: Essays in Sociology* (New York: Oxford University Press, 1958), esp. chaps. 3, 4, 7, and 8.

[4] For an elaboration of the argument that Weber was a "rational nationalist," see Wolfgang Mommsen, *The Age of Bureaucracy: Perspectives on the Political Sociology of Max Weber* (New York: Harper & Row, 1974), chap. 2.

Weber's political sociology, however, was biased toward the socio-logical determinism of politics. For him, the dominant impact of modern capitalism was the spread of rationality. The evolution of the modern European state, while partly a product of the centralizing actions of monarchs, was an integral aspect of this larger trend toward the rational reorganization of society. Weber's concept of the modern state thus remained focused on territoriality and on elements of centralized control. Bureaucracy as the efficient modern organization reflected the historical march of rationality. Even socialism was likely only to result in further bureaucratization of society and politics. The idea that the modern state, with all its powers, could not only dominate but transform societies in accordance with the ideologies of its leaders did not penetrate Weber's writings. The political determinism of socioeconomic change, and theo-rizing about it, were not major concerns of the 19th-century analysts; they belong to our times.

Marx, Durkheim, and Weber dominated the 19th-century study of social structural transformations in Western Europe;[5] problems of mod-ernization and development were not widely examined during the first half of the 20th century.[6] During this period, scholars were concerned primarily with the two World Wars and with issues of capitalism versus socialism. When, after World War II, most former European colonies became sovereign states and the United States emerged as the leading world power, the coincidence of these two global changes spawned considerable scholarly interest in the problems of development. This recent political-sociological scholarship on development has proceeded in three waves or "generations" of concerns: the concern with tradition, modernity, and modernization; the focus on the continuing legacy of colonialism in relations of dependency; and the emerging interest in the political determinants of socioeconomic development. After a brief re-view of the modernization and dependency perspectives, I will discuss the renewed scholarly interest in the state in developing countries.

THE MODERNIZATION PERSPECTIVE

In the 1950s and 1960s, a rich and diverse body of literature on modernization and development appeared in the United States, followed by numerous critical and some sympathetic reviews.[7] The main critical

[5] Because some of Weber's major writings were published after the turn of the century, the term "19th century" as I use it here includes work published before World War I.
[6] Exceptions are Joseph Schumpeter, *Capitalism, Socialism, and Democracy* (New York: Harper & Row, reprinted 1983), and various writings by Thorstein Veblen and Bronislaw Malinowski.
[7] For a sampling of these reviews, see Reinhard Bendix, "Tradition and Modernity

theme to be stressed here is the tendency in some of the modernization literature to treat the politics of developing countries as derivative of their cultures and social structure. Although this focus has occasionally generated important new insights, it has also diverted attention from the reverse causal relationship: the role of state authorities and politics in molding socioeconomic change in these countries.

Talcott Parsons' ambitious attempt to develop a general theory of society around the concept of a "functioning social system" provided the theoretical inspiration for the subfield of modernization. Although complex in detail, the structure of Parsons' approach was relatively straightforward.[8] He conceived of all societies as systems of interacting parts. The constituent parts of a social system were actors—with roles and status positions—sharing a common cultural orientation. As culture tended to define group membership ("insiders" and "outsiders"), social systems—characterized by shared culture—tended to be relatively self-sufficient. The parts within the social system were interdependent; change in one part often meant adjustment and change in others. In any case, social systems tended to survive beyond one generation.

Since social systems tended to persist, certain system-maintaining functions common to all of them helped to reproduce shared cultural orientations from one generation to the next. One task of comparative analysis has been to identify these common functions and to delineate the differing structures that actually perform them. Socialization, for example, was a function common to all societies; it could be performed by such different structures as the family, schools, religious organizations, political parties, or even the state. Parsons thus attempted to identify the common "pattern-maintaining" functions of social systems; he hoped that others would use them as a basis for structural-functional analyses of different societies.

Like Durkheim, Parsons sought to devise a classification scheme for social systems. The resulting conceptualization was dichotomous, as Durkheim's had been: all societies were either traditional or modern. Since social systems consisted of interdependent parts, traditional and modern social systems could be defined by "bundles" of co-existing and co-varying attributes. Modern society, for example, was likely to be

---

Reconsidered," *Comparative Studies in Society and History* 9 (April 1967), 292-346; Samuel Huntington, "The Change to Change," *Comparative Politics* 3 (April 1971), 283-322; Mark Kesselman, "Order or Movement? The Literature of Political Development as Ideology," *World Politics* 26 (October 1973), 139-54; and André Gunder Frank, *The Sociology of Development and the Underdevelopment of Sociology* (London: Pluto Press, 1971).

[8] The following discussion is based on Parsons, *The Social System* (New York: Macmillan, 1951), esp. chaps. 1, 2, and 7.

characterized by achievement orientation, functionally specific political
and economic structures, and differentiated roles. Traditional society,
by contrast, would be characterized by ascriptive orientations, low division of labor, and fused roles. Parsons expected that a scheme of this
type would help to classify all social systems and would thus provide
the basis for a more dynamic theory of modernization.

Parsons' abstract formulations had a profound impact on the subfield
of development. Some theorists built on his work in a deductive vein;
others preferred an inductive and empirical approach. Among the former, Neil Smelser extended Parsons' work in a more dynamic direction.[9]
He argued that, as societies industrialized, patterns of integration did
not always keep up with patterns of differentiation. Especially in the
case of late-industrializing countries, forces of differentiation often
moved more rapidly than those of integration. The result—reminiscent
once again of Durkheim—was the breakdown of social order. Maintenance of social order in late-industrializing countries thus required
the state to play a significant role and to utilize state ideologies such as
nationalism.

When the focus on politics in developing countries emerged from
this deductive sociological exercise, the role of the state was reduced and
subordinated to the "primary need" of a society's "pattern maintenance."
At the same time, political scientists were attempting to broaden their
legal-constitutional horizons. As some of them were attracted to Parsons'
work, the reductionist bias seeped into the comparative political study
of developing countries.

The reductionist mode of conceptualizing politics was clear, for example, in the influential work of Gabriel Almond.[10] He considered the
"political system" to be that subsystem of the social system which performed the tasks of "social integration" and "adaptation." Politics was
what it does; and what it did was to help a society integrate and to
adapt. Even though Almond referred favorably to Weber's writings, his
basic conceptualization of politics betrayed a tendency against which
Weber had warned stringently: to define the state in terms of the ends
of political action. It is therefore not totally surprising that this mode
of conceptualizing politics made it logically difficult to focus on the
state's autonomous and transformative role.

The concern with the political system also generated an attempt to

[9] See Smelser, "Mechanisms of Change and Adjustment to Change," in Bert F. Hoselitz
and Wilbert E. Moore, eds., *Industrialization and Society* (Paris: UNESCO, 1963), 32-54.
[10] See Almond's "Introduction," in Gabriel Almond and James Coleman, eds., *The Politics
of the Developing Areas* (Princeton: Princeton University Press, 1960), esp. p. 7.

define political development. The energy that went into this enterprise is legendary. In a review some years ago, Lucian Pye noted that there were at least ten different definitions of political development in the relevant literature. He concluded that all of these definitions tended to focus on one or more of the four salient characteristics of a developed polity: emphasis on equality; rational-legal political institutions; differentiated structures; and a high capacity for solving problems.[11] In another review some years later, Samuel Huntington pointed out that there were internal contradictions even in this succinct list; for example, equality and democracy may not always be compatible with a state's ability to deal with multiple problems. Thus, Huntington rang the death knell on this whole enterprise by suggesting that ten definitions were ten too many, and that the focus of study should be "political change" instead of "political development."[12]

Paralleling these deductive and abstract-definitional exercises, other scholars sought to generalize about the politics of development through more inductive and empirical approaches. Foremost among these were the attempts to trace the impact of economic development on prospects of democratic political change. Lipset, Deutsch, and others viewed the consequences of economic development for democracy in cautiously optimistic terms by analyzing such intermediate variables as the rise of a middle class, the spread of education, or, more generally, social mobilization.[13] By contrast, Huntington's path-breaking work had suggested that economic development was, at least over the short run, more likely to generate "political decay." Huntington's hypothesis focused on the gap between "social mobilization" and "institutionalization" as the explanation of the frequent crises of political order in developing countries.[14] The close parallel between this argument and the Durkheimian argument of Smelser—which focused on the gap between "differentiation" and "integration"—emphasizes the intellectual unity of the scholarship on the subject.

The tendency to reduce politics to socioeconomic variables was widespread in this whole body of modernization literature. Deductive theoretical exercises conceived of the state in developing countries primarily

[11] Pye, *Aspects of Political Development* (Boston: Little, Brown, 1966), chap. 2.

[12] Huntington (fn. 7).

[13] Seymour Martin Lipset, "Some Social Requisites of Democracy: Economic Development and Political Legitimacy," *American Political Science Review* 53 (June 1959), 69-105; Karl W. Deutsch, "Social Mobilization and Political Development," *American Political Science Review* 55 (September 1961), 493-514.

[14] See Samuel P. Huntington, *Political Order in Changing Societies* (New Haven: Yale University Press, 1968), esp. chap. 1.

as helping to maintain the basic patterns of the social system. Aside from its conservative bias, this conception detracted attention from the autonomous role of political authorities in bringing development about. In the more inductive exercises, the focus also was often on the impact of socioeconomic change on the political process. Although there is nothing wrong with this, it led to the neglect of an important political-economic reality in the developing world: socioeconomic change itself was being generated and controlled by the political authorities. Huntington probably went furthest in recognizing the autonomous significance of political institutions. Even he, however, conceived of the state primarily as an agent of political order and only secondarily as a force stimulating socioeconomic transformation.

The tension between theoretically generated concerns and the political realities of the third world was clearest in the works of empirically oriented scholars. Thus, the valuable country studies in Almond and Coleman's *Politics of the Developing Areas* were not well integrated with Almond's own elaborate introductory theoretical discussion.[15] And, despite David Apter's theoretical commitment to the modernization school, his work remains insightful and of continuing significance because his discussion of developmental capabilities of different types of political systems—traditional-autocratic, mobilizational, and reconciliatory—drew much more on his own rich empirical knowledge than on the Durkheim-Parsons approach to modernization.[16] Valuable individual country studies further reflected these tensions. The opening line of Kothari's modernization study of India is telling: "If 'modernization' is the central tendency of our times, it is 'politicization' that provides its driving force."[17] Clearly, the empirical reality of politics and politicians controlling socioeconomic development required a modification of the theoretically generated focus on autonomous socioeconomic development as the determinant of Indian politics. Henry Bienen's major work on Tanzania similarly paid as much attention to socioeconomic determinants of governmental capacities as it did to the role of the Tanzanian government in promoting socioeconomic development.[18]

This body of modernization scholarship, especially the theoretical literature, has come under considerable criticism over the last two decades. Often, preferred alternate approaches were implicit. A few examples demonstrate the variety of the criticisms: Weberian scholars like

---

[15] Almond and Coleman (fn. 10).
[16] Apter, *The Politics of Modernization* (Chicago: University of Chicago Press, 1965), esp. chaps. 6, 10, and 11.
[17] Rajni Kothari, *Politics in India* (Boston: Little, Brown, 1970).
[18] Bienen, *Tanzania: Party Transformation and Economic Development* (Princeton: Princeton University Press, 1967, expanded ed., 1970).

Bendix found the theoretical thrust to be far too evolutionary, over-generalized, and reductionist insofar as it collapsed the distinctions between authority and association, or between the state and society;[19] historically oriented scholars of Europe like Tilly similarly found a neglect of historical variety, and especially of the role of power struggles in historical cases of state building;[20] Mark Kesselman was upset by the ideological conservatism implicit in some of this scholarship;[21] and others on the left found the neglect of the impact of colonialism and neo-colonialism, as well as of political economy variables, so serious that they provided their own alternative dependency framework.[22]

It would be unfair not to note some of the lasting contributions made by scholars working within the modernization school. Intellectual credit must be given where it is due, and we must resist the facile and recurring tendency to reject the scholarship of the past. Many of the development-oriented case studies continue to be considered major works on the politics of the concerned countries.[23] The lasting theoretical contributions of this school of thought have been mainly in their analysis of political instability in the developing countries. The focus on the gap between differentiation and integration, or between social mobilization and institutionalization, has become a matter of common-sense understanding of political disorder. Because the modernization scholarship often drew its inspiration from the writings of Durkheim, and because one of Durkheim's main concerns was "social solidarity," it is not surprising that the lasting general insights have been explanations of social and political instability.

The sources of theoretical strength, however, have also been the root of important intellectual weaknesses. The focus on the destabilizing consequences of socioeconomic development was inspired by 19th-century intellectual concerns: Durkheim was observing a France in which entrepreneurial energies were propelling industrialization. The destabilizing consequences of this fundamental socioeconomic change must have appeared to be so important as to deserve to be placed at the center of intellectual inquiry.

The extrapolation of this mode of inquiry to contemporary concerns

[19] Bendix (fn. 7).
[20] Charles Tilly, ed., *The Formation of National States in Western Europe* (Princeton: Princeton University Press, 1975), Introduction and Conclusion.
[21] Kesselman (fn. 7).
[22] For examples, see Susanne Bodenheimer, *The Ideology of Developmentalism: The American Paradigm—Surrogate for Latin American Studies* (Beverly Hills, CA: Sage, 1971); Frank (fn. 7); and J. Samuel Valenzuela and Arturo Valenzuela, "Modernization and Dependency: Alternative Perspectives in the Study of Latin American Underdevelopment," *Comparative Politics* 10 (July 1978), 535-57.
[23] See, for example, Kothari (fn. 17), and Bienen (fn. 18).

assumes that developing countries are somehow similar to "developing" Western Europe; but they are not. The main agent of socioeconomic change within these countries is not the entrepreneur; it is the state. The absence of entrepreneurial initiatives is actually part of the explanation of underdevelopment. The state must therefore promote socioeconomic development in these countries. A theoretical framework that treats politics and the state as dependent variables, influenced and determined by the more fundamental socioeconomic changes, cannot focus attention on some of the most salient political-economic relationships in the contemporary, state-dominated third-world societies.

THE DEPENDENCY PERSPECTIVE

Strains of third-world nationalism and Marxism combined during the 1960s and 1970s to give rise to a trenchant line of criticism of the modernization perspective.[24] The radical critics found the modernization approach wanting, not only regarding substantial interpretations of the problems of developing countries, but also on methodological and ideological grounds. On issues of substance, dependency-oriented critics disagreed with the modernization school's assumption that the third-world countries were in "the early stages of development." For these critics, underdevelopment was a product of the encounter between the capitalist West and the colonized people of Asia, Africa, and Latin America. Colonialism fostered underdevelopment. Even after the granting of formal sovereignty, ties of economic dependency served to maintain neocolonialism; these contemporary relationships worked to the political-economic advantage of the developed West and to the disadvantage of the underdeveloped third world.

Beyond issues of substance, dependency advocates professed different methodological and ideological allegiances. Methodologically, these scholars found modernization approaches to be ahistorical and formal. They argued for historically oriented scholarship that was nevertheless rooted in theoretical assumptions about the primacy of the economic whole, especially the primacy of capitalism as a system of crossnational relations of dominance and dependency. Ideologically, they chastised modernization scholars for providing intellectual cloaks to cover continued Western designs for dominating and exploiting the third world. By contrast, they perceived themselves as championing the liberation of the third world from both capitalism and imperialism.

The strengths and the weaknesses of the dependency approach to

[24] For a review of the literature, see the essay by Tony Smith in this volume.

development are analyzed by Tony Smith in the first essay of this collection. There is therefore no need for me to review this body of scholarship further at this point. I will only reiterate some of the themes that are important for this volume.

Like the modernization approach, the dependency approach has made some valuable and lasting contributions to the political-economic study of development. The most significant of these are: (1) it recognizes that contemporary developing countries differ in important respects from the industrializing Western countries of the past; (2) it draws attention to world economic conditions as constraints on contemporary developing countries; and (3) it focuses on the interaction of political, social, and economic variables in the systematic study of development.

Numerous lines of criticisms have pointed out the problematic aspects of the dependency approach. The early dependency theory that asserted that the third world's integration into the world capitalist economy actually produced negative development—underdevelopment—is in tatters.[25] The revised dependency position, which suggests that dependent development is possible within the constraints of a world capitalist economy, has demolished the flawed but logical framework of early dependency thinking.[26] It is becoming increasingly clear that it is the respective third-world governments, and their chosen policies, that are responsible for the industrialization drives of some "newly industrializing countries" such as Brazil and South Korea.[27] The dynamics of development thus are being molded by the third-world states themselves rather than by international economic factors only.

This recognition of the significant role of state authorities and politics in development promises to dilute the theoretical thrust of the dependency framework. I do not mean to suggest that the role of the state has been ignored by dependency theorists. Indeed, several scholars who are

[25] For an early statement along these lines, see Paul Baran, *The Political Economy of Growth* (New York: Monthly Review Press, 1957), and André Gunder Frank, *Capitalism and Underdevelopment in Latin America* (New York: Monthly Review Press, 1969). In addition to the critical review of this line of thinking by Smith in this volume, see Robert Kaufman and others, "A Preliminary Test of the Theory of Dependency," *Comparative Politics* 7 (April 1975), 303-30, and Robert W. Jackman, "Dependence on Foreign Investment and Economic Growth in the Third World," *World Politics* 34 (January 1982), 175-98.

[26] The "dependent development" argument has been presented by Fernando Cardoso, "Associated Dependent Development: Theoretical and Practical Implications," in Alfred Stepan, ed., *Authoritarian Brazil: Origins, Policies and Future* (New Haven: Yale University Press, 1973), 142-78; also see Peter Evans, *Dependent Development: The Alliance of Multinational, State, and Local Capital in Brazil* (Princeton: Princeton University Press, 1979).

[27] For an argument along this line, see Atul Kohli, "Democracy and Development," in John Lewis, ed., *Development Strategies: A New Synthesis*, An Overseas Development Council Volume (forthcoming); also see Stephan Haggard, "The Newly Industrializing Countries in the International System," *World Politics* 38 (January 1986), 343-70.

sympathetic to the dependency approach have analyzed third-world states, especially in Latin America. For example, note O'Donnell's focus on the causes and consequences of bureaucratic-authoritarianism;[28] Cardoso's emphasis on populist regimes as harbingers of early Latin American industrialization;[29] and Peter Evans's conceptualization of the state as a significant actor in the alliance for "dependent development."[30]

A problem of much of the Marxist-inspired scholarship of third-world politics is that the logic of political explanation remains reductionist. Even though the significant role of the state in development has been widely recognized, varying explanations of this role share one blindspot: they insist that it must reflect the interests and goals, not of the political elite, but of specifiable economic actors. If the state exhibits "relative autonomy," that must be the consequence of a "Bonapartist" condition whereby the social situation does not permit the establishment of a clear class hegemony, and political authorities emerge as significant mediators.[31] If the state does not clearly pursue policies favoring capitalism, that must be the consequence of a peculiarity of the class structure of a developing society—such as being dominated by "petty bourgeois" or other "intermediate" classes.[32] If the state adopts policies further enmeshing domestic economies with the world economy, that must be a reflection of the altering class balance in favor of those representing the interests of world capitalism.[33] And changes in political organization, especially toward authoritarianism, must result from shifting economic needs to sustain and reproduce capitalism.[34]

I do not wish to dispute the accuracy of any of these specific propositions. The point is a more general one. At a specific level, important and profound insights concerning politics in developing countries have been generated by scholars working in both the modernization and the

---

[28] Guillermo O'Donnell, *Modernization and Bureaucratic Authoritarianism* (Berkeley: University of California Press, 1973). Also see David Collier, ed., *The New Authoritarianism in Latin America* (Princeton: Princeton University Press, 1979).

[29] Fernando Cardoso and Enzo Faletto, *Dependency and Development in Latin America* (Berkeley: University of California Press, 1977).

[30] Evans (fn. 26).

[31] For the development of such an argument with specific reference to South Asia, see Hamza Alavi, "The State in Post-Colonial Societies," *New Left Review* 74 (July-August 1972), 59-82.

[32] A general statement along these lines has been made by Michael Kalecki, *Selected Essays on the Economic Growth of the Socialist and Mixed Economy* (Cambridge and New York: Cambridge University Press, 1972), II, chap. 15. For an application of this idea to a contemporary developing country like India, see K. N. Raj, "The Politics and Economics of Intermediate Regimes," *Economic and Political Weekly* 27 (July 1973), 1189-98.

[33] This is of course a central idea in the dependency literature on Latin America. For example, see Cardoso (fn. 26).

[34] O'Donnell (fn. 28).

neo-Marxist traditions. More generally, however, there are limits to how far one can strain the logic of social determinism in political analysis. Many issues of state intervention for development are simply better analyzed by abandoning the 19th-century analytical commitment to a social logic of politics and admitting that political structures and processes result from a partially autonomous logic—a political logic that cannot be reduced to or derived from social variables.

II. The Concern with the Autonomy of the Political

Dissatisfaction with both the modernization and the dependency approaches has called forth numerous responses, many of which are theoretically anarchic. Some scholars have continued to work within modified modernization and dependency frameworks; others have wondered whether the attempt to generalize about all of the third world is really a meaningful exercise; and still others have attempted to follow new theoretical paths. No coherent "third" alternative to the modernization and dependency approaches has emerged and, in view of the accumulating knowledge concerning the diversity within the so-called third world, none is likely to do so.

Some analytical concerns have been voiced by scholars who are troubled by the tendency in both the modernization and the dependency approaches to reduce politics to socioeconomic variables. They have, in various ways, attempted to restore the significance of the autonomy of the political to their respective analyses of development issues.[35] The essays in this volume can be seen as part of such an ongoing reassessment. Although they were written independently, all are reacting to prevailing ideas. They are attempting to highlight the significance of political variables—state actions, relations among the political elite, political traditions, or patterns of state organization—for patterns of political-economic change in developing countries.

There are two main ways of interpreting the analytical assertion concerning the autonomy of the political. First, political variables may

[35] For examples, see Alfred Stepan, *The State and Society: Peru in Comparative Perspective* (Princeton: Princeton University Press, 1978); John Waterbury, *The Egypt of Nasser and Sadat: The Political Economy of Two Regimes* (Princeton: Princeton University Press, 1983); Ellen Kay Trimberger, *Revolution from Above: Military Bureaucrats and Development in Japan, Turkey, Egypt, and Peru* (New Brunswick, NJ: Transaction Books, 1978); Nora Hamilton, *The Limits of State Autonomy: Post-Revolutionary Mexico* (Princeton: Princeton University Press, 1982); Peter Evans, Dietrich Rueschemeyer, and Theda Skocpol, *Bringing the State Back In* (Cambridge and New York: Cambridge University Press, 1985); Robert H. Bates, *Markets and States in Tropical Africa* (Berkeley: University of California Press, 1981); Atul Kohli, *The State and Poverty in India: The Politics of Reform* (Cambridge and New York: Cambridge University Press, 1986).

be understood to have independent significance because those who control state power are in a position to take decisions of far-reaching socioeconomic consequences. Although these political decisions may on occasion reflect the interests and pressures of other powerful actors—at home or abroad—they usually manifest the interests and ideologies of the state authorities. State actions are thus political choices. While choices are always made within constraints, they are, nevertheless, choices. Patterns of state intervention in society can thus be empirically analyzed for understanding both why specific development strategies or options were adopted and, more importantly, the consequences of the political choices for political and economic change.[36]

The other sense in which political variables are of autonomous significance has to do with the continuity that political traditions often exhibit. Political cultures and structures do not alter readily in response to socioeconomic change. Authoritarian values and structures, for example, are not easily transformed by the spread of education or the rise of a middle class. Patterns of regime formation, as well as the mode in which political demands are made, and their intensity, are thus likely to be as much a product of the political past as of present socioeconomic patterns.

These analytical assertions clearly do not add up to a new theoretical perspective. They do, however, provide an alternative set of glasses through which some aspects of third-world development can be viewed and interpreted. The articles collected in this volume tend to adopt such a political perspective.

The first four essays are concerned with theoretical and conceptual issues. Tony Smith's article reviews the dependency approach to development in light of diverse empirical materials. Smith argues that the dependency perspective exaggerates the significance of the world capitalist economy and underestimates the autonomous capacity of sovereign third-world states for mobilizing their internal resources. He maintains that a more suitable perspective would highlight the diversity in state structures within the third world and the different capacities of these states to facilitate development.

Robert Bates criticizes the idea of "natural" and "peasant" views of precapitalist agrarian societies. Since the assumptions about the nature of precapitalism influence our understanding of contemporary issues, it

---

[36] I have developed this general argument in several of my recent writings. For examples, see Kohli (fn. 35), chap. 1; Kohli (fn. 27); and Atul Kohli and others, "Inequality in the Third World: An Assessment of Competing Explanations," *Comparative Political Studies* 17 (October 1984), 283-318.

is important to investigate them. Bates argues that the prevailing approaches are either overly culturally or overly economically determined. Many features of the "natural community" or "peasant society," like those of "precapitalism," are in part the products of an encounter with capitalism and in part the results of the effects of state authorities to control and dominate rural populations.

The arguments of the next two essays could apply to a number of countries, but the articles focus on specific issues. Nelson Kasfir finds the analysis of ethnicity by liberal and Marxist scholars wanting because of their neglect of the "fluid and intermittent" character of ethnic identity and ethnic conflict. Building on African materials, he argues that "the political situation—both the present moment and its historical development—contains the causal factors impelling an individual to prefer a particular social identity."

Dennis Rondinelli examines the problems of policy implementation. Although he makes specific policy recommendations on implementing integrated rural development programs, his point is of general significance: successful implementation of development policies, especially those that seek to reconcile growth with equity, presuppose political commitment and appropriate administrative design. Patterns of state organization and action are thus important variables in the understanding of both economic policy implementation and patterns of economic development.

These four general essays stress the significance of political variables in the analysis of development issues. A similar emphasis emerges in the empirical studies that follow.

Francine Frankel's discussion of India focuses on the causes of slow economic growth and the persistence of massive poverty in that country, asserting that these economic conditions are related to the political failure to reorganize India's agrarian structure and especially the failure to implement land reforms. She wonders whether an authoritarian regime that utilizes compulsion would be more successful in implementing far-reaching structural changes from above, and concludes by arguing against authoritarianism: a democratic regime with its power base among the poor is, to her mind, more likely to be a successful agent of redistributive reforms.

Henry Landsberger and Tim McDaniel trace the demise of Allende's left-of-center government in Chile to the "hypermobilization" of the working class. While some of this excessive social mobilization was part of the overall process of socioeconomic change (thus supporting Huntington's ideas), the process was accelerated by Allende's policies. The

UP government further mobilized the working class in order to strengthen its power base. The strategy backfired: excessive mobilization created economic expectations that could not be met; it increased support for the extreme left, made the right much more politically wary, and de-institutionalized established political patterns. Faulty mobilization strategies of state authorities thus contributed to the breakdown of a left-of-center democratic regime.

Douglas Bennett and Kenneth Sharpe analyze the bargaining process between the Mexican state and the transnational automobile industries. During the 1960s, the result turned out to be relatively favorable for the foreign automobile companies. In order to explain this outcome, the authors focus on issues of agenda setting and bargaining. They find that only those issues on which there was a considerable conflict of interest were placed on the agenda; a number of other important questions, like the consequences of the agreements for the Mexican working class, were simply not part of the discussion. The bargaining outcome, in turn, partly reflected the relative power resources of the transnationals vis-à-vis the Mexican state, but it was also determined by the failure of the Mexican state to utilize fully the power resources at its disposal.

Harold Crouch analyzes the military rule in Indonesia. Sukarno's regime, he suggests, had some of the characteristics that, according to Weber, defined patrimonial ruling arrangements: patronage among elites and exclusion of the masses. As the masses became politicized, however, elite cleavages developed on issues other than patronage. Significant ideological conflict emerged, leading to a breakdown of Sukarno's patrimonial style of rule and, eventually, to military rule. Ironically, the military rulers have, in turn, sought to establish stability by recreating arrangements of a patrimonial type. Over the short run, the military rulers have had some success. Elite conflict and unrest from below, however, make it increasingly difficult to govern purely through patrimonial arrangements.

Finally, Robert Jackson and Carl Rosberg seek to explain why and how Africa's weak and unstable states have survived as states. In an innovative argument, they suggest that the survival of weak states has been a function of the norms and imperatives of the international state system. Because of the value that is placed on state sovereignty in the international political system, even the weakest states, once created, tend to survive as juridical entities. The state system, though historically created by strong and centralized European states, has today become a precondition for the survival of weak third-world states.

The essays in this volume seek to explain issues of political stability and socioeconomic development. While some of the points they cover are not mentioned in this introduction, each of the articles can be read as highlighting the significance of the political determinants of development. Moving beyond reductionist tendencies in both modernization and dependency analyses, this volume thus seeks to draw attention to the significant role of the state in the contemporary third world.

Part I
Conceptual Issues

THE UNDERDEVELOPMENT OF DEVELOPMENT LITERATURE:

The Case of Dependency Theory

By TONY SMITH*

IN the midst of the turbulent seventies, when the ascendancy of the "South," or non-Communist industrializing countries, is everywhere in evidence, it is a bit difficult to remember back to the sixties when the social science establishment in the United States apparently dominated world literature on the topic of political and economic modernization in Africa, Asia, and Latin America. The end of colonialism and the expansion of this country's global power into the "vacuums" open to revolutionary activity were largely responsible for calling forth much of this scholarly effort; and, thanks to a growing interest in model building and to well-financed opportunities in area studies, solid professional careers were built in relatively short order. Some of this work has stood the test of time: monographs on delimited problems or, more rarely, theoretical explorations of general patterns of development. For the most part, however, standards of historical scholarship were not high, and to reread the methodological sections of these works with their jargon and their models is often a tedious affair, tempered only by amazement at the poverty of it all. Nor did this literature do much apparent good in influencing political judgment in Washington, if the last two decades of American policy in Southeast Asia or Latin America are any standard by which to measure.

Today a rival literature has appeared on the scene which might be called dependency theory. North Americans figure in its ranks, but the writers are more likely to bear African, Asian, or Latin American surnames. The term "dependency" originated with writings on Latin America; previously, work of this sort was better known for speaking of "neocolonialism," thereby betraying its African or Asian origins. As the different nomenclature suggests, the *dependencistas*, if we may use their Latin American name, are no monolithic group. Their general outlook has been in evidence for some time in a variety of places, so that substantial disagreements exist within this "school." Nevertheless,

* This work was done under the auspices of a grant from the Rockefeller Foundation Program on Conflict in International Relations.

it is useful to distinguish the *dependencistas* as a group, since in important respects these writers share an identity of outlook.

Probably the chief feature of the dependency school is its insistence that it is not internal characteristics of particular countries so much as the structure of the international system—particularly in its economic aspects—that is the key variable to be studied in order to understand the form that development has taken in non-communist industrializing countries. Such an emphasis is not the only distinguishing mark of dependency literature, of course: it tends to put more weight on the interaction of political and economic forces than does its developmentalist rival, and it often identifies itself as being unambiguously on the side of change in the South in order to benefit the poorest and most oppressed members of society there. But, as its name implies, dependency theory's most distinctive point is its insistence that the logic of contemporary southern development can only be grasped by placing this process firmly within a globally defined historical context. That is, contemporary political and economic change in the South must be understood as aspects of imperialism today and yesterday. From this perspective alone—from the standpoint of local histories globally understood—can the logic of the development process be comprehended correctly.

As a result, dependency literature has emerged as a powerful ideological vehicle joining southern nationalists and Marxists (together with their northern supporters) within the confines of a generally agreed-upon form of historical analysis. The importance of this union, whatever the tensions existing within it, should not be underestimated: dependency theory is not simply an academic exercise. For the most part, *dependencistas* are committed by their ideas to a form of political action (as they would maintain their developmentalist opponents in the United States to be, however much the latter might deny it). The literature stands out, therefore, because it is something more than a movement in the intellectual history of our day; it is an ideology as well—a form of discourse able to motivate significant political activity. That is, dependency theory represents far more than the intellectual association of Marxism and southern nationalism. It also represents an effort at the practical, concrete unification of two of the most important historical forces of our century, with potentially significant consequences for both local and world history.

This essay is an attempt to investigate what I believe to be a major historiographic failure of dependency theory. It is not intended to assess the relevance of this theory to concrete historical change, nor is it meant as a comprehensive review of the literature (needed as both of these studies are). My argument is simply that dependency theory in general substantially overestimates the power of the international system—or imperialism—in southern affairs today. This is not to deny that northern power is real in the South, nor to dispute that its effect may be to reinforce the established order of rank and privilege there, nor to suggest that imperialism is a term altogether lacking in meaning today. But it is to assert that dependency theory has systematically underestimated the real influence of the South over its own affairs, and to point out the irony of nationalists who have forgotten their own national histories. I hope to suggest not only a critical flaw in dependency theory as it is now written, but an alternative approach to the study of subordinate states in the international system.

I

Although it is an obvious oversimplification to reduce a complex and variously interpreted position to a few propositions, I will attempt to present a summary of the general tenets of the "dependency" or "neocolonial" form of historical analysis; further discussion will show that there are substantial disagreements among its different proponents. According to the best-known exponents of this perspective, the sovereign states of the South have long been dependent for an evolving mixture of technology, financing, markets, and basic imports on the international economic system dominated by the northern capitalist powers (including Japan). These less developed countries may be called "hooked": they cannot exist without their dependence, but they also cannot exist with it.

According to this thesis, the Third-World countries cannot do with their dependence because their form of incorporation into the international system has tended to inhibit their industrialization, relegating their economies to the less dynamic forms of growth associated with agriculture or the extractive industries. A surprising number of dependency theorists—until quite recently the great majority—have maintained that these countries would simply be unable to move beyond the industrialization associated with limited import substitution. As we shall see, such a basic error in analysis is typical of this group's way of thinking and of its preference for conclusions dictated by theoretically logical but empirically unsubstantiated concepts drawn on the grand scale. No wonder, then, that a number of statistically minded political economists have sought to test these propositions and have been unable to confirm them: it appears as a general rule that the countries most integrated into the world economy have tended to grow more quickly over a longer period than those that are not.[1] To those dependency theorists like Fernando Henrique Cardoso, however, who see the clear evidence that the manufacturing sector *is* expanding dramatically in many Third-World countries, the process remains nonetheless neocolonial, since the leading sectors are inevitably controlled by multinational corporations with headquarters in the North.[2] These corporations, despite whatever benefits they may bring in the form of managerial and technological know-how, take more than they give and—what is more important—make it virtually impossible for local, self-sustaining industrialization to occur. This form of analysis has affinities with Marxism, for it is the economic process which is seen as the dynamic of history. Thus, the stages of economic development of the international system (from mercantilism to free trade to finance capital to the multinational corporation, to take one possible way of marking its development through time) come to interact with the various pre-industrial economies in ways that may be different but that in every case soon establish the dominance of the world order over the form of growth followed locally. Over time, imperialism changes in form but not in fact.[3] Dependency theorists do not argue in any dia-

[1] See Robert Kaufman and others, "A Preliminary Test of the Theory of Dependency," *Comparative Politics,* VII (April 1975); David Ray, "The Dependency Model and Latin America: Three Basic Fallacies," *Journal of Interamerican Affairs and World Studies,* XV (February 1973); Patrick J. McGowan, "Economic Dependency and Economic Performance in Black Africa," *Journal of Modern African Studies,* XIV (No. 1, 1976); Elliot J. Berg, "Structural Transformation versus Gradualism: Recent Economic Development in Ghana and the Ivory Coast," in Philip Foster and Aristide R. Zolberg, *Ghana and the Ivory Coast: Perspectives on Modernization* (Berkeley: University of California Press 1971); and Patrick J. McGowan and Dale L. Smith, "Economic Dependency in Black Africa: An Analysis of Competing Theories," *International Organization,* XXXII (Winter 1978).

[2] Fernando Henrique Cardoso, "Associated-Dependent Development: Theoretical and Practical Implications," in Alfred Stepan, ed., *Authoritarian Brazil: Origins, Policies and Future* (New Haven: Yale University Press 1973), and Cardoso, "Dependent Capitalist Development in Latin America," *New Left Review,* Vol. 74 (July-August 1972).

[3] While the local economies as well as the international system are seen to change over time, in these analyses the dominant partner and therefore the shaper of the overall movement is always the world economy. The subordinate member develops as a "reflection" (Theotonio Dos Santos) or with a "reflex reaction" (Dieter Senghass) to these forces which it can neither escape nor control. Among others, see Theotonio Dos Santos, "The Structure of Dependence," *American Economic Review,* Vol. 60, (May 1970); Dieter Senghass, "Introduction" to a special number called "Overcoming Underdevelopment," *Journal of Peace Research,* XII (No. 4, 1975); Susanne Bodenheimer, "Dependency and Imperialism: The Roots of Latin American Underdevelopment," in K. T. Fann and Donald C. Hodges, eds., *Readings in U.S. Imperialism* (Boston: Porter Sargent 1971).

lectically recognizable fashion that the process is sowing the seeds of its own destruction. For the present at least, the system is still expanding and consolidating its gains.[4]

But if the Third World cannot do with its dependent status, neither can it do without it. For what has occurred is that the local political elites in these areas have almost invariably structured their domestic rule on a coalition of internal interests favorable to the international connection. Thus, it is not the sheer economic might of the outside that dictates the dependent status of the South, but the sociological consequences of this power. The result, as most dependency theorists see it, is that the basic needs of the international order must be respected by the South if this system is to continue to provide the services that the local elites need in order to perpetuate their rule in their turn. In other words, a symbiotic relationship has grown up over time in which the system has created its servants whose needs dictate that its survival be ensured, whatever the short-term conflicts of interests may be. In the case of decolonization, for example, the nationalists who led the drive against colonialism in Africa and Asia potentially faced two foes other than their colonial rulers: local rival class or ethnic groups whose loyalty the nationalists had not managed to secure; and hostile neighboring peoples who were anxious to ensure their interests in the wake of the departing northerners. The situation did not significantly alter once independence was obtained: civil war and jealous neighbors—in each case potentially abetted by the East-West confrontation—continue to jeopardize the independent regimes. Thus the system has at its disposal sanctions for transgressing its basic rules which are all the more powerful since their greatest force comes *not from an active threat of intervention* so much as *from a threat of withdrawal*, which would abandon these dependent regimes to civil and regional conflict; a great many of them would be quite unprepared to face such a fate. So far as I am aware, this last point has not been made by any of the dependency theorists. Nevertheless, it is clearly implicit in their form of analysis. Once again, there are affinities with Marxism: it is understood that economic forces do not act alone in any sense, but must be grasped sociologically as modes or relations of production creating specific configurations of political conflict over time.

---

[4] Immanuel Wallerstein does not foresee the end of the system for another century or two. See "Dependence in an Interdependent World: The Limited Possibilities of Transformation within the Capitalist World Order," *African Studies Review*, xvii (April 1974), 2.

Certain observations made by the dependency theorists are persuasive and serve as a useful antidote to the claims of those who see in decolonization's "transfer of power" more of a watershed in world history than was actually the case. But these insights exist alongside a number of arguments of dubious validity which I would link to a single yet fundamental theoretical shortcoming common to this style of thinking. Too many writers of this school make the mistake of assuming that since the whole (in this case the international system) is greater than the sum of its parts (the constituent states), the parts lead no significant existence separate from the whole, but operate simply in functionally specific manners as a result of their place in the greater system. They hold that it is sufficient to know the properties of the system as a whole to grasp the logic of its parts; no special attention need be paid to specific cases insofar as one seeks to understand the movement of the whole. "Apart from a few 'ethnographic reserves,' all contemporary societies are integrated into a world system," writes Samir Amin, an Egyptian working in Africa and known in Europe as a leading dependency theorist. "Not a single concrete socio-economic formation of our time can be understood except as part of this world system."[5] As a consequence, in the words of André Gunder Frank, one of the more influential members of this school working on Latin America, "underdevelopment was and still is generated by the very same historical process which also generated economic development: the development of capitalism itself."[6] In myriad forms, the argument appears again and again. A writer on contemporary African politics asserts that underdevelopment "expresses a particular relationship of *exploitation*: namely, the exploitation of one country by another. All the countries named as 'underdeveloped' in the world are exploited by others and the underdevelopment with which the world is now preoccupied is a product of capitalist, imperialist and colonialist exploitation."[7] A book comparing China's and Japan's economic growth after their contact with the West goes so far as to maintain that Ch'ing China and Tokugawa Japan were fairly similar up to the early 1800's, and that any later differences in their economic performance may be explained chiefly by the character of their contact with the West:

[5] Samir Amin, *Accumulation on a World Scale: A Critique of the Theory of Underdevelopment*, I (New York: Monthly Review Press 1974), 3.

[6] André Gunder Frank, "The Development of Underdevelopment," in James D. Cockcroft and others, *Dependence and Underdevelopment: Latin America's Political Economy* (New York: Anchor Books 1972), 9.

[7] Walter Rodney, *How Europe Underdeveloped Africa* (London: Bogle-l'Ouverture 1973), 21-22; emphasis in original.

This study argues that the paramount influence in the rise of industrial capitalism in Japan was . . . [that Japan] occupied a position of relative autonomy within the nineteenth-century world political economy. For a variety of reasons other societies were more strongly incorporated as economic and political satellites of one or more of the Western capitalist powers, which thwarted their ability to industrialize. . . . in contrast . . . China's location in the world political economy dominated by the Western capitalist nations, must be considered of prime importance in China's failure to develop industrial capitalism during the nineteenth and twentieth centuries. China was more strongly incorporated than Japan and thus lacked the autonomy to develop the same way.[8]

Other scholars report they "view Latin America as a continent of inadequate and disappointing fulfillment and seek to pinpoint the co-ordinates of sustained backwardness in examining the process of economic change in a dependent, peripheral, or colonial area."[9] And a book on the Middle East concludes,

The products of Turkish craftsmen, well known and in great demand in Europe during the seventeenth and eighteenth centuries, declined along with the products of the rest of the Middle East when Turkey failed to keep pace with the industrial development of the West. Machine production swept craftsmanship off the markets not only in Europe, but also in Turkey. The latter fell back on agriculture, but in 1908, under the Young Turk movement, she began to take an interest in industrial development.[10]

In the United States, this general argument has reached its fullest expression in the work of Immanuel Wallerstein.[11] In a companion essay written after the completion of *The Modern World System*, Wallerstein approvingly cites Georg Lukacs and says that a central tenet of Marxist historiography is that the study of society should "totalize," or begin with an understanding of the whole. The passage from Lukacs is worth quoting:

It is not the predominance of economic themes in the explanation of history which distinguishes Marxism from bourgeois science in a decisive

[8] Frances V. Moulder, *Japan, China, and the Modern World-Economy: Toward a Reinterpretation of East Asian Development* (New York: Cambridge University Press 1977), vii-viii.

[9] Stanley J. Stein and Barbara H. Stein, *The Colonial Heritage of Latin America: Essays on Economic Dependency in Perspective* (New York: Oxford University Press 1970), viii.

[10] Kurt Grunwald and Joachim O. Ronall, *Industrialization in the Middle East* (New York: Council for Middle Eastern Affairs Press 1960), 331.

[11] Wallerstein's first book in a four-volume series has been published under the instructive title *The Modern World System: Capitalist Agriculture and the Origins of the European World-Economy in the Sixteenth Century* (New York: Academic Press 1974).

fashion, it is the point of view of the totality. The category of the totality, the domination determining in all domains of the whole over the parts, constitutes the essence of the method Marx borrowed from Hegel and that he transformed in an original manner to make it the foundation of an entirely new science. . . . The reign of the category of the totality is the carrier of the revolutionary principle in science.[12]

Working from this perspective, Wallerstein declares that "the only kind of social system is a world-system, which we define quite simply as a unit with a single division of labor and multiple cultural systems." He explains:

But if there is no such thing as "national development" . . . the proper entity of comparison is the world system. . . . If we are to talk of stages, then—and we should talk of stages—it must be stages of social systems, that is, of totalities. And the only totalities that exist or have existed historically are mini-systems ["simple agricultural or hunting and gathering societies"] and world systems, and in the nineteenth and twentieth centuries there has been only one world-system in existence, the capitalist world economy.[13]

This tyranny of the whole over the parts can be easily illustrated in Wallerstein's own work on the sixteenth century; but I will look instead at the work that dependency theorists have done on the problems of underdevelopment in the world of the last two centuries. Here the American most frequently and favorably mentioned by the members of this school is Paul Baran. Appropriately enough, Baran chose as the epigraph for his book *Monopoly Capital* (written with Paul Sweezy) Hegel's dictum "The Truth is the Whole." And fortunately for our purposes, Baran's writing is a particularly egregious example of this form of reductionist historiography.

Taking the case of Indian economic development, Baran makes of the country under the pressure of British imperialism a *tabula rasa* such that whatever the land's problems past or present, they spring directly from this foreign presence. In a passage extraordinary in its exaggeration, he writes:

Thus, the British administration of India systematically destroyed all the fibres and foundations of Indian society. Its land and taxation policy ruined India's village economy and substituted for it the parasitic landowner and moneylender. Its commercial policy destroyed the Indian artisan and created the infamous slums of the Indian cities filled with

[12] Georg Lukacs, "Rosa Luxembourg, Marxiste," in *Histoire et conscience de classe* (Paris: Editions de Minuit 1960), 47-48.
[13] Wallerstein, "The Rise and Future Demise of the World Capitalist System," *Comparative Studies in Society and History*, xvi (September 1974), 390.

millions of starved and diseased paupers. Its economic policy broke down whatever beginnings there were of an indigenous industrial development and promoted the proliferations of speculators, petty businessmen, agents, and sharks of all descriptions.[14]

Baran speculates on what India's fate might have been without the British: "Indeed, there can be no doubt that had the amount of economic surplus that Britain has torn from India been invested in India, India's economic development to date would have borne little similarity to the actual somber record. . . . India, if left to herself, might have found in the course of time a shorter and surely less tortuous road toward a better and richer society."[15]

But surely this account—which is based on virtually no hard evidence —imputes far too much power (for evil or otherwise) to the British. Thus, despite his allegation that India without the British might have found its own autonomous way to industrial development with less human suffering, Baran makes no effort to assess the probability that Mogul India could have accomplished such a transformation or to evaluate what price the pre-British system exacted from its subjects. Life was surely not easy under the Moguls. Warfare was constant, particularly in the years preceding the British takeover, and the levels of taxation were quite high. The most significant accounts of which I am aware dismiss the likelihood that pre-British India had any capacity for sustained economic change. As M. D. Morris writes, "The British did not take over a society that was 'ripe' for an industrial revolution and then frustrate that development. They imposed themselves on a society for which every index of performance suggests the level of technical, economic and administrative performance of Europe five hundred years earlier."[16]

It is not at all accurate to suggest, as Baran so adamantly does, that pre-British India was without original sin or that the British were the authors of unmitigated evil. "Parasitic landowners and moneylenders" were not unknown before the British set foot on the subcontinent; British "commercial policy" is now thought by some to have "destroyed" far fewer artisans than was previously believed; British economic policy surely did more to create the foundations for industrial society in India than to "break down whatever beginnings there were" (however much the effort fails by comparison with Meiji Japan);

---

[14] Paul Baran, *The Political Economy of Growth* (2d ed.; New York: Monthly Review Press 1962), 149.

[15] *Ibid.*, 150.

[16] Morris D. Morris, "Towards a Reinterpretation of Nineteenth-Century Indian Economic History," *Indian Economic and Social History Review*, v (March 1968), 6-7.

British "land and taxation policy," far from "ruining" the village economy, was surely less exploitive than that of the Great Mogul and probably provided for a modest per capita increase of income during the nineteenth century; and British "administration" did not destroy "all the fibres and foundations of Indian society," but actually accommodated itself rather well to indigenous ways in the manner of most conquerors of large populations.[17] Of course there is no particular reason to sing hosannas about the British presence. For example, British rule clearly inhibited industrialization in the late-nineteenth century: the efforts of the Lancashire cotton processors especially were successful in keeping Indian customs duties low until World War I, and so stunted the growth of Indian manufactures.[18] But as the Great Mutiny of 1857 demonstrated, India herself possessed strong forces resisting change. In what seems to be a balanced judgment of the forces guiding India's development, Barrington Moore puts the effects of British policy within the context of the persisting strength of indigenous practices and institutions:

> In addition to law and order, the British introduced into Indian society during the nineteenth century railroads and a substantial amount of irrigation. The most important prerequisites for commercial agricutural and industrial growth would seem to have been present. Yet what growth there was turned out to be abortive and sickly. Why? A decisive part of the answer, I think, is that *Pax Britannica* simply enabled the landlord and now also the moneylender to pocket the surplus generated in the countryside that in Japan paid for the first painful stages of industrialization. As foreign conquerors, the English were not in India to make an industrial revolution. They were not the ones to tax the countryside in either the Japanese or the Soviet fashion. Hence, beneath the protective umbrella of Anglo-Saxon justice-under-law, parasitic landlordism became much worse than in Japan. To lay all the blame on British shoulders is obviously absurd. There is much evidence . . . to demonstrate that this blight was inherent in India's own social structure and traditions. Two centuries of British occupation merely allowed it to spread and root more deeply throughout Indian society.[19]

[17] See Barrington Moore, Jr., *Social Origins of Dictatorship and Democracy: Lord and Peasant in the Making of the Modern World* (Boston: Beacon Press 1966), chap. 6; Angus Maddison, *Class Structure and Economic Growth: India and Pakistan since the Moghuls* (London: Allen and Unwin 1971); Morris (fn. 16), and "Trends and Tendencies in Indian Economic History," *Indian Economic and Social History Review*, v (December 1968).

[18] Romesh Dutt, *The Economic History of India: In the Victorian Age, 1837–1900* (2d ed.; Delhi: Ministry of Information and Broadcasting, Government of India 1970), Book II, chap. 12, and Book III, chap. 9; Daniel Houston Buchanan, *The Development of Capitalistic Enterprise in India* (New York: Macmillan 1934), 465-67.

[19] Moore (fn. 17), 354-55.

When Baran takes up the question of the reasons for the success of Japanese industrialization, he advances the same reductionist formula: once again the part (Japan) disappears into the momentum of the whole (the dynamism of expansionist capitalistic imperialism):

> What was it that enabled Japan to take a course so radically different from that of all the other countries in the now underdeveloped world? ... reduced to its core, it comes down to the fact that Japan is the only country in Asia (and in Africa or in Latin America) that escaped being turned into a colony or dependency of Western European or American capitalism, that had a chance of independent national development.[20]

In explaining why Japan was not so incorporated, Baran refers once more to the properties of the international system: its preoccupation with other parts of Asia, its conviction that Japan was poor in markets and resources, its internal rivalries. That Japan may have escaped colonial rule and initiated the single successful attempt to industrialize outside of North America and Europe in the nineteenth century for reasons having to do with forces internal to the country is an idea to which Baran does not pay the slightest heed. Indeed, he is so ignorant of conditions in late Tokugawa Japan that he calls the Meiji Restoration a bourgeois revolution.

There is no doubt that the international system under the expansionist force of European and American capitalism has had an impact on the internal development of technologically backward areas of the world over the last two centuries. Dependency theorists make us aware how intense and complex these interactions were (and still are), and there is substance to their criticism that development literature as it is currently written in the United States tends to mask these linkages for its own ideological reasons.[21] Nor is my objection to the simple omission of evidence relevant to the construction of an historical argument. Selective judgment in the presentation of material is an inevitable part of the study of history. Rather, the objection is to a certain style of thinking which—to use two of the dependency school's favorite words —is biased and ideological, distorting evidence as much in its fashion as the "bourgeois science" that it claims to debunk.

As I suggested earlier, the chief methodological error of this kind of writing is to deprive local histories of their integrity and specificity, thereby making local actors little more than the pawns of outside

---

[20] Baran (fn. 14), 158.
[21] André Gunder Frank, "Sociology of Underdevelopment and Underdevelopment of Sociology," in Cockcroft (fn. 6); Susanne J. Bodenheimer, *The Ideology of Developmentalism: The American-Paradigm-Surrogate for Latin American Studies* (Beverly Hills, Calif.: Sage Professional Papers in Comparative Politics 1971).

forces. Feudalism as a force in Latin America? Nonsense, says Frank (to be applauded by Wallerstein); since capitalism has penetrated every nook and cranny of the world system, the concept of feudal relations of production cannot be validly used.[22] Destroy the particular, exalt the general in order to explain everything. Cite Hegel: "The Truth is the Whole." Tribalism as a force in Africa? Colin Leys cannot even bring himself to use the word without putting it in quotation marks, asserting that "among Africanists [this] point . . . perhaps no longer needs arguing." " 'Tribalism,' " Leys maintains, "is a creation of colonialism. It has little or nothing to do with pre-colonial relations between tribes. . . . In neo-colonial Africa, class formation and the development of tribalism accompany each other."[23] Why? Because the logic of the whole (capitalist colonialism) has found it expedient to work its will in the part (Africa) through creating, virtually *ex nihilo*, the divisive force of "tribalism." By such reckoning, all the social structures in history after a certain low level of development in the division of labor could be dissolved—feudal and bureaucratic estates, castes and clans, as well as tribes—in favor of class analysis, the only "real" social formation.

Because this approach is formulistic and reductionist, it is bad historiography. It is formulistic in the sense that it seeks to specify universal laws or processes in blatant disregard of the singular or the idiosyncratic. By the same token it is reductionist, since it forces the particular case to express its identity solely in the terms provided by the general category. The error of this approach is not that it draws attention to the interconnectedness of economic and political processes and events in a global manner, but that it refuses to grant the part *any* autonomy, *any* specificity, *any* particularity independent of its membership in the whole. Such writing is tyrannical. And it has its ties, I suspect, with other ways in which these writers view history. Thus, as late as 1962, in the preface to the second edition of *The Political Economy of Growth* (much lauded by dependency theorists), Paul Baran gives his *nihil obstat* to Stalin's forced industrialization of the Soviet Union in terms that depend for their authority on the author's ability to "totalize," to grasp the logic of the whole.[24]

[22] André Gunder Frank, "The Development of Underdevelopment," and "Economic Dependence, Class Structure, and Underdevelopment Policy," in Cockcroft (fn. 6); Wallerstein (fn. 13). For criticism of Frank's view, see Ernesto Laclau, "Imperialism in Latin America," *New Left Review*, Vol. 67 (May-June 1971); Michael Barratt Brown, *The Economics of Imperialism* (New York: Penguin Books 1974), chap. 11.

[23] Colin Leys, *Underdevelopment in Kenya: The Political Economy of Neo-Colonialism, 1964–1971* (Berkeley: University of California Press 1974), 198-99.

[24] Baran (fn. 14), xxxvi.

The problem of the relationship of the whole to the parts is, of course, a recurrent one in the social sciences. The only key to understanding their interaction, so far as I am aware, is to recognize that, while the whole does have a logic undiscernible from analysis of the parts considered separately, the parts too have an identity that no amount of understanding of the whole will adequately reveal. In his monumental *Critique de la raison dialectique*, Jean-Paul Sartre makes a telling criticism of Marxists who make "a fetish of totalizing." He illustrates it with an example of the problem of relating an individual biography to a social milieu: "Valéry is a petit bourgeois intellectual, no doubt about it. But not every petit bourgeois intellectual is Valéry. The heuristic inadequacy of contemporary Marxism is contained in these two sentences."[25] Part and whole must be comprehended at the same time as an aspect of each other and as analytically autonomous—although the degree of relative independence will obviously be more or less complete depending on the historical moment. The theoretical consequences are clear: systems composed of complex parts may expect change to come not only from the evolution of the whole (considered dialectically or otherwise), or from outside influences in the form of the impingement of other systems, but also from developments *within the parts* whose movements are endogenously determined. Therefore, in studying the changing configurations of power in North-South relations over the past several decades, we must be aware not only of the way the system is changing overall (for example, in terms of the growing role of the multinational corporation), or of the way the system is being challenged from outside itself (such as in the arms race with the Soviet Union), but also of the manner in which the units within it (both North and South) are evolving in response to locally determined forces whose ultimate development may have profound effects on the greater system outside. Historical analyses that hold to these premises may be difficult to write, since lines of movement tend to become more numerous and more difficult to see synthetically. But only such a form of writing can hope to portray at all adequately the complexity that history actually is.

II

At the risk of sounding hopelessly old-fashioned, I would suggest that, in order to understand the nature of their specificity apart from

---

[25] Sartre, *Critique de la raison dialectique* (Paris: Gallimard 1960), 44. For a criticism of Sartre on precisely the grounds that he also rides roughshod over the individual case on occasion, see Tony Smith, "Idealism and People's War: Sartre on Algeria," *Political Theory*, 1 (November 1973).

the international system, the primary single structure of southern countries to be studied is the organization of the state. Even in colonial situations, where the apparatus of the state was under foreign control at the highest levels, the natives invariably wielded significant power at lower levels of the government and in a variety of informal ways. Indeed, it was precisely these constellations of interests accommodating or opposing foreign rule that made for many of the significant differences in the pattern of postwar decolonization.[26] For the colonial regimes themselves had never amounted to more than a thin crust of European officials and officers atop complex networks of local collaborating groups. In the case of India, for example, Mahatma Gandhi tirelessly pointed out to his fellow countrymen that, in the 1930's, a mere 4,000 British civil servants assisted by 60,000 soldiers and 90,000 civilians (businessmen and clergy for the most part) had billeted themselves upon a country of three hundred million persons. The British had constructed a delicately balanced network through which they gained the support of certain favored economic groups (the zamindars acting as landed tax collectors in Bengal, for example), different traditional power holders (especially the native princes after the Great Mutiny of 1857), warrior tribes (such as the Sikhs of the Punjab), and aroused minority groups like the Muslims. Such a brokerage system was to be found in every colonial territory. In some there was a foreign economic presence: the Chinese in Vietnam, Malaya, and Indonesia; the Asians in East Africa; the Levantines in West Africa; the European settlers in Kenya and Algeria. In other cases, there were alliances with traditional ruling groups: the Native Authorities in Nigeria, the Princely States in Malaya, the imperial bureaucracies in Tunisia and Morocco, the Hashemite family in the Fertile Crescent, the ruling cliques in Cochin China and Tonkin which were interested in acting independently of Hue. Still another source of support came from the oppressed groups who found their rights protected and their interests secured by foreigners: Muslim sects in the Levant, Jews in Algeria, Christians in many parts of Asia and Africa. Simple rivalries also played their part: the *politique des races* practiced by Gallieni in Madagascar, or the support of competing religious brotherhoods in the British Sudan and French North Africa. There also were the agents of Western ways: caids in North Africa, native schoolteachers in West Africa, and economic middlemen (compradors). The latter entered into important collaboration with European overseas expansion when a rich Hindu

[26] See Tony Smith, "A Comparative Study of French and British Decolonization," *Comparative Studies in Society and History*, xx (January 1978).

merchant failed to bring his army to the support of his Muslim over-lord, the Nabob of Bengal, thereby assuring Robert Clive's great vic-tory at Plassey in 1757. This description should not give the illusion of a system of permanent alliances: old friends could become new enemies and old enemies new friends on the shifting grounds of po-litical competition; ultimately, the collaborative networks found them-selves superseded by indigenous forces determined to achieve inde-pendence. Thus, even when they failed to control the heights of the state, native political forces played a fairly powerful role in the colo-nies; it was their character and structure that profoundly influenced the process of decolonization.

Just as the variety of local political structures working for or against colonial rule must be understood in order to make sense of the intricate pattern of decolonization, so the range of state structures in the South in the nineteenth and twentieth centuries is the best general organiza-tional feature for sorting through the wide number of cases involved and for making sense of their experience. The spectrum of state struc-tures extends from those that are clearly the paramount power within their society (monopolizing the means of violence and thereby en-forcing a complete set of rules ranging from property ownership to the way political participation is permitted) to those that are states in little more than name, lacking either the party or the bureaucratic structures that would give them the scope of local control properly incumbent upon a state. Yet even in these latter cases (except perhaps for a few extreme examples among the sheikdoms of the Arabian Peninsula or in the poorest parts of Africa) the existence of an in-digenously controlled state does insulate the local society from the in-ternational system in a manner greater than was true under direct colonial rule. Short of military intervention, the leverage of the outside is significantly reduced, since foreign ties with local groups are in gen-eral restricted to certain economic interests and occasional religious bodies. Foreigners have neither the scope nor the intensity of ties within the independent southern country which they had under colonialism. Moreover, the power capacity of local interests and the state tends to grow as bureaucrats in the government and the army, jealous of their positions, show themselves likely to act on behalf of foreigners only when such behavior coincides with their own interests. Thus, no mat-ter how great the diversity among southern countries, they almost all have a state apparatus that depends on the aggregation of at least some local interests and is possessed of the ability to take at least some initiatives in regard to domestic and international issues. In this respect, the use of the word "neocolonial" is misleading to the extent that it suggests—as it apparently does to many—that the political distinctions between independent and colonial status are trivial. Surely Kwame Nkrumah overstated the case when he wrote in 1965, "The essence of neo-colonialism is that the State which is subject to it is, in theory, independent and has all the outward trappings of international sovereignty. In reality its economic system and thus its political policy is directed from outside."[27]

Many dependency theorists, seemingly persuaded of the correctness of the traditional Marxist reduction of the state to an administrative body of the ruling class, either overlook the function of the state entirely, or dismiss it as historically insignificant, or recognize its importance only to reduce it forthwith to a product of the international system. Thus, writing on the fate of independent Africa in relation to the world order, Frantz Fanon calls for a strong state, able to protect the nation from imperialist designs and improve the quality of life for the mass of the population; what he actually sees are weak governmental bodies, the servants of a new African bourgeoisie which itself has entirely sold out to foreign interests:

> The national middle-class which takes over power at the end of the colonial regime is an under-developed middle-class. It has practically no economic power, and in any case it is in no way commensurate with the bourgeoisie of the mother country which it hopes to replace. . . . Since the middle-class has neither sufficient material nor intellectual resources . . . it limits its claims to the taking-over of business offices and commercial houses formerly occupied by the settlers. From now on it will insist that all the big foreign companies should pass through its hands, whether these companies wish to keep their connections with the country, or to open it up. The national middle-class discovers its historic mission: that of intermediary.[28]

In this descriptive account of a number of post-independence African regimes, Fanon is undoubtedly correct. But as an analytical principle for the study of Third World countries past, present, and future, his point is surely inadequate.

Nevertheless, it is precisely as an analytical point that Immanuel Wallerstein means to press the issue. He writes:

> . . . the world-economy develops a pattern where state structures are relatively strong in the core areas and relatively weak in the periphery.

[27] Kwame Nkrumah, *Neo-Colonialism: The Last State of Imperialism* (New York: International Publishers 1966), ix.
[28] Frantz Fanon, *The Wretched of the Earth* (New York: Grove Press 1966), 122.

. . . What is necessary is that in some areas the state machinery be far stronger than in others. What do we mean by a strong state-machinery? We mean strength vis-à-vis other states within the world-economy including other core-states, and strong vis-à-vis local political units within the boundaries of the state.[29]

Apparently not even these strong states can compare with the real mover of international affairs—the dynamic of economic forces: "It is the social achievement of the modern world, if you will, to have invented the technology that makes it possible to increase the flow of surplus from the lower strata to the upper strata, from the periphery to the center, from the majority to the minority, by eliminating the 'waste' of too cumbersome a political superstructure."[30] Thus, Charles V was the last to make the impossible attempt of putting the entire economic apparatus of the West under a single political authority. The present eclipse of the United States, Wallerstein believes, should in no way endanger the system: "such a decline in United States state hegemony has actually *increased* the freedom of action of capitalist enterprises, the larger of which have now taken the form of multinational corporations. . . ." Indeed, he minimizes the role of the state to such an extent that he can say: "There are today no socialist systems in the world economy any more than there are feudal systems because there is one world system. It is a world-economy and it is by definition capitalist in form." But history does not move blindly, free of human agency. If not states, then what social force coordinates this activity, fights its battles, projects it into the future? The obvious answer is class:

We must maintain our eye on the central ball. The capitalist world economy as a totality—its structure, its historic evolution, its contradictions—is the arena of social action. The fundamental political reality of that world-economy is a class struggle which, however, takes constantly changing forms: class-consciousness versus ethno-nationalist consciousness, classes within nations versus classes across nations.[31]

As we have seen, this set of assumptions is somewhat similar to that of many dependency theorists who make little reference to the state and hold that the international system has established its interests locally through the medium of an alliance with the dependent classes of the Third World.

Although there may be many instances when state action is not important, Wallerstein's abrupt dismissal of the potential significance of

[29] Wallerstein (fn. 11), 355.   [30] *Ibid.*, 15-16.
[31] Wallerstein (fn. 13), 412, 415; Wallerstein "Class Formation in the Capitalist World-Economy," *Politics and Society*, v (No. 3, 1975), 375.

the state is in error. I have recited his argument at some length in order to illustrate the theoretical importance of correctly understanding what a strong state may be able to accomplish. For even on his home ground, the sixteenth century, Wallerstein is surely wrong in his discussion of state power. As Theda Skocpol has pointed out, the strong states of the sixteenth century were not at the core (in England and Holland), but on the periphery (in Spain and Sweden). Holland was ruled by a federation of merchant oligarchs while the English crown, deficient in terms of a bureaucracy or a standing army, was beholden to merchants and local notables.[32] Later history substantiates Wallerstein's position no better. Alexander Gerschenkron has demonstrated that the "late industrializers" in every case were successful because of exceptionally strong state structures that were determined to modernize. One-time peripheral countries like Russia, Germany, and Japan could not possibly have developed as they did without the vigorous leadership of the state.[33] Nor is it clear today that the state structure of the United States corresponds to the Leviathan one might expect of the "core country of the world-economy" any more than that many governments on the periphery are the weak structures which Wallerstein declares them to be.

Granted, some of the literature associated with dependency does recognize the importance of southern states. But in its discussion, these governments sound more like products of the international system than of local circumstances; thus it loses by one set of assumptions part of what it has gained from another set. A large number of essays and books appearing in recent years on Latin America have maintained that the "bureaucratic-authoritarian" or "authoritarian-corporatist" regimes so prevalent there since the mid-1960's are the most recent result, in the words of Philippe Schmitter, of situations of "delayed, dependent capitalist development and non-hegemonic class relations."[34] In an essay on authoritarian government in Brazil, Argentina, and Mexico, Robert R. Kaufman, drawing heavily on the work of Guillermo O'Donnell, comes to much the same conclusion: "such regimes are linked to a particular phase (or crisis) of capital accumulation en-

[32] Theda Skocpol, "Wallerstein's World Capitalist System: A Theoretical and Historical Critique," *American Journal of Sociology*, Vol. 82 (March 1977), 1083ff.

[33] Alexander Gerschenkron, "Economic Backwardness in Historical Perspective," in *Economic Backwardness in Historical Perspective* (Cambridge: Harvard University Press 1963).

[34] Schmitter, "Still the Century of Corporatism?" *Review of Politics*, XXXVI (January 1974), 108. Also see fn. 35.

countered in the maturation of dependent industrializing economies";
he points out that their advent is related to increasing local investments
by multinational corporations.[35] And several contributors to an anthol-
ogy of essays on Latin American authoritarianism observe that since
this kind of regime occurs not only in South America, but in other
parts of the Third World, what they all have in common is their dependent status internationally. *Ergo*, the character of the world system
is said to be the factor that is basic to the genesis of all authoritarian
Third-World regimes. O'Donnell asserts that the focus of his work is
on Latin America "only in a trivial sense; the pertinent historical context is provided by the political economy of nations that were originally
exporters of primary materials and were industrialized late, but extensively, in a position of dependency upon the great centers of world
capitalism."[36]

It should be emphasized that these authors do not intend to provide
a simplistic explanation of how the dependent status of these countries
engendered authoritarian regimes. From their perspective, the fact that
the United States reacted to Castro's coming to power by increasing
aid to the militaries of Latin America, thereby encouraging them to
topple civilian governments, is only incidental to the process. They
point to the long-term evolution of South America's social structure,
insisting that the strains and tensions that were the product of dependent development set the stage for the wave of authoritarian regimes of
the past fifteen years. The indirect molding power that the North
exercised through the international economic system did more to cause
these developments than direct political intervention alone could have
accomplished.

But the obvious question is by what line of reasoning we are brought
to see that authoritarianism grew out of dependency; that in assigning relative weights of importance to domestic and external factors
in such developments, it is the latter that emerge as decisive. Is there
not historical evidence—provided, for example, by Germany and Japan

[35] See Kaufman, "Mexico and Latin American Authoritarianism," in José Luis Reyna
and Richard S. Weinert, eds., *Authoritarianism in Mexico* (Philadelphia: Institute for
the Study of Human Issues 1977), 195, and the chart derived from O'Donnell, 197.
Nevertheless, neither Kaufman nor Schmitter should be classified as dependency theorists: see Kaufman (fn. 1), and Schmitter, "Desarrollo retrasado, dependencia externa
y cambio político en America Latina," *Foro Internacional*, XII (December 1971).
[36] Guillermo O'Donnell, "Corporatism and the Question of the State," in James M.
Malloy ed., *Authoritarianism and Corporatism in Latin America* (Pittsburgh: University of Pittsburgh Press 1977), 54. For similar observations in the same volume, see
Silvio Duncan Baretta and Helen E. Douglass, "Authoritarianism and Corporatism
in Latin America: A Review Essay."

—to suggest that authoritarian regimes do not reflect dependency but the effort to avoid subordination? And does the case of India not suggest that at times dependency has contributed to liberal forms of government outside Europe? More to the point, there are reasons to link authoritarian governments in Latin America to domestic rather than to foreign causes. One internal factor (usually conceded by dependency theorists themselves) is that three hundred years of rule by Catholic Spain and Portugal left Latin America a legacy of authoritarian government complete with a corporatist ideology. The vertical ties of patron-client relations for which the continent is well known, especially in its agrarian structures, and the traditions of regional caudillo rule must have made their contribution to the form of governments we see today.

Or we could move forward in time, pointing out that the political heritage of the last hundred years set the pattern for authoritarian government in more recent years. For example, both Lorenzo Meyer and Roger Hansen see more continuity than change in style between the Porfiriato (1876–1910) and present-day government in Mexico.[37] An even better line of reasoning linking Latin American authoritarianism to domestic factors would be to maintain that it is the fruit of unsuccessfully resolved problems born of the populist nationalism common to most of the continent after 1930. World War I and especially the Great Depression brought populist leaders such as Vargas and Perón to the fore in Latin America; they were opposed to foreign influence and its local collaborators (chiefly the landed oligarchs of the export sector), and committed to developing their countries through import substitution industries. In this sense, Latin America "decolonized" in the 1930's; populist nationalism appeared triumphant. By the 1950's, import substitution had exhausted itself as a means of domestic economic expansion; at the same time, the market for Latin exports weakened, thus beginning a period of decline in the terms of trade for these commodities. The result was economic crisis.

The civilian governments in power proved unable either to correct the situation or to muster enough support to ensure stability. The drastic inflation rates of the period were symptoms of the government's trying to please rival sectors of the polity. Ultimately, the situation was

---

[37] Meyer, "Historical Roots of the Authoritarian State in Mexico," in Reyna and Weinert (fn. 35). Meyer speaks of Díaz's "inability to transform an authoritarian situation into an authoritarian system" and states that "the Mexican Revolution did not destroy the authoritarian nature of Mexican political life, it modernized it" (pp. 9, 4); Roger Hansen, *The Politics of Mexican Development* (Baltimore: The Johns Hopkins Press 1971), 149.

exacerbated to the point that the populist alliance disintegrated, with the middle and upper classes choosing authoritarian military governments over their quasi-democratic republican predecessors. This choice provided stability, but it did not ensure growth. Only when the authoritarian governments enlisted the multinational corporate community in their development drives could the Latin American economies once again experience expansion at a significant pace. In this (admittedly schematic) account, it is unquestionably the domestic factors that emerge as the predominant force behind the creation of authoritarian states—however much one may wish to blame external influences for making the failure of populist ambitions inevitable and for supplying aid to military dictatorships once the crisis had come. For populism *itself* bred corporatist government, albeit of the kind that initially included significant mass participation. As the governing structure was elaborated, however, it became fairly easy to exclude this same political membership. Argentina and Brazil certainly fit this pattern, but the case of Mexico is especially clear-cut: the Partido Revolucionario Institucional which has ruled Mexico since the Revolution (under various appellations) took its most important steps toward institutionalizing itself in its present corporatist form around 1938, at the very time the Cárdenas Government was dramatically bearding Washington with its expropriations of American utility and oil companies in Mexico. The chief explanation for the contemporary spread of authoritarianism through the continent is not the dependent status of Latin America internationally, but the internal evolution of its social and political forces.

Histories of the nineteenth century have too often painted the states of the pre-industrial world in drab, uniform colors, depicting them as *reacting* to European expansion in a helpless manner, rather than as active centers of development in their own right. But the power of the Great Mogul in Delhi was already in disarray by 1757—the date of Clive's victory—as a result of maladministration and the incursions of the Persians, Afghans, and especially Marathas over the preceding decades. Similarly, in West Africa, former slave kingdoms such as Dahomey, Bonny, and Lagos had successfully converted their economic base to the export of palm oil and groundnuts; but in the latter part of the nineteenth century they proved quite unable to administer the hinterlands effectively when new European steamships began to ply the upstream waters and caused struggles with the African middlemen who were handling this trade. Even with more effective governments, Africa might not have been treated as Latin America was after 1875;

but the fact that these African states were relatively rudimentary institutions surely contributed to the Partition.[38]

By contrast, the Ottoman state in the 1800's was a complex, long-lived institution; but when the pressures of Western expansion reached it in earnest, it proved unable to reverse a decline of some two hundred years. In contrast to Tokugawa Japan which, while also in decline, had, in the words of Barrington Moore, been sapped by more than two hundred years of "peace and luxury," the Sublime Porte entered the nineteenth century after more than two hundred years of internecine warfare and economic decay. Admittedly, the Anglo-Turkish Commercial Convention of 1838 and the large debts to foreign creditors that the Sultan ran up later in the century played a part in making the Empire more difficult to hold together. But were these factors more the cause or the effect of a deficient state authority? Surely it is the effect that deserves the emphasis.

There seems to be no disagreement among historians that, by the seventeenth century at the latest, the state left by Suleiman at his death in 1566 was in decline. An attempt by Selim III to imitate Peter the Great and to modernize defensively in order to protect his realm against Russia and the West met with defeat in 1808 when the Janissaries (backed by religious authorities) assassinated him. The state's next ambitious attempt at reform, the Tanzimat proclaimed in 1839 under Abdul Medjid, achieved some notable results, but it proved quite unable to live up to the expectations of its creators—not because of foreign opposition (indeed, Britain and France were eager for the reforms to succeed in order to build Turkey up against Russian expansion), but because the Ottoman government could not overcome *internal* obstacles to the Tanzimat's proposals. It was not until Kemal Ataturk took charge of the Turkish government after World War I that the state gained the strength to define its objectives and to attain them as the result of a concerted effort at internal reform.[39]

[38] Kenneth Onwuka Dike, *Trade and Politics in the Niger Delta, 1830–1885* (New York: Oxford University Press 1956); C. W. Newbury and A. S. Kanya-Forstner, "French Policy and the Origins of the Scramble for West Africa," *Journal of African History*, x (No. 2, 1969); A. G. Hopkins, *An Economic History of West Africa* (London: Longman 1973), chap. 4.

[39] Frank Edgar Pailey, *British Policy and the Turkish Reform Movement: A Study in Anglo-Turkish Relations, 1826–1853* (New York: Howard Festig 1970); Z. Y. Hershlag, *Introduction to the Modern Economic History of the Middle East* (Leiden: E. J. Brill 1964); Charles Issawi, ed., *The Economic History of the Middle East, 1800–1914* (Chicago: University of Chicago Press 1966); Stanford J. Shaw, "The Nineteenth-Century Ottoman Tax Reforms and Revenue System," *International Journal of Middle East Studies*, vi (October 1975); Edward C. Clark, "The Ottoman Industrial Revolution," *International Journal of Middle East Studies*, v (January 1974); Z. Y.

What a more powerful state might have accomplished in the Middle East is suggested by the history of the amazing Albanian adventurer Mehemet Ali, who became pasha, and then viceroy, of Egypt. Having arrived in Egypt in 1801 with the Ottoman forces that were to reclaim the land after Napoleon's withdrawal, Mehemet Ali managed to gather a following around himself; in 1811, he completed the work of internal reform of the local elite structure by smashing the Mameluke ruling class and emerging as the undisputed leader of the land. Ali was thereupon free to begin an effort which can be best described as the forced industrialization of Egypt. His state created marketing monopolies in agriculture, and dramatically increased the production of export crops, particularly cotton. With the substantial revenues gained from these sales abroad, the state created protected industrial monopolies within Egypt. By the 1830's, there was a work force of at least 30,000 in modern iron foundries, cotton mills, ammunition works, and a shipyard. Industrial employment did not reach this figure again for nearly a century.[40]

The obstacles Ali faced were tremendous. Egypt in 1800 was a very backward land. Its population, between six and seven million in Roman times, now numbered no more than two-and-a-half million. Wheeled vehicles were unknown, transportation unsafe, and the formerly great city of Alexandria had a citizenry of only 8,000 living in its ruins. But if these internal factors did not cause Ali's fall, his overweening ambitions to claim for himself the entire Ottoman Empire finally did. In 1831, under the pretext of pursuing 6,000 escapees from forced labor in Egypt into Syria, Ali began the first of two campaigns whose ultimate goal was to take Constantinople. The result was consternation in Europe, as Britain and France saw Russia offer its aid in defense of the Sultan. A second campaign, begun at the end of the decade, finally prompted British intervention; in 1842, Ali was obliged to reduce the size of his army (the chief market for his factory production) and to dismantle his industrial monopolies, permitting the import of cheap European goods.

Now the stage was set for the "underdevelopment" of Egypt, much

Hershlag, *Turkey: The Challenge of Growth* (Leiden: E. J. Brill 1968); Ellen Kay Trimberger, *Revolution from Above: Military Bureaucrats and Developments in Japan, Turkey, Egypt, and Peru* (Edison, N.J.: Transaction Books 1977).

[40] Charles Issawi, *Egypt in Revolution: An Economic Analysis* (New York: Oxford University Press 1963), chaps. 1 and 2; A. E. Crouchley, *The Economic Development of Modern Egypt* (London: Longmans, Green 1938), chap. 2; *Encyclopaedia Britannica*, 11th ed., XVIII, s.v. "Mehemet Ali." The figures for industrial workers may be found by comparing Hershlag, *Introduction* . . . (fn. 39), 86, with Issawi, 43.

in the manner schematized by the dependency school. Ali's successors converted Egypt into a single-crop export economy based on cotton, and contracted larger debts than they could repay. Ultimately, the nationalist reaction to these foreign pressures alarmed the British to such an extent that they saw no choice but to occupy Egypt in order to assure the security of the Suez Canal. "It would be detrimental to both English and Egyptian interests to afford any encouragement to the growth of a protected cotton industry in Egypt," wrote Lord Cromer, Consul General of Egypt in 1891. During his tenure in office (1883–1907), Cromer refused to protect any Egyptian manufacturers, going so far as to levy an excise tax on certain products made within Egypt so that they had no protection behind a revenue-raising import duty.[41] It was not until 1920, with the founding of the Bank Misr by Egyptian capital, that a stable foundation was finally provided for the growth of an Egyptian entrepreneurial class. Tariff autonomy (1930) and fiscal autonomy (1936) followed, permitting the Egyptian state to take a more forceful hand in the country's economic development. Thereafter, as Charles Issawi reports, there was a shift of economic power in three primary directions: of business over landed interests; of national over foreign investment; of state over private initiative. After Nasser came to power and the Suez Invasion of 1956, the role of the state emerged as the decisive element in Egypt's economic development.[42] One can, to be sure, mark the principal periods of Egyptian economic activity in terms of the movements of the international system. But I would suggest that a better way to understand the Egyptian experience is by reference to the vicissitudes of the Egyptian state.

Certainly the ability of Japan to industrialize and to become in its turn an important member of the international community cannot be understood apart from the actions of the state. For in the aftermath of the Meiji Restoration (1868), it was the state, acting on behalf of the nation and not at the behest (although in the interests) of any particular group or class, that undertook a fundamental reordering of the Japanese government and economy. It was the state that insisted on agrarian reform in order to accelerate industrial development; it was the state that invested in a whole range of industrial enterprises where merchant capital at first feared to enter; it was the state that absorbed

[41] E.R.J. Owen, "Lord Cromer and the Development of Egyptian Industry, 1883–1907," *Middle Eastern Studies*, II (July 1966).
[42] Robert L. Tignor, "Bank Misr and Foreign Capitalism," *International Journal of Middle East Studies*, VIII (April 1977); Charles Issawi, "Shifts in Economic Power," in Issawi (fn. 39), 505ff.

as many samurai as it could into its bureaucracies and broke the resistance of the rest; it was the state that began modern systems of banking, taxation, and education in Japan.[43] To be sure, these dramatic developments cannot be isolated from the assault Japan correctly feared from the international system, nor from the advantages given the state in its social and economic heritage from the Tokugawa period. But to underestimate the independent role of the state—to see developments in Japan as the product either of international factors alone or as the reflection of no more than domestic class interests—is to miss the central feature of Japan's exceptional economic performance.

By the middle of the nineteenth century, it was only in Latin America that a group of states had escaped direct colonial control and had also managed, in contrast to Peking and Constantinople, to expand their capacity to rule. A good part of the explanation surely has to do with the continent's geographic remoteness from the centers of geopolitical rivalry, and with the Monroe Doctrine which had a real, if limited, influence on keeping the area free of competitive annexations. But a more basic reason for the success of these states in establishing themselves locally had to do with the strength they drew from participation in the international system. In China, the Ottoman Empire, and Africa, the international connection functioned mainly *to undermine* the local political systems (however much the Europeans may have hoped to do otherwise); in Latin America, these same linkages worked instead *to reinforce* the position of the ruling elite. *Not so much designs formulated at the center, but rather conditions among the states on the periphery were the fundamental factors determining the impact of European economic power abroad.* As John Gallagher and Ronald Robinson put it in regard to the concerns of the British early in the century:

> Ideally, the British merchant and investor would take into partnership the porteños of Argentina, the planters of Alabama, the railway builders of Belgium, as well as the bankers of Montreal and the shippers of Sydney. . . . At the same time, the trader and missionary would liberate the producers of Africa and Asia. The pull of the industrial economy, the prestige of British ideas and technology would draw them also into the Great Commercial Republic of the world. In time the "progres-

[43] Moore (fn. 17), chap. 5; Trimberger (fn. 39); Angus Maddison, *Economic Growth in Japan and the USSR* (London: George Allen & Unwin 1969); G. C. Allen, *A Short Economic History of Modern Japan: 1867–1937* (New York: Praeger 1962); Henry Rosovsky, "Japan's Transition to Modern Economic Growth, 1868–1885," in Rosovsky, ed., *Industrialization in Two Systems: Essays in Honor of Alexander Gerschenkron* (New York: Wiley 1966).

sive" native groups within the decaying societies of the Orient would burst the feudal shackles and liberalise their political and economic life. Thus the earlier Victorians hoped to help the Oriental, the African and the Aborigine to help themselves. Many would be called and all would be chosen: the reforming Turkish pasha and the enlightened mandarin, babus who had read Mill, samurai who understood Bentham, and the slaving kings of Africa who would respond to the Gospel and turn to legitimate trade.[44]

The history of nineteenth-century Africa and Asia is, of course, largely that of the failure of this dream. But the same is not true of British commerce with Latin America: although it eventually came to have a retarding influence on the industrialization of the continent, for a period it exercised a strong influence in favor of economic development. A simple comparison illustrates the point: by 1880, Egypt and Argentina had each received British investments totaling between 20 and 25 million pounds sterling, and each was permeated with foreign influence. Egypt was on the verge of collapse, however, while Argentina was moving into position to become Britain's most important economic satellite in South America. An observer interested in proving the all-pervasive power of the international system over the pre-industrial states within it might take the history of these two countries, *considered separately*, as proof of his argument. But I am more impressed with the *different impact* European expansion had on these two areas, and would suggest that a major explanation (certainly not the only one) has to do with internal differences between Egypt and Argentina, which can best be approached through a study of their respective state structures.

From the struggle for independence from Madrid, Spanish America had emerged economically impoverished and politically divided. Although Foreign Secretary Canning is widely quoted for his remark at the time that "Latin America is independent, and unless we mismanage our affairs she is English," the economic record suggests that this prize amounted to very little indeed until after the middle of the century.[45] By that time, a symbiotic relationship was establishing itself in which political stability in Latin America increased foreign economic interest in the continent in the form of loans and commerce; at the same time, these links to the outside provided assistance to the various

[44] John Gallagher and Ronald Robinson, *Africa and the Victorians: The Climax of Imperialism* (New York: Doubleday 1968), 3-4.
[45] D.C.M. Platt, *Latin America and British Trade, 1806–1914* (New York: Harper & Row 1973).

national governments intent on solidifying their power locally. Richard Graham describes the case of Brazil between 1850 and 1865:

> Whereas up to that point the landed aristocrats had viewed the central government with suspicion—first as foreign and then as radical—they now saw it wedded to their own interests. They therefore submitted to the control of the central government and, by allowing the tradition of a centralized national administration to arise, unwittingly contributed to the weakening of their own position once the central government became more responsive to the pressures of rising urban groups.[46]

The emergence of the state in nineteenth-century Latin America was therefore characterized not only by its Iberian heritage and by its contemporary need to control a population that was geographically and especially ethnically quite heterogeneous (ranging from the Indian, mestizo, and creole populations in Mexico to the large number of slaves in Brazil), but also by its ability to create an economic basis for rule through sales to the international system. It is well to recall in this connection that the American Confederacy initially believed Britain would intervene on its behalf once the Union blockade of cotton exports was felt in Lancashire, and that Prime Minister Palmerston and Foreign Secretary Russell at first hoped for a Southern victory.

Yet I have difficulty in understanding by what obvious measure one can say that the British connection "delayed," "distorted," or "exploited" Latin American economic development. To be sure, trading interests within Latin America sought to obstruct high protective tariffs before the turn of the century and so might perhaps be viewed at first glance as "enemies within," willing to sell out the national interest for their own private gain. Certainly most *dependencistas* suggest that this was the case. But, as Graham points out in his study of Brazil, whatever costs were thereby incurred must be weighed against the substantial benefits the international connection provided in economic terms. Indeed, it may well be that a closer analysis will reveal that what has been accepted as an article of faith—that it took the Great Depression, throwing Latin America on its own, to stimulate industrial production on the continent—is an exaggeration. For where is the evidence that Latin America was so in thrall to export interests that it lay completely open to a flood of cheap foreign manufactures—an argument almost invariably advanced by nationalists or Marxists. To the contrary, it should be recalled that tariffs on imports were the chief source of

[46] Graham, *Britain and the Onset of Modernization in Brazil, 1850–1914* (New York: Cambridge University Press 1968), 27-28.

revenue for these states in the nineteenth century. In 1870 in Argentina, for example, at least $14 million of the $14.8 million state budget came from trade duties. D. C. M. Platt writes:

> It is clear that by the last decades of the nineteenth century there were no serious institutional obstacles to the development of manufacturing. In Mexico, at least, import substitution had become a prime element in government tariff policy, and to a lesser extent the same was true of the other Latin American nations with industrial pretentions—Brazil, Argentina, Chile, Peru.[47]

Nor was the phenomenon limited to Latin America. In the 1890's, the British found themselves obliged to impose excise taxes on Indian and Egyptian textile production in order to reduce the effect of the protection revenue duties on imports which worked to the detriment of the Lancashire cotton industry.[48] In other words, revenue tariffs were in effect protective walls for infant industries in these two countries, and probably in Latin America as well. Latin America may not have been the plaything of international economic forces to the extent often supposed. Indeed, it appears to Carlos Díaz Alejandro, one of the most respected historians of Latin American economic development, that in terms of economic rationality, Argentina probably withdrew overly from the international system. Comparing the case of Argentina to those of Canada and Australia in the twentieth century, Díaz writes:

> The most ironic lesson of postwar Argentine experience is that if there had been less discrimination against exports, manufacturing expansion would have been greater. Indeed, the annual growth rate of manufacturing during 1900–1929 (5.6%) was higher than during 1929–1965 (3.7%). The ratio of imported to total consumption of manufactured goods probably would have been higher, but there is little to be said on economic grounds for minimizing this ratio.[49]

Of course it may be maintained that because Latin America did not grow economically along the lines of what is today called "basic human needs," its development was "delayed" and "distorted." For example, Rene Villarreal refuses to speak of "development"—as do many other dependency theorists—unless it involves full employment, equal income distribution, and external economic independence.[50] Ethically

---

[47] Platt (fn. 45), 78, 84.

[48] On Egypt, see Owen (fn. 41); on India, see Dutt (fn. 18), Book II, chap. 12, and Book III, chap. 9.

[49] Carlos F. Díaz Alejandro, *Essays on the Economic History of the Argentine Republic* (New Haven: Yale University Press 1970), 138; for his comparisons with Canada and Australia, see 110-14.

[50] Villarreal, "The Policy of Import-Substitution Industrialization, 1929–1975," in Reyna and Weinert (fn. 35).

speaking, this concern with words may be commendable; but when matters of definition become the key issue, as they frequently do, it is fairly obvious that major issues of structural analysis are being lost sight of. That is not to say that moral concerns should not make themselves felt in the study of history, but rather that their pursuit should not interfere with our appreciation of structural historical development. To cite but one example, Bradford Burns describes early nineteenth-century Latin American economic development in the ambiguous language one finds recurrent in the literature:

> The elite proudly regarded the new railroads, steamships, telegraph lines, and renovated ports as ample physical evidence of the progressive course on which their nations had embarked. In their satisfaction, they seemed oblivious to another aspect of modernization: that those very steamships, railroads, and ports tied them and their nations ever more tightly to a handful of industrialized nations in Western Europe and North America. . . . They failed to take note of the significance that many of their railroads did not link the principal cities of their nations but rather ran from plantations or mines directly to the ports, subordinating the goal of national unification to the demands of the industrial nations for agricultural products and minerals. As foreign investment rose, the voices of foreign investors and bankers spoke with greater authority in making economic decisions for the host countries. Local economic options diminished. In short, modernization magnified Latin America's dependency.[51]

The clear inference to be drawn from such writing is that the process victimized Latin America and that some alternative form of economic development was possible. But the author defends neither allegation. Was an alternate path available? In his own account Burns gives evidence aplenty that, following the struggle against Spain, national populations were small, the agrarian structures of the countries were rigid, political instability was rampant, and capital for investment simply did not exist in any quantity. Men can hardly be blamed for being "oblivious" to options that did not exist. Nor is it so apparent that the choices made victimized Latin America as a whole. Díaz writes that the rapidity of growth in Argentina from 1860 to 1930 "has few parallels in economic history," it was so rapid, and he points out the compelling logic of reliance on the international system:

> Pre-1930 growth can be said to have been "export-led" [because] . . . exports and capital inflows led to an allocation of resources far more efficient than the one which would have resulted from autarkic poli-

---

[51] Burns, *Latin America: A Concise Interpretive History* (Englewood Cliffs, N. J.: Prentice-Hall 1972), 130-31.

cies. In particular, the domestic cost of capital goods, which would have been astronomical under autarky, say in 1880, was reduced to a low level by exports of commodities produced by the generous use of an input—land—whose economic value under autarky would have been quite small.[52]

With very good reason one may of course object that the social form economic development has taken in Latin America is ethically objectionable (and has been for some time). But to suggest—as many influenced by dependency theory appear to do—that because the social form is objectionable, growth itself was "delayed" and "distorted" is to mix the arguments, to draw empirical conclusions from normative premises in an unacceptable manner.

During the nineteenth century, world trade grew tremendously under the impetus of the industrial revolution, and European and American investments abroad grew apace. In 1820, world trade was valued at 341 million pounds sterling; by 1880, its value topped 3 billion pounds. In 1810, British investments abroad were approximately 10 million pounds sterling; by 1890, they approached 200 million and probably represented about half the European and American investments abroad.[53] How could this dramatic increase fail to have repercussions on the pre-industrial countries of the globe as the industrial leaders sought primary materials and markets as well as strategic vantage points in their competitive race? Indeed, any specific southern area *looked at in isolation* will show clear signs of the impact. But when the range of southern countries is *placed side by side*, what also emerges is the *variety* of responses to this global experience of the expansion of the industrial revolution. The Ottoman Empire disintegrated while Japan modernized successfully; Africa was partitioned while Latin American governments were more effectively expanding and consolidating their rule. Although the study of the international system as such may suggest some reasons for these differences, it is by no means able to substitute for an inspection of each specific case.

The key variable to be analyzed in order to explain these significant differences lies in the abilities and behavior of the various southern states as they encountered the technologically superior force of Europe

[52] Díaz (fn. 49), 2, 11. For a similar argument on Brazil, see Carlos Manuel Peláez, "The Theory and Reality of Imperialism in the Coffee Economy of Nineteenth-Century Brazil," *Economic History Review*, xxix (May 1976).

[53] For trade figures, see E. J. Hobsbawm, *Industry and Empire* (London: Pelican 1969), 139, and J. Forbes Munro, *Africa and the International Economy, 1800–1960* (London: Rowman and Littlefield 1976), 40; for investment figures, see Michael Barrett-Brown, *After Imperialism* (New York: Humanities Press 1970), 93.

and the United States over the last century-and-a-half. Some states, such as the kingdoms of West Africa which had been built up partly through a preceding period of trade with the North, were taken by assault; others, like the Ottoman Empire and the Manchu Dynasty, collapsed—for reasons fundamentally caused more by internal factors than by the overwhelming power of the North; Japan managed to mount a rival industrial establishment; and the Latin American states drew strength from the international connection—albeit of a sort that made them satellites of the economic dynamism of the North. Both Theda Skocpol and Ellen Kay Trimberger have suggested that the key to whether a nineteenth-century agrarian order could preserve itself in the face of internal and external threats may lie in whether the state was functionally independent enough of the economic elite to take initiatives despite the opposition of this class. Skocpol writes of governmental responsiveness to the threat of revolution:

> The adaptiveness of the earlier modernizing agrarian bureaucracies was significantly determined by the degree to which the upper and middle ranks of the state administrative bureaucracies were staffed by large landholders. Only state machineries significantly differentiated from traditional landed upper classes could undertake modernizing reforms which almost invariably had to encroach upon the property or privileges of the landed upper class.[54]

Trimberger makes the same general point with reference to the ability of the Meiji State and Kemalist Turkey to undertake economic modernization, and she goes on to link these experiences with contemporary developments in Latin America. The central characteristic of a strong state, she argues, is that its bureaucracy—and particularly the military officer corps—be neither recruited from nor responsible to the classes economically dominant in society.[55] The autonomy from vested reactionary interests allows such a state to undertake the necessary (and always, to some, unpopular), reforms necessary for modernization. At the same time, however, it is well not to overemphasize the autonomy of the state: any ruling apparatus must have some allies, potential or actual, in the population at large. For all the usefulness of Skocpol's and Trimberger's distinctions, Bill Warren's point on the multiple forms that vigorous state rule may take calls attention to the danger of defining the issue too narrowly:

---

[54] Theda Skocpol, "France, Russia, China: A Structural Theory of Social Revolution," *Comparative Studies in Society and History*, XVIII (No. 2, 1976), 185.

[55] Trimberger (fn. 39); Trimberger and Irving Louis Horowitz, "State Power and Military Nationalism in Latin America," *Comparative Politics*, VIII (January 1976).

Significant capitalist industrialization may be initiated and directed by a variety of ruling classes and combinations of such classes or their representatives, ranging from semi-feudal ruling groups (northern Nigeria) and including large landowners (Ethiopia, Brazil, Thailand), to bureaucratic-military elites, petty bourgeoisies and professional and state functionaries (especially in Africa and the Middle East). These "industrializers" may themselves become industrial bourgeoisies or may be displaced by the industrial Frankensteins they have erected. . . . the crucial point is this—that it is the characteristic of the post-war period throughout the underdeveloped world that the social forces compelling industrialization have developed with more massive impetus and greater rapidity than ever before in history. . . . This partly explains the importance of the state in most underdeveloped countries where it often assumes the role of a bourgeois ruling class prior to the substantial development of that class.[56]

The style of state action will thus vary with time and place. Alexander Gerschenkron has described not only what is common to "late industrializers"—the speed of industrial growth and its concentration in large enterprises favoring capital goods production, for example— but also how different countries use different structures to further the same functional end of growth—England used accumulated capital, Germany the investment banks, and Russia the state budget.[57] Barrington Moore makes the same general point when he insists that historical timing is a crucial factor in the style of state action:

To a very limited extent these three types—bourgeois revolutions culminating in the Western form of democracy, conservative revolutions from above ending in fascism, and peasant revolutions leading to communism—may constitute alternative routes and choices. They are much more clearly successive historical stages. . . . The methods of modernization chosen in one country change the dimensions of the problem for the next countries who take the step, as Veblen recognized when he coined the now fashionable term "the advantages of backwardness." Without the prior democratic modernization of England, the reactionary methods adopted in Germany and Japan would scarcely have been possible. Without both the capitalist and reactionary experiences, the communist method would have been something entirely different, if it had come into existence at all. . . . Although there have been certain common problems in the construction of industrial society, the task remains a continually changing one.[58]

[56] Warren, "Imperialism and Capitalist Industrialization," *New Left Review*, Vol. 81 (September-October 1973), 42-43.

[57] Gerschenkron, *Europe in the Russian Mirror: Four Lectures in Economic History* (New York: Cambridge University Press 1970), 99, 102-3. See also Rondo Cameron, ed., *Banking and Economic Development: Some Lessons of History* (New York: Oxford University Press 1972).

[58] Moore (fn. 17), 113-14. See also David Collier, "Timing of Economic Growth and Regime Characteristics in Latin America," *Comparative Politics*, vii (April 1975);

III

Whether industrializing countries today will imitate any of the historical models of growth, or will find new forms of development, or indeed will succeed at all in their ambition to become autonomous centers of technological advance is a key question. Albert O. Hirschman notes that "late, late industrializers" seem unable to move as decisively as their historical predecessors.[59] Dependency theorists would link this to the role that external forces have played in the growth of southern countries, and insist that the impetus for forward movement does not yet come from inside. A strong state would seem to be an indispensable prerequisite for success. And few of the states of the Third World today have developed governing institutions appropriate to the social forces they must integrate and control. Regional, ethnic, and class demands are not effectively aggregated through party structures (if, indeed, they are capably articulated at all), while bureaucracies, which determine the ability of governments to act, are frequently incompetent and corrupt. In a strong polity, party and bureaucratic structures parallel and reinforce one another. But in a weak state, the shortcomings of each system feed the vices of the other.[60] Some governments are obviously stronger than others on the same continent—India in Asia, Tanzania in Africa, Mexico in Latin America; meanwhile, military regimes converting themselves into civilian governments, or popular parties with roots in a variety of social groups may yet succeed in institutionalizing political authority. Few are as weak as some of the former French territories of Black Africa, where Europeans continue to staff many of the important government positions and the presence (or absence) of a metropolitan paratrooper company or two determines political stability. And few are as corrupt as Zaire, where one apparently informed source reports the disappearance in 1971 of 60 percent of the state's revenues (not counting under-the-table transfers).[61]

Peter A. Gourevitch, "The Second Image Reversed: The International Sources of Domestic Politics," paper for the American Political Science Association, Annual Meeting 1977.

[59] Hirschman, "The Political Economy of Import-Substituting Industrializing in Latin America," in *A Bias for Hope: Essays on Development and Latin America* (New Haven: Yale University Press 1971).

[60] Samuel P. Huntington, *Political Order in Changing Societies* (New Haven: Yale University Press 1968); Fred W. Riggs, *Administrative Reform and Political Responsiveness* (Beverly Hills, Calif.: Sage 1970).

[61] J. P. Peemans, "The Social and Economic Development of Zaire since Independence," *African Affairs*, Vol. 74 (April 1975), 102.

For most southern countries, the Algerian dilemma seems familiar: the failure of the party system engenders the failure of the bureaucracy —which in turn makes the eventual success of the party all the more difficult. Thus the present attempt in Algeria to bring about wide-scale land reform is every bit as much a political as an economic effort. What the Boumédienne regime requires to achieve modern stability is power dispersion; that is, the creation of institutional linkages throughout the country by means of a party structure and organized interest groups. Of course a risk is involved. An increasingly participant peasantry may challenge well-designed programs as well as inefficiency and corruption in government. Thus, increased mass participation is at once a possible salvation for the regime and a real threat to it. The result has been to temporize. Now the Peasant Unions, like the Communal Assemblies, will be participatory in form but carefully controlled in practice. The attempt may succeed; or again, it may not. Since the summer of 1972, the idea of the Agrarian Revolution has been broadcast to every corner of Algeria in an official campaign quite without precedent in the country's history. The media have long and actively promoted it, thousands of students have been mobilized to come to its assistance, and religious as well as military and political authorities have pronounced favorably on its ambitions. One thing is becoming evident: Algeria must somehow institutionalize the participation of its peasantry if its political order is to find strength and stability and its economic order is to create prosperity. The peasantry has a genuine interest in participation. The overriding question is whether the state, through its party and bureaucratic structures, can acquire a mature form in the process.[62] The task is not unique to Algeria. Throughout the Third World, similar problems of political development are being confronted by equally bold programs of reform.

The job of the modernizing state in contemporary domestic terms therefore appears paradoxical: it must have autonomy, yet it must sink roots. It must have the autonomy of a unitary actor if it is to make long-term plans and to implement them despite some opposition (and on occasion those who object will eventually benefit more than those who truly pay the price). Particularistic interests of every variety must be weaker than the state, which is competent to act on behalf of what it will call the collective good. At the same time, the state must sink roots, both as a precondition and as a result of this very effort at change. If some interests must be checked or broken, others must be mobilized

[62] Tony Smith, "The Political and Economic Ambitions of Algerian Land Reform, 1962–1974," *Middle East Journal*, xxix (Summer 1975).

and controlled if the state is to attain its ends. In Samuel Huntington's terms, state power must be both concentrated and expanded in a complex process that will depend in each case on specific configurations of social forces.[63] Different regimes will choose to promote different sectors of their populations, and a variety of political structures may be used to the same functional end. But the final product must be a state apparatus that can effectively knit together the social forces under its jurisdiction, and provide for future growth.

Is a state that is strong domestically also a state that is strong internationally? No obvious direct relationship holds. For a society may be possessed of a strong state in the sense that governmental structures have a demonstrated capacity to integrate the social forces of the land, while at the same time it may lack military strength and hence be weak on the world scale. Or else, a state may be strong internally while its economic system is highly dependent on world trade over whose rules it has no power. As a result, this state is weak internationally, since the coalition of domestic forces on which it depends would be upset if the world economy failed to perform in certain necessary ways. On the other hand, internal strength would seem a precondition of strength internationally. For a globally powerful state must be possessed of an ability to extract resources from its citizenry and coordinate them in a fashion that suggests that its government is strong internally as well.

It is thus legitimate to say that an aspect of the growing international power of southern states is their ability to grow strong internally. As their economies become more diversified and their societies are better organized politically, the probability is that they will gain in international strength. It would be a mistake to think that this process is unidimensional, however: a society may over time vary in its dependence on outside influences. In Mexico, for example, the Porfiriato (1876–1910) signified one type of incorporation to the hegemony of the United States, only to be ended when Mexico in effect "decolonized" by the Revolution of 1910–1917, and by the subsequent economic Mexicanization of the country until 1945. Subsequently, however, Mexico once again became more closely involved with the United States, although in ways significantly different from the pattern that ended nearly seventy years ago. The complexity of the modern Mexican economy and the demonstrated ability of the state to control the social forces under its jurisdiction make the Mexican state today stronger

[63] Huntington (fn. 60), chap. 2.

domestically than it was before the Revolution; but how do we describe its international position?

One recent event confirms the growing power of the South in striking fashion. More clearly than the defeat of the Italians at Adua in 1896 and the Japanese victory over Russia in 1904, the ultimate triumph of nationalist communism in Vietnam stands as an historical benchmark of the first order in the process of reversing nearly five hundred years of European overseas expansion. Direct leverage over the political and bureaucratic institutions in the South may have ended with colonialism, but the North could retain the belief that if a southern state failed to respect basic northern interests (defined not only economically and strategically, but in some cases ideologically or symbolically), it ran the risk of military intervention. So at least it had been in Asia and the Middle East since the time of the First Opium War in 1840. We are witness to the failure of the United States to continue the tradition, as called for by George Liska in a widely read book that appeared in 1967:

> The Vietnamese War . . . may well come to rank on a par with the two world wars as a conflict that marked an epoch in America's progress toward definition of her role as a world power. . . . This role implies the necessity to define—by force if necessary—the terms on which regional balances of power are evolved and American access to individual regions is secured. . . . Had it been less dramatized, the Vietnamese War would have been an ideal ground for evolving, training, and breaking in . . . a combined political-military establishment as well as for educating the American people to changing facts of life. It may still prove retrospectively to have been such. . . .[64]

It was under the shadow of America's military reversal in Vietnam that the rise in petroleum prices occurred. In 1972, the OPEC states received $29.2 billion for their exports, which constituted 7 percent of world trade by value; by 1975, the value of their exports reached $114 billion and represented some 13 percent of world commerce (down from 16 percent in 1974).[65] Nor is the success of OPEC the only sign of strength in southern economic development. Statistics on manufacturing output in the Third World show this sector to have been the pacesetter in most Third-World economies for approximately the past two decades. Even during the recession of 1974, so called "middle income" countries, those with per capita incomes of $200 to $700 a year,

---

[64] Liska, *Imperial America: The International Politics of Primacy* (Baltimore: The Johns Hopkins Press 1967), Preface (unpaginated), and 180.
[65] United Nations, *Monthly Bulletin of Statistics*, June 1976.

managed to expand their manufacturing output by 8 percent, while the OECD countries registered a zero growth rate. The following index numbers of industrial production for all southern countries are striking evidence of this development.[66]

TABLE I

INDUSTRIAL OUTPUT AS A
PERCENTAGE OF 1970 PRODUCTION

	Year	Heavy Industry	Light Industry	Total
Developed Market	1960	53	66	57
Countries	1970	100	100	100
	1974	122	114	119
	1975	112	110	111
	1976	123	120	122
Developing Market	1960	43	64	54
Countries	1970	100	100	100
	1974	148	127	137
	1975	150	132	141
	1976	165	141	152

One must be careful not to push this point too far and thereby fail to recognize the substantial power that the North still retains over the South. In my opinion, dependency theory is certainly correct when it maintains that northern power is not only preponderant, but that its effects significantly influence the course of economic, social, and political development in southern countries. Nor would I dispute the use of the word "imperialism" to characterize this relationship.[67] But I would repeat that it is essential not to assume that the power of this interaction between North and South is so great as to mold single-handedly all aspects of social life in the South. Not for a moment should the strength and independence of local factors be forgotten. In the case of Mexican industrialization, to take but one example, the role of northern multinational investment is indisputable in providing capital and technology for development. But much more important were changes within Mexico itself, chief of which was the Revolution of 1910. Here the groundwork was laid, as William Glade recounts it, for the economic, social, and political infrastructure basic to industrialization.

[66] United Nations, *Monthly Bulletin of Statistics*, August 1977.
[67] For a fuller discussion, see Tony Smith, "Changing Configurations of Power in North-South Relations since 1945," *International Organization*, XXXI (Winter 1977).

And the Revolution was achieved not *because* of the international system, but *against* it and its local allies.[68] Nor should it be assumed that southern leaders, even when heavily dependent on the North, are mere puppets of the international system. It was Porfirio Díaz, after all, who not only opened Mexico to American economic penetration on an enormous scale at the close of the nineteenth century, but who also coined the phrase still dear to Mexicans, "Pobre México, tan lejos de Dios, tan cerca de los Estados Unidos" (Poor Mexico, so far from God, so close to the United States). In short, the system is far more fluid than dependency theory allows. It is fluid in the sense that it has weaknesses permitting important actors to escape its direct influence, in the sense that it contains contradictory movements within it (American support for Israel has been no way to run an imperial system, for example), and in the sense that in many respects the very success of the system prepares the ground for its own displacement.

Let us look at this last point more closely. Even if the North were to advance a blueprint for North-South economic relations more comprehensive than anything suggested to date, are we to suppose that it would unquestionably succeed in perpetuating the present international distribution of power? Such might be the short-term consequences, which for a generation or two might perhaps be able to improve the mechanisms of northern control; but what about the longer term? Marxist and southern nationalist rhetoric notwithstanding, where is the evidence that the system is operating to make the Third World perpetual "hewers of wood and drawers of water" as the now standard cliché has it? If that were the northern intention—and I have never seen it seriously alleged that the countries of the OECD or the United States alone have the cunning or the organization to be able to draw up such a scheme—then the attempt would be a notable failure. Where is the whole-hearted effort to prevent southern industrialization, monopolize southern raw materials, break up domestically integrated southern markets, oppose southern regional integration schemes, and develop a greater degree of international specialization that would heighten southern reliance on northern goods and markets? Neither the OECD nor the United States gets high marks for imperialist strategy: plans are neither clear nor resolute in purpose; the means whereby to gain the ends have not been specified; interests at home

[68] Glade, "Revolution and Economic Development: A Mexican Reprise," in William Glade and Charles W. Anderson, eds., *The Political Economy of Mexico* (Madison: University of Wisconsin Press 1963).

have not been harmonized so that such a strategy would seem enticing. Unlike the influence of Britain in Egypt, India, and Latin America at the end of the nineteenth century, and unlike Nazi policy toward Southeastern Europe, the impact of the North today would seem to accelerate rather than retard southern industrialization.[69]

The standard reply in the dependency literature is to maintain that foreign enterprise holds the commanding heights in Third World industrialization, thereby "decapitalizing" and "denationalizing" southern industry. It is held that whatever gains are being made would be greater and less vulnerable without this presence. The favored way to document the alleged decapitalization is to present figures of capital inflow and outflow over time to show that foreign investment is taking more out of southern countries than it is bringing in. For instance, in the case of Latin America, Dale Johnson repeats the standard charge, declaring that "between 1950 and 1961, 2,962 million dollars of U.S. private capital flowed into the seven principal countries of Latin America, while the return flow was 6,875 million dollars."[70] Although this state of affairs might suggest that northern investment is no assistance in terms of southern balance-of-payments problems, it is obvious that these figures, cited by themselves, cannot establish the case for southern exploitation. For unless we know what this surplus in favor of the United States amounting to $4 billion means in relation either to American investment in Latin America or to the output of American firms there, the sum says very little. The available statistics suggest that "decapitalization" is a nationalist/Marxist myth, at least in the terms in which it is usually presented. For example, in 1975, Latin America received $178 million from the United States to be invested in private manufacturing there. At the same time, American corporations remitted $359 million in profits and $211 million in fees and royalties from this sector to the United States. Apparently, therefore, United States private investments "decapitalized" Latin America of $392 million that year in terms of manufacturing alone. Yet, if we compare this to United States manufacturing investments in Latin America of $8.6 *billion*, the sum repatriated to the North amounted to a mere 4.6 percent, hardly an extortionist outflow. The sum of $392 million is all the more insignificant when we compare it to the total sales of United States manufacturing affiliates in Latin America in 1974, which amounted to $20.9

[69] Smith (fn. 67), 21ff.
[70] Johnson, "Dependence and the International System," in Cockroft (fn. 6), 75n.; repeated with other dates, 94n.

billion. In other words, if we consider the $392 million as return either on investment or on volume of business generated, it can scarcely be maintained that Latin America is being "decapitalized."[71]

It is more difficult to refute unambiguously the charge that Third-World economies are being "denationalized"—a term that refers to the tendency of northern industries to buy out successful local businesses and to control local capital through encouraging its minority participation in northern ventures there. For example, the Department of Commerce provides figures showing that from 1968 to 1972, Latin Americans provided from 33 to 54 percent of the capital called for by United States companies in the region.[72] Should that be interpreted as southerners financing the takeover of their own countries? Similarly, Richard J. Barnet and Ronald E. Müller cite a study by the Harvard Business School for the years 1958–1967 to underscore the familiar allegation of *dependencistas* that Americans are buying up able southern firms and are thereby stifling southern entrepreneurs: "About 46 percent of all manufacturing operations established in the period were takeovers of existing domestic industry."[73] A closer inspection of this argument suggests that once again the dependency school is presenting its statistics selectively. For if we look more thoroughly through the material assembled by the Harvard Business School survey, it appears that through liquidations or expropriations, or sales of an entire affiliate or a substantial part thereof, American interests had divested themselves of nearly as many manufacturing concerns as they had acquired: 332 lost as compared with 337 gained.[74] Nor do sheer numbers of firms present the most interesting statistics; it is the *value* of affiliates bought or sold that may be more important. And, so far as the figures for 1975 and 1976 are concerned, Department of Commerce statistics show that United States firms sold off about as much in value of their manufacturing affiliates in the South as they acquired through takeovers.[75]

[71] See Department of Commerce, *Survey of Current Business*, "U.S. Direct Investment Abroad in 1976" (August 1977), for all figures except those on sales; for sales, see *ibid.*, "Sales by Majority-Owned Foreign Affiliates of U.S. Companies, 1974" (May 1976). Other years could be cited where American profits were far *less*.

[72] Department of Commerce, *Survey of Current Business*, "Sources and Uses of Funds for a Sample of Majority-Owned Foreign Affiliates of U.S. Companies, 1966–1972" (July 1975).

[73] Barnet and Müller, *Global Reach: The Power of the Multinational Corporations* (New York: Simon and Schuster 1974), 154-55.

[74] James W. Vaupel and Joan P. Curhan, *The Making of Multinational Enterprise* (Cambridge: Graduate School of Business Administration, Harvard University 1969), 240-41 for expansion; 376-77, 505 for losses.

[75] Department of Commerce, *Survey of Current Business*, "U.S. Direct Investment Abroad in 1976" (August 1977), Table 4, p. 35 and Table 5, pp. 36-37.

Moreover, there seems to be unanimous agreement that as a percentage of gross business volume, the multinational corporations are declining in importance in the South: it is only in terms of their control over certain of the leading sectors of the economy that their presence is dominant. Even in these sectors, the emerging pattern seems to be for the southern governments to restrict foreign investment to those areas of the economy where local abilities cannot yet provide adequate capital or skills, and to push the foreigners out once conditions warrant it. To be sure, in many instances foreigners continue to operate behind the scenes: the custom of *prestanombres* (borrowed names), whereby locals act as figurehead directors and owners of establishments that are actually controlled from abroad is by no means restricted to Latin America, as the Spanish term might suggest. However, as the state and domestic interests gain in strength, there is little reason to think the letter of the law will not be increasingly applied.[76] In the process of the "nationalization" of these foreign concerns, might not the investors in such enterprises, those who hold minority shares as reflected in the Commerce Department survey cited above, be considered the logical next majority owners? "Denationalization" of southern industry has as little substance to it as "decapitalization."

The moral of these considerations is that the system of North-South relations is not only too weak to determine all aspects of change in the South—a fundamental point bearing reiteration—but that even in those areas where its influence is real, its long-run effect may well be to hasten the end of the international predominance of the North. For example, Algeria had managed to run up an external public debt of over $9 billion as of the end of 1975, and the United States had moved into position as the country's largest trading partner and substantial creditor.[77] Yet, one would mistake this involvement with the outside world if one were to see it as anything other than an Algerian effort to practice that skill of the martial arts whereby the strength of the opponent

[76] For a particularly strong essay stressing the growing role of the South relative to the North, see Theodore H. Moran, "Multinational Corporations and Dependency: A Dialogue for Dependentistas and Non-Dependentistas," *International Organization*, xxxii (Winter 1978); on Nigeria, see editorial notes in *African Development*, x (December 1975); on Mexico, Richard Weinert, "The State and Foreign Capital," in Reyna and Weinert (fn. 35); and on Southeast Asia, Franklin Weinstein, "Multinational Corporations and the Third World: The Case of Japan and Southeast Asia," *International Organization*, xxx (Summer 1976).
[77] World Bank, *Annual Report* (1977), Table 5, p. 111; Department of Commerce, *Overseas Business Report*, "World Trade Outlook for Near East and North Africa," OBR 77-45 (September 1977); Department of State, *Foreign Economic Trends and their Implications for the U.S.*, "Algeria," 77-033 (March 1977).

is used against himself. The same point of view has predominated in the Soviet Union since 1920, when Lenin actively sought to recruit capitalist trade and investment in his effort to build up his country's economic base. It is the unhistorical dogmatist, a familiar fellow in dependency literature, who asserts solely on the basis of certain grand ideas that, whatever the situation, the international system is a "trap," and that "self-reliance" through socialism is the only road to economic development.[78]

In this essay I have attempted to deal only with a major historiographic shortcoming common to most of dependency theory. I have made no claim to review the literature in full, to deny its genuine insights, or to analyze the ideological "united front" the theory is sponsoring between southern nationalists and Marxists. Instead, I have tried to encourage skepticism about propositions alleging the all-pervasive and self-perpetuating character of northern power with respect to the South, and to establish some measure of the relative autonomy of the various Third-World countries which comes from the real strength of local traditions and institutions.

[78] Johan Galtung, "The Lomé Convention and Neo-Capitalism," *African Review*, VI (No. 1, 1976).

SOME CONTEMPORARY ORTHODOXIES IN THE STUDY OF AGRARIAN CHANGE*

By ROBERT H. BATES

INTRODUCTION

THE purpose of this paper is to present a critical review of two major approaches to the analysis of agrarian societies, and to do so in light of evidence taken from the literature on Africa. The African data provoke considerable skepticism concerning the validity of these contemporary orthodoxies and support the following three major counter-arguments.

1. The very traits that have caused these societies to be classified as "precapitalist"—e.g., the existence of common land rights; the avoidance of market exchanges; the turning to subsistence production, reciprocity, and such social institutions as the family system for economic support—are themselves arguably products of the encounter of agrarian societies with agents of capitalism.[1]

2. Agrarian institutions represent compromises and adaptations; equally as often, they represent impositions from above by more powerful external agents. In either case, they cannot represent institutionalized expressions of agrarian values; subjectivist, value-based accounts of these institutions are therefore false.

3. Not only are the current orthodoxies overly culturally determined; they are also overly economic. Many of the distinctive traits of agrarian societies, I argue, result from the efforts of the state to secure domination and control over rural populations. Insofar as the institutions and behaviors exhibited by agrarian societies define a peasantry, in short, it is the state that creates peasants.

THE DOMINANT ORTHODOXIES

Among the most prominent of the current approaches, two stand out: the "natural economy" and "peasant economy" models of rural society.

* Original title: "Some Conventional Orthodoxies in the Study of Agrarian Change"

[1] By capitalism I mean an economic system in which there exists: (1) market exchange of both products and factors of production; (2) in particular, private markets for labor; and (3) economic accumulation, thus securing the reproduction and expansion of the means of production.

The Myth of the Natural Economy

The critical elements of the model of the natural economy are presented in Table 1.

TABLE 1
Schematic Presentation of the Model of a Natural Economy

Initial Conditions
1. Agrarian economy
2. Production for use rather than exchange
3. Insignificance of markets

Institutional Characteristics
1. Communal land rights
  a. Use rights accorded to producers if, and only if, producer is a member of the community
  b. Rights to land revert to community when use rights are no longer exercised
2. Importance of the primary community and, in particular, the village

Social Values
1. Self-sufficiency
2. Status
3. Equality

Patterns of Change
1. Initial opposition to "commoditization"
2. Social disintegration in the face of markets
3. Radicalization under the impact of capitalism

Implications
The preference of agrarian societies for communal forms of economic organization

---

Initial conditions. According to the model of the natural economy, "primitive" agrarian societies produce not for exchange but for use; as a consequence, "market exchanges are usually peripheral [and] all important output and factor flows are carried on via reciprocity and redistribution."[2] In the absence of markets, resources are not allocated in accord with their value in exchange; rather, the patterns of allocation are determined by social relationships. As Dalton states, "There is no separate economic system to be analyzed independently of social organization."[3]

---

[2] George Dalton, "Traditional Production in Primitive African Economies" in Dalton, ed., *Tribal and Peasant Economies* (Garden City, N.Y.: Natural History Press, 1967), 75.
[3] George Dalton, "Subsistence and Peasant Economies in Africa," *ibid.*, 157.

Institutional characteristics. Nowhere is the determining influence of social organization over the allocation of economic resources more clearly seen than in the area of property rights. In precapitalist societies, according to Marx, "an isolated individual could no more own land than he could speak."[4] The acquisition of property is thus a social act; it requires membership in a community.

Particularly critical is membership in the village. Along with kin-based organizations, the village is viewed as the central social institution of agrarian societies.[5]

The two themes of communal restrictions on landed property and the pervasive significance of villages are often fused. They combine in the discussion of the corporate village. In the words of Eric Wolf, such villages "maintain a measure of communal jurisdiction over land ... restrict their membership, maintain a religious system, enforce mechanisms which ensure the redistribution or destruction of surplus wealth, and uphold barriers against the ... outside."[6] Although the initial writings of Wolf make it clear that the corporate village is but one of many forms of rural settlement, the analysis of these villages dominated much of the subsequent literature on agrarian society.[7]

Social values. The social institutions of rural society, this literature contends, facilitate the attainment of basic cultural values. One such value is a sense of membership. Another is equality. A third is an outgrowth of the first two: the value placed on guarantees of subsistence. All members of society possess an equal right to sufficient income to guarantee their survival. "It is the absence of the threat of *individual* starvation which makes primitive society, in a sense, more human than market economy, and at the same time less economic."[8]

Patterns of change. The initial condition of the natural economy is said to be the absence of markets. But, according to this model, markets inevitably penetrate into even the most isolated communities; and this alteration in the initial conditions generates characteristic patterns of change.

[4] Karl Marx, "Precapitalist Economic Formations," in Karl Marx and Friedrich Engels, *Pre-Capitalist Socio-Economic Formations: A Collection* (London: Lawrence & Wishart, 1979), 98.
[5] See, for example, the discussion in James C. Scott, "Protest and Profanation: Agrarian Revolt and the Little Tradition," *Theory and Society* 4 (Summer 1977), 213.
[6] Wolf, "Closed Corporate Peasant Communities in Mesoamerica and Central Java," *Southwestern Journal of Anthropology* 13 (Spring 1957), 6.
[7] A prime illustration would be Joel S. Migdal, *Peasants, Politics, and Revolutions* (Princeton: Princeton University Press, 1974).
[8] Karl Polanyi, quoted in James C. Scott, *The Moral Economy of the Peasant* (New Haven and London: Yale University Press, 1976), 5.

One response is to resist the market; Robert Redfield maintains that these societies attempt to keep the market "at arm's length."[9] With the inevitable triumph of the market, however, a second response arises: social disintegration. Eric Wolf states that "capitalism cut through the integument of custom, severing people from their accustomed social matrix in order to transform them into economic actors, independent of prior social commitments to kin and neighbors."[10] A third response is rural radicalism. Agrarian protest is considered radical in the sense that it asserts the entitlement of all people to subsistence, the validity of communal property as a means of securing this entitlement, and the rejection of the private market.

> It is precisely the fact that peasants and artisans have one foot in the precapitalist economy that explains why they have provided the mass impetus for so many "forward looking" movements. Their opposition to capitalism, based as it is on a utopian image of an earlier era, is as tenacious, if not more so, as the opposition of a proletariat which has both feet in the new society.[11]

Policy implications. An important implication of this theory is that rural dwellers will subscribe to collective forms of economic organization that reject private property, and thereby forestall the emergence of economic inequality and exploitation. Goran Hyden notes that the promotion of cooperative societies in Africa derives in part from the conviction of political leaders that African rural society is communitarian by preference.[12]

THE PEASANT ECONOMY

A second model of agrarian society that is frequently applied to rural Africa is the model of the peasant economy. Its distinctive features are summarized in Table 2.

Initial conditions. Peasant economies are held to be precapitalist in the sense that, in peasant societies, labor is not separated from the means of production. Nonetheless, peasant societies represent a more "advanced" form of agrarian society than do natural economies. Peasant economies do not stand isolated and self-sufficient; rather, they reside within state systems and within economies that contain cities, industry, and manufacturing. They are linked to these other sectors through relations of political domination and economic exchange.

[9] Redfield, *Peasant Society and Culture* (Chicago: University of Chicago Press, 1956), 46.
[10] Wolf, *Peasant Wars of the Twentieth Century* (New York: Harper & Row, 1969), 279.
[11] Scott (fn. 5), 231.
[12] Hyden, *Efficiency versus Distribution in East African Co-operatives* (Nairobi: East African Literature Bureau, 1973), 4.

TABLE 2
SCHEMATIC PRESENTATION OF THE MODEL OF A PEASANT ECONOMY

INITIAL CONDITIONS
  1. Post-agrarian economy; importance of urban industry and manufacturing
  2. Fully elaborated markets both for products and factors of production
  3. Production for exchange as well as for use

INSTITUTIONAL CHARACTERISTICS
  1. Private rights in land
  2. Prevalence of inequality
      a. State coercion
      b. Class formation
  3. Limited participation in the markets for products and labor

BEHAVIORAL CHARACTERISTICS
  1. Subsistence ethic
  2. Rejection of pure profit maximization

PATTERNS OF CHANGE
  1. Creation of the peasant mode: impact of capitalism on the natural economy
  2. Conflicts between peasant mode and capitalism

Institutional characteristics. Nearly all discussions of peasant economies emphasize that peasant societies are "part-societies." In the cultural sphere, peasants are bearers of the "little" tradition; they define their rituals in response to the "great" tradition of the ritual centers of the larger society.[13] In the political sphere, they are part, but not governors, of the system. Not only are peasants politically subordinate to the state, but they also are politically dominated by other classes, which are often rural classes: in the context of a market economy and with the help of state power, certain elements of the rural society are able to accumulate large-scale private landholdings. This pattern of inequality is so important that Welch asks: "Without . . . landlords, could there be peasants?"[14]

In the economic sphere, peasants are "part" societies in the sense that they participate in markets and are reliant upon them to fulfill their subsistence needs—but only partially. *Limited* market participation exists where there is a tendency to consume large proportions of one's own

[13] Redfield (fn. 9), 46.
[14] Claude Welch, "Peasants as a Focus in African Studies," *African Studies Review* 20 (No. 3, 1977), 2.

production and to rely primarily upon family, as opposed to hired, labor.[15]

Behavioral characteristics. Peasants are held to exhibit characteristically "precapitalist" or "non-market" forms of behavior. As production units, peasant households differ from profit-maximizing firms in that they are driven by the need to secure sufficient subsistence to guarantee their survival and their reproduction. As a consequence, they will, if necessary, engage in internal exploitation to cover the requirements of domestic consumption. They will work longer hours, cultivate the lands they hold more intensively, or surrender greater revenues for lands they wish to buy than purely commercial considerations would justify.[16]

Patterns of change. The origins of peasant economy, it is held, lie in the impact of market forces upon the natural economy. Under the stimulation of the market, property rights become individualistic; households are no longer self-sufficient, but become dependent on the market; and "self-sufficient communities founded largely upon kinship ties are 'turned outwards,' as it were, and made dependent ... upon external structures and forces."[17] In the third world, the primary agency for this expansion of the market is imperialism. Post contends that "the colonial powers ... greatly extended the market principle, to the point where the impersonal forces of the world market dominated the lives of millions. ... It would appear, then, that many of the conditions for the existence of a peasantry were suddenly created, but from outside."[18]

The subsequent trajectory of change in peasant societies is said to be largely characterized by protracted periods of conflict between capitalism and the peasant mode of production. Some scholars, such as Hyden, find that peasants retard the growth of capitalism by their tendency to avoid markets and by their preference for subsistence production.[19] Others, such as Williams, contend that peasants resist the growth of capitalism but nonetheless fail, for they are inherently a "transitional class, which will inevitably be displaced by the technical superiority of capitalist production."[20]

[15] Eric R. Wolf, "Types of Latin American Peasantry: A Preliminary Discussion," *American Anthropologist* 57 (June 1955), 454.

[16] A. V. Chayanov, Daniel Thorner, Basile Kerblay, and R.E.F. Smith, eds., *The Theory of Peasant Economy* (Homewood, Ill.: Richard D. Irwin for the American Economic Association, 1966).

[17] Ken Post, " 'Peasantization' and Rural Political Movements in Western Africa," *Archives Européennes de Sociologie* 13 (No. 2, 1972), 225-26.

[18] *Ibid.*, 233. See also Wolf (fn. 10).

[19] Goran Hyden, *Beyond Ujamaa in Tanzania* (Berkeley and Los Angeles: University of California Press, 1980).

[20] Gavin Williams, "The World Bank and the Peasant Problem," in Judith Heyer, Pepe

THE MODELS REVIEWED IN LIGHT OF THE AFRICAN EXPERIENCE

As outlined above, the foregoing represent two of the dominant models of rural society. What is devastating is how poorly these models perform when applied to the African data.

INITIAL CONDITIONS

To an Africanist, one of the most striking deficiencies in these theories is posited in their initial conditions: a world of subsistence production in which there are no markets, no buying, no trading. This assumption, it should be stressed, cannot be dismissed as a mere romantic overtone in the arguments; rather, it provides an essential underpinning. Movements away from these initial conditions precipitate the change from a subsistence-oriented, egalitarian, isolated natural society to a market-dependent, class-riven, peasant society that is inextricably tied to centers of wealth and power. The initial conditions also help to account for the growth and behavior of political forces: outrage at the loss of a "state of virtue" provides a demand for agrarian revolution, and the moral values that are threatened through the spread of capitalism provide the revolutionary ideology.

If the initial conditions of the model of the natural economy were to hold anywhere, one would expect them to hold in Africa. And yet, time and time gain, historical research reaffirms that in precolonial Africa there was trade, there was commerce, and there was the widespread use of money in exchange economies. Jack Goody, who best summarizes these findings, is worth quoting at length:

> The concept of non-monetary economics is hardly applicable to precolonial Africa, except possibly for certain hunting groups of minimal importance. Africa was involved in a vast network of wide-ranging trade long before the Portuguese came on the scene. For East Africa we have a late first-century sailors' guide, the *Periplus of the Erythrean Sea*, to the trade along the coast. Long before the Europeans arrived there were trade routes from Madagascar up the East African coast, through the Red Sea and into the Mediterranean, along the Persian Gulf to India, South-east Asia, and Indonesia. By the time the Portuguese had reached East Africa, the Chinese had already been active there; before the development of the gun-carrying sailing ship on the Atlantic seaboard, the maritime commerce of the Indian Ocean made western Europe seem an underdeveloped area. Indeed, the trade between Ethiopia, the Mediterranean, and the Indian Ocean had much to do with the developments in the Arabian peninsula, including the rise of Muhammed.

Roberts, and Gavin Williams, eds., *Rural Development in Tropical Africa* (New York: St. Martin's Press, 1981).

In West Africa the medieval empires of the Niger bend were built up on the trade which brought salt, cloth, and beads south from the Sahara across to West Africa and took gold and ivory and slaves back to the Barbary coast and from there into medieval Europe.[21]

From the point of view of mercantile economy, parts of Africa were similar to western Europe of the same period. Metal coinage was in use on the East African coast. In the west, currencies consisted of gold, brass, and salt, but more especially cowrie shells which, coming as they did from the Maldive Islands off the south of Ceylon, filled most of the necessary attributes of money.[22]

Isolation, subsistence, and lack of involvement in an exchange economy were not commonly found in the "primitive" economies of Africa. Where they were, these traits characterized so small and insignificant a group of African societies that it would be nonsensical to base a general theory of social change upon them.[23]

TRANSITION ARGUMENTS

The reigning orthodoxies in the study of agrarian economies are defined not only in terms of their initial conditions; they are also defined in terms of their dynamics—i.e., assertions are made concerning their characteristic patterns of change. Agrarian societies are portrayed as locked in conflict with a powerful alternative: the capitalist economy, where private property exists, where everything can be bought and sold, and where people are driven to maximize profits by the imperative of market competition. In the face of the encroachment of the capitalist economy, rural dwellers are said to attempt to keep the market at arm's length and to resist commoditization. In light of the expectations generated by these arguments, it is therefore disconcerting to find that in Africa the roles of the supposed antagonists are sometimes the reverse of what these models would lead us to expect.

Buying and selling. Despite myths to the contrary, indigenous peoples throughout much of Africa turned quickly, vigorously, and skillfully to production for colonial markets. The rapid and astonishing growth of the cocoa industry in West Africa has been told by Hill and Berry; within one generation, Ghana became the world's leading producer of cocoa; it did so on the initiative of indigenous agrarian interests.[24] Ho-

---

[21] Jack Goody, "Economy and Feudalism in Africa," *The Economic History Review* 23 (December 1969), 394-95.

[22] *Ibid.*, 395.

[23] There is evidence that extensive trade existed in precolonial Africa for agricultural products as well. See William O. Jones, "Agricultural Trade Within Tropical Africa: Historical Background," in Robert H. Bates and Michael Lofchie, eds., *Agricultural Development in Tropical Africa: Issues of Public Policy* (New York: Praeger, 1980), 10-45.

[24] Polly Hill, *Studies in Rural Capitalism in West Africa* (London: Cambridge University

gendorn has shown how in Northern Nigeria indigenous entrepreneurs organized the large-scale production of groundnuts for export to colonial markets.[25] Similar histories exist for palm oil production in Nigeria and groundnut production in Senegal.[26] Giovanni Arrighi notes that in the Rhodesias change was not limited to the sphere of exchange but was also introduced in the methods of production: "Africans were equally prompt in investing and innovating in response to market opportunities."[27] The peasants acquired wagons, carts, maize mills, pumps, ox-drawn ploughs and other equipment; they radically altered their farming system; and they invested in higher-grade cattle and the fencing and dips required for their survival.[28]

Property rights. Change went even deeper: it extended to the definition of property rights. In light of the expectations formed by the orthodox treatment of agrarian change, the stunning irony of the matter is that it was often the governments of the colonial powers—the primary agents of capitalism—who advocated "communal" property rights, whereas members of the indigenous agrarian societies championed the cause of private ownership.

In order to avoid confusion on the matter of property rights, let me recall the definition outlined in Table 1. By communal land rights, I mean a system wherein

1. Use rights are accorded a producer if, and only if, that producer is a member of the community. In other words,
    (a) Community membership is a sufficient condition for rights to land: no member of the community can go without land.
    (b) Community membership is a necessary condition for rights to land: land cannot be alienated outside of the community.
2. The community holds revisionary rights in land. That is, when individuals no longer use the land, rights to it revert to the community. The land can then be reallocated to other users.

Press, 1970); Sara Berry, *Cocoa, Custom and Socio-Economic Change in Rural Western Nigeria* (London: Oxford University Press, 1975).

[25] Jan S. Hogendorn, "Economic Initiative and African Cash Farming," in Peter Duignan and Lewis H. Gann, eds., *Colonialism in Africa, 1870-1960* (London: Cambridge University Press, 1975), 283-328.

[26] Donal Cruise O'Brien, *The Mourides of Senegal* (Oxford: Clarendon Press, 1971); G. K. Helleiner, *Peasant Agriculture, Government, and Economic Growth in Nigeria* (Homewood, Ill.: Richard D. Irwin, 1966).

[27] Arrighi, "Labor Supplies in Historical Perspective: A Study of Proletarianization of the African Peasantry in Rhodesia," in Giovanni Arrighi and John S. Saul, *Essays on the Political Economy of Africa* (Nairobi: East African Publishing House, 1973), 185.

[28] See also the cases described in Robin Palmer and Neil Parsons, eds., *The Roots of Rural Poverty in Central and Southern Africa* (Berkeley and Los Angeles: University of California Press, 1977).

Under a system of private property rights, membership in the community is no longer sufficient to guarantee access to land; nor is it a necessary condition. Thus, land can be alienated to persons outside the community. Moreover, land that is not in use does not revert to the community; it can be held for purposes of speculation, transferred to other private individuals, or bequeathed to persons of the owner's choosing. It is a consequence of this system, of course, that even in the presence of abundant land, people may starve for want of access to it; a primary attraction of a communal system of land rights is that under similar circumstances such deaths would not occur.

Conflicts between capitalist governments committed to communal rights and spokesmen for agrarian societies committed to private land rights broke out in both West and East Africa. In 1912, the British colonial government appointed the West African Lands Committee to investigate land laws in British West Africa. The Committee's report called for the reinforcement of "pure native tenure." It stressed that "legislation should have as its aim the checking of the progress of individual tenure and the strengthening of native custom," which, it held, "did not recognize the concept of individual tenure and forbade the ... sale of ... community land."[29] In these recommendations, the Committee was vigorously opposed by local interests. One expert on local practices, Sir Brandford Griffith, noted that in opposing private ownership and a free market in land, the government was in fact flying in the face of "local custom." Grier comments that

> So definite and so common a practice was the sale of land ... by the end
> of the nineteenth century that Griffith (whose association with the colony
> dated back to his father, Sir William Brandford Griffith, Governor 1886-
> 1895) could say that he "never had occasion to consider the question."[30]

In West Africa, then, the putative agency of capitalist expansion—the government of the colonial power—actively promoted communal rights, while members of the agrarian societies demanded the unrestricted right to purchase and to alienate land. In East Africa, a similar "reversal" obtained. In opposition to the penetration of private market forces into the rural sector, for example, the postwar governor of Kenya, Sir Philip Mitchell, argued that soil degradation, environmental spoilage,

---

[29] Beverly Grier, "Underdevelopment, Modes of Production, and the State in Colonial Ghana," *The African Studies Review* 24 (March 1981), 35. For an excellent discussion of the issue of property rights, see also John Cohen, "Land Tenure and Rural Development in Africa," in Bates and Lofchie (fn. 23).

[30] Grier (fn. 29), 33.

and avaricious exploitation of land inevitably followed the creation of private property. What was needed, he maintained, was "the proper control of the community. Each Native Land Unit, or a portion of a unit, was to be regarded as an 'estate of the community'; each occupier of land was to be a 'tenant of the tribe'."[31]

The indigenous people opposed the land policy of the government of Kenya. As long ago as 1912, a Kenya District Officer had investigated local tenurial practices among the Kikuyu and had found that land was held by families who occupied it unconditionally—that is, not at the pleasure of any higher communal authority. He had also found that many of these family estates had been purchased. Land was in fact bought and sold both within and between tribes.[32] It is therefore not surprising that the Kikuyu opposed the government's policy and demanded individual registration of land holdings and the enforcement of private rights to land. The urgency with which they pressed their demands was of course intensified by the insecurity they felt in the face of the uncompensated seizure of lands by the colonialists.

Characteristically, the transition arguments of the orthodox models of agrarian change have made the assumption that rural dwellers are assaulted by capitalism. They counterpoise the communal attributes of these societies against the forces of capitalism that promote private interests. They make allowance for some members of rural society to demand private property rights: rural elites, for example, are expected to seek a regime of private property rights in order to defend their economic privileges. But it could never be the case under these theories that agents of capitalism would seek to establish communal rights while the members of agrarian societies seek private ones. And yet, as we have seen, the literature on Africa documents at least two instances of this "reversal."

Our attention is thus deflected from the economist orthodoxies. In particular, the discordant set of facts suggests that *governments* may act in ways that differ from what one would expect, given their societies' "stage of development"; they may confront an independent set of political imperatives.

Ideology. In the case of the British, there existed a genuine conviction that precapitalist societies were communitarian; that Western man, in the personage of the imperialist, was introducing forces that promoted self-interested behavior; and that, because indigenous institutions were

---

[31] Quoted in M.P.K. Sorrenson, *Land Reform in Kikuyu Country* (Nairobi: Oxford University Press, 1967), 56.

[32] *Ibid*, 20-21.

scarce and inherently valuable, they should be protected by government. In his discussion of Norman Humphrey, an influential figure in the postwar development of Kenyan land policy, Sorrenson notes:

> Humphrey—and indeed a good many other officials—doubted the moral right of Europeans to impose ... a system [of economic individualism] on Africans, thus destroying the supposed communal spirit of tribal tradition. Humphrey wanted to establish a series of locational, divisional, and district councils to manage land along communal lines ... and he hoped this would lead to a 'reawakening of [the individual's] sense of duty to his fellows and his land and the instilling of a desire to abandon those false values that have been a major product of his sudden contact with our civilization.'[33]

Humphrey was, of course, echoing the sentiments of far more powerful figures in the British colonial regime: Lugard, Cameron, Perham, and Hailey, to mention but a few.[34]

Empowerment. Tactical calculations made in the course of securing political domination in Africa were also important. The colonial governments sought, and needed, political allies through whom they could secure control over Africa's largely agrarian population. A prime reason for insisting on communal land rights, it would appear, was that a system of communal rights empowered locally based confederates: it gave control over the allocation of the key resource in an agrarian economy to those who would govern the agrarian population on behalf of the colonialist powers—the tribal chiefs.

In the British case, the policy of governing through "traditional rulers" was known as "indirect rule." C. K. Meek clearly articulates the link between indirect rule and the formation of property rights; at the beginning of his semi-official treatise, *Land Law and Custom in the Colonies*, he states:

> The authority of chiefs, sub-chiefs and heads of clans and families is bound up with the land. The grant, therefore, to individuals of absolute rights of ownership would tend to disrupt the native policy, and so, too, would the indiscriminate sale of tribal lands by chiefs.[35]

So compelling is this thesis that Meek returns to it toward the end of his work, contending that "there is a political danger in allowing

[33] *Ibid.*, 58.

[34] See, for example, Lord Hailey, *An African Survey: Revised, 1956* (London: Oxford University Press, 1957); Frederick D. Lugard, *The Dual Mandate in British Tropical Africa* (London: F. Cass, 1965); and Margery Freda Perham, *Native Administration in Nigeria* (London: Oxford University Press, 1937).

[35] Meek, *Land Law and Custom in the Colonies* (London: Oxford University Press, 1949), 10.

individuals to become owners of 'freeholds,' without owing any allegiance to the local Native Authorities." He concludes, "If 'indirect rule'
is to continue to be a cardinal principle of British policy, it would appear
to be essential that the local Native Authorities should remain the ultimate 'owners' of as much land as possible. . . ."[36]

The best system, from Meek's point of view, was one in which political
loyalty to an agent of the colonial power served as a prerequisite for
access to land. Robert L. Tignor, in examining the operation of this
system, finds it to operate roughly as one would expect. Friends and
relatives of the chief secured land; indeed, the chiefly families became
the richest land owners in the districts studied, while political enemies
of the chiefs lost rights to land. Tignor also notes that the more valuable
the control over land—i.e., the scarcer the land in relation to the population—the greater the power which the British policy of customary
land rights conferred to the chiefs. The Ibo and Kikuyu chiefs, for
example, who ruled in densely populated agricultural areas, proved far
more effective as "modernizing agents" of the British than did the chiefs
of the Kamba or Masai, who lived in areas where population was far
less dense and land therefore relatively more abundant.[37]

Counter-factual observations—that rural dwellers favor private property rights while capitalist governments favor communal property—
have thus driven us to a departure from orthodox theories of rural
change. We have moved instead to an approach in which key rural
institutions—in this case, property law—are interpreted as political outcomes. As a corollary to this approach, it might be assumed that the
institutions that were adopted in any particular situation would represent
the outcome of political bargaining. Viewed in this light, there is no
particular reason to expect one or another form of agrarian institution
to emerge as a consequence of social change. The outcome would depend
on the configuration of power.

This inference is supported by the literature. In some areas of Africa,
both the colonial powers and the native chiefs were notably weak. In
Zambia, for instance, the occupying forces were small and chiefly powers
had been based largely upon warfare and slave raiding, both of which
were abandoned following the imperial occupation. It was also true in
Kenya; not only were the British forces small in number, but acephalous

[36] *Ibid.*, 193.
[37] Tignor, "Colonial Chiefs in Chiefless Societies," *Journal of Modern African Studies* 9
(1971), 350. See also Marshall Clough, *Chiefs and Politicians: Local Politics and Social Change
in Kiambu, Kenya, 1918–1936*, Ph.D. diss. (Stanford University, 1978).

societies were the rule—the institution of chieftaincy was nonexistent. From the point of view of the colonial administration in both places, the result was a need for power. In the case of Kenya, the response of the British was the virtual creation of chiefs and tribal authorities, and the assignment of the power to regulate the allocation of "native" lands to these native authorities. In the case of Zambia, the British forbade any registering of individual titles of land ownership, and created tribal rights in land; land allocation became the responsibility of the chiefs. As Gluckman states, government policy promoted tribalism.[38]

Where there was a need to create rural power, then, the colonial state promoted the establishment of communal property rights as part of its effort to elaborate systems of rural political control over an agrarian population. Where the colonial authority possessed decisive power and was not reliant upon the creation of rural elites, the situation was different. In essence, it was no longer purely political; commercial considerations could be decisive. For example, if an industrial labor force was needed, the agrarian society could be "proletarianized," as it was in some regions of southern Africa. Where food or export crops were desired, the rural population could be left in place as a free peasantry and agrarian society, a collection of smallholders working virtually within a regime of private property.

In other regions, where rural elites did exist, the outcome of the bargaining between the colonial power and the indigenous agrarian society often reflected the composition and preferences of the latter. In Ghana, for instance, indigenous commercial elites profited from the use of land. Exports of rubber, timber, and palm oil had long flourished in the territory, and the local political leaders themselves were deeply involved in commerce and trade. The colonial power, in securing the terms of the political settlement by which to govern the territory, had to concede the rights of these rural elites to exercise unrestricted control over their property. In Uganda, by contrast, the rural elite was not commercialized, and land was not exploited to secure pecuniary profits from agriculture. Rather, the elite was almost purely political and consisted of the chiefs and their administrators. In order to secure allies within the rural sector, then, the imperialists had to accommodate themselves to this structure of power. The result was yet another form of property settlement: the virtual "Junkerization" of landed relations. In return for their collaboration with the British occupying powers, the

---

[38] Max Gluckman, "Foreword" to W. Watson, *Tribal Cohesion in a Money Economy* (Manchester: Manchester University Press for the Rhodes-Livingstone Institute, 1958), x-xi.

chiefs were given freeholders' rights to the best lands in Uganda; the peasants virtually became serfs. When cash crop production began, the chiefs reaped vast economic benefits through the appropriation of labor dues and other "feudal" services.[39]

The argument that African indigenous societies embodied collective property rights and that it was the influence of capitalism that led to the formation of private rights in land is an overly economist one. Rather, the form of property law was shaped by the desire of the colonial state for political domination of an agrarian population and by the nature of the political accommodations it had to make in order to secure its hegemony.

Finances. States that are driven by the need for domination thus develop land rights in efforts to create rural centers of power. In shaping their policies toward rural property, their behavior is also influenced by financial imperatives. One of the best illustrations of the influence of fiscal considerations comes from Zambia. As is well known, Zambia depends on the production of copper. The copper deposits, first located early in the 20th century, gave birth to one of the world's leading copper industries; by 1930, the mines of what was then Northern Rhodesia employed 30,000 people. As the largest industry in this small territory, and by a vast measure the most profitable, the copper industry constituted the major element in the colonial government's tax base.

When copper prices rose, both the government and the mining companies prospered; when copper prices fell, both suffered. But the costs imposed by lower prices were borne unequally: while both the government and the firms experienced decreasing revenues, the efforts of the firms to lower their costs when income declined imposed increased costs upon the government.

The mines were capitalist enterprises. When prices fell, they maximized their profits (or, equivalently, minimized their losses) by curtailing their use of the variable factor of production: labor. While it was cost-minimizing on the part of companies to release labor at times of lower prices, unemployed labor threatened to add to the costs of government. These costs might take the form of the state's providing food and shelter; or they might take the form of police protection in the face of threats posed by masses of unemployed workers. Even though both the government and the mining companies derived their revenues from mining, then, the government's need for additional funds increased just when revenues became most scarce.

[39] Henry W. West, *Land Policy in Buganda* (London: Cambridge University Press, 1972).

This fiscal dilemma was, in a sense, created by capitalism. Since the means of production were in private hands, production decisions were made solely with a view to private, as opposed to social, consequences. In addition, the state's revenues were subject to cyclical shocks originating from the capitalist economies. L. H. Gann quotes the Chief Secretary of Northern Rhodesia at the time of the most cataclysmic of these shocks—the depression of the 1930s:

> The wealth of the country is in the minerals which it does not own ... and direct revenue from this source is at present negligible.... The fact ... that the companies are not earning taxable profits does not diminish the services which the Government is compelled to supply to the mining areas.[40]

To deal with this dilemma, the state advocated an ironical solution: the development of communal forms of rights to landed property. The government created a form of citizenship in which rights were dependent not only on national membership, but also on membership in a sub-nationality, a tribe. Access to land became a function of tribal affiliation. Land could be acquired in a rural community by affiliating with its political officials and by establishing membership in a kin group that belonged to that political community. To retain rural land rights, then, urban dwellers had to be "tribalized." Rural lands could not be sold; they were retained as "tribal trusts." The reason for these policies was clear: at times of fiscal stress, the government wanted to be able to avoid the costs of large-scale unemployment. It wanted the disbanded urban labor force to reincorporate itself into the rural economy quickly and peacefully. The costs of guaranteeing subsistence were thus to be borne by the rural community.[41]

Thus, the origins of communal land rights lay at least as much in capitalism and in the fiscal problems it created for the state as they did in the inherent cultural traditions of the rural population.[42]

---

[40] Gann, *A History of Northern Rhodesia* (London: Chatto & Windus, 1964), 253.

[41] Excellent discussions are included in Elena L. Berger, *Labour, Race and Colonial Rule: The Copperbelt from 1924 to Independence* (Oxford: Clarendon Press, 1974); Charles Perrings, *Black Mineworkers in Central Africa* (New York: Africana Publishing Company, 1979); A. L. Epstein, *Politics in an Urban African Community* (Manchester: Manchester University Press for the Rhodes-Livingstone Institute, 1958); and Helmuth Heisler, *Urbanization and the Government of Migration* (New York: St. Martin's Press, 1974).

[42] For additional arguments, see Claude Meillassoux, *Maidens, Meal and Money: Capitalism and the Domestic Community* (London: Cambridge University Press, 1981); Harold Wolpe, "Capitalism and Cheap Labour Power in South Africa," *Economy and Society* 1 (No. 4, 1972), 425-56; and Palmer and Parsons (fn. 28). I differ from these approaches in my acknowledgement of the divergence of interests between the state and private enterprises, and in my conviction that the state was set upon solving *its own* fiscal problem by controlling the formation of land laws.

ANOTHER INSTITUTION: THE VILLAGE

Thus far I have employed the African data to criticize several major components of the currently orthodox theories of agrarian change—their statement of initial conditions; their specification of characteristic trajectories of change; and their analysis of a key agrarian institution, property rights. The African experience provokes a skeptical reappraisal of arguments pertaining to a second major rural institution, namely, the village.

In Africa, village dwelling was often not the basic form of rural settlement; many people preferred to live in isolated homesteads. Where villages were formed, it was often at the behest of states. Many of these states were profoundly capitalist.

At the time of the establishment of the Pax Britannica in north-eastern Rhodesia, for example, people generally resided in family home-steads. In the late 19th century, however, the British South African Company (B.S.A.C.)—the creation of that most dedicated proponent of capitalist expansion, Cecil John Rhodes—determined that the region's rural population properly belonged in villages. George Kay notes that "throughout the whole of north-eastern Zambia ruthless regrouping for administrative convenience was systematically carried out."[43] He quotes from the B.S.A.C.'s own records that "many ... resisted and were sent to prison before the order was finally obeyed."[44] In this area, then, it was the administrators who sought to form the villages. That the agents of one of the most dedicated embodiments of capitalism were the pro-ponents of villagization adds an ironic note to our reappraisal of the orthodox position.[45]

Even today it would appear that village dwelling is preferred by the governments rather than by the rural people. Tanzania is a notable case in point. In the name of "development," the government of Tanzania has sought to group rural dwellers into communities large enough for it to provide dispensaries, clinics, schools, water supplies, agricultural inputs, marketing facilities, and other services; it thereby hopes to strengthen the productive forces of the country's agrarian society.[46] It is notable that the state legitimated its reconstruction of rural society by propound-

---

[43] Kay, *Social Aspects of Village Regrouping in Zambia* (Lusaka: Institute for Social Research, University of Zambia, 1967), 11.

[44] *Ibid.*, 10.

[45] In the case of Kenya, Sorrenson notes: "The Kikuyu did not live in villages, but in dispersed households. ... During the Mau Mau Emergency the Kikuyu, the Embu and some of the Meru population were concentrated in 732 villages. ..." Sorrenson (fn. 31), 3.

[46] The best studies are Michaela Von Freyhold, *Ujamaa Villages in Tanzania* (New York and London: Monthly Review Press, 1979); Dean E. McHenry, Jr. *Tanzania's Ujamaa Villages* (Berkeley: Institute of International Studies, 1979); and Hyden (fn. 19).

ing a theory of African agrarian history in which "colonialism [had] encouraged individualistic social attitudes,"[47] whereas prior to colonialism, Africans had lived cooperatively in socially integrated, mutually supportive, "village communities." Tanzanian scholars have not hesitated to question the validity of these claims.[48]

In evaluating the presumption that village-living is the natural form of agrarian settlement in Africa, we should be disposed toward caution. In some areas, villages appear not to have been the preferred mode of habitation. In other cases, where they *were* preferred, it was the states that preferred them. Some of these states were socialist, as in the case of Tanzania; in the case of the late British South Africa Company, however, the authorities were rampantly capitalist.[49]

A Behavioral Characteristic: The Preference for Subsistence

The three elements of initial conditions, institutional traits, and characteristic patterns of change help to define the orthodox models of agrarian society. So, too, does a fourth element: the psychological traits of rural dwellers. Of these traits, the one that is central to the conventional models is the preference for subsistence production.

In contradistinction to the conventional orthodoxies, I argue that the reversion to subsistence can be viewed as a rational response to prevailing conditions in the political and economic environment of the rural producers. The actions of the states that control the markets in efforts to extract resources from rural populations constitute an important source of these conditions.

Many of Africa's export crops are cash crops, pure and simple; they have no direct use in consumption and are grown purely for the market. Recently, the volume of agricultural exports from Africa has declined, creating shortages of foreign exchange; this decline has been taken by Hyden and others as evidence of the disruptive power of a precapitalist peasantry.[50] But I would argue that it should be viewed in a different light.

In Africa as a whole, over 80 percent of the population is engaged in agriculture, and over 50 percent of the gross domestic product is derived from agricultural production. Most African states therefore rely

---

[47] *Ibid.*, 98.

[48] See, for example, Samuel S. Mushi, "Modernization by Traditionalization: Ujamaa Principles Revisited," *Taamuli* 1 (No. 2, March 1971).

[49] For further evidence concerning "state origins" of village communities and a brilliant exposition of this argument, see Samuel L. Popkin, *The Rational Peasant* (Berkeley and Los Angeles: Unversity of California Press, 1979).

[50] Hyden (fn. 19).

on agriculture for financial resources. One way in which the industry can be taxed is by regulating the market for export crops. In many cases, the government is the sole legal buyer of these crops. By purchasing them at an administratively set price in the domestic market and selling them at prices prevailing in the world market, the government accumulates revenue generated by the difference between the domestic and world market prices. In this way, the producers of cash crops are heavily taxed.[51]

One implication of such governmental fiscal policies is that the rewards for participating in the market place are lowered for many farmers; they are certainly lowered in comparison with the returns attained by producing crops that can be consumed on the farm or sold outside of official marketing channels.[52]

A government's use of market controls to levy resources from agriculture thus lowers the returns farmers can expect from production for the market, both in absolute and relative terms. *In and of itself, this fact would account for the peasants' turning away from cash crop production.* There is therefore no need to posit the existence of an antimarket peasant mentality. Indeed, such an imputation would be wrong: withdrawal from exchange is the appropriate market response to the economic conditions that at present characterize many agricultural markets.

THE MARKET ORIGINS OF POLITICAL BONDAGE

Governments are interested not only in securing public revenues from export markets; they are also interested in securing foreign exchange. Toward this end, they tend to overvalue their currencies. One consequence is the taxation of export agricultural products for the benefit of those who seek imports: the industrialists (who seek cheap imports of plant and capital equipment) and the elites (who seek to gratify their tastes for imported products more cheaply). Another consequence of overvaluation is the generation of political power by establishing an excess demand for foreign exchange. At the artificially pegged price of the domestic currency, the market cannot allocate foreign exchange; the demand for it exceeds the supply. Those in charge of the foreign exchange "market" therefore become enormously powerful because they control the allocations of a scarce and valuable resource.

In this system, the beneficiaries are those in the Central Bank or those who make appointments to it. They are members of the foreign exchange

[51] See Robert H. Bates, *Markets and States in Tropical Africa* (Berkeley and Los Angeles: University of California Press, 1981).
[52] See, for example, the data contained in Government of Uganda, Ministry of Agriculture and Forestry, "Pricing Policy and Agricultural Production," (Entebbe: Ministry of Agriculture and Forestry, August 1978).

allocation committees and of the committees that allocate import licenses, or persons who designate the appointees to these committees. Those who receive import licenses also stand to benefit.

The losers in this system are those who are not located in positions of access to this scarce resource and who nonetheless must purchase imported goods. Typically, there are no peasant farmers in the Central Bank or on the committee that allocates foreign exchange or import licenses. Yet the farmers rely on imports. Farm implements such as hoes, cutlasses, sprayers, pesticides, ox ploughs and other tools, sacks and bags, milling machines, and so forth often have to be imported. Moreover, many consumer goods, such as shirts, shoes, blankets, soap, and batteries are imported, or are manufactured with imported equipment. But, in this administratively structured market, the farmers must, in effect, bribe their superiors to secure needed imports; they must pay the premium exacted by the excess demand for foreign currencies and imports to satisfy those who have sufficient political power to secure privileged access to foreign exchange or to the imports it can buy.

Overvaluation thus lowers the price of exports, increases the costs of farming, and raises consumer prices for farmers. And it does so while involving the farmers in a system of regulated foreign exchange markets in which they are subject to political and economic domination by persons with influence in the national capital.

An analysis that is based on the political manipulation of markets thus reveals three features of the conventional models of precapitalist societies. One is the withdrawal from markets; another—a virtual corollary—is the preference for subsistence; and the third is the powerlessness of peasants. Rather than posit these characteristics as three separate traits, I regard them as joint consequences of the way in which markets have been manipulated by states to extract resources from agrarian societies. The approach is more powerful than the conventional orthodoxies.[53]

Conclusion

In this paper I have summarized two of the dominant models of agrarian change and reviewed them in light of evidence drawn from rural Africa. The traditional approaches require initial conditions that

[53] Catherine Coquery-Vidrovitch, in writing about precolonial African societies, defined the African mode of production as one in which states did not directly control producers (e.g., through enserfment or slavery), but controlled and manipulated trade in order to accumulate resources from them. Her analysis is at least as applicable, in my view, to contemporary Africa as it was to the precolonial period, and very likely more so. See Coquery-Vidrovitch, "Recherches sur un mode de production Africain," *Le Pensée* 144 (1969), 61-78.

have rarely existed historically. They are overly subjectivist, attributing the existence of institutions to preferences under circumstances in which these institutions have clearly been imposed. Moreover, they are overly economic, in that they place too strong an emphasis on the impact of the market on agrarian societies and too little on the impact of states. Time and again throughout this essay, an approach has proved fruitful that looks at the effect upon rural society of the demand for power and resources on the part of states under conditions in which people and wealth are concentrated in agriculture.

EXPLAINING ETHNIC
POLITICAL PARTICIPATION

By NELSON KASFIR*

FAR too many explanations of the role of ethnicity in political behavior, particularly in Africa, vastly understate or overstate its relevance. For every writer who insists that "tribalism is Africa's natural condition, and is likely to remain so for a long time to come,"[1] another will assert that "tribalism is not an explanation but an ideology, one which itself needs to be explained."[2] That observers of these matters—whether they be liberal modernization theorists or Marxists—are so often wide of the mark poses an interesting question about unrecognized biases hidden within Western social science. The conclusions of Marxist writers and of students of modernization usually conflict because their analyses begin from opposite assumptions. It is the restrictiveness of each set of assumptions that prevents an accurate assessment of ethnicity in particular political situations.

The concept of ethnicity developed here comprises both schools of thought. By converting the assumptions of both approaches into empirical questions, a more subtle and useful inquiry into the political force of ethnicity can be articulated. The essential feature that underlies this conjunction is the observer's acceptance that ethnic identity is both fluid and intermittent. Thus it is one of many possible identities that could become the motivation for political action. The political situation—both the present moment and its historic development—contains the causal factors impelling an individual to prefer a particular social identity. The individual's choice may be fundamentally ethnic, class, religious, or—it is worth stressing—a combination of these identities. This choice may be constant or it may change from one situation to another. Indeed, even when an ethnic identity is preferred, an individual may, within limits, change from one ethnic category to another. This choice is a political resource over which individuals have varying degrees of control.

* An earlier version of this paper was presented to the 1977 Annual Meeting of the African Studies Association in Houston. I would like to thank James Mittelman for his suggestions.
[1] Colin Legum, "Tribal Survival in the Modern African Political System," *Journal of Asian and African Studies*, v (January–April 1970), 102.
[2] Mahmood Mamdani, *Politics and Class Formation in Uganda* (New York and London: Monthly Review Press 1976), 3.

When political participation is based on ethnicity, individuals are necessarily constrained (though to a greater or lesser degree) by those objective indicators of common ancestry thought to be especially salient —culture, myths, language, or territory. Whether these objective indicators are the product of a history of traditional usage or the result of recent manipulation, subjective perception by others involved in the same political situation is essential for credible political participation. Shared perception permits, but does not necessarily create, sufficient social solidarity to turn individuals assigned to an ethnic category into an active ethnic group. Even then, the likelihood of social solidarity being channeled into participation depends on the opportunities created by the specific political situation.

Each of the foregoing steps introduces a new set of empirical questions that take the place of the starting assumptions of the modernization and Marxist schools. The research task created as a result is immeasurably more complicated than most observers of ethnicity realize. However, it permits the observer to develop a more sophisticated explanation of the different possibilities and changing interrelationships between ethnicity and class in political action. The assumptions concerning politicized ethnicity common to writers on modernization, and those of Marxist or radical analysts are presented below. The utility in combining these postulates to resolve various empirical issues is then demonstrated. The argument is illustrated here by presenting a brief account of what it means to call the Nubians in Uganda an ethnic group —particularly now that they have spectacularly improved their political fortunes. In the final section, the tendency toward reification of the role of ethnicity in explanations based on cultural pluralism and consociationalism is highlighted by applying the situational notion of ethnicity in politics.

Political participation, understood in its broadest sense, includes any form of political involvement from voting to rioting, from nepotism to revolution. It may or may not be based to some measure on ethnic considerations.[3] When two cases of ethnic political participation are compared, differences almost always emerge—not only in the kind of political involvement, but also in the nature of ethnicity espoused.

Before examining the conflict in assumptions between the two approaches, it is worth noting the points on which there is some agree-

---

[3] The concept of participation is analyzed in Kasfir, *The Shrinking Political Arena: Participation and Ethnicity in African Politics with a Case Study of Uganda* (Berkeley and Los Angeles: University of California Press 1976), 5-14; six ethnic case studies from Uganda are presented, 119-52.

ment. First, ethnic political participation is concerned with actions of a group or an individual arising from the imputation of common ancestry to themselves or to others. It makes little difference whether that ancestry is genealogically factual or fictitious. Where common ancestry is not at least indirectly implied, ethnicity is not involved and the roots of political action must be sought elsewhere. Second, for Africa in particular, there is an important difference between "tribe" in the precolonial sense of a small, remote, culturally distinctive, and self-sufficient unit, and "tribalism," involving certain political actions taken in the colonial or independence periods.[4] To the extent that tribalism is taken to refer to the act of a tribesman who is defined in the former sense, it has virtually disappeared from Africa. Few Africans are so untouched by outside influences that they can be considered members of the tribes that social anthropologists have attempted to reconstruct. Third, ethnicity and tribalism refer to the same political actions. Unfortunately, the latter term suggests that political behavior in Africa is not only qualitatively different from ethnic participation elsewhere, but also inferior.[5] Although "tribalism" is in constant popular usage in Africa, wider generalizations and less emotional discussion are more likely to result if "ethnicity" is the operative term.

OPPOSING SETS OF ASSUMPTIONS

Anyone wishing to discuss ethnicity as a political variable has to consider the following questions: (1) Is ethnicity to be regarded as a characteristic of the mental state of the political actor or of the social milieu in which he lives? (2) Are the advocates of ethnicity those of high position within society, or those without power, wealth, or status? (3) Is the decision to act on ethnic motives based on rational calculation or deeply held values? Each of these questions has been stated in "either-or" terms to focus attention on the assumptions that analysts often make, usually implicitly, on each of these themes. A more comprehensive notion of ethnicity requires, however, that each of these themes be treated as an empirical continuum on which instances of politicized ethnicity can be placed according to the characteristics of each case studied.

[4] Aidan Southall, "The Illusion of Tribe," *Journal of Asian and African Studies*, v (January–April 1970), 28.
[5] An explicit comparison showing the similarity of "nationalist" movements in Europe and "tribal" movements in Africa can be found in W. J. Argyle, "European Nationalism and African Tribalism," in P. H. Gulliver, ed., *Tradition and Transition in East Africa: Studies of the Tribal Element in the Modern Era* (London: Routledge & Kegan Paul 1969), 41-58.

The restrictiveness of basic assumptions are illustrated by the dominant view on ethnicity in the late colonial period, particularly in the British colonies.[6] Fortified by acceptance of the proposition that all people move in a unilinear, irreversible path from tradition to modernity, observers took ethnicity to be a set of primordial values growing out of the coincidence of culture, political organization, language, and territory. As people were educated in schools with a Western curriculum, converted to a Western religion, or entered the cash sector by growing new crops or taking wage employment, they were believed to be shedding the trappings of tradition and embracing the modern (that is, the colonial) world. The growth of African cities was regarded as evidence of this shift, which came to be called "detribalization." Behind this point of view were three assumptions: (1) that ethnicity was based on objective indicators (2) which produced values held deeply (3) primarily by the masses—that is, those who had not gained elite status by entering the colonial cash economy.

A variety of difficulties afflict this point of view, even though it probably remains the most widely held conception of ethnicity today. The survival and intermixture of tradition and outside influences raise serious questions about the notion that social change leads ineluctably to an easily specified modernity. The coincidence between culture, political organization, language, and territory was questionable before colonial rule began; it was increasingly distorted afterwards. Seeing ethnicity as a primordial value meant overlooking the fact that new ethnic groups were suddenly appearing under colonial rule—sometimes in rural areas, but more inexplicably, in the towns.

The older perspective has recently also been subjected to a thoroughgoing attack by analysts influenced by Marxist modes of inquiry.[7] In their view, it is economic relationships that carry critical political importance. The economic factors that shaped the colonial situation permitted those who acquired control over one or another aspect of the means of production to use new forms of ethnicity as weapons to mystify peasants and workers. In this sense, members of disadvantaged classes who enter politics to pursue ethnic goals are the victims of "false consciousness." At the root of this point of view are the three assumptions (1) that ethnicity

[6] For example, see Daniel F. McCall, "Dynamics of Urbanization in Africa," *The Annals of the American Academy of Political and Social Science*, No. 298 (March 1955); and Clifford Geertz, "The Integrative Revolution: Primordial Sentiments and Civil Politics in the New States," in Geertz, ed., *Old Societies and New States: The Quest for Modernity* (New York: Free Press 1963).

[7] For example, see Archie Mafeje, "The Ideology of 'Tribalism,'" *Journal of Modern African Studies*, ix (August 1971); and Ken Post, "'Peasantization' and Rural Political Movements in Western Africa," *Archives européenes de Sociologie*, xiii, No. 2 (1972).

is subjective (since it is the direct consequence of ideology rather than of economic material relationships), (2) that its political uses can frequently be traced to members of the recently formed middle classes who (3) advocate ethnic demands as a consequence of their rational calculations in pursuit of desired resources. These assumptions, of course, are the polar opposites of those adopted by the writers on modernization.

The basic problem with the radical approach is the willingness of its proponents to "throw out the baby with the bathwater." False consciousness is still consciousness, whether or not the actor recognizes his "true" interests. Where his life is in danger on the basis of an ethnic threat, it would be foolish to expect him to ignore ethnic considerations. To dismiss all manifestations of politicized ethnicity as irrelevant is to ignore a range of motives many of which will, on empirical examination, turn out to be strongly felt. Even where ethnic symbols are merely the façade for economic grievances, they often structure the political situation and thus affect the outcome.

A More Comprehensive Notion of Ethnicity

By accepting that a combination of the assumptions in both perspectives may sometimes explain an aspect of ethnic politics, we may examine how these different factors can vary from one case to another. It is useful, though, to begin with the issue of whether ethnicity is the product of subjective perception or whether it is an objective indicator, because we may then ask how pervasively ethnicity occurs in political participation. Or, to put a closely related question, when ethnicity is put forward to explain political participation, are other variables—notably class, but also religion and status—automatically ruled out?

Because ethnicity implies common ancestry, kinship is the most obvious objective indicator of membership in an ethnic group. Since many people cannot trace their genealogy through more than three generations, however, language, culture, and territory become more useful signs of membership in a larger group. The central difficulty—as in the case of using objective indicators to demonstrate affiliation with economic classes—is that the individual's perception of the group in which he considers himself a member may differ substantially from the group in which he would be classed on the basis of his first language, customs, or place of birth. The consequences for explaining his political participation are likely to be equally significant.

Thus, the subjective alternative—that an individual is a member of a group when he so thinks of himself—seems more attractive. However, political action is the result not only of an individual's beliefs (presuming for the moment that he acts on the basis of those beliefs), but also of the reaction of others to his assertion. Insiders may classify him as an outsider despite his desire to join their ethnic category. This is particularly apparent where a person who bears the objective indicators of a low-prestige ethnic unit attempts to become a member of a more desirable category. The problem is parallel to that which faces analysts who infer class membership solely from class consciousness.

The solution is to take objective indicators as well as subjective perceptions into account without assuming that they will be combined in precisely the same way in every ethnic group. There are, so to speak, standard paraphernalia that each ethnic group must display in order to make a political claim that will be taken seriously. A traditional history that stretches back many centuries or a standard language that is widely spoken will give plausibility to the assertion of group identity. But, where these are missing, they can often be constructed—as many local cultural enthusiasts and political entrepreneurs set out to do during the colonial period. The question then is whether these indicators are matched by equally widespread perceptions of ethnic membership. It may seem unduly restrictive to require both insiders *and* outsiders to share a perception of ethnic membership before labeling participation as ethnic. But since self-perception and external perception affect one another in most instances, widespread agreement can often be achieved on membership boundaries. Where it is not, the political value of ethnic assertion will be dubious.

The combination of subjective perception and objective indicators shared by insiders and outsiders may be related, either closely or distantly, to the traditional heritage of particular individuals. The work of urban anthropologists has shown how much ethnic identities can change as people migrate to the city and find that new skills and new associations are necessary, first for survival, and then for economic advancement.

Many of the newly defined urban ethnic groupings brought together migrants whose traditional homes in the countryside were close to each other and whose languages were closely related, but who had never previously thought of each other as possessing the same ethnic identity. These new groupings often developed intense social solidarities and then became the successful vehicles of political entrepreneurs. Sometimes, consciousness of the enlarged group seeped back to the countryside, where it stimulated the basis of political unity of much larger rural groupings. Relatively small ethnic units thus coalesced into much larger ethnic groups during the colonial period, creating the Ibo, Yoruba, Bagisu, Iteso, and Kikuyu as we know them today. On the other hand, a new ethnic consciousness created in the city might be resisted in the countryside. The urban migrant would then develop two ethnic identities: one that was appropriate for his urban life, and a different set of loyalties that was activated whenever he returned to the countryside. A third possibility, typical of "target workers," was to import one's traditional lifestyle into the city and avoid new loyalties as much as possible.[8] Finally, some migrants chose to break their ties to their rural ethnic units when they moved to the city.

Because of the changes created in ethnic loyalties by colonial influences, particularly urbanization (and too often we overlook the changes in ethnic identities that occurred in the precolonial period), the problem of the "proper" ethnic label for the people one met, for one's friends, and for one's self became immensely complicated, especially in the cities. The solution, as in any complex social situation, was to stereotype by creating a small number of ethnic categories. Social distance and relative prestige have been shown to be important elements in constructing these categories on the Zambian copperbelt, for instance,[9] though the elements undoubtedly vary from one place to another and often also involve differences in economic position. Ethnic categories imposed by others may also become the basis of self-definition—at least in situations in which those categories are regarded as relevant.[10]

The categories themselves are not necessarily stable. They may vary over time, depending upon the degree to which they are reinforced. S. R. Charsley builds on Mitchell's work in a useful manner by treating ethnic categories as proposals by the identifier that may be accepted or rejected by the person so identified. If the "transaction" is not completed (that is, if the proposal is rejected), the parties must find a new category—not necessarily ethnic—or fail to interact.[11]

[8] For a discussion of the varieties of responses by migrants to the city, see David Parkin, "Tribe as Fact and Fiction in an East African City," in Gulliver (fn. 5), 286-92.

[9] The argument was originally developed by J. C. Mitchell, *The Kalela Dance*, Rhodes-Livingstone Institute, No. 27 (Manchester: Manchester University Press 1956).

[10] In his research, Mitchell used objective indicators (based on *rural* criteria) to establish the ethnic units whose social distance he then measured in an *urban* area by asking respondents to classify *others*. Both the uncritical reliance on objective indicators and the use of rural definitions in the urban setting make his findings dubious, though the conceptual implications greatly advanced the study of ethnicity. Mitchell rediscusses his own work, though without reference to these difficulties, in "Perceptions of Ethnicity and Ethnic Behavior: An Empirical Exploration," in Abner Cohen, ed., *Urban Ethnicity* (London: Tavistock Publications 1974).

[11] Charsley, "The Formation of Ethnic Groups," in Cohen, *ibid.*, 360-61.

If ethnic categories are understood to be subjective and changeable, there are several implications for the observer of political behavior. First, the relationship between traditional culture and ethnicity is empirical and variable, rather than definitional and constant.[12] Thus, any demand for a political solution to satisfy an economic grievance or bolster local prestige on the basis of ethnicity will not necessarily involve primordial customs, though some sort of objective indicators must be asserted to make the appeal credible. Second, identifying someone as a member of an ethnic category at a particular time and in a particular place does not mean that, for political purposes, he will continue to hold that identity in other places and at other times. Again, the question must be decided empirically. Third, if categories are fluid, identity may shift dramatically not only from one ethnic category to another, but from ethnicity to class or religion. Fourth, and most important, by accepting that the identities people assume are both multiple and intermittent, the researcher must consider the situation that activates the particular identity the individual chooses.[13]

The identity chosen may be rationally selected by calculating costs and benefits, or it may be conditioned by deeply held values. Threats to personal survival because of membership in a particular ethnic group are likely to cause a potential victim to think in terms of his ethnic identity when objective indicators (characteristic scarification, for example) make it impossible for him to escape this label. The same individual may, in another situation (for example, where a strike is called to demonstrate against a government-ordered wage freeze), perceive himself and be perceived by others solely in terms of his class. Both cases point to the necessity for empirical research to establish how the choice of a particular identity, however constructed, is activated in the pursuit of a particular goal.

In taking this approach, it would be a mistake to assume that all social action must be reduced to fluctuating individual perceptions. A variety of factors help to stabilize political situations that reduce the choices open to an individual over a period of time. The possibilities of migration, economic opportunities, and social stratification may not change rapidly. The presence of entrepreneurs who assert a cultural identity by

[12] The point is developed by Frederick Barth, "Introduction," in Barth, ed., *Ethnic Groups and Boundaries: The Social Organization of Culture Difference* (London: George Allen & Unwin 1969).

[13] For valuable analyses articulating this point, see Crawford Young, *The Politics of Cultural Pluralism* (Madison: University of Wisconsin Press 1976), 41-44, 64-65, and particularly 140-62; Robert Melson and Howard Wolpe, "Modernization and the Politics of Communalism: A Theoretical Perspective," *American Political Science Review*, Vol. 64 (December 1970).

reinforcing traditional values or creating new ones may establish a mass consciousness among the relevant public that firmly stabilizes an ethnic label accepted by insiders and outsiders. J. S. La Fontaine describes the process by which members of the "Bagisu-to-become" created an "ideology of unity" by standardizing the dialects spoken by several smaller groups to create a single language, and by emphasizing that everyone should carry out particular ceremonies, especially those involving circumcision.[14] A "tribal" welfare association was founded, and new administrative boundaries demarcating "Bagisu" land were claimed in colonial and postcolonial arenas.

The most important factor in the political situation in Uganda that stimulated the formation of the Bagisu, as well as other large ethnic units containing people who were conscious of the political advantages of a shared identity, was the favored position of the Baganda.[15] Others emulated the Baganda, both to avoid cultural and political domination and to improve their own share of economic rewards. Political mobilization took place when the process of ethnic formation so dominated the consciousness of people who might otherwise have chosen other identities that it became the basis of strong feelings of social solidarity. The vigorous Bagisu response to the Mbale dispute (in which two recently created ethnic groups were involved in disturbances in the late 1950s and early 1960s over "control" of a town) shows the intense passions that even newly created ethnic loyalties can arouse.[16]

The concept of ethnicity so far developed can be summarized in four steps:

(1) Particular objective indicators associated with common ancestry
(2) become the focus of subjective perceptions both by members within the unit and by non-members
(3) through social solidarity created by a resurgence, or the fictive creation, of traditional unity
(4) so that in certain situations political participation will occur.

The creation of social solidarity in response to a situation turns the members of an ethnic *category* into an ethnic *group*. Political mobiliza-

[14] La Fontaine, "Tribalism among the Gisu: An Anthropological Approach," in Gulliver (fn. 5).

[15] Kasfir (fn. 3), 104-113.

[16] For a brief account of this controversy, see *ibid.*, 139-41. In some ways, the "Bakedi," the opponents of the Bagisu, are a more extreme case because they had no basis on which to build a homogeneous "traditional" culture due to the extraordinary variation in local customs. The "Bakedi" were merely disparate groups who found themselves in a single administrative district. This circumstance did not prevent them from acting as if they were an ethnic group, and even demanding a traditional head like the Kabaka at the time of Uganda's independence.

tion may occur at the same time, thus producing ethnic political participation. However, the third step may also be bypassed where individual ethnic political action occurs in the absence of social solidarity. (An example would be a client-patron relationship based on personal loyalty.) A much debated issue—whether the ethnic group is the small subgroup or the larger coalition into which the subgroups have united—can easily be resolved in this framework. By examining the political situation, the boundaries of the politically active ethnic group can be determined. For purposes of participation no other group matters.

We can now more directly consider the opposition between ethnic and economic explanations of political action. By analyzing the second and third set of opposed assumptions in liberal and Marxist discussions, we come to a more complex perspective than the simple presumption that class and ethnicity are antithetical. Political action stemming from economic class may be conceived along the same lines as those just developed for ethnicity. There are objective indicators of class (occupation, salary, place of residence, education, and even language and culture) which may or may not be the focus of subjective perceptions of those within them, and of outsiders. Consider, for example, the members of the bourgeoisie who organize proletarian action, or members of the fallen petite bourgeoisie who intensely oppose the workers. The formation of social solidarity (shared class consciousness) *may* lead to political mobilization in response to particular situations. There is a peculiar blindness among some Marxist writers who presume that, when they have demonstrated a common objective class membership, they have proved that political action will occur on the basis of class.[17]

Political situations that evoke participation along class lines may appear and disappear just as they do for participation along ethnic lines. A well-known example involves the Nigerian workers who participated in a general strike in June 1964, only to vote along ethnic lines the following December.[18] Robin Cohen correctly argues that "class and class consciousness have a partial manifestation that may be activated in certain conditions and in certain measure."[19] It is a short step to recognizing that class and ethnicity may involve the same political participants in different situations, and that both may be involved in the same

[17] For a typical example, despite careful attention to definitional problems, see V. L. Allen, "The Meaning of the Working Class in Africa," *Journal of Modern African Studies*, x (July 1972), 177-78.
[18] Melson and Wolpe (fn. 13), 1127.
[19] Robin Cohen, "Class in Africa: Analytical Problems and Perspectives," in Ralph Miliband and John Savile, eds., *The Socialist Register 1972* (London: Merlin Press 1972), 243.

situation. In the latter case, class motives may either conflict with or reinforce ethnic motives.

By conceiving the relationship of ethnicity and class in this manner, we recognize a subtle variation in the possible answers to the questions whether political action is based on rational calculation or deeply held primordial values, and whether the active agents are leaders or followers. Where the persistence of ethnic groups can be directly attributed to the desire to acquire the fruits of the modernization process,[20] rational calculations are probably more important than long-held fundamental values. Thus, "tribal" unions were often willing to pay for the education of those possessing the same objective indicators of ethnicity in hope of gaining tangible benefits for their members when these men achieved professional status or political office. Abner Cohen provides a case in point in his study of "retribalization" of the Hausa in Ibadan who maintained their separation from their co-religionists among the Yoruba in order to protect their control over an economic speciality.[21]

On the other hand, the traditional values that form the basis for an ideology of unity may not be a recent fabrication, but the product of a long cultural history. Threats to their kingdom, the cultural inheritance of several centuries, have evoked deep responses among many Baganda —whether rich or poor, educated or illiterate. Of course, particular Baganda often have manipulated this response to their own economic advantage. For ethnic groups to persist, their members must rally to a shared set of definitions of common ancestry. The legitimacy and enrichment provided by a historical culture may (or may not) underlie the group's political coherence. Despite the stress Abner Cohen places on rational calculations in his account of the Ibadan Hausa mentioned above, he appropriately insists that explanations of ethnicity depending solely on maximizing self-interest are "one-sided and *cannot account for the potency of the normative symbols* which the individual manipulates in his struggle for power. An ethnic group is not simply the sum total of its individual members, and its culture is not the sum total of the strategies adopted by independent individuals."[22]

As Cohen goes on to argue, a political entrepreneur who attempts to advance himself by manipulating ethnic beliefs is necessarily *constrained* by the symbolic implications and cultural participation that

[20] Robert Bates, "Ethnic Competition and Modernization in Contemporary Africa," *Comparative Political Studies*, vi (January 1974).

[21] Abner Cohen, *Custom and Politics in Urban Africa: A Study of Hausa Migrants in Yoruba Towns* (London: Routledge & Kegan Paul 1969).

[22] "Introduction: The Lesson of Ethnicity," in Cohen (fn. 10), xiii; emphasis added.

make these beliefs meaningful to those whom he intends to persuade. The transaction between the entrepreneur and others receptive to these symbols occurs in the creation or reinforcement of the ethnic group. This transaction limits the choices open to the entrepreneur, no matter how disingenuous his motives may be. To understand this behavior, it is important to recognize that there may be differences in motives among those claiming membership. But in no way is it logically contradictory to recognize that some will respond to rational calculations and others to primordial values, while all intensely assert their ethnic membership.

Of course, any empirical examination of subjective perceptions that is carried out by means of Western techniques of social science will run the risk of substituting explanations of motives that are familiar to foreigners for those held by the actors. In Malaysia, for example,

> in some contexts where westerners would perceive class and party divisions, the Malaysian will see ethnic divisions so that the ethnic unit supports similar functions and ideology as does class in western society. . . . this is particularly noticeable in relations of greatest social distance and antipathy.[23]

The danger is greatest where the researcher is so eager to find either objective cultural or economic consequences for political participation that he presumes that the motives of the actors were determined by these consequences.

On the issue whether leaders or followers (or members of the middle or lower classes) are the active agents in ethnic political participation, there is a range of possibilities that are more useful than the opposed assumptions of those who adopted the tradition-to-modernity proposition in the late colonial period or of the Marxists who wrote approximately fifteen years later. Elites and masses cannot exist without each other. An ethnic group may evolve in response to frustration on the part of unemployed urban migrants unable to break into an ethnically stratified labor market, or to threats felt by poor villagers fearing domination from another group whom they perceive in terms of *its* ethnic charter. Or an ethnic group may be carefully constructed by an upwardly mobile entrepreneur looking for a political base, or by introducing ethnic disputes into the civil service or university. The educated man, lamented

---

[23] Judith Nagata, "The Status of Ethnicity and the Ethnicity of Status: Ethnic and Class Identity in Malaysia and Latin America," *International Journal of Comparative Sociology*, xvii (September–December 1976), 251.

Kenneth Dike in July 1966, is "the worst peddler of tribalism in Nigeria."[24]

However, examination of either type usually reveals a complicated mixture of motives, often by self-designated leaders and their followers. Members of the political elite, for example, may find themselves at least temporarily outflanked by their followers or by marginal men eager to raise their own status. The Kabaka of Buganda and his (well-to-do) advisors took full advantage, and ultimately full control, of the *Kabaka Yekka* (the "King Alone") movement which swept all opposition in the kingdom's elections of 1962 with an extraordinary display of intense ethnic unity. But two years earlier, with ferment growing over Buganda's place in an independent Uganda, a wildcat anti-Asian boycott organized by low-level Baganda politicians and traders had succeeded for a time in taking the initiative from the Kabaka's hands. In eastern Nigeria, on the other hand, the rise in "Ibo consciousness" among peasants, which facilitated the creation of Biafra, was to a large degree the work of academics and civil servants who fled to the East following the massacres of 1966.[25]

In some cases, class or ethnicity alone may explain political action. For example, in 1968 the *Egbe Agbekoya* (the "Farmers are Suffering") movement in western Nigeria was a protest carried out by rural peasants who took violent action over several months, responding to peasant leaders from their own villages rather than to members of an elite or an urban bourgeoisie.[26] Aside from the apparently liberal use of traditional magic (which provided some ethnic reinforcement within the movement), this was basically a class action. The massacres of Ibos in May and September of 1966, in which the victims were chosen on the basis of objective indicators of ethnicity, on the other hand, were primarily ethnic political actions. Even here, however, elements of class motivation were involved. To many Hausa-Fulani and Middle Belt peoples, the Ibos symbolized exploitation and, after the January 1966 coup d'état, humiliation. Dudley finds that in both massacres the participants were predominantly petty hawkers and urban unemployed.[27] In Uganda the agitation—soon after Amin's coup in 1971—

[24] Quoted in Robin Luckham, *The Nigerian Military: A Sociological Analysis of Authority and Revolt* (Cambridge: Cambridge University Press 1971), 278.

[25] B. J. Dudley flatly states that "it was the academics who spearheaded the movement for secession." *Instability and Political Order: Politics and Crisis in Nigeria* (Ibadan: Ibadan University Press 1973), 195n.

[26] C.E.F. Beer, *The Politics of Peasant Groups in Western Nigeria* (Ibadan: Ibadan University Press 1976), 179-205.

[27] Dudley (fn. 25), 132-33 (May); 166 (September).

for the return of the Kabaka's body for a funeral and for the coronation of his son as the new Kabaka seems primarily to have been an ethnic response—the release of long repressed cultural sentiments. Yet, members of the Baganda elite surely recognized that recapture of a strong political and economic position within Uganda would have been promoted by a resurgent Buganda.

Alternatively, both ethnicity and class may be organizing principles of equal fundamental importance within the same political situation. The two may be in conflict where, for example, migrants of rising economic status are involved in political disputes with indigenous inhabitants of a town—as occurred in Port Harcourt, Ibadan, and Kampala. Or, ethnicity and class may reinforce each other, as in the case of Ibo and Hausa-Fulani in pre-civil war northern Nigeria, where "conflict of any sort—whether over jobs or markets or political office—threatened an all-out communal struggle."[28] Differential modernization during colonial rule created similar cases in virtually every African country. In each of these four types of situations—class alone, ethnicity alone, class and ethnicity in conflict, and class and ethnicity in concert—the research problem is to untangle and assess the mixture of motives held by the actors.[29] In every case, the observer must seek the causes in the political situation that stimulate people to think of (and organize) themselves in class, ethnic, or other terms—or some combination of them.

Nubians in Uganda: An Illustrative Case

The abrupt but spectacular political and economic prominence achieved by the Nubians under their most illustrious member, Idi Amin, provides an apt illustration of much of the foregoing analysis. The Nubians have stretched the notion of common ancestry to its fictive limits by opening membership to Africans possessing objective traits of other ethnic units. Their "tribe" is a product *not* of the colonial situation, but of the pacification that established colonial rule. They live almost exclusively in urban communities, but have received little exposure to Western education and thus have taken little advantage of the opportunities of modernization. Their decline in status following colonial pacification in the early years of this century and their rise

[28] Melson and Wolpe (fn. 13), 1116.
[29] See Cohen (fn. 19), 250-52. It seems unnecessary to accept his additional categories of class structure within ethnic groups and of interethnic hostility within a class, as these can be adequately handled within the four types of situations identified here.

since the 1971 coup d'état suggest the usefulness of relying on *both* class and ethnicity in explaining political participation.

The Nubians take their name from 19th-century slave traders (primarily from Dongola and as far south as Khartoum in northern Sudan), who commanded small military forces in their raids on what is now southern Sudan and northern Uganda. Some of these slave traders could trace their ancestry to the former Kingdom of Nubia in northern Sudan, which was Arabicized in the 13th century.[30] The militia they raised included freed slaves and camp followers, and consisted predominantly of people indigenous to southern Sudan. Some of these soldiers were recruited by Emin Pasha to continue his administration of Equatoria Province after this outpost of the Egyptian Khedive's dream of an empire was cut off by the successful rebellion of the Mahdi. When H. M. Stanley "rescued" Emin in 1888, these soldiers were abandoned. They turned to a life of banditry in the countryside. Their ties to the different cultural backgrounds from which they came were broken, at least while they remained away from home. They developed a group solidarity based on the adoption of a form of pidgin Arabic and acceptance of Islam—originally propagated by the slave traders they followed and by Emin's officers. These traits were strongly reinforced by the rewards of soldiery in comparison with the disastrously uncertain lot of the cultivators in the villages they had left behind.

In 1893 Sir Frederick Lugard recruited 900 Nubians from the remains of Emin's army to strengthen his alliance with Baganda chiefs.[31] Pain estimates that 18,000 more Nubians came into Uganda in the next four years; some of them were brought into the Uganda Army. There was continual military unrest during this time, culminating in a major mutiny in 1897.[32] Over the next several years, Nubian troops saw duty in Lango, Acholi, Karamoja, Buganda, Bunyoro, Ankole, and what is

[30] Dennis Pain, "The Nubians: Their Perceived Stratification System and Its Relation to the Asian Issue," in Michael Twaddle, ed., *Expulsion of a Minority: Essays on Ugandan Asians* (London: Athlone Press 1975), 177-79. Barri A. Wanji disagrees on the name of the people, calling them "Nubis," and locating the origin of their original military officers in the Nuba mountains in what has become Southern Kordofan province in central Sudan. "The Nubi Community: An Islamic Social Structure in East Africa," Sociology Working Paper No. 115 (Makerere University, n.d.), 21-22. P. L. Shinnie (*Uganda Argus*, December 23, 1957, p. 4), also argues for nominal origin in the Nuba mountains. However, cultural influences emanating from the homelands of the founders are slight enough to make irrelevant the question which place happened to be the origin of the name. Both terms seem to be in use in Uganda.

[31] Aidan Southall, "General Amin and the Coup: Great Man or Historical Inevitability?" *Journal of Modern African Studies*, XIII (March 1975), 87.

[32] Pain (fn. 30), 179.

now Kenya. Because the Khedive disowned responsibility for them, and because the British had relied upon them in early battles, they were permitted to settle in towns and trading stations throughout Uganda. Several were appointed chiefs of counties in West Nile. In addition to reaping the rewards of a soldier's life in the disturbed conditions of Uganda in the 1890s, the Nubians perceived themselves to be partners of the British in the colonization of Uganda.[33] From this rather minor pinnacle of social stratification they steadily declined until civilian rule came to an abrupt end in Uganda.

During the colonial and independence periods, the Nubians lived in urban settings, primarily because there was no territory in Uganda which they could claim as their own. (That particular objective indicator is not available to them.) Without land or special skills, they often became petty traders. In Gulu, they set up stores near cotton collection centers, where they sold beer and distilled *enguli*.[34] However, the forces structuring modernization in Uganda worked against the economic and social acceptance of the Nubians. As Muslims, they were placed below Protestants and Catholics in the colonial social order.[35] As northerners, they took second place to southerners. Nor were these the only disadvantages. Since they were ignored by missionaries, there were fewer schools for their children to attend, and consequently fewer civil service positions for which they could qualify.

A revealing discussion that appeared in the letters column of the *Uganda Argus* in 1957 suggests both the distress felt by some Nubians over their lack of educational opportunities and the importance at least some of them attached to developing channels of cultural communication. "Without Education," Ahmad Juma Abongo wrote from Kira, "one cannot cope with modern civilization. I am exceedingly surprised and distressed to see that my tribe, the so-called Nubians in Uganda, have neglected their duty to send their children to school." Few, he asserted, had gone through three years of secondary school. Perhaps aware that the low estate of the Nubians might be remedied by greater cultural unity, Abongo complained that "because of this lack of education, there is not a single publication in the Nubian language in Uganda. The excuse they give is that it is a complicated language or

[33] Some British felt they owed "a very real obligation to these natives who have followed and fought under our flag, and who are now strangers in a strange land; and that obligation, I claim also, extends in some degree to their children . . ." J.R.P. Postlethwaite, *I Look Back* (1947) quoted in Pain (fn. 30), 228.

[34] Dennis R. Pain, "Ethnicity in a Small Town," paper delivered to the East Africa Universities Social Science Council Conference, Nairobi, December 1972, p. 8.

[35] F. B. Welbourn, *Religion and Politics in Uganda, 1952–62* (Nairobi: East African Publishing House 1965), 8.

rather cannot be written, which I strongly disagree with. I only know that they have not made any attempt to write it."[36]

In response, two other letter writers indignantly insisted that many Nubians were indeed trying hard to educate their children and cited particular cases of students who had reached the engineering school at Nakawa and the Royal Technical College in Nairobi. The first of these, Mustapha Ramathan, asserted that Nubians had become more active in sending their children to school in the past ten years. However, he was forced to conclude that "about six" had passed the Cambridge School Certificate examination and none had yet gone to Makerere University College.[37] The other writer, A. M. Ally, blamed the lack of publications on the fact that "the Nubians, as immigrants, have no strong position in this country," but "that many . . . are working hard to see the existence of a paper in the Nubian language."[38] These comments suggest the Nubians' rather late awareness—in contrast to members of other Ugandan ethnic units—of the importance of ethnic solidarity for political protection as the possibility of independence began to seem likely. But they also demonstrate that Nubians "remain a byword for low education."[39] Still, a widespread consciousness of a Nubian identity had become firmly implanted.

But, although the Nubians were a marginal group, they possessed some important economic advantages during the colonial period, as well as a special status that created social solidarity and made them attractive to some outsiders. They formed a trading network which, on a very small scale, connected different Nubian settlements in the towns of Uganda. Because the British had created a Special Native Court in Bombo (a large Nubian settlement near Kampala) for Nubians, they were outside the jurisdiction of the Native Courts of Buganda until 1940.[40] For the remainder of the colonial period they were able to avoid local courts on an informal basis. Their continuing special status in the army was of great importance. Barri Wanji notes:

> The British built an exclusive military school for Nubi children. In that school they were taught crafts such as carpentry, mechanics and other trades. After the completion of seven or eight classes, they went straight

[36] *Uganda Argus*, December 18, 1957, p. 4.
[37] *Uganda Argus*, December 28, 1957, p. 4. Mustapha Ramathan is himself an example of the Nubian network (discussed below) on which Amin relies heavily. A teacher at about the time the letter was written, he became the Ugandan Ambassador to the United States in September 1971; in October 1973 he was recalled to Uganda to become Minister of Cooperatives and Marketing.
[38] *Uganda Argus*, December 31, 1957, p. 2.
[39] Pain (fn. 30), 184.   [40] *Ibid.*, 183.

into the army. The logical result of that policy was to create an elite corps of N.C.O.'s predominantly Nubi and Sudanese by origin.[41]

They created a network within the army: "For almost every Nubi man a brother, father or uncle must have at one time or another served in the army."[42] Amin was part of this Nubian network at least from the time he joined the Ugandan Army just after World War II.[43] He rose through the ranks until chosen by his British officers as one of the first two Africans to receive a commission. When the officer corps was Africanized following the mutiny in 1964, Amin was appointed second in command. He was the officer who commanded the army during the troubles of 1966.

Caught by surprise by the sudden appearance of soldiers at his home just after the attempted assassination of Obote in 1969, Amin fled to the Nubian settlement in Bombo before trying to find out what was happening. The coup d'état of 1971 occurred in large part because Milton Obote attempted to maneuver Amin out of the chain of field command, and perhaps into prison. Amin had assiduously built up his Nubian contacts in the army. As men with little education but a respected military heritage, these soldiers had been unable to rise beyond the noncommissioned ranks. Thus, Amin's political network within the army leapfrogged the more highly educated Sandhurst graduates in the higher ranks, to reach the less well-educated noncommissioned officers who were in closer contact with ordinary soldiers. Still, his coup d'état was only barely successful and produced the instability which in part accounts for the continuing violence in Uganda.[44]

[41] Wanji (fn. 30), 22.

[42] *Ibid.*, 8-9. Southall asserts that "the core tradition of the Uganda army is a Nubi tradition" (fn. 31), 89.

[43] Amin, like many Nubians, can choose between two accepted ethnic identities—in his case Kakwa as well as Nubian. The Kakwa, unlike the Nubians, have land and a traditional history on which to draw in constructing their ethnic identity. Amin's birthplace is often asserted to be in the Northwest corner of Uganda (or in Sudan), because large numbers of people objectively identifiable as Kakwa live there. But Ugandans who have known Amin for a long time maintain that he grew up in Bombo, which became the site of a large Nubian settlement because it was the headquarters of the King's African Rifles until 1939. Amin himself has said that he was born in the Police Barracks in Kampala, and, significantly, that his father had been a policeman. As explained below, these facts suggest that he had close early associations with Nubians—which are entirely consistent with his Kakwa ties.

[44] David Martin, *General Amin* (London: Faber and Faber 1974), 27-66, offers an excellent account of the coup d'état that includes details of Amin's reliance on Nubian noncommissioned officers in its execution.

The widespread assertion (accepted by Martin), that Anya-nya guerrillas fighting in the southern Sudan secessionist forces helped Amin to take over the government, is probably false. As it happened, the Southern Sudan Liberation Movement was under heavy military pressure from Sudan's national army at this time, and the site of the SSLM's headquarters was taken in battle by Khartoum forces on the same day as the

Since the coup d'état, Amin has increasingly come to rely on Nubians in the army and civil service and has made opportunities in the private sector available to them far out of proportion to their numbers. By expelling the Asians in 1972, Amin made possible the rapid creation of an entirely new indigenous commercial class. The implications were not lost on Ugandans. Those with greater wealth and education may have anticipated receiving the juiciest plums. But because Nubian traders had relatives in the army, they were brutally effective in preventing richer Baganda businessmen (many of whom withdrew their applications for new businesses without explanation) from acquiring predominance in large-scale trade. However, the actual proportion of Nubians acquiring (and keeping) control of businesses is not known at present.[45]

These economic rewards are the consequence of the political importance Amin places on Nubian ethnicity, so intimately associated with his own survival. The economic advantages of Nubian status in contemporary Uganda suggest the danger of relying solely on a class explanation for military participation there. Ali Mazrui, for example, imaginatively borrows from Marx to create the notion of a *lumpen militariat* to describe the response to opportunities for wealth suddenly available to uneducated soldiers who leapt directly from village life to ruling positions.[46] But the notion underplays the importance of ethnic designation in determining *which* soldiers are powerful and likely to gain control of businesses, and which are likely to remain as disadvantaged as ever.

Even more fascinating in the context of the concept of ethnicity has been the open ethnic boundary maintained by the Nubians for the past 100 years. Formed into an ethnic category by a distinctive life of banditry and military operations far different from the culture of their home villages, the first Nubians followed a pattern of establishing new social identities that is morphologically identical to contemporary explantations of urban ethnicity—even though few of these forerunners ever set foot in a town.

Ugandan coup d'état. After March 1972, when the civil war in Sudan ended, 6,000 members of the SSLM (Anya-nya guerrillas) were admitted into the Sudanese national army as one of the terms of settlement. Far more than this number presented themselves for potential induction; most of the excess were attracted by the job opportunity and had not been part of the guerrilla forces during the past decade. It is entirely plausible that some of those rejected *then* found their way across the border and were recruited into the Ugandan Army.

[45] Data on the social composition of those to whom abandoned Asian businesses were allocated have been collected by Horace Campbell and E. A. Brett.

[46] Mazrui, *Soldiers and Kinsmen in Uganda: The Making of a Military Ethnocracy* (Beverly Hills, Calif.: Sage Publications 1975), 127-44.

One of the enduring results of the original Nubian pattern of socialization has been the ease with which an individual can cross ethnic
boundaries and become a Nubian. The basic requirements are ability
to speak the Nubi language (pidgin Arabic), adoption of Islam, and
acceptance of certain typical dress and social customs. Since military
service is regarded as the most prestigious occupation a Nubian can
undertake, joining the army can cement one's perceived identity. Thus,
certain southern Sudanese can come to Uganda and quickly become
Nubians.[47]

Though Nubians have been marginal in the Ugandan system of
stratification for the past seventy years, their involvement in trade and
the army has been attractive to others without any power or wealth.
Thus, other Ugandans have adopted a Nubian identity for many years.
The possibility exists of becoming a Nubian intermittently—for example, when in town or in the barracks—while maintaining one's original
ethnic identity in the village. Alternatively, a person may make a fuller
commitment to a Nubian identity.[48] Amin was thus able to invite other
Africans "to become members of the Nubian tribe," and to observe that
"in Uganda there are Nubians who are Baganda, Basoga, Banyoro,
Acholi, Langi, Batoro and Kakwa. In Kenya there are also Kikuyu,
Kamba and Luo Nubians."[49] Support for Amin's statement can be
found in the language survey conducted by Pain in Gulu. Consistent
with the assumption that many have changed their ethnic status,
Nubians knew more languages well than did respondents from any
other ethnic unit.[50] In addition, theirs was the only ethnic category in
which everyone knew more than one language.

The remarkable changes in the basis on which Uganda's political
process now rests and the extraordinary (though probably temporary)
reversal in the pattern of social stratification have created new political

[47] The general category of southern Sudanese in Uganda overlaps but is not identical
with Nubian: the former includes many non-Muslims as well as persons not attracted
to trade or the military.

[48] Whether insiders among the Nubians are making efforts to close the group's boundaries, particularly in light of their current good fortune, would be of great interest.
Investigation might also indicate other cultural traits held by outsiders that facilitate (or
prevent) their full assimilation into Nubian status. Wanji (fn. 30, 71-72) points out that
many Nubian cultural traits are identical to those found in southern Sudan, and unlike
those in East Africa.

[49] *Voice of Uganda*, April 23, 1973, p. 1. Wanji (fn. 30, 69-70) found that Nubians
discourage marriages with those whom they objectively identify as Baganda—even if
Muslims—though not with most other Bantu or Nilotic speakers.

[50] Pain (fn. 34), 19. Nubians also formed the only unit all of whose members could
speak Swahili, which has always been the official language of the Ugandan Army. They
did poorly, relative to other ethnic categories, in the number of respondents who could
speak English well—a further indication of their low access to formal education.

situations that are likely to have attracted many to adopt a Nubian identity for their own particular purposes. Given the present political and economic advantages in possessing Nubian status, and given Uganda's growing population of unskilled, semi-educated, and disaffected urban dwellers, it is quite probable that more than half of those claiming Nubian identity today grew up with the objective indicators of other ethnic units. Pain's metaphor of the chameleon is strikingly appropriate.

The Nubian case demonstrates the fluidity of ethnic identity and its responsiveness to changes in political situations. The potentially intense yet intermittent focus implied by these characteristics points to the importance of research into the subtle and dynamic interconnections between class and ethnic factors in political participation.

Reification of Ethnicity in Theories of Cultural Pluralism and Consociationalism

In terms of the concept of ethnicity articulated here, the use of ethnic groups in theories relating cultural pluralism and consociationalism to political stability or instability should be reconsidered, since the logic of these theories requires that ethnic groups be conceived as separate communities. These theories therefore cannot cope with ethnic groups that are fluid and intermittent in character. Imposing false concreteness on the boundaries of ethnic solidarity produces a generous measure of unreality.

The concepts of cultural pluralism and consociationalism were developed to explain political and social relations in societies presumed to be deeply divided. They begin from opposite starting points. Cultural pluralists assert that the institutions into which people are segmented are deeply and rigidly unequal so that political stability is ensured through domination.[51] Consociationalists argue that the leaders of institutions from each segment can form an elite cartel that makes political decisions satisfactory to members of all segments, so that political stability is ensured through accommodation.[52] There is not necessarily a contradiction here, since cultural pluralists have focused primarily on authoritarian societies containing highly stratified racial or cultural groups such as colonies in Asia and Africa and countries like South Africa, while the consociationalists have directed their attention to European democracies which exhibit pronounced cleavages.

[51] For a recent statement, see the essays in Leo Kuper and M. G. Smith, eds., *Pluralism in Africa* (Berkeley and Los Angeles: University of California Press, 1969).

[52] See the useful collection of articles in Kenneth D. McRae, ed., *Consociational Democracy: Political Accommodation in Segmented Societies* (Toronto: McClelland and Stewart, Carleton Library 1974).

The danger in relying upon the notion of ethnicity developed to support the concept of cultural pluralism is vividly illustrated by two sophisticated uses of aggregate data analysis based on information from 32 black African countries. Both test the proposition that an increase in cultural pluralism is positively correlated with greater political instability. In one case, a positive correlation was found; in the other, no correlation (with one limited exception) could be discerned.[53] Since both studies drew on the same data bank, the differences in the conclusions are somewhat distressing. The test variables are constructed somewhat differently, however, which may explain the variation in findings.

But, no statistical measure can do better than the concepts on which it is based. The data used to construct the concept of cultural pluralism in both studies were differences in cultural traits of groups identified in national censuses and in the ethnographic literature. As a result, the authors of both articles include distortions caused by (1) colonial governmental definitions of ethnic units for census purposes, and (2) idealized accounts by social anthropologists attempting to reconstruct a precolonial description of cultural practices "purified" of colonial influence. In addition, these two analyses based on cultural pluralism assume that in all cases *traditional* cultural traits (which may never have been practiced by contemporary ethnic advocates) somehow "explain" participation in *current* violence or coups d'état. And the writers argue this despite the fact that they cite the literature dealing with the situational nature of ethnicity!

Consociational procedures, on the other hand, have been suggested as an appropriate instrument of government in ethnically divided societies. Arend Lijphart, for example, speaks of separate "subcultures" and makes references to Lebanon, Cyprus, and Nigeria (when those countries were under parliamentary rule).[54] The notion of subculture remains an unexplored concept for Lijphart except where he finds it necessary to elaborate it to develop his theory. To support consociation-

---

[53] The positive correlation is argued in D. G. Morrison and H. M. Stevenson, "Cultural Pluralism, Modernization, and Conflict: An Empirical Analysis of Sources of Instability in African Nations," *Canadian Journal of Political Science*, v (March 1972). The absence of correlation (with the exception of the relationship of "ethnic pluralism" and instability when controlling for the category of "civil servants/wage earners") is asserted in Walter L. Barrows, "Ethnic Diversity and Political Instability in Black Africa," *Comparative Political Studies*, ix (July 1976). Indeed, Barrows (pp. 161-62) concludes from the lack of statistical association that researchers ought to examine other variables instead of ethnicity in studying instability.

[54] Lijphart, "Consociational Democracy," in McRae (fn. 52), 70-89. For one appeal in support of extending this particular approach to ethnically divided societies, see Young (fn. 13), 527-28.

alism, subcultures must have distinct boundaries on the basis of which the political cleavages of the society rest; they must also possess a high degree of political cohesion, permitting their leaders to strike compromises with each other without losing their status within the subculture.[55]

Although Lijphart's model was constructed as an alternative to pure majoritarian rule in a typology of *democratic* governments, the concept —in principle—might be used to explain national decision making where democratic institutions are absent.[56] Thus, consociationalism has been taken up with enthusiasm in certain heterogeneous societies in which governments have insisted upon separation of ethnic communities as a matter of policy. In South Africa, for example, a radio commentator recently went so far as to cite Lijphart in support of the principle that it was more important to guard the rights of different communities than to preserve majority rule in order to protect what he called "democratic rights."[57] But the South African notion of separate development, or *apartheid*, is strictly based on the *government*'s definitions of ethnic units and their appropriate boundaries. In view of the immense inequalities that have been legitimated on this basis, this use of the term consociationalism amounts to nothing more than a fashionable façade to hide white domination.

Brian Barry presents a more general argument against the extension of consociationalism to ethnic cleavage; but it is based on the inadequate assumption that ethnic groups are continuous political units.[58] He argues that ethnicity, unlike other cleavages, is not manageable through bargaining by group representatives. In his view, "gross inhumanity" is more likely to occur in ethnic conflicts than in disagreements based on other cleavages. Organizations, and therefore leaders, have less relevance for ethnic groups than they have for religious or class conflict. Ethnic definitions of issues permit greater clarity of goals sought, and

[55] Lijphart (fn. 54), 82-84.

[56] Cf. Ian Lustick, "Stability in Deeply Divided Societies: Consociationalism versus Control," *World Politics*, xxxi (April 1979), 334.

[57] "South Africa's Answer to the World," Johannesburg Radio broadcast, October 5, 1977, British Broadcasting Corporation, *Summary of World Broadcasts*, Part 4B, ME/5634/B/1-2, October 7, 1977. In an extremely interesting paper, "Consociational Authoritarianism: Incentives and Hindrances toward Power Sharing and Devolution in South Africa and Namibia," John Seiler reviews efforts by Afrikaner intellectuals to make use of consociationalism. American Political Science Association Conference, Washington, D.C., September 1977, pp. 21-22.
Lijphart left himself open to this sort of interpretation by referring approvingly to "a kind of voluntary *apartheid* policy as the best solution for a divided society," in his argument that separation of subcultures may reduce conflict (fn. 54), 83.

[58] Barry, "Political Accommodation and Consociational Democracy," *British Journal of Political Science*, v (October 1975), 502-3.

thereby reduce the ability of leaders to bargain. Thus, ethnic leaders have a more difficult time agreeing to compromises in the elite cartels that consociationalism requires. Finally, ethnic issues often raise the question of secession, but class and religious issues do not.[59] Thus, Barry insists that ethnic cleavages are too intense for consociational arrangements. But he can succeed in this argument only by assuming (contrary to the analysis presented above) that ethnic groups are necessarily based on deeply held primordial values against which rational calculations are unavailing.

The most serious theoretical problem for most proponents of cultural pluralism and consociationalism is their insistence that ethnic categories be treated as self-contained communities. Any useful concept of ethnicity must embody the possibility that situations evoking ethnic identity may stabilize over a period of time and may give birth to reinforcing institutions. Long-term racial domination is a case in point. But racial attitudes may change, and ethnic identity may turn out to be too evanescent a basis to support political institutions that are separate and parallel, and also durable. The fact that polarization of ethnic identities may in some situations create civil strife does not necessarily mean that ethnic identities have stabilized. Political solutions which remove the factors that evoke ethnic identification may produce greater stability than those which explicitly build upon and reinforce such identification. One of the great mysteries of the post-civil war period in Nigeria is what has happened to Ibo ethnic solidarity. No one would argue that ethnicity is absent from Nigeria now, but the creation of 12 states in 1967, increased to 19 in 1976 (dividing into two the so-called heartland identified with the Ibos), has certainly reduced its political relevance.[60]

The central point of any situational analysis of ethnicity is that the range of possible degrees and duration of ethnic group coalescence should not be converted into a rigid assumption of presence or absence of a continuous subculture. If comparative analysis based on cultural pluralism, or the creation of consociational solutions for ethnic problems, must therefore be narrowly constricted or abandoned, that may be the price that must be paid in order to stay in touch with the complexities of social reality.

[59] Oddly, Barry insists (*ibid.*, 504) that political parties in Northern Ireland are ethnically (rather than religiously) based. In so arguing, he appears to plant the seeds of a tautology by implying that all cleavages too intense to be amenable to consociational solutions are ethnic.

[60] There is evidence that political disagreements produced demands among those objectively identified as Ibos that the 1975 panel considering the number of new states divide the old East Central state into *four* new ones. *Daily Times* (Lagos), June 27, 1977, p. 3.

ADMINISTRATION OF INTEGRATED
RURAL DEVELOPMENT POLICY:
The Politics of Agrarian Reform
in Developing Countries

By DENNIS A. RONDINELLI*

THE directions of development policy have shifted drastically over the past decade, from a predominant concern with promoting rapid growth in gross national product, through capital-intensive industrialization, export production, and construction of large-scale infrastructure, to ways of stimulating domestic markets, expanding economic participation, and reducing disparities in income and wealth. The new policies, less concerned with the rate of aggregate economic growth than with its composition and the distribution of its benefits, seek to increase agricultural productivity, expand employment opportunities, and meet basic human needs of the poorest groups in society.

Changes in government policy in developing countries resulted in part from the growing realization that post-World War II macroeconomic development strategies did little to reduce the dependence of these countries on industrialized nations, spread the benefits of growth, or improve the conditions of the majority of the poor. The new strategies also emerged from internal social and political pressures: from widespread recognition of the social injustices perpetuated by dual economies and from the realization by national leaders that political stability and national unity could not be achieved or maintained only by narrow support from a small, wealthy, urban elite. The success of experiments with more equitable growth policies in some communist and socialist societies created further pressure on governments with mixed economies to reduce the growing gaps in income and wealth; in some nations it encouraged insurgency movements to challenge incumbent political regimes. The new policies in no small measure reflect pressures for agrarian reform by international funding institutions, whose own strategies place increasing emphasis on reaching the "poor majority."

* An earlier version of this paper was presented in the Seminar Series on Land Management Issues in Developing Countries, sponsored by the Lincoln Institute of Land Policy and the John Fitzgerald Kennedy School of Government, Harvard University, March 1978.

Since the late 1960s, nearly all developing countries have embraced the new strategies in varying degrees, and some governments have established elaborate programs of implementation. Although goals and approaches of Third-World governments differ, their integrated rural development policies and those of international funding institutions are remarkably similar in their basic thrust. They attempt to coordinate a "package" of investments and services that will accomplish the following:

1. Increase agricultural output and productivity, thereby transforming rural regions from subsistence to commercial agricultural economies in order to meet the basic food needs and raise the incomes of the rural poor.

2. Stimulate agro-processing, agri-business, and related rural industries in order to diversify local economies, provide greater employment opportunities, and generate internal demand for domestically produced goods.

3. Increase access of the rural poor to the social services, facilities, technologies, and infrastructure needed to improve health, nutrition, literacy, and family planning—thereby increasing the productivity of individual workers, raising the overall standard of living in rural areas, and stemming the tide of rapid rural-to-urban migration. The intended beneficiaries are small-scale farmers, rural entrepreneurs, migrant workers, shifting cultivators, and landless laborers, as well as squatters and low-income workers on the fringes of the urban economy.

Although Third-World governments and international lending institutions have engaged in agrarian reform for more than a quarter of a century, integrated rural development is a new experiment in terms of its dominant place in development policy, the scope and variety of inputs that must be coordinated, and its administrative complexity. In adopting the new policy, however, few governments or assistance agencies seriously considered the political and administrative preconditions for successful implementation. Instead, most governments focused their attention on the technical components, either assuming the existence of adequate administrative capacity or relying on marginal adjustments in administrative structure and procedures after policies were initiated. But progress in strengthening indigenous capacity to mobilize and sustain political support, build decentralized administrative networks for implementation, and organize the rural poor to participate in productive activity has fallen far behind advances in agricultural research and technology development. Few countries have dealt seriously with the underlying political forces that maintain poverty and inhibit agrarian reform. In Asia, for instance, Griffin found the causes of the Green Revolution's failure to improve the conditions of most small farmers "not so much in inadequate technology as in inappropriate institutions and poor policy. The explanation for the latter, in turn, lies not in the ignorance of those who govern but in the powerlessness of most of those who are governed."[1] Integrated rural development policies are replete with paradoxes; they pose serious dilemmas for developing nations and generate political tensions and conflicts that are at the heart of complex administrative problems.

Equitable growth policies, for instance, require strong national political support. Socialist regimes see them as a way of consolidating ideological commitment, and therefore provide a basis for economic redistribution and political reform; but in most mixed economies any meaningful dispersion of economic and political resources to rural groups is considered potentially subversive of central authority. It is equally paradoxical that the strong commitment by the central government which is needed to initiate rural development is not sufficient to ensure implementation or effectiveness. Most governments in developing countries have been unwilling or unable to create the decentralized institutional structure that seems essential to meet the needs of the rural poor. Unless control is decentralized, functions are devolved, and a strong institutional network is created within rural areas to deliver services and elicit participation, there is little hope of sustaining rural reform. But in almost every country pursuing rural development, central administrative control has been carefully protected and reluctantly dispersed.

Nearly all analyses of rural poverty and underdevelopment have concluded that well-designed, closely coordinated, multiple-policy interventions, sustained over long periods of time, are essential for stimulating equitable growth. Still, integrated rural development programs often depend for their success on those political and administrative resources that are least likely to be found in developing countries and least susceptible to rapid development. Indeed, the problems of rural poverty persist in most developing countries precisely because of the weakness of political commitment to change, and because administrative structure and coordinative capacity are inadequate for expanding participation in economic activity.

[1] Keith Griffin, *The Political Economy of Agrarian Change* (Cambridge, Mass.: Harvard University Press 1974), 255.

The Emergence of Integrated Development Policies

Integrated rural development emerged as a focus of international assistance strategies in the late 1960s for a number of related reasons. One motivation for change undoubtedly was the growing realization by government leaders and development analysts that the "trickle-down" effects promised by conventional economic theory had not materialized in most of the developing world and could no longer be used as a basis for planning or as an excuse for governmental inaction. By the mid-1960s it had become clear that the emphasis on rapid macro-economic growth through capital-intensive industrialization had neither improved economic conditions in most developing nations nor reduced the growing disparities between rich and poor. Despite the growth of GNP in many countries over the past two decades, nearly half of the 187 nations surveyed by the World Bank in 1974 had a per capita GNP below $500 a year, only 19 reported levels above $5000.[2] The majority of countries with a per capita GNP below $300 during the 1960s also had an annual growth rate of less than 5 percent.[3] About 30 desperately poor countries with intransigent social and economic problems, and with a substantial portion of the world's population, had been totally bypassed by economic and social progress. Moreover, the distribution of income and wealth, even within growing economies, remains highly inequitable. In 35 of the 43 developing nations examined by Adelman and Morris, less than 20 percent of the population received 50 percent or more of total income, with concentrations among the upper fifth rising as high as 90 percent. In many countries, the poorest 40 percent of the population received less than 20 percent of income; in some, only 10 to 15 percent of income went to the poorest half of the population.[4]

The new directions in development policy were also shaped by the realization that gaps in income and wealth among nations and within them were growing rather than diminishing. Even countries with high levels of growth have large concentrations of poor that remain relatively untouched by, or entirely excluded from, the benefits of development. The World Bank estimates that nearly 85 percent, or more than 750 million, of the people in developing nations live in relative poverty, earning less than $150 a year, and that two-fifths survive in absolute

[2] International Bank for Reconstruction and Development, *World Bank Atlas 1976* (Washington: World Bank 1977).

[3] See Gerald M. Meier, "The Dimensions of Development: Indicators of International Poverty—A Note," in Meier, ed., *Leading Issues in Economic Development* (3rd ed.; New York: Oxford University Press 1976), 12-18.

[4] See Irma Adelman and Cynthia T. Morris, *Economic Growth and Social Equity in Developing Countries* (Stanford: Stanford University Press 1973), 152.

poverty on annual incomes of less than $50.[5] The U.S. Agency for International Development, using both social and economic measures, calculates that 800 million people live in poverty in the nations it assists.[6]

Not only did capital-intensive industrial investments in urban centers fail to produce the "trickle-down" benefits promised by economic planners but, as Myrdal expected, the "backwash effects" far exceeded the spread effects: in many countries the urban centers drained their rural hinterlands of resources, capital, and productive manpower.[7] Rural areas were left without the preconditions or resources needed to benefit from potential backward and forward linkages of urban industrialization. Areas with high concentrations of poverty provided little internal demand for domestically produced goods, and received inequitably small portions of national investments in infrastructure and services that would enable them to increase their agricultural output or attract private investment. Urban centers became modern enclaves, tied to industrialized nations by dependence on imports, exports, and capital and technical assistance, while their rural hinterlands remained isolated subsistence economies, unable to provide for even the basic human needs of a majority of their populations.[8]

Without sufficient economic, social, political, and human resources, moreover, leading sector, or "unbalanced," investment strategies cannot work in rural regions of developing nations. Entrepreneurs are not readily available, savings are low, capital is scarce and expensive. Without sufficient collateral for loans, small-scale businessmen and farmers are considered high-risk borrowers and rarely can obtain credit or investment capital. The infrastructure and the services necessary to operate profitable ventures either do not exist or are not reliable. Land tenure is uncertain for many small farmers; ownership is concentrated among wealthy elites who generally reinvest their profits in urban centers where returns are higher and risks are lower. Markets are often inaccessible to small producers, or the terms of trade are adverse. Government subsidies and services that help make private investment profitable in more developed areas are either not provided in rural regions, or access to them is highly restricted.

[5] International Bank for Reconstruction and Development, *Rural Development Sector Policy Paper* (Washington: World Bank 1975).

[6] See *Implementation of the "New Directions" in Development Assistance*, report prepared by the U.S. Agency for International Development, U.S. House Committee on International Relations, 94th Cong., 1st sess. (Committee Print 1975), 63-64.

[7] Gunnar Myrdal, *Rich Lands and Poor: The Road to World Prosperity* (New York: Harper 1957).

[8] See Dennis A. Rondinelli and Kenneth Ruddle, *Urbanization and Rural Development: A Spatial Policy for Equitable Growth* (New York: Praeger 1978).

Attempts to stimulate agricultural productivity through single-purpose government programs also yield poor results. Subsistence and small-scale farmers—especially those in the economically most depressed regions—simply will not increase agricultural production unless many or all of the conditions necessary to make low-risk profits are at hand. In order to increase output, the government must make simultaneous investments in services, facilities, technical inputs, and marketing in rural areas. The failure of agrarian reform in countries such as Sri Lanka, for instance, has been directly attributed to fragmented programs. "The segmentary approach has resulted in attention being paid to particular aspects of a problem to the neglect of others," one Sri Lankan analyst complains. For example, "new lands have been developed without provisions for irrigation; production of diversified crops has been stimulated without developing agro-based industries; mechanized cultivation has been promoted without ensuring adequate supplies of tractors."[9]

Adelman, Morris and Robinson, in a historical review of development policy, confirm this finding on a larger scale. They maintain that even quite extensive single-policy interventions do not have lasting effects on the rural poor. Transfer policies are somewhat more effective, but their impact is limited in most countries. They conclude that "only when a significant number of different interventions are applied simultaneously so that there is, in effect, a change in development strategy, are more sizable or lasting effects possible."[10] The benefits of single-purpose programs have usually gone to richer farmers or the middle class, only temporarily increasing the incomes of smaller farmers and largely bypassing landless laborers and shifting cultivators.

By the late 1960s, it became apparent that the only hope for achieving more socially equitable economic development would lie in increasing agricultural productivity and diversifying rural economies through integrated development programs. Under Mao, for instance, Chinese economic policy sought to balance sectoral and regional development. It focused on agricultural production as the basis for both small-scale rural and capital-intensive urban industrialization. Reduction of disparities in urban and rural wages and dispersal of infrastructure, technology, and services to the countryside were an integral part of the strategy. By establishing a "consumption floor"—a standard of living

[9] V. Kanesalingham, "The Impact of Government Policies and Programmes on Villages in Sri Lanka," in Asian Centre for Development Administration [hereafter cited as ACDA], *Approaches to Rural Development in Asia*, III (Kuala Lumpur: ACDA 1975), 145.

[10] Irma Adelman, Cynthia T. Morris and Sherman Robinson, "Policies for Equitable Growth," *World Development*, IV (July 1976), 561-82, at 575.

below which no one was allowed to fall—China has been able to satisfy basic human needs, eliminate abject poverty, distribute income more equitably, and provide the organization for expanded participation in economic activity.[11]

Requirements for Integrated Rural Development

Equitable growth strategies were adopted by international assistance agencies and by governments in most developing countries without a clear understanding of the ways in which poverty might be alleviated and rural economies stimulated, and without the political and administrative commitment to make the drastic changes in economic structure which were needed to implement these policies. The U.S. Agency for International Development, perhaps more frank in admitting the limits of knowledge than most other assistance organizations, reports that "determining the precise application of general development approaches in specific cases remains, despite all our efforts and those of thousands of practitioners and scholars alike, a very murky, difficult, uncertain, complex and intractable business."[12] Few governments have had much experience with programs of the magnitude and complexity of integrated rural development, and fewer still seem intent on providing the economic and political resources required to make them effective. The ultimate beneficiaries, in many cases, have not been clearly identified; their characteristics, behavior patterns, institutional practices, and motivations are rarely understood by national planners and administrators. The drastically different conditions found among countries, and among rural regions within them, make prescription of universally applicable strategies nearly impossible.

At the same time, experience with single-purpose development programs and with larger-scale, more complex agrarian reforms, with land development and resettlement schemes, and with multi-purpose community development activities, points to specific elements essential to the success of integrated rural development.[13] Those elements include:

1. *Strong national political commitment.* Experience with rural development and agrarian reform indicates that they simply will not

[11] See Suzanne Paine, "Balanced Development: Maoist Concept and Chinese Practice," *World Development*, iv (April 1976), 277-305, and John G. Gurley, "Rural Development in China," in E. O. Edwards, ed., *Employment in Developing Nations* (New York: Columbia University Press 1974), 383-403.

[12] *Implementation of the "New Directions" in Development Assistance* (fn. 6), 4.

[13] See Dennis A. Rondinelli and Kenneth Ruddle, "Local Organization for Integrated Rural Development: Implementing Equity Policy in Developing Countries," *International Review of Administrative Sciences*, xliii (January 1977), 20-30, and Rondinelli and Ruddle (fn. 8), chap. 4.

succeed without strong and sustained commitment by national political leaders to the goals of equitable economic growth. High-level political commitment is necessary for at least three reasons. First, it is required to articulate strategy in national policies, legislative declarations, national plans, and administrative orders. The history of rural development in Asia and Africa indicates that political initiatives, often by charismatic leaders and ideological movements, were prime forces in articulating the need for and setting the goals of rural development. In Tanzania, Pakistan, Taiwan, Malaysia, and the People's Republic of China, widely varying yet equally forceful political commitments were needed to generate national policies for rural development.[14]

Political commitment is needed, in addition, to ensure high priority for rural development in resource-allocation decisions over a long period of time. A steady and reliable flow of budgetary resources is one of the most important inputs for rural development. Even in countries where agriculture is the sector of the economy that contributes the most to national production, and where the population is overwhelmingly rural, budgetary allocations for agriculture have often been low. In Ethiopia, for instance, less than 10 percent of the expenditures of the central government are for agriculture.[15] In Nicaragua, the agricultural sector's share of public funds declined during the 1960s, while overall governmental spending was increasing.[16] It is often assumed that financial support will be automatically provided by the national government once it commits itself to rural development, but agrarian reforms have regularly been beset with budgetary problems. Between 1965 and 1971, the Philippine Government released less than one-third of the amount authorized for agrarian reform and, since 1972, high rates of inflation have reduced the value of allocations to rural development.[17] In the Dominican Republic, an average of less than 70 percent of budget allocations was released to the Secretariat of Agriculture between 1966 and 1973, with over $40 million withheld during that period.[18]

Finally, political commitment is required to motivate groups and

[14] See David F. Roth, "Political Structure, Policy Adaption and Rural Change: The Cases of Thailand, Malaysia and the Peoples' Republic of China," and A. N. Seth, "Agrarian Changes in Asia," both in ACDA (fn. 9), II, 162-264, 266-316.

[15] Jacob Meerman, "Evaluation of the Agricultural Sector Loans Funded by USAID Ethiopia" (Washington: USAID 1973), mimeo.

[16] U.S. Agency for International Development, *Nicaragua–Rural Development Sector Loan, Capital Assistance Paper* AID-DLC/P-2091 (Washington: USAID 1975), Annex V-C.

[17] J. E. Rocamora and C. Conti-Panganiban, "Rural Development Strategies: The Philippines Case," in ACDA (fn. 9), II, 267-68.

[18] J. B. Robinson and J. M. Stone, *Agricultural Sector Assessment for the Dominican Republic* (Washington: USAID 1974), V-18.

organizations throughout society to reverse or eliminate centuries-old practices and behavior that have kept rural people in poverty. Observers of Tanzania's rural development have noted the intensity of political pressure needed to achieve reform: the unrelenting pressure by President Nyerere who "pushed, prodded, cajoled, persuaded and led the people" in order to reorganize the economic and political structure of that nation.[19] Such steadfast commitment is needed to achieve results even in centrally controlled societies. Thirty years of forceful leadership by Mao were required to achieve more equitable development in China, in the face of political opposition from national and provincial leaders and powerful landowners before the revolution, and in order to overcome conflict among party officials over appropriate means of establishing a communist society after the revolution.[20] In India, without the political commitment to break the barriers raised by entrenched interests, national and local elites were able to distort and redirect rural reform programs to their own advantage, successfully "insulating the poor from the benefits of development."[21]

2. *Pervasive administrative support.* It cannot simply be assumed that national officials and lower-level administrators will support programs of rural development even after they have been enacted. Indeed, it has often been the national administrative agencies that have blocked or delayed reforms. High-level officials may themselves be large landowners, and technical personnel within rural development agencies may be subjected to the influence of or to threats by landholding elites.[22] Without pervasive administrative support or the mobilization of sufficient political power among rural beneficiaries to maintain steady pressure on ministries of the national government, reform will slowly dissipate.

Integrated rural development, in addition, requires strong central coordination. Evaluations of rural development programs in Africa note that their "multiple, and at times, conflicting objectives have rendered overall rural development strategy inconsistent and even self-defeating."[23] In the Philippines, for instance, programs to improve land

---

[19] Richard N. Blue and James H. Weaver, "A Critical Assessment of the Tanzanian Model of Development," *Agricultural Development Council Reprint*, No. 30 (July 1977), 18.

[20] See Gurley (fn. 11), 385-89.

[21] Kuldeep Mathur, "Administrative Institutions, Political Capacity and India's Strategy for Rural Development," in ACDA (fn. 9), III, 1-62, at 52.

[22] Judith Tendler, "What Happens in an Agrarian Reform," *Inter-country Evaluation of Small Farmer Organizations: Honduras* (Washington: USAID 1976), mimeo.

[23] Uma Lele, *The Design of Rural Development: Lessons from Africa* (Baltimore: The Johns Hopkins University Press 1975), 142.

tenure, develop agriculture and physical infrastructure, strengthen marketing and cooperative institutions, and deliver credit to farmers must be coordinated among the following: the Departments of Agrarian Reform, Agriculture and Natural Resources, Local Government and Community Development, and Public Works; the Bureaus of Lands, Public Schools, and Agriculture Economics; extension programs in at least three different agencies; and more than a half-dozen government or semi-independent financial institutions. Even under a martial-law government, the agencies often are at odds with each other on administrative and budgetary matters, and rarely integrate their activities within rural areas. Coordinating committees have been established to coordinate the coordinators.[24] Israel's experience with integrated agricultural development—one of the more successful models—reveals that coordination can only be achieved when planning is closely related to budgeting and programming. "Planning and implementation must be closely interwoven," Israeli analysts note, "with the plan continuously modified to fit real conditions. The institutional framework must be such that this dynamic interaction can proceed smoothly."[25]

3. *Complementary domestic and foreign trade policies.* The International Labor Organization's analysis of development problems in Kenya, Colombia, Liberia, Sudan, the Philippines, and Ethiopia, all indicate that successful rural development depends heavily on national policies that seek to expand participation in economic activity.[26] Domestic economic policies and foreign trade strategies must be clearly and deliberately formulated to reinforce rural development. Generally included in such policies are land reform measures that promote an equitable distribution of ownership, with opportunities for rural workers to acquire enough land to support their families and produce a surplus; investment incentives that will promote small- and medium-scale manufacturing as well as craft and cottage industries; noninflationary wage policies that encourage and protect labor-intensive industries while assuring adequate levels of income for individual workers; and ade-

[24] See Russell Cheetham and E. K. Hawkins, *The Philippines: Priorities and Prospects for Development* (Washington: World Bank 1976), chap. 13.
[25] Raanan Weitz and Avshalom Rokach, *Agricultural Development Planning and Implementation: An Israeli Case Study* (New York: Praeger 1968), 329.
[26] See United Nations, International Labor Organization (ILO), *Employment, Incomes and Equality: A Strategy for Increasing Productive Employment in Kenya* (Geneva: ILO 1972); *Towards Full Employment: A Programme for Colombia* (1970); *Total Involvement: A Strategy for Development in Liberia* (1972); *Growth, Employment and Equity: A Comprehensive Strategy for the Sudan* (1976); *Sharing in Development: A Programme of Employment, Equity and Growth for the Philippines* (1974); *Employment and Unemployment in Ethiopia* (1973).

quate price supports for essential agricultural commodities so as to provide incentives for individual farmers to increase output, adapt improved practices, and experiment with new techniques without fear of catastrophic losses in income owing to drastic fluctuations in price. National programs for family planning, public works, and social services must be designed specifically to reach the rural poor. And a complex set of international trade policies, creating exchange rates, import and tariff regulations, and export practices favorable to rural production, must be established. Both domestic and foreign trade policies must be aimed at reducing a nation's reliance on external resources and at building a viable internal economy.

4. *Integrated package of technical inputs.* An effective combination of technical, organizational, and service inputs within rural areas is required to stimulate agricultural production. The technical components must be tailored to the needs and conditions found in rural regions. They usually consist of improved seed varieties, marketing assistance, credit, extension services, nonformal education, technical training, and rural savings mobilization. Schemes for land reform, improvement, and settlement are an integral part of many rural development projects; most countries emphasize the extension of farm-to-market roads, provision of utilities and rural electrification, dissemination of appropriate technology for rural industrialization and agricultural processing, as well as irrigation and flood control where they are required. Projects dealing with health and social services, family planning, and nutritional improvement are part of integrated rural development in some countries, as are technical assistance to local governments and promotion of agricultural research and experimentation in others.

5. *Investments in productive activities.* In mixed economies, the aim of governmental intervention is to stimulate private investment or to provide goods and services directly where private markets are weak or nonexistent. Nearly all countries pursuing integrated rural development also attempt to promote small-scale, labor-intensive industrialization—either on a communal basis in socialist societies, or through entrepreneurial development in mixed economies. Where such programs have been successful, small-scale industrialization has significantly stimulated resource mobilization, capital investment, and entrepreneurship. Smaller industries are usually the primary, and sometimes the only, means through which rural people, serving as apprentices, can obtain specialized skills and vocational training. Smaller industries are also considered important generators of off-farm employment opportunities. In

Japan, which strongly supported such entrepreneurial efforts during its period of development, small- and medium-size firms now account for more than 90 percent of all manufacturing establishments, employing almost 70 percent of the nation's nonagricultural industrial workers. Small industries provide a greater quantity and diversity of goods in smaller cities, towns, and villages in rural areas, at prices within the reach of lower income groups, and in India, Korea, and Japan they also contribute to production for export. Where they have been successful, small-scale industries usually require lower investment costs per job, use labor more intensively, have lower capital requirements, and make use of more local resources and materials than large industries would.[27]

Even in communist countries, where private enterprise is not officially encouraged, a good deal of small-scale private activity is tolerated. Privately controlled family enterprises carried on within Chinese communes through "sideline production"—farming on private plots, raising animals, fishing, handicrafts, selling firewood, and so forth—provide rural families with an important part of their annual incomes.[28]

6. *Local political support and administrative capacity.* The success of integrated rural development depends heavily on the creation of a strong network of local institutions to support and implement projects and programs. Evaluations of rural development in China, India, and Pakistan indicate that local governments can mobilize political support and induce popular participation by extending institutional procedures for local involvement in planning and decision making; strengthening communications between rural areas and urban centers, and with higher levels of government; expanding opportunities for local leadership; and supporting politically responsible and socially conscious bureaucracies in rural areas.[29] But in few developing nations do local governments perform these functions effectively. Social and economic transformation requires that the local government's capacity to plan for and manage public facilities and to deliver basic social services be strengthened. It must be able to raise revenue; plan, budget, and imple-

[27] See Rondinelli, "The Importance of Project Management in Asian Development: An Integrated Framework for Planning and Implementation," paper prepared for delivery at Project Management Seminar, Manila, 1977; processed by Asian Productivity Organization, Tokyo.
[28] Benedict Stavis, *People's Communes and Rural Development in China* (Ithaca, N.Y.: Cornell University Center for International Studies 1974), 54-55.
[29] G. S. Cheema, "Rural Local Government and Rural Development in China, India and Pakistan," in ACDA (fn. 9), I, 149-50.

ment programs; and maintain facilities and equipment. Local political leaders must be committed to the goals of rural transformation, and the adverse influences of those elites who oppose the expansion of participation in economic activity must be countered or neutralized.

In addition, either through regional decentralization or local devolution, organizational capacity must be expanded within rural areas to plan and manage individual projects. Innovative attempts at integrated rural development in East Africa clearly show that success depends on the assignment of projects to strong, well-staffed organizations, with sufficient resources to coordinate and integrate a variety of technical and administrative inputs within the project area. Lele describes projects in Kenya, Tanzania, and Malawi that required effective procedures for programming, monitoring, and control, and for mobilizing the support and participation of beneficiaries.[30] But since such projects are, by their very nature, temporary and narrowly focused, they depend on and should contribute to the administrative capacity of public and private institutions in rural areas.[31]

7. *International financial and technical assistance.* Finally, appropriate forms of international funding and technical aid are also needed in many countries to supplement and reinforce the government's efforts to assist the rural poor. Although international agencies have been a primary source of pressure for adopting integrated rural development, their lending policies often fail to reinforce governmental programs. Because of the tendency of aid agencies to support large-scale, capital-intensive projects; their lack of concern, in appraising projects, for income distribution and social impact; and their unwillingness to take risks in making loans, national governments often have little flexibility for experimentation. In some countries, block grants, continuous financing, and general budgetary support may be more appropriate for agrarian reform than project-funded assistance. Most importantly, aid should be used to build administrative capacity and technical expertise within developing countries to identify, design, appraise, finance, implement, and evaluate their own projects rather than to create greater dependence on foreign consultants and experts. Increased use of sectoral, block-grant, and untied concessional lending might greatly encourage developing nations to be more innovative and responsive.

[30] Lele (fn. 23), chap. VIII.
[31] See, for instance, experiences with Kenya's Special Rural Development Program: Institute of Development Studies, University of Nairobi, "An Overall Evaluation of the Special Rural Development Programme," Occasional Paper No. 8 (Nairobi: Kenya: IDS 1972), mimeo.

ADMINISTRATIVE IMPLICATIONS OF INTEGRATED RURAL DEVELOPMENT

Ultimately, the success of integrated rural development depends on the ability of governments and international assistance agencies to solve three sets of problems that create serious tensions, if not outright conflicts, in most developing societies. They are the paradox of power, problems of national administrative structure, and strategies for delivery of local services.

THE PARADOX OF POWER: CENTRAL POLITICAL COMMITMENT AND
DIFFUSE POLITICAL SUPPORT

A paradox inherent in agrarian reforms is that, although strong central political commitment is unquestionably necessary to initiate them, they cannot be effectively implemented or sustained without diffused political support and widespread participation by the intended beneficiaries. But those whose political commitment is necessary to initiate the reforms often consider such a diffusion of participation and power as a serious threat. Rural development programs that reallocate economic resources, increase income, and expand participation in the economy also create new and potentially more powerful interest groups that can make claims on and challenge central authority. Indeed, the creation of countervailing power is often a *precondition* for sustaining rural development in market economies. The success of agrarian reform in India's Punjab during the late 1960s, for instance, not only tended to equalize political power between peasants and former landowners, but also provided a new and more powerful political base that allowed a unified state government, committed to development, to bargain with the central government from a position of strength. It succeeded in obtaining financial and technical resources for agriculture, as well as highly favorable grain prices.[32] Rural development may not only intensify conflicts between peasants and elites, but also generate new cleavages among various beneficiaries of reform. In Tanzania, for instance, the government's attempts to assist landless peasants and poor farm workers are often opposed by small-scale commercial farmers and landholding peasants who fear loss or diminution of government benefits, and who join with some technical personnel in national ministries to oppose further expansion of *ujaama* villages or collectivization projects.[33] In many countries, the fear of loss of power and control inhibits

[32] See A. Hague, N. Mehta, A. Rahman, and P. Wignaraja, *Towards A Theory of Rural Development* (Bangkok: U.N. Asian Development Institute 1975), 20.
[33] G. K. Helleiner, "Socialism and Economic Development in Tanzania," *Journal of Development Studies*, VIII (No. 2, 1972), 183-204.

central authorities from creating the political organization necessary for successful rural development.

The history of agrarian reform clearly shows that, in order to mobilize widespread political support for rural development, two tasks must be successfully carried out: first, the hold of clientelist politics in rural areas must be broken; and second, it must be replaced with organizations or coalitions strong enough to represent the interests of rural people when decisions on development are made.

1. *Breaking the hold of clientelist politics.* Little can be done to reorder the economic structure in areas where peasants are dependent on wealthy landowners or elites for their livelihood and survival, and where such dependence manifests itself in the patrons' domination of local and national politics through personalism, favoritism, and the manipulation and control of large peasant voting blocs.[34] In places where rural people depend on patrons to purchase their labor and products, provide shelter, offer credit, loans, and aid in emergencies or crises, and assist in paying for marriages and funerals, those government programs that threaten to weaken or destroy the patron-client relationship will receive no sympathy from the elite and little support from the peasants. In many rural areas, the patron-client relationship provides whatever small amount of security the peasants can expect in an uncertain and precarious life. Rural development programs will have little impact unless they are accompanied by massive political reorganization, and unless the government can displace the functions performed by patrons by providing demonstrably better, more reliable services, with little risk for the peasant.

2. *Creating an organizational base of political support and local participation.* The difference between more effective and less effective rural development has been the willingness and ability of the government to assist in creating an organizational framework for the mobilization of leadership, sharing of power and decision making, and expansion of economic participation. Gurley notes that communist land reform in China during the late 1950s not only redistributed the productive assets by which the peasantry could economically sustain itself, but also—and perhaps more importantly—organized rural people to break the hold of the landlord-gentry class:

[34] See J. D. Powell, "Peasant Society and Clientelist Politics," *American Political Science Review*, LXIV (June 1970), 411-25, and J. C. Scott, "Patron-Client Politics and Political Change in Southeast Asia," *American Political Science Review*, LXVI (March 1972), 91-113.

The Chinese land reform did not *give* land to the poor peasants. It encouraged them to organize themselves to *take* it, and in the process to crush their former oppressors. This was the prerequisite for later social development in the countryside, for, without it, the old class structure and wealth ownership patterns would have been regenerated by the persistence of old attitudes and of institutions favorable to the rich.[35]

Similarly, in Taiwan and Japan the success of agrarian reform depended on first breaking the control of wealthy landowners and then substituting strong local government and a network of farmers' associations, irrigation associations, land reform committees, and cooperatives that allowed participation by rural people and provided a channel of communication and influence. In both China and Taiwan, as well as in Tanzania and under other one-party political regimes, a strong, integrated, and responsive party system extending down to the village level has been a necessary adjunct to government agencies in mobilizing political support, eliciting participation, generating leadership, and ensuring administrative compliance with rural development policies. Countries without either a strong party structure or effective local organizations have made little headway in rural reform.

Perhaps the most carefully planned dispersion of political power and mobilization of support has been in China, where more than two decades of experimentation were necessary to create workable arrangements. The Chinese system, as Stavis notes, is based on two principles of political organization—inclusiveness and integration. Each level of government and all levels of the communist party are involved in development, and all are mutually dependent:

> The result is a very complex situation in which power is decentralized to different levels with regard to different policies. Moreover, the distribution of power changes from time to time. Always, no matter where power is focused, no level of administration is autonomous, and each level will interact with and respond to demands from the other levels.[36]

In China, Vietnam, and a few other communist countries, rural development depends heavily on the use of political cadres to mobilize and control the participation of the rural poor. Cadres are carefully chosen young volunteers, often high school or college students of peasant stock, who are intensively indoctrinated, and are highly motivated to suffer the deprivations and hardships of working and living in the poorest rural areas for long periods of time.[37]

[35] Gurley (fn. 11), 389; emphasis in original.
[36] Stavis (fn. 28), 53.
[37] Antonio J. Ledesma, "Land Reform Programs in East and Southwest Asia: A Com-

In nearly all countries, the tensions and conflicts over control and distribution of political power are an underlying factor in the planning and administration of rural development. The tensions between the desire to maintain central control and the need to diffuse support and elicit participation are evident in all societies attempting to cope with rural poverty. China's ambivalence toward decentralization, and the recurring shifts during Mao's regime between delegation of authority and recentralization, resulted from fear of the growing power of provincial leaders during periods of decentralization and from their pursuit of regional self-sufficiency in economic development—sometimes in conflict with national plans and policies. In the 1960s, when decentralization threatened to give provincial leaders the power to challenge national policies, communist party leaders pressured Mao to recentralize because "it became more difficult for the central leadership to elicit compliance from the provinces." As Parris Chang points out, "the center [had] increasingly found itself compelled to use negotiations, bargaining, cajoling and manipulation in dealing with province authorities." Central control was re-exerted because, on a number of occasions during the 1960s, "the provincial leaders appear to have exercised an effective veto power over policy decisions made in Peking."[38]

PROBLEMS OF NATIONAL ADMINISTRATIVE STRUCTURE

Within developing nations, rural development policies also create a set of administrative problems that are related to, or indistinguishable from, conflicts over the distribution of power. In addition to the strong and pervasive administrative support that is needed to initiate and sustain rural reform, a highly dispersed structure of participation, coordination, supervision, and management is essential for successful implementation. Agrarian reforms controlled exclusively from the center often become bogged down in national political conflicts, interagency rivalries, serious disagreements between national and local interests, and the inefficiencies of large-scale bureaucracy. Moreover, conventional principles of administration—especially Western, and particularly American, standards of management—that are adopted by developing countries or imposed on them by international assistance agencies are usually inappropriate for organizing integrated rural development. Short-range inefficiencies and seemingly irrational arrangements must

parative Approach," University of Wisconsin Land Tenure Center, Research Paper No. 69 (Madison 1976), mimeo.
[38] Chang, "Centralization vs. Decentralization in the Chinese Political System, 1949-1971," *Asian Forum*, IV (1972), 14-36, at 29.

often be accepted as the price of social reorganization. Relationships among efficiency, redundancy, and the role of central coordination must be seriously re-examined in the light of the low levels of administrative capacity in much of the developing world.

1. *Central control and decentralized implementation.* Although rural development programs need central guidance and support, their implementation must be localized to meet the needs of subsistence and small-scale farmers, either by decentralization through field organizations, or by devolution of functions to local institutions. Evaluations of rural development suggest that devolution has generally been more effective in reaching the intended beneficiaries. In his review of land reform in 25 countries, Montgomery concludes that devolution of administrative functions to local, non-career officials "produced significantly better results for peasant welfare than arrangements using professional administrators, whether in a centralized or decentralized administrative system."[39] Nelson's study of 24 land development and colonization projects in 9 Latin American countries seems to reinforce Montgomery's conclusions. Nelson finds no projects with "dynamic performance" among those undertaken by the national government: all economically viable projects were spontaneous colonizations, private efforts, or publicly supported but privately executed ventures. On the other hand, Nelson contends that "practically all recorded failures have been state-directed projects. The inadequate technical and administrative capacity of government agencies has been evident in all phases of the process. . . ."[40]

The inability of national ministries to control rural development from the center or to coordinate their efforts in the field has contributed to the failure of Nepal's agrarian reforms. One Nepali's assessment voices a familiar refrain of evaluations in many other countries:

> . . . the field offices of relevant agencies could not work together as a team and in the spirit of cooperation. It is evident that there were many instances where critical inputs, especially credit, were not provided in time and in sufficient amounts. Since credit was extended through activities of various agencies, coordination among these agencies was vital for effective implementation of the program. Due to the long processing

[39] John D. Montgomery, "Allocation of Authority in Land Reform Programs: A Comparative Study of Administrative Process and Outputs," *Administrative Science Quarterly*, XVII (March 1972), 62-75, at 62.
[40] Michael Nelson, *The Development of Tropical Lands: Policy Issues in Latin America* (Baltimore: The Johns Hopkins University Press 1973), 267.

needed and because of inadequate coordination, private moneylenders continued to dominate.[41]

In most countries of Asia and Africa that made an attempt at decentralization, poor motivation, high turnover, inadequate equipment and funds, poor communication between headquarters and the field, and shortages of trained manpower have limited its effectiveness.[42]

The record of devolution is also mixed, but there are some clear examples of success. To the extent that communes were given responsibility for a wide variety of local decisions in China, devolvement seems to have created motivation and interest on the part of local leaders; it allowed national programs to be tailored to the needs of villages, and gave rural people more control over selecting and implementing small-scale social service projects and programs. Taiwan and Japan both successfully implemented agrarian reform through a network of local institutions.[43] Montgomery observes of land reforms in 10 Asian and Latin American countries that devolvement seems to have worked better because it allowed easier access to knowledge, better communications among various levels of organization, and increased community solidarity and support.[44]

Other countries have also attempted to decentralize or devolve functions to the regional level. Regionalization can have a number of advantages: it often allows rural programs to be designed to exploit unique resources and opportunities, provides convenient units of analysis for disaggregating national plans, extends greater opportunities to develop local leadership, and permits the testing of experimental or pilot projects. Regions with well-defined geographical boundaries facilitate the monitoring, supervision, and evaluation of national programs and the coherent integration of sectoral investments.[45]

But serious obstacles to decentralization and devolution have appeared in most developing countries. Few governments have been willing to establish regional development authorities or administrative units with sufficient autonomy and resources to carry out their tasks,

[41] Kiran Nath Pyakurayal, "Paddy Production Program in the Third Plan (1967–1970): A Nepalese Experience," in G. U. Iglesias, ed., *Implementation: The Problem of Achieving Results* (Manila: Eastern Regional Organization for Public Administration 1976), 35-61, at 57.

[42] See Dennis A. Rondinelli and Kenneth Ruddle, "Political Commitment and Administrative Support: Preconditions for Growth with Equity Policy," *Journal of Administration Overseas*, XVII (January 1978), 43-60.

[43] Theodore Reynolds Smith, *East Asian Agrarian Reform: Japan, Republic of Korea, Taiwan and the Philippines* (Hartford, Conn.: John C. Lincoln Institute 1974).

[44] Montgomery (fn. 39), 73.   [45] Rondinelli and Ruddle (fn. 8), chap. 6.

or with sufficient power to coordinate the work of different ministries operating within their jurisdictions. The fear of loss of central control and the threat of political fragmentation and rivalry block decentralization. In most countries, moreover, devolution is inhibited by the weakness of local governments, their lack of independent sources of revenue, their dependence on the central ministries for trained manpower and expertise, and their subservience to local elites unsympathetic to the cause of small-scale farmers. Experience in India suggests that even when functions were delegated, diffidence on the part of local leaders in exercising authority and in making legitimate claims allowed higher-level officials to maintain control.[46] In other cases, local elites managed to maintain their domination because of political conflicts at the local level and squabbles among contending factions over government allocations.[47] Studies of local government in Central Africa and Southwest Asia, moreover, found that the attitudes and behavior of traditional tribal leaders or village elders were often obstacles to effective participation in government development programs: feelings of helplessness concerning their ability to solve local problems through deliberate action, acceptance of "fate" rather than belief in their ability to control their environment, and disinterest in problems beyond their immediate concern or the boundaries of their villages. In addition, the deep mutual distrust between rural people and government officials often makes decentralization and devolution difficult.[48]

2. *Efficiency, redundancy, and effectiveness.* National governments and international agencies have paid relatively little attention to alternative ways of organizing for rural development. The funding agencies have either left governments to their own devices or insisted on administrative arrangements that conform to Western management practices. But the application of Western administrative principles—emphasizing economic efficiency, technical rationality, avoidance of "overlap" and "duplication," and central coordination—may seriously inhibit innovation and be inappropriate for serving the rural poor.

Programs that depend on cooperation among government agencies are vulnerable in any country, but in much of the Third World they are

[46] See R. Hooja, "The District as a Planning Unit: Style and Locus," and N. R. Inamdar, "District Planning in Maharashtra," both in *Indian Journal of Public Administration*, xix (July-September 1974), 393-406, 320-27.

[47] See J. M. Cohen, "Rural Change in Ethiopia: The Chilalo Agricultural Development Unit," *Economic Development and Cultural Change*, xxii (July 1974), 580-614.

[48] African Training and Research Centre in Administration for Development, "Regional Conference on Management of Rural and Urban Development in Africa," *African Administrative Studies*, ix (January 1973), 33-41.

simply doomed to failure. The creation of rural development programs that require large numbers of inputs from different ministries and the coordination of their activities in rural areas imposes insuperable administrative burdens on governments in most developing nations. Formal mechanisms of coordination rarely work in traditional cultures. In much of Asia and Africa, interaction among various levels of the bureaucracy is often highly constrained: evaluation or "feedback" from subordinates is often construed by superiors as criticism, and is neither expected nor encouraged in bureaucracies where hierarchies reflect and reinforce differences in social status. Time is valued differently in most developing nations than in the West: promptness is not necessarily considered a virtue; deadlines or schedules are met "in good time" rather than on time. The seeming rigidity of hierarchical organizational structures, however, may belie the lack of real control at the top and mask the informal processes of interaction through which tasks are actually performed. Corruption, favoritism, dependence on political authority outside the bureaucracy, and the inability to match skills with job needs, may all undermine the capacity of governmental organizations to coordinate.[49]

In her evaluation of agrarian reform projects in Latin America, Tendler found that those requiring a great deal of coordination were often quickly stymied, and that better results could frequently be obtained by assigning all rural development activities to a single organization with sufficient resources and personnel to perform its functions, even if it duplicated existing activities.[50] In making a choice of organizational structure in developing countries, the cost of redundancy and duplication must be traded off against increased probabilities of success in meeting the program's objectives. Some analysts argue, in fact, that the creation of redundancy, far from being inefficient and wasteful, is essential for increasing the reliability of service delivery. Caiden and Wildavsky contend that the ability of rich countries to obtain resources needed for production, and to deliver services, owes less to efficiency of management than to complex redundancy—that is, to a large number of organizations with an overabundance of resources and skills, which perform the same or similar functions; if one organization fails, others

[49] See Jon R. Moris, "The Transferability of Western Management Concepts and Programs: An East African Perspective," and Gabino A. Mendoza, "The Transferability of Western Management Concepts and Programs: An Asian Perspective," both in L. D. Stifel, J. S. Coleman, and J. E. Black, eds., *Education and Training for Public Sector Management in Developing Countries* (New York: Rockefeller Foundation 1977), 73-83 and 61-71, respectively.
[50] Tendler (fn. 22), 25-30.

in the institutional network fill the gap, thereby greatly increasing reliability and reducing uncertainty. "Arrangements in poor countries," they note, "lack the benefits of redundancy—the surplus, the reserve, the overlapping networks of skill and data—to cushion the reverberating effects of uncertainty."[51]

3. *Diffusion of administrative capacity.* Some governments and international assistance agencies, such as the World Bank, hedge against risk and avoid the weaknesses of central coordinating mechanisms by creating autonomous implementation units for each large-scale project. These institutions are usually outside of the formal structure of government, and are given all the resources needed to carry out their functions. To the extent that these autonomous units add to national organizational capability, are highly visible and therefore held responsible for achieving results, can obtain the resources and manpower needed to perform their functions, are able to work compatibly with other government agencies, and can focus their attention on specific objectives, they may have significant advantages over regular ministries in implementing rural development, even when they duplicate, or overlap with, existing agencies. They often have other advantages, such as the ability to offer higher salaries, better benefits, and sufficient amenities to attract the most competent personnel; in addition, they may have greater flexibility to innovate and make decisions expeditiously, and to act as training grounds for young administrators.[52]

Tendler suggests that a key factor in determining whether to establish an autonomous unit or to assign integrated rural development to existing ministries is the degree to which the latter are committed to reaching the rural poor. "The institution should be hand-picked for its commitment to small farmers rather than only for its ability to carry out a certain conventionally defined task."[53] If existing agencies are captured or influenced by elite or large-farmers' groups—as are many development banks and ministries of agriculture in the Third World— there is little hope that they can be reoriented toward serving the rural poor; they should therefore not be used to implement rural reform programs. In these cases, the creation of a new agency or the assignment of tasks among agencies in such a way that little coordination is required may be better alternatives.

Creation of large numbers of semi-independent development authori-

[51] Naomi Caiden and Aaron Wildavsky, *Planning and Budgeting in Poor Countries* (New York: Wiley 1974), 63.
[52] See Rondinelli and Ruddle (fn. 13), 22-24.
[53] Tendler (fn. 22), 33.

ties may also have serious disadvantages, of course, which must be weighed in the balance. Too often such authorities become powers unto themselves, and over time amass enough political influence to pursue their own interests—as did *Pertamina* in Indonesia—sometimes in conflict with national development policies. Or they may become so dependent on external financial and technical support—as did the Water and Power Development Authority in Bangladesh—that they respond more readily to international priorities and technical and professional standards than to the needs of their own clientele, and become involved in damaging conflicts with government ministries. A serious problem arises in countries with limited technical and managerial manpower, where autonomous implementation units compete with regular ministries for the same people and resources, draining existing agencies of their best talent. On the other hand, they may become dependent on expatriate personnel and not develop indigenous administrative capacity at all.

Thus, integrated rural development may create serious tensions and potential conflicts over the organization of national administrative structure. If rural reform is to be effective, those problems must be anticipated and resolved.

STRATEGIES FOR DELIVERY OF LOCAL SERVICES

Although creation of semi-autonomous institutions may effectively solve immediate administrative problems in developing nations, the ability to sustain rural development depends on a complex, integrated, and appropriate organizational network in rural areas. Thus, the third problem facing development planners is to establish or stimulate the growth of an effective institutional structure for delivering services and technology to the rural poor.

To a large extent, subsistence farmers and landless laborers are poor because they lack access to public and private institutions that have the resources needed to increase productivity and thereby raise incomes. In many rural regions, organizations that provide public and private services are missing altogether or are found only in traditional forms. The institutions that do exist may not serve the majority of the poorest people, and indeed may severely exploit them. Moreover, institutions in rural areas are rarely linked into a network or "hierarchy" of supporting institutions in such a way as to provide continuous, reliable, and efficient flows of services; others have low levels of administrative capacity to deal with the complex problems facing the rural poor. And new institutions introduced by government or international agencies are frequently so incompatible with traditional practices, customs, and behavior that they not only fail to serve, but may further alienate rural people.[54]

Analysts attribute the failure of past attempts at integrated rural development to the absence, or weak linkage, of rural organizations. The design of future strategies, Ruttan argues, must be aimed at "a unique combination of technical and institutional change." Private markets are inaccessible or exploitive, and the public markets "through which political resources are brought to bear on institutional performance in rural areas are often more imperfect—more biased against rural people—than the credit and product markets."[55] Although the concept of *appropriate technology* is well established, relatively little attention has been given to its organizational dimensions or, more importantly, to the characteristics of *appropriate institutions* for delivering social services and technological improvements to rural areas.

Appropriate institutions for integrated rural development have a number of important characteristics:

First, like appropriate technology, they must be highly adaptable to the wide variety of problems and conditions found in rural areas. Beneficiaries are often quite heterogeneous; small farmers have needs different from those of shifting cultivators, and both have problems and characteristics that differ from those of landless laborers. Moreover, their patterns of settlement are usually so unalike that a delivery system designed to meet the needs of only one group will overlook others or serve them inadequately. Organizational solutions can no more be designed and universally prescribed for all rural areas than they can for all developing countries.

Second, rural institutions must be complementary and integrated. Services and technologies in support of rural development must be mutually reinforcing and interlocking in order to stimulate local economies. Credit delivered without the provision of technical assistance in improved agricultural methods, higher-yielding seed varieties, fertilizers, irrigation, and improved marketing, will, as noted earlier, have little impact on production and income in rural areas. Institutions must be linked both vertically and horizontally to provide a hierarchy of services and to increase the quality and reliability of delivery. In their study of

[54] For a detailed description, see Dennis A. Rondinelli and Kenneth Ruddle, "Appropriate Institutions for Rural Development: Organizing Services and Technology in Developing Countries," *Philippine Journal of Public Administration*, xxi (January 1977), in press.

[55] Vernon Ruttan, "Integrated Rural Development Programs: A Skeptical Perspective," *International Development Review*, xviii (1975), 9-16, at 12.

16 countries in Asia, Uphoff and Esman "found no case where only one institution was carrying the full responsibility for rural development or where *complementarities* among institutions were not as important as what the institutions themselves did."[56]

Third, appropriate institutions must be built on culturally accepted arrangements, practices, and behavior. Understanding the operation of traditional institutions that have served rural people for decades or centuries, and accepting their strengths, inadequacies, limitations, and potentials for transformation, is essential for modifying old arrangements and introducing new ones. The success of agrarian reform in Taiwan and Japan was largely attributable to the adaptation of traditional farmers' associations to new functions in land redistribution and community development. Even after the revolution on mainland China, Mao's planners were careful to adopt acceptable local arrangements as the basis of communal structure. The communal system, as Stavis points out, "did not emerge from an historical and social vacuum; it was not simply proclaimed according to a vision of society." On the contrary, the communes were "intimately related to centuries of economic and political history and to almost a decade of gradually expanding organs of economic cooperation, slowly increasing in size, complexity, responsibility and degree of socialization."[57]

Fourth, as the Chinese experience demonstrates, the institutional network must be designed to transform traditional practices and behavior into procedures more suitable for economic growth and equitable income distribution. Although they must be based on and compatible with rural custom and tradition, they must also be catalysts for change, transforming developmentally inadequate practices and behavior at a locally acceptable pace. Moreover, they must gradually displace those traditional institutions that are incapable of change, while remaining flexible enough themselves to adapt to changing conditions as development occurs.

Fifth, appropriate institutions must tailor arrangements for service delivery to the locational requirements of their rural clientele; in most cases, that means modifying the "central service point" locational bias of large-scale organizations. Rather than locating operational and distribution units at large cities, provincial capitals, or district towns— which are usually not very accessible to rural people—appropriate insti-

---

[56] Norman T. Uphoff and Milton J. Esman, *Local Organization for Rural Development: Analysis of Asian Experience* (Ithaca, N.Y.: Cornell University Center for International Studies 1974), xi; emphasis in original.
[57] Stavis (fn. 28), 48.

tutions would deliver services to rural clients through mobile or widely dispersed delivery mechanisms. Rural people would be sought out at farmsteads, or services would be brought to marketplaces; officials would travel to the rural areas rather than requiring rural people to go to centrally located government offices. Taiwan, Korea, and to some extent the Philippines have been able to mobilize rural savings and provide financial services by extending banking functions through widely dispersed branch offices, the use of mobile and temporary facilities in villages on market days, and the creation of agricultural and fishing financing associations and credit cooperatives in rural areas.[58] The short-term costs of these arrangements undoubtedly are higher than they would be for service delivery at fixed points, but their impacts are more widespread and effective in reaching small-scale farmers and rural workers.

Finally, appropriate institutions for service delivery must be designed in conjunction with beneficiaries and open to local leadership and participation. Studies of small-farm rural development projects in Latin America and Africa show that participation by farmers can lead to ideas for more effectively designed projects—particularly those components dealing with agricultural production techniques. Local people can help to adapt components that have been tested and proven successful in other projects to local conditions, and they can test new technologies and organizational arrangements prior to introduction on a broader scale. Surveys of more than 80 development projects for small farmers found that the following factors contributed to increased local participation: (1) Geographical boundaries of the projects were well defined, and the client population easily identifiable. (2) The project staff held a series of meetings with local leaders and farmers, delegating to them control over or participation in specific decisions in the design of the project. (3) Farmers were involved jointly with project staff in testing technological packages and organizational arrangements to be used in the project. (4) Participants were generally homogeneous in terms of social group and economic class. (5) The project staff developed an effective process of communication with and among local participants. (6) Organizational arrangements were created to give farmers a voice in decisions concerning management of the project. (7) High priority was placed on the technical training of participants;

[58] See D. P. Villanueva, "A Survey of the Financial System and the Saving-Investment Process in Korea and the Philippines," *Finance and Development*, II (1971), 16-19, and B. Maithreyan, "Savings in a Developing Economy—Certain Suggestions for Reform and National Coordination," *Economic Bulletin for Asia and the Pacific*, xxvi (1975), 188-201.

many were used as paraprofessionals to teach technical skills to others. (8) Involvement was related initially to single-purpose activities, such as credit or crop promotion, and was broadened only after success with initial activities. (9) Systems of accountability were established to permit changes in leadership among local participants and to ensure that services were provided efficiently. (10) Opportunities were offered initially for participants to engage in income-generating activities.[59]

In short, efficient and effective delivery of services to the rural poor can rarely be attained through standardized locational criteria or by mechanisms designed by professional technicians and administrators. It depends on an intimate understanding of rural life, behavior, and motivation, which is unlikely to be brought to bear on the planning and implementation of integrated rural development programs without participation by the intended beneficiaries.

CONCLUSION

Ultimately, equitable growth is a matter of political will and effective organization. Technology is merely a means to an end; in most cases even sophisticated, proven technologies will be unable to stimulate growth or alleviate poverty if a developing nation cannot mobilize political commitment, break institutional barriers to economic participation, and structure administrative agencies in such a way as to serve rural beneficiaries.

Equitable growth requires expanding participation in economic activities. It involves drawing larger numbers of people into processes of production, exchange, and consumption, as well as mobilizing savings and investing them in directly productive activities and social services. It also means expanding the administrative capacity of public and private organizations, and increasing the access of individuals to resources and opportunities needed to meet basic human needs, raise productivity, and develop human potential. The solution of these societal problems depends, as Lindblom has so forcefully argued, on an understanding of the fundamental political and economic mechanisms of authority, exchange, and persuasion, through which governments and political groups committed to a policy of equitable growth must influence development decisions.[60]

In order to solve social problems, development planners and administrators must not only understand the characteristics of these mecha-

---

[59] Development Alternatives Inc., *Strategies for Small Farmer Development: An Empirical Study of Rural Development Projects*, I (Washington: USAID 1975), 95-96.
[60] Charles E. Lindblom, *Politics and Markets* (New York: Basic Books 1977).

nisms; they must also be able to combine them in new ways. Lindblom's observation on India applies to most developing countries: "India's difficulties in economic development are in part the consequences of her leaders' inability to understand that growth requires a growth mechanism: if not the market, which Indian policy cripples, then the authority of government, which India has never chosen to mobilize."[61] The success of integrated rural development policies depends not so much on the technical inputs that international agencies and Third-World governments have so strongly emphasized, as it does on the ability of governments to expand domestic markets and mobilize authority in order to increase participation in productive activities. Unless means can be found to resolve the paradox of power, solve the problems of national administrative structure, and create institutional networks of service delivery, neither integrated rural development nor any other policy of rural reform will have much impact on economic conditions in the developing world.

[61] *Ibid.*, 6.

Part II
Empirical Cases

COMPULSION AND SOCIAL CHANGE:

Is Authoritarianism the Solution to India's Economic Development Problems?

By FRANCINE R. FRANKEL*

HISTORIANS, sociologists, and psychologists have by now all challenged the notion that conditions determining economic development can be adequately explained through the use of growth models limited to economic variables. They have stressed the importance of preconditions, whether national integration, social structure, value systems, or political organization. Economists, for their part, have graciously acknowledged the utility of these critiques, but have nevertheless continued to formulate their theories of development in terms of economic variables. They seem to have decided, as Albert Hirschman aptly observed twenty years ago, that "in spite of the many valuable insights gained from these [non-economic] theories, their cumulative impact on the unwary reader could well raise serious doubts about the possibility of any economic development at all."[1] If economists now appear chastened, it is not because of rival theories, but as the result of experience. The great majority of new states have failed to make a significant impact on the problem of mass poverty. They seem unable to achieve the economic transformations that the economic theories were so painstakingly designed to help bring about.

Attention has turned to the peculiarities and special conditions that constitute the historical and social setting in which economic development must take place in each state. A decade has passed since Gunnar Myrdal advanced the most influential statement of an alternative "broad institutional approach" in his *Asian Drama*, a ten-year, three-volume study that is "mainly about India with numerous and systematic attempts at comparisons with other countries of South Asia."[2] Myrdal's

* I am grateful to the Institute for Advanced Study (Princeton) for providing support to me as a visiting member during the time this article was written. I also want to express my appreciation to John P. Lewis and Philips Talbot for their careful comments on an earlier draft of this paper.

[1] Albert O. Hirschman, *The Strategy of Economic Development* (New Haven: Yale University Press 1958), 2.

[2] Gunnar Myrdal, *Asian Drama, An Inquiry into the Poverty of Nations,* I (New York: Pantheon 1968), 40.

critique of the narrowly "economic" framework of analysis rests largely on the argument that Western theories, models, and concepts have distorted the study of economic development in South Asia by separating economic theories from the radically different—and unfavorable—environment in the attitudes, cultures, and institutions of the area.

If we accept the proposition that economic development is a function of overall social development, the prospects of new states assume an even more hopeless aspect than disappointment about poor performance might warrant. The erratic gains, the narrow spread effects, and the reverses or stagnation characteristic of many of the economies of the underdeveloped countries (which otherwise might be rationalized as the result of still imperfect growth models), take on an aspect of inevitability and permanence once they are traced to the intractable obstacles of an unfavorable environment. Myrdal's attempt to carry out a "realistic" analysis of development problems, which restores the initial conditions of the South Asian context—conditions that were ignored by the more abstract Western theories—ends, in fact, with little to offer either in the realm of theory or of practice that could solve these problems, short of a complete social transformation.

The obstacles to development in the South Asian context turn out to be the very same limitations that were "prominent in the thought of the old European colonial masters."[3] They include the irrational beliefs sanctioned by religion, cultural attitudes deprecating manual labor, and styles of living and working accepted as immutable on the strength of these beliefs—all inimical to development. Myrdal considers the "inefficiency, rigidity and inequality of the established institutions and attitudes" and the "economic and social power relations embodied in this framework of institutions and attitudes"[4] to be the primary reasons for the new states' inability to implement economic plans effectively. The "precondition" for economic development that logically follows from this kind of reasoning is that old religious attitudes, cultural patterns, and social structures have to be destroyed before development can take place.

The possibility of achieving such a revolutionary social transformation through democratic processes of government is, of course, remote. Arguments that accept the need for a direct attack on traditional attitudes and modes of economic and social stratification have therefore inevitably stressed the need for compulsion. In this view, countries that limit themselves to democratic planning are doomed to failure since they cannot use force to impose obligations. They are, in Myr-

---

[3] *Ibid.*, 20.   [4] *Ibid.*, 47.

dal's increasingly fashionable terminology, "soft states."[5] Indeed, he considers assertions by the first generation of the post-Independence leadership in India that they were ideologically committed to political democracy to be an opportunist political compromise with powerful propertied interests, for the purpose of remaining in office. By contrast, the litmus test of genuine commitment to development is said to be the willingness to take direct action in a frontal assault on religion and the attitudes and institutions sanctified by it which perpetuate inequalities inimical to change.

The notion that development requires revolutionary social change (which can be accomplished only through imposing greater obligations and social discipline by resort to force) has only recently assumed the aspect of official dogma in India. "Talk Less Work More" became the rationale as well as the political slogan of the authoritarian regime imposed by Prime Minister Indira Gandhi during the period of National Emergency declared on June 26, 1975, when leading members of the opposition were arrested and all the civil liberties that had been guaranteed by the constitution were suspended. The 20-point Economic Program that followed the Proclamation of Emergency by only five days promised to apply the government's sweeping new powers to enforce long-standing policies for basic social change, including the redistribution of agricultural assets and the "socialization" of urban land.[6]

The experiment with authoritarian social transformation was brief. It was cut short in March 1977, by the completely unexpected rout of Mrs. Gandhi and her ruling Congress Party at the first opportunity afforded the population to openly express its opinion on the new political order. The majority of India's electorate remained illiterate and impoverished, but had little difficulty in drawing up a balance sheet of the economic gains and social costs of the new forms of authoritarian planning. On the one hand, the Congress Party's policies of redistribution, designed to improve the condition of the "poor and downtrod-

---

[5] Myrdal uses this term to characterize the governments of South Asia where "policies decided on are often not enforced if they are enacted at all, and . . . the authorities, even when framing policies, are reluctant to place obligations on people." *Ibid.*, 66.

[6] The 20-Point Program, announced by Prime Minister Indira Gandhi on July 1, 1975, was designed to rally maximum public support for the Proclamation of National Emergency by pledging to meet the unfulfilled demands of diverse social groups. The government promised, among other things, to implement agricultural land ceilings, provide house sites for landless laborers, abolish bonded labor, liquidate rural debt, increase agricultural wages, bring prices down, step up agricultural and industrial production, socialize urban land, prevent tax evasion, confiscate the property of smugglers, provide cheaper books for students, and increase overall employment. For a full description of the 20-Point Economic Program by one of the Prime Minister's strong supporters, see J. S. Bright, *Emergency in India and 5 + 20 Point Programme* (New Delhi: Pankaj Publications 1976).

den," had remained confined largely to schemes that could not be effectively implemented. On the other hand, the stepped-up family planning programs of the Government bureaucracy had scored dramatic successes in overfulfilling targets, through methods that ended in the abuses of enforced mass sterilization. Similarly, the administrative machinery had been successful in carrying out its accelerated "slum clearance" projects, by bulldozing the makeshift shacks and shops of the urban squatter population who were subsequently "relocated" outside the cities. India's voters—that is, the poor, both rural and urban—once given the chance to endorse or reject the kind of social discipline enforced during the Emergency, rallied behind the hastily combined opposition (the Janata Party and the Congress for Democracy) to remove the Congress Party from power after 30 years of uninterrupted rule. The poor responded once again to the promise, this time by the leadership of the anti-Congress opposition, of "both bread and freedom."[7]

The renewed vote of popular confidence in democratic methods of social change appears all the more poignant in the face of the doubts about the efficacy of the democratic process that still trouble not only Western intellectuals (and business leaders), but even the leading architect of the opposition's momentous triumph. Jayaprakash Narayan, who became the most revered political figure in India after the resumption of normal democratic government, apparently was not convinced himself that the problems of unemployment, high prices, and mass poverty could be solved even if the opposition were to win. Not unlike Myrdal, he had concluded that solutions to these problems were impossible without "radical change in the whole society" amounting to a "total revolution," that is, "an all-round revolution, political, economic, social, educational, moral and cultural."[8] While still under detention during the Emergency, Narayan confided in his prison diary:

> The question is can the picture be fundamentally altered through the ordinary democratic process? Even if the opposition wins, will the picture change? I fear no. Laws will be passed and applied, monies will be spent—even if all this is done, possibly without corruption creeping in, will the structure, the system, the "order" of our society change? I think no.[9]

Although Narayan, a Gandhian, originally hoped to bring about a "total revolution" through peaceful means by mobilizing "people's

[7] *Times of India*, February 27, 1977.
[8] Jayaprakash Narayan, "Why Total Revoluiton?" *Everyman's Weekly*, December 22, 1974.
[9] *New York Times Magazine*, March 27, 1977, p. 88.

direct action" in the form of civil disobedience against an unresponsive (albeit democratically elected) government, radical Marxists despair of using the democratic process at all in carrying out a fundamental social transformation. They accept the view that democracy has failed, and that, as in the Soviet Union and China, an element of compulsion will ultimately be necessary if the institutional changes essential to economic development are to be achieved.

In this article, I shall offer a somewhat different perspective on the extraordinarily complicated problems confronting India. Like Myrdal and a growing number of critics who reject narrowly economic solutions to problems of underdevelopment, I will argue that India's poverty cannot be overcome solely through the evolutionary growth models of neoclassical theory. In India, in the absence of prior institutional change —and no matter how sophisticated the investment plans for "inducing" other investments that have backward and forward linkage effects— one set of investments will not lead to another, or will lead to only a few others and then very quickly to a dead end, if the past is any guide.

At the same time, it is difficult to endorse the opposite view; namely, that revolutionary social transformation is a necessary or, perhaps more important, a realistic precondition for breaking down the social barriers to development. Whether presented as the "broad institutional approach" of the social theorist or the "total revolution" of the political activist, the solution is indeed too comprehensive. In particular, it fails to differentiate between what may be called the *direct* and *indirect* obstacles to economic advance which are part of the social setting in India. I shall argue that the direct constraints are found in the patterns of land distribution and tenure relations. By contrast, the cultural attitudes, caste structures, and power relations which are also part of the Indian environment are more accurately characterized as indirect obstacles, in the sense that they strengthen ideological and political patterns that stand in the way of agrarian reform.

Two important consequences follow from this type of distinction. First, obstacles to economic growth turn out to be more narrow—and therefore somewhat more tractable—than the broad institutional critique allows. Second, by differentiating between direct and indirect social causes of economic underdevelopment, it becomes possible to devise ideological and organizational strategies aimed at undermining the beliefs and attitudes that continue to legitimate inequalities as well as the structures that fragment the peasantry into vertical alignments led by upper-caste, landed elites. Indeed, it was the basic assumption of India's leadership during the days of Gandhi and Nehru that an informed and organized peasantry could build direct relationships with outside centers of power in both the administration and the political parties, to convert its strength of numbers under a democratic political system into a "nonviolent" sanction for radical reform.

This notion was not based merely on self-delusion or self-interest. The fact is that theories calling for revolutionary social transformation are "non-theories" under Indian conditions, once they are tested against political constraints. Not only are such strategies outside the intention or capability of the government or any organized opposition movement; even worse, they are prescriptions that in practice can only retard social change or trigger social chaos. In India, a frontal assault on the existing social order would, in the best case, delay or abort desired egalitarian changes by fragmenting large numbers of the poorer classes along the more potent allegiances to religion, language, or caste. In the worst case, such an assault would be likely to lead to a prolonged period of disorder and the prospect of eventual national disintegration. In sum, India seems to present a unique case: a society that is unresponsive both to neoclassical models of evolutionary economic change and to direct confrontation for the purposes of sweeping away social obstacles to development.

I

An account of India's development since Independence is itself the most eloquent critique of neoclassical growth theory and the inability of its labor-surplus models to solve problems of mass poverty in the absence of prior institutional change. The basic fact is that only a small minority of the population has been incorporated into the high-productivity, high-wage modern sector of the economy. Despite substantial expansion in industrial output and social overhead capital, the spread effects from the creation of more jobs have been narrow. Eighty percent of the population continue to live in rural areas. Of this vast majority, about the same proportion earn their livelihood directly from agriculture, as cultivators or laborers.[10] Overall increases in per capita net national product have been modest. Reverses in recent years have substantially neutralized earlier gains.[11]

[10] India, Registrar General and Census Commissioner, *Census of India, 1971*, Provisional Population Totals, Paper 1 of 1971—Supplement, 3-33, 49.

[11] The annual growth rate in per capita net national product registered its highest levels in the first decade of planning. Increments during the First Plan (1951–56) and the Second Plan (1956–61) were 1.6% and 1.8% per annum respectively. By contrast, the annual rate of growth during the Third Plan (1961–66) declined to 0.3% at constant prices. Except for a brief spurt in 1967-68, and again in 1975-76, annual growth

There are two reasons for this failure. The first is highly visible and easily quantified. Population, which increased by more than 50 percent in the first half of this century (at annual growth rates of about 1 percent), almost doubled during the next 25 years (as the rate of growth increased to a peak of 2.5 percent per annum). Altogether, the current population of India is at least 100 million higher than economic planners were able to anticipate.[12] This population explosion makes it clear that, for decades to come, new employment opportunities created in the modern industrial sector will be able to absorb only a small fraction of the unemployed and underemployed. Estimates made in 1971—on the basis of population increases that had *already* occurred— project an additional 65 million entrants into the labor force by 1986. This increase alone represents more than three times the existing level of employment in the entire organized sector, including private industry and public enterprise.[13] In addition, there was a backlog of unemployment (as of 1971) estimated at 15 million persons.[14] Chronic underemployment within the rural sector, as measured by a series of pilot studies in the early 1970's, was estimated to affect one-third of the rural population.[15]

The second reason for this failure is less readily apparent, but it takes on greater practical significance for the future, when most new entrants into the labor force will have to find productive employment within the agricultural sector. It is the chronic inability of the vast agricultural economy to achieve the higher levels of output and productivity that are well within the potential of existing technology.

---

rates have tended to remain at levels of less than 1%. During the Fourth Plan (1969–74), per capita gains in net national product per annum averaged 0.5%. India, *Economic Survey, 1974-75,* 59; India, *Economic Survey, 1969-70,* 61.

[12] In 1952, the Planning Commission estimated that "for the purposes of our calculations regarding possible rates of development in India in the next few decades," population would continue to grow at the rate of about 1¼% per annum—the rate during the previous ten years. At the end of 25 years, the population was projected to reach 500 million. India, Planning Commission, *The First Five Year Plan* (New Delhi 1952), 20, 23.

[13] India, Planning Commission, *Draft Fifth Five Year Plan, 1974-79, Part I* (New Delhi 1973), 3.

[14] India, Planning Commission, *Fourth Five Year Plan, A Draft Outline* (Delhi, August 1966), 106-8.

[15] These data were generated through the Pilot Intensive Rural Employment Project launched by the Department of Community Development in 1972-73, as part of the Government's Crash Scheme for Rural Employment. A survey of unemployment and underemployment was conducted in 15 selected blocks, each in a different state, to get data representative for the country as a whole. The results showed that there were approximately twice as many unemployed wage-seeking laborers as anticipated in statistical computations based on 1961 census data. The earlier estimates had projected levels of "surplus" manpower at about 17% of the agricultural work force. (India, Ministry of Agriculture, Department of Community Development, unpublished.)

Such a constraint has been apparent since the turn of the century. The British created railways and road networks, new export markets, and a rising demand for raw materials by domestic industries, all of which spurred a steady increase in the rate of output and per-acre yield of non-foodgrain crops (especially tea, sugarcane, and oilseeds).[16] But they accomplished these changes without a significant diversion of land from food crops or any substantial stimulus to the adoption of commercial practices in the rest of the agricultural economy. More striking, during the 40 years ending in 1947, the percentage increase in output of foodgrains, estimated at 12 percent, lagged far behind the increases in population growth, of over 40 percent.[17] Yield levels, among the lowest in the world, showed almost no increase. What is even more remarkable, small negative growth rates emerged—both in output and yield per acre—for rice, which, accounting for about one-half of India's foodgrain output, is her chief crop. In Greater Bengal (an area which had seven-eighths of its acreage under rice), the yield declines occurred at the same time in which "intensity of cultivation increased considerably," with an estimated addition of six million people to the agricultural labor force.[18] India's experience during this period provides a direct contrast to the pattern of "agricultural involution" reported by Clifford Geertz for Java under similar circumstances; there, it proved feasible to raise per hectare yields to match population growth rates through the application of more labor-intensive techniques of cultivation.[19] In Greater Bengal, the marginal productivity of labor clearly could not be maintained. Per capita availability of foodgrains declined.[20] These decreases were cushioned, but not compensated, by imports. When the imports stopped during the Second World War (after Burma had been occupied by the Japanese), three million persons died of starvation in the famine of 1943.

After Independence, the obvious gap between the actual average yields and the technical possibilities spurred optimism about India's potentiality for rapid agricultural growth. This provided the rationale of the Community Development Program that was inaugurated in 1952. It

[16] George Blyn, *Agricultural Trends in India, 1891–1947: Output, Availability and Productivity* (Philadelphia: University of Pennsylvania Press 1966), 107-18.

[17] *Ibid.*, 96.

[18] *Ibid.*, 209-10. On the most favorable assumptions, Blyn estimates that after 1911-12, yields per acre for foodgrains in Greater Bengal declined by −0.10% per annum. The raw data indicate a higher rate of decline of −0.55% per annum. The actual rate probably lies between these two limits. *Ibid.*, 219-24.

[19] See Geertz, *Agricultural Involution: The Processes of Ecological Change in Indonesia* (Berkeley: University of California Press 1963), 28-38; 77-82.

[20] Blyn (fn. 16), 104-5.

assumed that expansion of 50 percent or more in yield per acre over a fifteen- to twenty-year period was technologically possible with only relatively small changes in production techniques, and using mainly indigenous inputs. Those responsible for the program actually insisted that "even a hundred percent increase (in yields) is not so much a problem of high science. Seeds, composts and green manures, chemical fertilizers to the extent available, line sowing, interculture, irrigation, field bunding and plant protection measures are by no means technical problems. They are mainly matters of organization."[21] The Planning Commission which had been established in 1950 was also persuaded of these possibilities. Launching the drive for rapid industrialization at the beginning of the Second Five-Year Plan in 1956, the Commission adopted the goal of "doubling within a period of 10 years of agricultural production, including food crops."[22] Yet, these potentialities were only partially realized. Despite large-scale investments on major and medium-size irrigation projects, the compound rate of increase in production of all crops between 1949–50 and 1968–69 was somewhat less than 3 percent per annum, while gains from productivity averaged 1.3 percent annually.[23]

India's inability to realize her agricultural production potential has emerged in even sharper relief since the introduction of the new agricultural strategy in the mid-1960's. Major departures from previous policies were devised to achieve rapid gains in production, this time through concentration of modern scientific techniques in the 20 to 25 percent of the cultivated area where assured water supplies provided the most favorable environment for increasing yields. The economic rationale was considerably strengthened, moreover, by the technical breakthrough reported in 1965 from the Philippines and Mexico, of the development of highly fertilizer-responsive paddy and wheat varieties with yield capacities of 5,000 to 6,000 pounds per acre—almost double the maximum potential output of indigenous Indian varieties; it was also encouraged by the development at Indian research stations in the late 1950's of higher-yielding hybrid varieties of maize, bajra, and jowar. During the Fourth Five-Year Plan, 1969–74, two-thirds of the target for additional production of foodgrains was supposed to come from the 30 percent of the total acreage under high-yielding varieties of wheat, paddy, maize, jowar, and bajra.[24] Overall, the rate of increase in agri-

[21] S. K. Dey, *Community Development: A Chronicle* (New Delhi: Ministry of Community Development 1958), 91.

[22] India, Planning Commission, *The Second Five Year Plan* (New Delhi 1956), 62.

[23] India, Planning Commission, *Fourth Five Year Plan, 1969–74* (New Delhi, July 1970), 117.

[24] *Ibid.*, 138.

cultural output that was projected as the result of planting the high-yielding varieties was about two-thirds higher than the level of previous achievements—a minimum of 5 percent per annum.

New requirements for a "package" of complementary modern inputs, including chemical fertilizers, pesticides, and agricultural machinery, did stimulate potentially important backward linkages with the industrial sector. New factories, and increases in installed capacity of factories producing fertilizers and pesticides, were put into operation. Firms manufacturing tractors, power tillers, and other agricultural machines proliferated.

The government's initial concern was that bottlenecks of supply would prove to be the greatest constraint on the rapid introduction of modern techniques, given the meager domestic output of essential inputs, shortages of foreign exchange for imports, and political inhibitions against a major role for foreign private enterprise. That concern, however, was soon replaced by worry over the weakening demand for modern inputs. After a dramatic initial spurt in production, the output of foodgrains actually declined. Partly due to a succession of several years of poor weather, harvests in 1973–74, the last year of the Fourth Plan, were somewhat smaller than they had been in 1970–71.[25] The overall rate of growth in agricultural production at 2.8 percent per annum was far short of the plan's target of 5 percent. The distribution of gains, moreover, was extremely uneven. Rapid agricultural transformation was mainly confined to the irrigated wheat area, primarily in three northern states (Punjab, Haryana, and western sections of Uttar Pradesh). By contrast, only small pockets of rapid growth could be created in the much larger area under rice and other foodgrain crops. Indeed, despite the fact that targets for steady expansion of *area* under the high-yielding varieties of paddy were fulfilled (extending to 25 percent of the total acreage under rice), an official evaluation in 1973–74 found that "thus far, the new agricultural strategy does not appear to have made any visible impact on the production of rice."[26]

Modern agriculture, coexisting alongside much larger subsistence sectors, has simply extended and proliferated the scattered enclaves of development into the hinterland. This dual agricultural economy mirrors many of the features characteristic of the overall dualism between the modern and the traditional sectors. Productivity, employment, wage rates, and absolute levels of income are much higher in the modern agricultural sector than in the traditional subsistence economy.

[25] Production of foodgrains reached a peak level of 108.4 million tons in 1970–71, but dropped back to 103.6 million tons in 1973–74. India, *Economic Survey, 1974–75*, 6.
[26] *Ibid*.

Just as the modern industrial sector has not expanded horizontally but has achieved higher rates of growth through more intensive investment of capital, the modern sector in agriculture shows signs of stabilizing at its present size, and making additional gains in productivity through greater capital investments in mechanization.

Perhaps the most dramatic evidence of this persistent dualism is provided by the large proportion of the rural population that continues to live below the poverty line. According to estimates made by the Planning Commission in 1960–61—after the first decade of planning—50 to 60 percent of the rural population, or approximately 211 million people, subsisted below the minimum level of consumption (calculated primarily in terms of caloric intake necessary to avoid the onset of malnutrition).[27] Available estimates for the early 1970's reveal a reduction in the proportion of the poor, but a moderate increase in their absolute numbers. About 40 to 50 percent of the rural population, at least 220 million people, are still believed to be subsisting below the poverty line.[28]

Ideologically and politically—not to say morally—it is impossible to ignore these millions. Economic objectives of expanding growth rates, of generating greater investment from domestic production and savings, and of achieving self-reliance (or self-sustaining growth) also require much more rapid increases in agricultural output. Low and erratic gains in agricultural production have been a major factor in India's failure over the period of four Five-Year Plans to achieve its target of overall economic growth of 5 to 6 percent per annum. Indeed, during the 1960's and 1970's, the average rate of growth of the net national product at constant prices actually declined from levels achieved in the early years of planning. Annual increases during the First Plan (1951–56) and the Second Plan (1956–61) of 3.4 percent and 4 percent respectively compare with gains during the Third Plan (1961–66) of 2.6 percent; and, after a three-year plan holiday (1966–69), with the progress during the Fourth Plan (1969–74) of 2.8 percent.[29] These reverses were accompanied by a sharp deceleration in the rate of growth of industrial production—from an average annual increase of over 8 percent in 1956–64 to less than 4 percent per annum during 1969–74.[30] Recurrent food shortages, sharp inflationary price spirals, low availability of domestic

[27] India, Perspective Planning Division, Planning Commission, "Perspective of Development: 1961–1976, Implications of Planning for a Minimum Level of Living," August 1962, 4-5 (mimeo).

[28] India, Planning Commission, *Towards Self-Reliance, Approach to the Fifth Five Year Plan* (New Delhi, June 1972), 4.

[29] *Economic Survey, 1974–75* (fn. 11), 59; *Economic Survey, 1969–70* (fn. 11), 61.

[30] *Economic Survey, 1974–75* (fn. 11), 10.

raw materials, shortfalls in industrial output, underutilized capacity (especially in consumer-goods industries), and stagnant or declining rates of public investment have all contributed to the prospect that India will return to a low-level equilibrium in which growth rates do not significantly exceed the rate of population increase.

Any serious effort to prevent what appears to be an incipient enclave pattern from hardening into a permanent separation between the modern and traditional sectors requires a strategy for raising overall productivity in agriculture to levels that at least approach the possibilities already present in the potential of either the traditional or the modern techniques.

II

It is at this point that the process of development runs into direct obstacles because of the pattern of land distribution and land tenure. Although it is "dramatic" to attribute low levels of productivity to irrational religious beliefs and cultural patterns (such as the large numbers of festivals, holidays, and ceremonial occasions which presumably interfere with work schedules that would allow efficient utilization of labor), that explanation is almost entirely gratuitous. The chronic gap between the potential for productivity and actual output can be more parsimoniously (if prosaically) explained by examining the institutions of land tenure that prevent efficient allocation of land, labor, and capital.

The agrarian pattern does not have its origins in religious beliefs, cultural attitudes, or even the exotic social structure of caste. Rather, it derives from the decision taken by the British in the mid-19th century to replace communal forms of landownership with individual proprietary rights in land. The characteristic features of the present agrarian pattern can be summarized as follows:

(1) The overriding constraint is the unfavorable ratio of land to population in the rural areas, which is estimated at 0.71 acre per capita.

(2) The overall scarcity of land is accompanied by extreme inequalities in the distribution of ownership. More than one-quarter of all rural households (26 percent) own no land at all. Another 15 percent own fragments of land of less than one acre. An additional 15 percent own uneconomic or marginal holdings of between 1 and 2.49 acres (i.e., less than one hectare). In brief, the *majority* of all rural households, approximately 57 percent, either own no land or small fragments, or

uneconomic and marginal holdings of less than one hectare. Together, they own only 7 percent of the land. This is the population that is chronically unemployed and underemployed, the millions of rural poor precariously subsisting just at the border of, or slipping below, the line of poverty. In addition, approximately 31 percent of all rural households operate small and medium holdings of between 2.5 and 10 acres and account for over 33 percent of the land. All of these landless and land-poor households can be contrasted with what passes for large land-owners in India, the upper 12 percent of all households who have 10 acres or more and own about 60 percent of the land. Within this group, an even smaller elite, the upper 4 percent, own 20 acres or more each, or 35 percent of the area.

(3) The upper 12 percent or so of rural households can be considered "large" landowners only from the perspective of their size *relative* to the mass of landless and subsistence cultivators. Among this group, for example, only a fraction of 1 percent own holdings of 50 acres or more.[31] Even then, there are considerably *fewer* large *farms* than large landowners. Holdings in all size groups are subdivided into separate parcels that are scattered within and between villages. The tiniest frag-ments are, of course, contained in the smallest holdings. They may be subdivided into plots of one-quarter or one-third of an acre. However, "large" holdings of 10 acres or more are commonly separated into 7 or 8 parcels of 2, 3, 4 or 7 acres.[32] "Large" landowners, therefore, tend to *operate* small holdings. They do not enjoy advantages associated with economies of scale.

(4) The foregoing pattern of land distribution is associated with a complex system of tenurial relationships in which sharecropping plays a central role. Landowners with tiny plots lease out their holdings to other cultivators and seek additional employment outside the village. "Large" landowners lease out part of their holdings because they tend to have several scattered plots which they find impossible to manage without the aid of tenants. The incidence of tenancy is highest in the densely populated rice deltas where the man/land ratios are least favor-able. It is not unusual for 30 to 40 percent of all cultivators to take some

[31] The above estimates are based on a projection for 1969–70 from National Sample Survey data collected in 1960–61, and have been computed by the Indian economist, B. S. Minhas. See B. S. Minhas, "Mass Poverty and Strategy of Rural Development in India" (Economic Development Institute, International Bank for Reconstruction and Development, March 1971), 37 (mimeo).

[32] National Sample Survey, No. 140, "Tables with Notes on Some Aspects of Land-holdings in Rural Areas" (State and all-India Estimates), "Seventeenth Round, Septem-ber 1961–July 1962," (Calcutta: Indian Statistical Institute, April 1966), Draft, 70.

land on oral lease, or for the proportion of the area operated under such sharecropping arrangements to reach levels of 40 percent or more.[33]

If Marx had not long ago advanced the thesis that production relations can become fetters on the forces of production it would have to be invented to explain India's dilemma at her current stage of development. The present patterns of land distribution and land tenure put major obstacles in the way of increasing per-acre yields, *either* through the more efficient application of traditional labor-intensive techniques *or* the introduction of modern methods. Vast numbers of the landless and those engaged in subsistence agriculture remain unemployed or underemployed for long periods during the year. They have neither the incentive nor the capacity to carry out labor-intensive production schemes that could increase yields within the traditional framework of production. The most obvious case is that of sharecroppers who pay 50 percent or more of their output in rent. They rarely invest in modern inputs, and they certainly do not lavish any extra attention on the cultivation of leased-in land. Nor is there much scope for carrying out overhead labor-investment projects—construction and maintenance of water courses, field channels, wells, tanks, drainage systems—which are critical for increasing productivity through traditional techniques. Individuals are unable to undertake such land-improvement schemes, and groups of individuals find no incentive to do so. The government's efforts after Independence, to establish village councils with statutory authority to carry out construction of capital projects, have foundered on the inequalities of the land-tenure system. It has proved impossible to mobilize "surplus" or underemployed labor on a voluntary basis when the expected gains in productivity will increase economic concentration even more in favor of "large" landowners. It has also proved fiscally impossible—given the large numbers of the underemployed involved—

[33] It is difficult to make accurate estimates of the incidence of tenancy. Most leasing arrangements involve sharecropping agreements that are undocumented in village records. According to interview data collected by the Census Commission in 1961, about 23% of all cultivators were pure tenants, operating wholly leased-in land; in many states, 30 to 40% of all farmers took some land on oral lease. (*The Statesman*, June 1, 1968.) This situation has probably not changed significantly in recent years. Early in 1977, the Agriculture Ministry's Director of Land Reforms offered an "informed estimate" to the effect that approximately 20 to 25% of all agricultural holdings are cultivated by tenants; probably as much as 40% in the densely populated rice regions of eastern India. Interview, New Delhi, January 8, 1977. Reports of field research in diverse regions of the rice areas confirm that sharecropping is a pervasive feature of the tenurial pattern. See Wolf Ladejinsky, *A Study on Tenurial Conditions in Package Districts* (New Delhi: Planning Commission 1965); Frankel, *India's Green Revolution: Economic Gains and Political Costs* (Princeton: Princeton University Press 1971), 61-64; 87-88; 127-31; 165.

for the government to mount rural works programs on the scale required, and still pay normal market wages to laborers for work done on such projects—not only because the cost is staggering, but also because inflationary pressures are generated as the result of scarce wage goods, especially foodgrains.

The patterns of land distribution and land tenure also present intractable obstacles to carrying out the productivity revolution promised by the capital-intensive technologies under the programs that employ high-yielding varieties. Except in areas where landholdings are consolidated and two or three times the size of the national average (conditions which exist only in the "green revolution" wheat areas),[34] "large" landowners, like small and marginal cultivators, find it uneconomic to invest in modern agricultural techniques. The large landowner is rarely able to realize the maximum return from his investment because the size of his *operational* holding is usually less than the optimum area for the efficient cultivation of the high-yielding varieties. In fact, this problem is a pervasive one in the rice areas, where the installation of minor irrigation works (percolation wells, pumpsets, and tubewells) is necessary to supplement supplies of water from surface irrigation projects,[35] but where the command area of the smallest mechanized

[34] Punjab and Haryana, the heartland of the green-revolution wheat area, are the only two states in which consolidation operations have been carried out over the entire sown area. In the majority of states, land consolidation is still in the early stages of implementation. (India, Planning Commission, *Report of the Task Force on Agrarian Relations*, New Delhi 1973, 97.) There were also fewer small operational holdings in these states than in India as a whole. According to data collected in 1960, the average size of operational holdings in India (i.e., all lands that are part of the same economic unit, including leased-in land) was 6.6 acres; almost three-quarters of all holdings were less. By contrast, data for the undivided Punjab (before it was bifurcated into Punjab and Haryana in 1966), showed that 42% of all holdings were 10 acres or more. "Data collected in the 16th Round of NSS on Operational Holdings," 1 (mimeo).

[35] The existing canal irrigation systems are inadequate for the efficient cultivation of the high-yielding varieties on several counts. They were initially designed with traditional cultivation techniques in mind to spread water as widely and thinly as possible, and to provide protection in time of drought, rather than to supply the higher water levels per acre that are necessary for the introduction of scientific agriculture. In addition, the canals have no cross-regulators to allow for controlled rotation of watering. They also lack channel systems that reach directly into the farmer's field. The result is that cultivators cannot be certain of receiving supplies at the exact time and in the amounts required. None of the irrigation systems, moreover, have master drainages. Finally, irrigation water is usually sufficient for only one wet-rice crop during the main growing season. The growth cycle of the high-yielding varieties is basically unsuited to the monsoon patterns of much of the rice-growing area. The new varieties are best cultivated as a second crop during the sunny, dry season. In practice, therefore, the efficient adoption of modern techniques requires the installation of minor irrigation works to tap underground water as an assured source of supply all year round. See B. Sivaraman, "Scientific Agriculture is Neutral to Scale—The Fallacy and the Remedy," Dr. Rajendra Prasad Memorial Lecture, December 27, 1972, Indian Society of Agricultural Statistics, 26th Annual Conference, Kalyani.

works is a minimum of five to ten acres. It is, moreover, financially difficult for even large landowners to install several such facilities, costing $400-$1,000, on a number of scattered holdings. But without assured water, neither the large cultivators nor the small and marginal holders will make higher outlays for modern inputs—especially the fertilizers and pesticides required by the high-yielding varieties—when the investment is likely to be lost if rains are inadequate or there is flooding.

Some landowners simply have no interest in land development or in maximizing output from their holdings. Under existing tenurial arrangements, they receive reliable income effortlessly by collecting rent and interest on loans. If they own land in irrigated areas, they can look forward to the additional pleasing prospect that their holding is bound to steadily appreciate in value.[36]

If it appears plausible that direct obstacles in the pattern of land distribution and tenurial relations are sufficient in themselves to account for a large part of India's problems of stagnation and mass poverty, it is reasonable that solutions should first be sought in a change of the agrarian pattern rather than in an undifferentiated assault on the entire social system. At the same time, although the former focus is narrower —and appears at first glance somewhat more manageable—the effective implementation of agrarian reform would ultimately amount to a program of radical social change.

It is possible, of course, to consider a strategy for raising agricultural output that does not go much beyond consolidation of existing ownership holdings and is aimed at increasing economies of scale. However,

[36] Tenurial arrangements have been directly blamed for the slow progress of agricultural modernization in the Kosi area of North Bihar, where major new irrigation projects carried out during the 1960's and early 1970's were expected to irrigate about 1.8 million (gross) acres annually. In 1973, however, figures showed that utilization had reached only about 25% of the potential. A field investigation by the Land Reforms Commissioner concluded that, while technical difficulties explained part of the problem during the main growing season, "the reasons for the gross under-utilization of water during the [autumn] and summer seasons are rooted in the agrarian structure of the Kosi area. The concentration of ownership of land and widespread sharecropping on terms grossly unfair to the sharecroppers are the main reasons for the under-utilization of water during the [autumn] and summer seasons." In particular, landlords with large holdings found it difficult to prepare the land for a second crop within two to three weeks after the main harvest, especially since most of the farms were fragmented and operated by bullock power. At the same time, sharecroppers, who were expected to provide all production inputs and pay one-half the produce to the landowner, could not afford the higher costs of the new techniques, the more so since they usually borrowed money on usurious terms. Landowners, for their part, were not interested in sharing in the costs of modern inputs, because they "look upon their land essentially as a form of wealth, the value of which is appreciating year after year. They are not overly concerned about annual returns." P. S. Appu, "Kosi Area Development, The Pivotal Role of Institutional Reform" (New Delhi, April 1973, mimeo).

in the absence of any policy for redistribution of ownership rights in land, consolidation will only aggravate the problems of technological dualism and income disparities. Recent data reported by G. S. Bhalla on structural changes in the economy of the Punjab[37]—the heartland of the "green revolution"—suggest that although the growth of total output and income was "phenomenal" after the introduction of the new wheat technology, "dualism has become further entrenched." The basic causes for this pattern are not hard to find. Over the ten-year period, 1961–71, there was little diversification in the economy. The proportion of workers engaged in manufacturing actually declined somewhat, even though the share of state income generated by industry increased—for the now familiar reason that the "whole process of industrialization seems to be the traditional labor saving capital intensive process."[38] Similar tendencies emerged in the tertiary sector, where proportionately fewer workers generated a higher share of income. As a result, income per male worker in manufacturing doubled during this period, and increased by over 60 percent in the tertiary sector. The gains of these urban workers, however, only widened the gap in income disparities between them and the workers employed in agriculture. Between 1961 and 1971, the agricultural sector had to absorb a growing share of the total working population. Yet, these workers, whose numbers as a proportion of the labor force increased from approximately 55 percent to about 62 percent, were producing almost the same share of the state's income over the entire ten-year period. Gains in income per male worker in agriculture increased at a lower rate of about 30 percent. This aggregate figure masked growing disparities within the agricultural sector. Although all classes of cultivators who managed to adopt the new technology experienced some improvement in output and income, the gains from the introduction of modern methods were very unevenly distributed. In the Punjab, the size of holding required for economic viability using the new technology is estimated at 8 acres; therefore a large number of cultivators with very small holdings were simply unable to make the transition. Worse yet, the number of marginal holdings of less than 5 acres increased by three times between 1961 and 1971, from 17 percent to over 56 percent of total cultivating households. Such figures clearly indicate

[37] The data on the Punjab economy presented in this paragraph are drawn from the analysis prepared by G. S. Bhalla, *Punjab Economy: Growth and Prospects*, Occasional Papers, No. 2 (New Delhi: Centre for the Study of Regional Development, Jawaharlal Nehru University 1976).

[38] *Ibid.*, 15.

that a majority of the rural population in even the most advanced and prosperous agricultural area of India were still having difficulty meeting their minimum needs. In fact, according to official surveys, more than 40 percent of the rural population were living below the poverty level.

The consequences of introducing the "Punjab model" of agrarian modernization into the rice areas are not difficult to imagine. In these regions, the *initial* problems of inequality in land ownership, number of marginal holdings, incidence of sharecropping, and percentage of landless laborers are all more extreme. By comparison with the Punjab, gains are likely to be even more heavily skewed, increases in disparities larger, and the rate of displacement greater relative to the pace of creation of alternative job opportunities outside agriculture. Thus, while dispossessed sharecroppers and marginal farmers swell the ranks of "surplus" laborers, a small minority of big farmers operating consolidated holdings will find it economically advantageous to mechanize farm operations.

If, for these reasons, we rule out the undiluted "capitalist" pattern of agrarian reorganization, we are confronted with alternatives that require (a) some significant redistribution of land, and (b) some degree of change in agrarian organization from individual to cooperative patterns of economic activity. Such a new pattern might take one of several forms, but it must provide opportunities for development schemes that cut across the boundaries of individual fragments and farms. Possible organizational models range all the way from the "integrated" programs of area development now popular with the World Bank (involving mainly a compulsory consolidation of landholdings, and government-funded complementary land- and water-development works at the local level, with costs recovered from taxes on the beneficiaries) to more radical proposals, endorsed in India's first three Five-Year Plans, for the reorganization of all economic activity in agriculture, including production, into cooperatives. Whatever the ultimate pattern, however, the first step, once we rule out free-market models, involves the prior need for land redistribution to ensure minimum levels of economic viability to larger numbers of small holdings. Yet, because of the overall constraint of the unfavorable man/land ratio, even "moderate" proposals for land redistribution set a very low ceiling on the size of household ownership holdings.[39] If, for example, a ceiling

[39] A household is defined for survey purposes as a group of persons who normally live together and take their meals from a common kitchen. The household ownership holding includes all plots of land, whether cultivable or not, owned by the household.

is placed on household ownership holdings at the low level of 20 acres, only those households who already own *some* land (although less than 5 acres), would be provided with a minimum holding of roughly one hectare. Such a redistribution alone could reduce the number of persons living below the poverty line to approximately one-third of the rural population.[40] Most of these persons—the landless—would presumably improve their condition as the result of additional employment opportunities that are generated in the wake of agrarian reorganization. Specifically, small farmers who pool their resources can create additional capacities for investment in capital projects (for instance, construction of communal tubewells to serve several small contiguous holdings) that spur higher overall levels of economic activity in the agricultural sector.

Even this "moderate" proposal requires the redistribution of 43 million acres of land, that is to say, 13 percent of the cultivated area. It also affects large numbers of landowners who, along with their families, amount to not less than 30 million persons.[41] At that, such a land reform is not revolutionary. It poses no challenge to the institution of individual property rights. It is, however, radical. It involves a substantial redistribution of assets that are the chief source of wealth and income in an agricultural society. On that account, it inevitably threatens the entire structure of social prestige and power relations that closely parallel the pattern of land ownership. It certainly goes far beyond reforms that have previously been achieved through legislation. Under existing land-ceiling laws, a total of only 4.1 million acres of surplus land has been formally transferred from private landowners to the government.[42]

III

If the direct cause of India's development problem lies in her patterns of land ownership and land tenure, and the solution to the problem is radical land reform, the need for compulsion could presumably

[40] Minhas (fn. 31), 6, 7. There are normally four to five persons per household in the size class of holdings of less than five acres.
[41] *Ibid.*, 6, 36.
[42] Approximately 2.3 million acres of surplus land were vested in the government under land ceiling legislation enacted by the states during the 1960's. *Report of the Task Force of Agrarian Relations* (fn. 34), 96. Another 1.8 million acres were taken over by the government under amendments to existing legislation enacted after 1972 (as of December 31, 1976), with the possibility that effective implementation of the amended Acts might yield an additional 2.6 million acres. Estimate provided by the Director of Land Reforms, Interview, New Delhi, January 8, 1977.

be justified by historical precedent. It has often been pointed out that drastic land reforms have taken place only by fiat from above or as part of a major revolutionary upheaval of the type experienced in Russia and China. Alternatively, dissent has been repressed by the state from above or swept away by mass violence from below.

The prospect that land reform in India could be carried out through the first means, that is, by government fiat from above, is extremely dim. Even if an authoritarian government professing commitment to social reform were to gain control of the major means of repression in the state, not enough power would be concentrated in the central government to carry out land redistribution in the face of probable strong opposition from local elites. In actual fact—as the performance of the central government during its almost two years of unlimited emergency powers suggests—an authoritarian political system is as likely to be a "soft state" as the democratic political system it replaces. The national government has no direct administrative apparatus reaching down to the village level. The ruling Congress Party had depended on intermediaries drawn from among those with power and influence in local linguistic, religious, and caste groups to mobilize the peasantry for political participation. The new Janata Party is a coalition based on the Congress (O)—created by dissident former members of the Congress Party after the 1969 split in the parent organization—the Socialists, the Bharatiya Lok Dal (centered in Uttar Pradesh), and the Jan Sangh. It has virtually no political machinery of its own reaching down into the villages. On the contrary, in parts of north India, it was heavily dependent for election workers on the Rashtriya Swayamasevak Sangh (National Volunteer Association), the militant Hindu nationalist youth organization that had provided the backbone of the Jan Sangh party apparatus. Indeed, precisely *because* old beliefs, attitudes, and established religious and caste institutions—rather than class—have been such vital rallying points for popular organization in large parts of rural India, the government would find it virtually impossible to use compulsion for the purpose of carrying out social change.

The political constraints on imposing radical social change from above are not, as is now frequently asserted, located in inappropriate parliamentary institutions imposed during and inherited from the days of colonial rule. Rather, they are deeply rooted in the diverse internal cleavages which have traditionally divided the Indian subcontinent and still compete with more recent class divisions as the basic principle of political interest and political action.

Within India's boundaries there are fourteen major linguistic groupings, each claiming a unique cultural heritage; a large Muslim religious minority, accounting for one-sixth of the total population; and, at the core of the social structure, over three thousand endogamous caste groups. The entire national political structure is, in fact, built upon accommodation of these linguistic, religious, and caste sentiments and structures as the only way to accelerate national integration, enhance the legitimacy of the political system, and maximize the possibility of peaceful adjustments of social conflict that arise during the development process.

Language has been granted formal recognition as a legitimate principle of political organization since 1956, when the states were reorganized around linguistic boundaries and kept their wide federal powers over public order, welfare, and development, *including land reforms*. If, for example, we were to apply Stalin's definition of nationality, it can be argued that there are fourteen "nations" in India, in the sense that each linguistic State is "an historically evolved stable community of people formed on the basis of a common language, territory, economic life and psychological make-up manifested in a common culture."[43] There is, moreover, no dominant national group comparable to the Great Russian, nor is the largest linguistic group—Hindi speakers—dispersed throughout the country.[44] On the contrary, the linguistic state rather than the national government has provided a main focus of extended feelings of political solidarity, especially since state leaders have successfully claimed access to government resources on a regional-linguistic basis.

Diverse linguistic communities are not the only subnational unit around which the peasantry is politically organized. Indeed, within each "nation" there are multiple centers of personal and parochial loyalty that have played an even greater role in arranging peasant participation. Caste, in particular, has been used as a natural building block, both by political interest groups and by party organizations in ways that have split the solidarity of the poor.

Caste associations—at the district, state, and regional levels—have united previously isolated but essentially comparable subcastes to emerge as active pressure groups in local and state politics. They have

[43] Joseph Stalin, *Marxism and the National Question* (Moscow: Foreign Languages Publishing House 1950), 16.
[44] Whereas Great Russian accounts for the language of over 58% of the population and Great Russian speakers are dispersed throughout the Soviet Union, Hindi users total about one-third of the national population in India and are concentrated in the northern Ganges plains. See Selig Harrison, *India: The Most Dangerous Decades*, (Princeton: Princeton University Press 1960), 304.

encouraged an exclusive and intense loyalty among their members, which inhibits the development of overlapping memberships or cross-cutting class pressures. Although in theory the caste associations enable the lower castes (and, what is often the same, the poorer classes) to use their large numbers to gain influence, access, and power for the community as a whole, in practice it is only the very small, upwardly mobile element that is able to benefit from government concessions won in the name of the group. The caste associations, therefore, have made little contribution to the growth of equality or direct peasant participation in politics. On the contrary, the leaders of caste associations have often been able to extract political concessions precisely *because* they were known to be able to mobilize large numbers of people by appealing to traditional ascriptive loyalties.[45]

Even more important than the adaptation of caste structures to new roles as interest groups has been the direct use of caste by politicians in building party organizations. In general (although with notable exceptions at the state level), national political parties have not recruited from among the poor peasantry. Instead, they accommodated themselves to the existing power structures as the easiest way to win votes. The advent of universal suffrage did displace the tiny English-educated upper-caste urban professionals from key positions in party organizations; but the major beneficiaries of the change were individuals in the most prosperous sections of the dominant landowning castes— individuals who could exploit a wide network of traditional caste, kinship, and economic ties (of dependent sharecroppers and laborers) to organize a large personal following. The rate of politicization of low-caste, lower-class members was slowed down by this process. Such groups did not act independently in making demands on the political system. Rather, they related to the political process only through the dominant caste leadership.

The prototype for this pattern of vertical political organization was pioneered by the Congress Party, which developed the art of accommodation to its highest degree. The Congress Party succeeded by adapting to local power structures. Typically, it recruited from among those who were members of the dominant landowning castes, and, within this caste, were the leading members of the large landowning group.[46]

[45] See Frankel, "Democracy and Political Development: Perspectives from the Indian Experience," *World Politics*, XXI (April 1969) 448-68, esp. 450-56.

[46] The most comprehensive empirical study of the grass-roots political organization of the Congress Party is Myron Weiner, *Party Building in a New Nation: The Indian National Congress* (Chicago: University of Chicago Press 1967), 467-68. Data collected in five districts in widely separated parts of India showed that "district party organiza-

Such local notables put together the basic units of the Congress Party organization. The units were composed of the leaders' kin, caste fellows, and economic dependents. The wider district, state, and national party organization represented a complex pyramiding of these vertical (multicaste and multiclass) factional alliances. Significantly, the majority of Congress Party members retained primary loyalty to their faction or, if the party dissolved, to the kinship and caste groupings at its core rather than to the party. As a result, the relationship between the leaders of the local faction and state and national political parties was often asymmetrical: the authority of the former was largely independent of party identification; in many cases, the power of the latter depended on support of the rural elites.

Under such conditions, the obstacles to land reform by fiat from above are obvious. In order to rally the support of the poor peasantry who are the potential beneficiaries of its land reform policies, the ruling party would have to operate through the very local elites it wants to displace.

The alternative of carrying out land reform from below appears equally implausible in the absence of a class-based party organization. It is, of course, conceivable that the central government could use radical populist rhetoric denouncing the large landowners as "exploiters" in order to encourage "spontaneous" action, such as strikes by laborers and seizures of land by tenants. It could also restrain the police and the courts from intervening to provide protection for those members of the landed classes whose granaries are looted, homes burned, lands occupied, and so on. The danger of such a strategy—especially where class consciousness or the degree of peasant organization is low—is that large-scale social struggle will spill across class boundaries and trigger civil violence. Under Indian conditions, that could threaten national unity. The potential for widespread social violence is almost boundless. There is, first of all, the "national" issue. To cite Stalin once more:

> The bourgeoisie of the oppressed nation, repressed on every hand, is naturally stirred into movement. It appeals to its "native folk" and begins to shout about the "fatherland," claiming that its own cause is

---

tions are usually run by peasant proprietors. At the village and district levels, the prominent Congress leaders are property owners and typically, although not always, members of the dominant caste within the local community." The major qualifications to this generalization are that conflict within village elites made it impossible for the Congress Party to recruit all local leaders; and lower-status, but more numerous, peasant-proprietor castes were challenging traditional elites for positions of local leadership.

the cause of the nation as a whole. It recruits itself an army from among its "countrymen" in the interests . . . of the fatherland. . . . As far as the peasants are concerned their participation in the national movement depends primarily on the character of the repressions. If the repressions affect the "land" . . . then the mass of peasants immediately rally to the banner of the national movement.[47]

Second, there is the possibility of large-scale communal violence. Animosity has, in fact, smoldered and occasionally flared between Hindu and Muslim communities since the partition of the subcontinent into India and Pakistan in 1947. In that year alone, half a million persons died when Muslim minorities in Hindu-dominated areas and Hindus in Muslim majority regions were slaughtered. Conflicts between Hindu landlords and Muslim tenants would not necessarily be any easier to contain.

Third, in parts of rural India and particularly in the South, there are possibilities of cruel caste conflicts. Cleavages drawn on the basis of landed and landless classes closely parallel the traditional divisions between pure and polluted castes. In many villages, the landlord is a Brahmin, and the landless farmworkers are Harijans, descendants of the despised untouchables.

Finally, even within the lower castes, poor peasants may be divided by different perceptions of their economic interest into those who own some land and those who own none at all. Some peasants will simply choose to remain loyal to their old patrons. In such cases, relations between landlords and the landless may settle into a permanent adversary pattern, with both sides organizing rival private armies or "volunteer" groups that polarize the poor into "loyal" workers and tenants, and those who join the rebels.

Whether it instigates reform from above or below, an authoritarian form of government is therefore not likely to be any more successful than the "soft" democratic state in carrying out institutional change—given practical political constraints on the use of compulsion for this purpose. On the contrary, an authoritarian political system might be counter-productive at this time, by creating even more unfavorable conditions for social reform because it may freeze existing power relationships at the local level while dominant landowning castes still have the upper hand.

Is there any solution? In the immediate future, the realistic answer is that one is not likely to appear. But if we are thinking in longer time horizons about the direction in which India should move in order to

[47] Stalin (fn. 43), 28-29.

generate the political capacities necessary to carry out social change, the assumption that authoritarian political structures offer the best hope appears unfounded. On the contrary, democratic institutions may contain a better possibility of weakening both the legitimacy and the power of landed elites without risking the social disorder of a direct confrontation.

The basic condition for nonviolent social change, or social change that holds out at least the potential for limiting violence short of the point at which it threatens national unity, is the solidarity of the poor. The basic obstacle to mobilizing the poor on the principle of their shared poverty is the vertical pattern of political organization which in the past has fragmented the peasantry around ties of religion, caste, kinship, and economic dependence.

Such structures can be indirectly undermined even if they cannot be directly destroyed. Traditional values and attitudes that legitimate ascriptive inequalities sanctified by the religious myths of caste can be eroded by political ideologies endorsing egalitarian norms. The dominant landed castes who until now have played a strategic role as intermediaries between the peasantry and the wider political system can be outflanked if the more numerous lower castes are organized for political participation in horizontal class alignments. Under Indian conditions, democratic rather than authoritarian institutions offer the best prospect for indirect ideological and organizational assaults on the dominant position of the landed castes.

Indeed, the first part of a process of ideological change is already well advanced. After thirty years of Independence, during which the Constitution, the Parliament, the dominant political party, and the basic principles of national policy embodied in the Five-Year Plans all endorsed egalitarian and socialist goals as an integral part of the development approach, low-caste landless and land-poor groups are making the first tentative distinctions between the sacred and secular spheres. Literacy, education, the demonstrable liberative powers of modern science and technology, and, not least, the principle and practice of adult suffrage itself, have created a receptive environment for new slogans of economic and political equality. In the landmark elections of 1971 and 1972 at the center and in the states, Mrs. Gandhi, deserted by large numbers of local influentials in the wake of a split in the Congress Party, still managed to win unprecedented majorities among the rural poor by cutting across regional, parochial, and caste lines with a direct class appeal to "abolish poverty," including a promise to carry out land reforms.[48] The most recent national election of 1977, which ironically brought about Mrs. Gandhi's defeat, offered further confirmation that large numbers of the peasantry have begun to participate directly in the national electoral process in response to political issues and appeals that transcend religious, factional, and caste divisions.

In the years since the 1971 and 1972 elections, the grass-roots organizational effort that was required, state by state, to transform such nascent sentiments of solidarity into effective pressure from below for the implementation of land reforms was, unfortunately, never undertaken. The reasons are complex and outside the scope of this article.[49] Even if such organization had been attempted, of course, the outcome would still be uncertain.

One conclusion seems warranted. The political conditions for a democratic restructuring of India's agrarian economy are more favorable now than they have been at any time in the recent past. New egalitarian norms are beginning to erode the old caste and factional loyalties that buttressed the previous patterns of vertical political mobilization. At the same time, an organizational vacuum is in the process of developing in the rural areas. The leadership of the democratic parties that have once again been entrusted with power can seize this opportunity to organize the most disadvantaged sections of the rural society with the aim of institutionalizing popular participation—and pressure—as an integral part of the political process. Or, fearing the consequences of a genuine shift in the balance of social forces, they can temporize and attempt to slow down the pace of social mobilization by mending the old patterns of clientelist politics.

It is likely to be a historic choice. The unexpected election of 1977 restored the democratic political order established 30 years earlier, an order that had all but completely collapsed as a result of previous failures to carry out essential social reforms. Should a further breakdown occur, the improbable events of March 1977 are unlikely to be repeated.

[48] See All India Congress Committee, *People's Victory—An Analysis of 1971 Elections* (New Delhi, April 1971); All India Congress Committee, *People's Victory—Second Phase (An Analysis of the 1972 General Election to State Assemblies)* (New Delhi, June 1972).

[49] A detailed analysis of the reasons for this organizational failure is presented in Frankel, *India's Political Economy 1947–1977*, chap. XI (Princeton: Princeton University Press, forthcoming).

HYPERMOBILIZATION IN CHILE, 1970–1973

By HENRY A. LANDSBERGER and TIM McDANIEL

MOBILIZATION, REVOLUTION, AND DEVELOPMENT

DR. ALLENDE'S death and the violent end of his presidency on September 11, 1973, were tragedies not only in themselves. They were also part of a larger, more complex tragedy as his attempt to lay the foundations for a future socialist society came to a bloody halt. The exact sequence of events and, above all, their causes will surely be discussed for decades to come, just as are those of the Spanish Civil War, with which the Chilean situation had startling parallels.[1]

Major roles in these events were, of course, played by those who always had been—and those who over time came to be—the bitter enemies of the *Unidad Popular* (UP), the coalition of parties of the left whose successful candidate Dr. Allende had been in the 1970 presidential elections.[2] We can take for granted, for purposes of this paper, the role of the regime's internal and external enemies.

The focus of this paper, both descriptively and analytically, is on sectors supposedly supporting the UP. Specifically, it is on labor—both as an aggregate of individuals and in its organized form—as trade unions and a constituent unit of several political parties. Labor, al-

---

[1] Reputedly, this ominous parallel was recognized by Chilean intellectuals of the left months before the coup. Largo Caballero's role in pulling the Spanish Socialists away from a moderate stand toward left extremism, thereby helping to polarize the political situation, was played, in Chile, by Carlos Altamirano, General Secretary of the Socialist Party (PS). The unnecessary alienation of small landholding peasants in Spain (see Edward Malefakis, *Agrarian Reform and Peasant Revolution in Spain* [New Haven: Yale University Press 1970]) had a direct parallel in Chile. It also had a broader one in the sense that in Chile the entire bourgeoisie was alienated at a time when, according to Marxist analysis, the working class did not yet have enough power by itself to implement Dr. Allende's program. For a frank appraisal of the errors of "petit bourgeoisie ultra leftism," see the analysis by Rene Castillo (the *nom de plume* of a member of the Central Committee of the Communist Party of Chile), "Chile: Ensenanzas y Perspectivas de la Revolución" (Prague: Editorial Internacional Paz y Socialismo 1974).

[2] *Unidad Popular* could be translated, awkwardly, as "Popular Unity." The more graceful "Popular Front" cannot be used because in 1938, a coalition with that exact name came to power. In both 1970 and 1938 the Socialist and Communist Parties were key elements in these coalitions. But in 1938 they were overshadowed by the Radical Party, whereas in 1970 the much-diminished Radical Party was but one of several minor members of the coalition. The doctrinal position of the Socialist Party in 1970, although it covered a wide range, was on the whole distinctly to the left of the Communist Party (PC). Dr. Allende, a Socialist, was for the most part right-of-center of his party, i.e., relatively close to the Communists; he was accepted as a presidential candidate with considerable reluctance by his own party, and with much greater alacrity by the PC.

though in a broad and vague sense basically in favor of the kinds of objectives and policies pursued by the UP, played an important part in aggravating the mounting difficulties which Dr. Allende's government faced almost from the very beginning of his presidency. These difficulties were only briefly obscured by the successes of his first year in power. While the UP's desire may have been to be "the government of the workers,"[3] some of the ways in which the workers responded presented the government with severe problems. It is the aim of this paper to undertake a preliminary analysis of what these working-class responses to the UP government were; what their causes and consequences were; and to place this analysis of one country into a much broader perspective.

An analysis of the role of the working class in Chile before September 11, 1973, raises several critical issues. One set of issues views the working class statically, and inquires into the nature of working-class consciousness and unity at certain stages of development. Put more dramatically, we ask whether "the working class" can be said to exist as a unified actor at all. More specifically, to what degree and on what issues can working-class consciousness be described as "revolutionary" or "radical"?

Our thesis will be that—unfortunately for the UP's policies—the Chilean working class was not united behind *any* ideological position and that it certainly was not, in so far as an "average" can be struck, very revolutionary. And this despite the fact that the Chilean working class, as we shall see below, was an exceptionally politicized and, in that sense, mature one for an "underdeveloped" country. Similarly, in 1918, the German working class may have been an exceptionally knowledgeable and experienced one in comparison with those of other, then *developed*, countries—the working classes of France, Britain, the United States. It was therefore of exceptional analytical and practical importance that the German working class failed to be either sufficiently united or radical to put itself massively behind the revolutionary attempts of December 1918 to January 1919. Lenin and the Russian Communist Party took years to assimilate this fact, if they ever did.

And so, too, is it of exceptional significance for the analysis of the *underdeveloped* countries that a working class as relatively mature as the Chilean, showed itself—on the key issues on which it mattered most in practical terms, such as productivity—to be so unsupportive of

---

[3] This phrase and others similar to it were frequently used by high officials of the government. An example may be found in Gonzalo Martner, ed., *El pensamiento del gobierno de Allende* (Santiago: Editorial Universitario 1971), 119.

its own (relatively moderate) government. Nor was it any more united behind a more extreme, revolutionary alternative available to it. (The role of the "revolution-now" *Spartakists* who, in the Germany of 1918–1919, were highly critical of the German Social Democrats, was played in Chile by the Movement of the Revolutionary Left, the MIR, which was highly critical of Dr. Allende and the UP government, regarding them as merely reformist.)

Marxist thought, beginning with Marx himself, displays a peculiar duality in its assessment of the unity and revolutionary potential of the working class. On the one hand, it is one of the basic tenets of Marxism, and certainly of the "Young Marx," that the working class—symbolizing in its most extreme form the alienation in fact suffered in varying degrees by all humanity—will come to a clear revolutionary consciousness of the state of society. Yet the later Marx certainly was fully aware that parts, or even the entirety, of the working class of one or another country failed to move in the direction of a truly Marxian understanding of the situation. This was true, at one end of the spectrum, of the backward Spanish working class, partly seduced by Bakuninist anarchism. It was true also, at the other extreme, of the highly advanced British (and American) working classes, bourgeoisified by prosperity, and split by ethnic and racial divisions (in the case of Britain, the presence of Irish laborers).

Precisely in order to prevent the working class from losing its way, Lenin and his followers emphasized the role of the Communist Party in indoctrinating and orienting the working class in backward countries, in which—rather than in the metropolitan countries themselves—imperialist exploitation was now seen as most likely to produce a revolutionary crisis. Thus, while Lenin continued to accord the working classes (and, increasingly, the peasantry) of developing countries a key role in any revolution, he was more systematically aware than Marx had been that this role would be played only if the working classes were properly guided. With such guidance, however, the outcome still seemed secure to Lenin.

More recent non-Marxist radicals have reverted *de facto* to Marx's more straightforwardly optimistic assessment. Left-wing Catholics such as the Brazilian educator Paulo Freire appear to be guided by the assumption that "conscientization," and the mobilization of the poor in all its forms, will lead to relatively unproblematic support by the lower classes for change-oriented groups and regimes. Many of those seeking moderate changes share the same optimistic premise. For example, Eduardo Frei, the Christian Democratic President who preceded Dr. Allende in the period 1964–1970, argued that:

> the broadening of the electoral base to include youth in the political process, the recognition of the role of unions in the micro- and macro-economic decisions, the new organization of the people into Neighbor-hood Committees, the creation of mechanisms for participation at various levels of decision of the state, agrarian reform, social promotion, the necessary reform of the constitution to eliminate vices incompatible with the very survival of democracy . . . all these are steps toward real popular participation to preserve our liberty and to promote economic and social progress.[4]

It is our thesis that although this hypothesis may be true in a very broad sense, it neglects to distinguish among the various forms that the mobilization of the underprivileged may take, and therefore the different consequences which it may have. Some of these forms can present severe practical problems even to a government sympathetic to changes favoring the underprivileged, especially when its power for propelling major social changes is limited.

Western social scientists have also been interested in what has been termed the "mobilization" of the lower classes in the developing nations. And although their theoretical orientation has hardly been Marxist, their assessment of the effects of mobilization has shown very much the same wavering between optimism and caution.

Karl W. Deutsch, who introduced the concept "mobilization" into the literature in the early 1960's, saw the process in highly positive terms: an essential prerequisite for modernization. He defined mobilization as "the process in which major clusters of old social, economic and psychological commitments are eroded . . . and people become available for new patterns of socialization and behavior . . . including potential or actual involvement in mass politics."[5] He goes on to emphasize the subsequent stage of "new levels of aspirations and wants," in which "actual participation" rises. The process, then, has both a subjective aspect, with increasing economic, political, and cultural aspirations, and a behavioral one: actual attempts to participate, to obtain greater rewards, to share authority, to have more leisure, to behave less respectfully to traditional authority, and to demand more respect. Of late, however, second thoughts have set in about the benefits of

---

[4] Frei, *Mensaje del Presidente, May 21, 1969*, Presidencia de la Republica, Santiago, Chile; translations here and elsewhere in this article are the authors'.

[5] Deutsch, "Social Mobilization and Political Development," *American Political Science Review*, Vol. 55 (September 1961), 493-511; quote from p. 494.

mass mobilization. Unlike Lenin, who merely wanted to be sure that it was channeled in the right direction, political scientists such as Samuel P. Huntington do not want too high a level of it. Arguing that change requires power, and that power is manifested through strong, effective institutions, Huntington sees mobilization as a threat to effective institutional functioning. The rising expectations which mobilization entails almost by definition imply greater discontent with any given level of institutional performance. And discontent undermines the perceived legitimacy of institutions on which they in part depend for their power. Moreover, participation in its behavioral form is likely to represent a difficult challenge to new, weak, and still not very flexible institutions, resulting in violence, instability, and ineffectiveness.[6]

Latter-day wisdom therefore holds that political change requires some degree of control of mobilization. That this belief is not simply a conservative prejudice is evident from Fidel Castro's remark that in democracies the people "begin trying to satisfy all their needs as quickly as possible. Then, since the tremendous problem is precisely that there are not enough resources to satisfy their needs, since the resources available do not reach far enough, all kinds of conflicts arise."[7]

The foregoing brief review of some perspectives on mobilization leads us to believe that it is a double-edged sword. Its consequences depend not only upon the form it takes, but on the political context in which it operates: it may either support or weaken change-oriented social actors (including organizations). Accordingly, our theoretical task is to suggest conditions under which mobilization may have negative implications for social change in developing countries. Our conclusions must be tentative. We hope that they will nonetheless be of some value, both theoretically and practically.

THE CHILEAN BACKGROUND

I. WORKING-CLASS INSTITUTIONS: PARTIES AND TRADE UNIONS

If one is to understand the relationship between "labor" and the government of Dr. Allende in the years 1970–1973, one needs to know the historical evolution of the Chilean trade-union movement; the history of the two main parties sustaining the government (the Social-

---

[6] Huntington, *Political Order in Changing Societies* (New Haven: Yale University Press 1968).

[7] Castro, "Plan for the Advancement of Latin America" in Paul E. Sigmund, ed., *The Ideologies of the Developing Nations* (New York: Praeger 1963), 262-66; quote from p. 263.

ists and Communists), which were also the dominant parties in the trade union movement; and the role of the Christian Democrats and Radicals who, while weaker in the labor sector than the Socialists and the Communists, were strong enough to play very important parts. We also insist that "labor" be understood as an aggregate of individuals: trade unions, like parties, do not in any simple sense represent all their members. Opinion surveys and voting statistics can help us determine coincidences as well as divergencies between members and organizations. Such analysis is especially necessary for crisis situations, when the relation between member and organization (be it union or party) is put under particular strain. It is clearly impossible, within the confines of this article, to even attempt a historical summary of these elements.[8] We will limit ourselves to pointing out the most important characteristics of the situation up to 1970, for it is our thesis that the characteristics which had by then evolved into salient ones illuminate many of the difficulties which the UP government encountered in its relationship with labor.

The Chilean trade union movement was both old (dating back to the nineteenth century in one form or another) and mass-based. Angell estimates that by the late sixties, about 30 per cent of the organizable labor force was unionized; as much as 70 per cent in manufacturing establishments with more than 25 workers. The law made organization difficult in smaller plants, so these figures are fairly impressive.[9] As to the political parties of the left, the PC (Communist Party) was formally established in the 1920's, but had precursors earlier; the PS (Socialist Party) was formed in 1932. These two parties, together with the Christian Democrats (PDC) and Radicals (PR), between them represented a very substantial sector of Chilean labor. Thus, in a general sense, Chilean labor was organizationally committed and politically highly conscious.

But it was also divided, and its strength vis-à-vis its opponents was thereby reduced. This division also implied (though this was not foreseen clearly) that no government, not even a friendly one, would ever be able to count on the unified support of labor. Indeed, the fact of division, together with labor's high organizational commitment, implies that opposition within its ranks to the efforts of any one group—extreme left, center left, or center—would be strong and at least partially

[8] This has been done admirably by Alan Angell in his *Politics and the Labour Movement in Chile* (London: Oxford University Press 1972).
[9] *Ibid.*, 45-47.

effective. Not only was there understandable hostility inside the union movement between the representatives of the two old established Marxist parties on the one hand, and, on the other, the recently arrived Christian Democratic Party (PDC), with its very different vision of "the good society" and how to reach it. (The PDC, though founded in 1938, did not acquire a large following until the late fifties.) In addition, there was a long record of feuding (at its height in the 1940's) between the PS and the PC, both in the political-electoral and in the trade union sphere, which is understandable in view of their competition for the same clientele (workers, peasants, intellectuals), as well as in ideological terms. There would be no need for two basically Marxist parties if they did not believe that their differences were difficult to reconcile. Indeed, the Socialist Party itself had always been a heterogeneous collection of ideological (and partly opportunistic) groups, not much subject to party discipline. One of the frequent party splits of its forty-year history played a role in a most embarrassing and costly confrontation between labor and the Allende government: the strike of copper workers in Chuquicamata in March 1972.

Moreover, in terms of "pure" organizational efficiency—i.e., a well-functioning means of formulating policy and implementing it, speed and accuracy of communication, rational division of labor, and specialization of tasks within the union—the Chilean labor movement (like most labor movements) was weak. This weakness was due not only to political rivalries, but also to the labor code. It facilitated bargaining primarily at the plant or company level, severely inhibiting the strength of industry-wide unions, not to mention the growth of a single central body such as the CUT (*Central Unica de Trabajadores*). In a country where almost half the labor force works in establishments of ten persons or fewer, it meant that plant unions were often small, weak, and isolated. During the years 1970–1973, there was consequently no single body, or limited group of entities, with whom the government could arrive at an agreement *and* know that it would be adhered to. Although the Allende Government did sign annual wage agreements with the CUT, these were partly nullified by separate industry and company agreements that went beyond the wage increases envisaged by the master agreements.

In the absence of strong bodies of a purely trade-union type, the political parties belonging to the UP might in theory have performed an orientating role for labor, especially since a substantial proportion of labor was—in the abstract, and in the voting booth—favorable to the government (though to a lesser extent than one might think, as we shall see below). But in practice, the long chain that extended from a party's central committee to its trade union department,[10] through the union leader loyal to the party, down to the rank and file, was not strong enough to act as an effective guide and control of labor action—even in the absence of party rivalries and contradictory policies. The symbiotic relationship between unions and leftist parties was held together not by firm, legitimated interorganizational controls, but by much vaguer elements, such as mutual sympathy, ideological affinity, and overlapping concrete interests. The inability of political parties to control unions definitively is, of course, an old story in pluralistic parliamentary democracies, beginning with Britain, France, and Germany in the late nineteenth and early twentieth centuries.

We appear to have contradicted ourselves in the previous discussion: we began by highlighting the strength and maturity of the Chilean labor movement but thereafter emphasized its division and organizational weakness. Actually, there is no contradiction, because two different criteria were used. There was substantial mass-participation of workers in union organizations and political parties; through such organizations, workers certainly had a voice in political and economic affairs. But the potential control of this mobilization was insufficient, both because of political differences and because of organizational deficiencies. In Huntington's terms, the institutions called upon to channel workers' mobilization were simply too weak. And controlled mobilization was precisely what a minority government needed as it sought to embark on immensely ambitious schemes of social and political change. Otherwise, it could not count on the kind of support from its friends which would allow it the freedom to deal with its enemies.

Let us now examine more closely the all-too-facile assumption that even in a general sense labor was committed to the UP. In the literature about the radicalism of the Chilean working class as an aggregate, two views are to be found. One, associated with writers committed to the far left, emphasized—with reservations, of course—that the working class either was, or could very readily become, a "cohesive force that can be politically and socially mobilized by the Left."[11] The other view,

---

[10] Typically, Chilean parties with a labor constituency had a trade-union department that served as a two-way contact point between the party and the union officials "out there" who were party members.

[11] This is a summary statement by James W. Prothro and Patricio Chaparro of the position of Maurice Zeitlin and James Petras, who have written extensively on the Chilean working class. See Prothro and Chaparro, "Public Opinion and the Movement of

to which we subscribe, as do Prothro and Chaparro, and Rodriguez and Smith, is that although industrial workers may be the core of the Socialist and Communist Parties, the class taken as a whole shows a wide range of opinion. "Things are not as clear-cut as we are often led to believe."[12]

2. WORKING-CLASS ATTITUDES

As individuals, Chilean workers were spread over a wide ideological range, and a vast majority were certainly not ready for violent activism. A study conducted in the early 1960's revealed that 23 per cent of the presidents of industrial union locals were Christian Democrats, and only twice as many (43 per cent, still fewer than one-half) were Socialists and Communists. That was at a time when the Christian Democrats had only begun to penetrate the trade-union movement. Moreover, this amount of non-Marxist affiliation was found in a part of the working class (blue-collar, industrial) where the PDC's strength was likely to be smallest (as compared with white-collar and service sectors).[13] The "economist" orientation of even the Marxist union officials was evidenced by their choosing the economic betterment of their members as the most important long-term (five year) goal for their union, rather than "awakening the political conscience of workers" (59 per cent as against 8 per cent).[14] The impression is reinforced that these working-class leaders, and even the Marxists among them, were not as ideologically committed as might have been expected. Only 42 per cent of the Marxist leaders wanted a "total and immediate restructuring of society;" 13 per cent were even satisfied with a "gradual evolution of the present structure."

Alejandro Portes surveyed 382 slum dwellers in the late sixties. Since many of the urban land invasions which took place at that time were made by slum dwellers, there is no a priori reason for thinking of them as less radical than industrial workers. In any case, given the small size of the industrial working class, no party could base itself on it alone and claim to be broadly representative. The left parties, the PDC,

---

Chilean Governments to the Left, 1952–1972," *Journal of Politics*, xxxvi (February 1974), 2-43.

[12] José Luis Rodriguez and Brian Smith, S.J., "Political Attitudes and Behavior of the Chilean Working Class, 1958–1968" mimeo (Dept. of Sociology, Yale University 1973), p. 6.

[13] Henry A. Landsberger, Manuel Barrera and Abel Toro, "The Chilean Labor Union Leader," *Industrial and Labor Relations Review*, xvii (April 1964), 399-420.

[14] Landsberger, "Do Ideological Differences Have Personal Correlates?" *Economic Development and Cultural Change*, xvi (January 1968), 219-42.

and any party that lays claim to representing "the masses," very much include slum dwellers in their clientele. Table 1 shows the results of Portes' study which are relevant to us. Sixty-two per cent of these slum dwellers thought a popular revolution would be bad or very bad for Chile; only 6 per cent thought it would be "very good"; and 27 per cent thought it would be "good." They wanted the electoral route to be adhered to, and did not want to see force used. They were *not* anti-U.S., nor overly pro-Cuban. On the other hand, a hefty majority (over 60 per cent) *did* want the property of the rich to be under state control.

TABLE 1

FREQUENCY DISTRIBUTION ON PORTES' SEVEN-ITEM "LEFT RADICALISM INDEX" FOR A SAMPLE OF 382 SLUM DWELLERS

Item	Categories	Percentage $(N = 382)$
1. Do you believe that a popular revolution would be:	Very good for Chile	6
	Good for Chile	27
	Don't know	5
	Bad for Chile	49
	Very bad for Chile	13
2. A progressive government should break diplomatic relations with the United States	Should not be done—Not very important	77
	Very important that it be done	23
3. A progressive government should establish friendly relations with Cuba	Should not be done—Not very important	60
	Very important that it be done	40
4. A progressive government should expropriate the properties of the rich and put them under state control	Should not be done—Not very important	38
	Very important that it be done	62
5. John says: A social change must be revolutionary. It is necessary to sweep away the past.	John	27
	Neither Don't know	3
Peter says: A social change should not be revolutionary. It is necessary to maintain many things from the past. Who is right?	Peter	70

TABLE I (*Continued*)

Item	Categories	Percentage (N = 382)
6. Tom says: The best way for a progressive government to attain power is through elections.	Tom	75
Paul says: The best way for a progressive government to attain power is through	Neither Don't know	2
a popular revolution. Who is right?	Paul	23
7. Jim says: Force does not lead anywhere. To achieve true social changes it is necessary to seek the cooperation of all.	Jim	66
Bill says: To achieve true social changes it is necessary to use force against	Neither Don't know	2
the powerful. Who is right?	Bill	32

Source: Adapted from Alejandro Portes, "Political Primitivism, Differential Socialization, and Lower-Class Leftist Radicalism," *American Sociological Review*, xxxvi (October 1971), 820-35; Table 1, p. 824.

Reinforcing Portes' findings are those of Goldrich and his collaborators. Their study, conducted in 1965, shows that between 51 and 76 per cent of slum dwellers in Santiago agreed "strongly" that "our system of government is good for the country"; that the interviewees were very heavily against "social changes which provoke disorder," as well as the use of violence (percentages ranged from 61 to 85). Yet, at the same time, between 44 and 62 per cent agreed strongly that "only if things change very much will I be able to affect what the government does."[15]

Obviously, our point is not to deny that Chilean workers and the lower classes in general leaned to the left. They clearly did so, but to different degrees, depending on the exact nature of the issue. Specifically, they did not want to see violence. Further, even though the per-

[15] Daniel Goldrich, Raymond B. Pratt and C. R. Schuller, "The Political Integration of Lower-Class Urban Settlements in Chile and Peru," in Irving L. Horowitz, ed., *Masses in Latin America* (New York: Oxford University Press 1970), 175-214.

centage among the working class whose vote was committed to Marxist parties is probably in the range of 45 to 65 per cent (which leaves a sizeable minority), being a Marxist may not mean the same to a member of the lower classes as it does to a middle-class intellectual, especially in the matter of readiness to use force, and concerning matters of foreign policy, including anti-U.S. policies.

These pluralistic tendencies continued during the Allende years. Let us take the 1970 presidential elections, and focus, as does Petras, on the male vote in the mining zones (coal, copper, and nitrate).[16] With the exception of the three coal districts (Coronel, Lota, and Coranilhue), where Dr. Allende's vote was in the 70 to 80 per cent range, his vote in the remainder was in the 50's and low 60's. Votes of 69 and 71 per cent are offset by 43 per cent in Chuquicamata and 41 per cent in Lagunas. These are not overwhelming percentages, and Petras's unusual ratios ("Votes for Allende for each 100 votes for . . .") may be rather confusingly high, because the remaining vote was split. Even in San Miguel (a large working-class district of Santiago) Allende obtained only 52 per cent of the vote. In Chile as a whole, he obtained only 36 per cent of the vote, 3 per cent less than in 1964.[17]

Finally, in a survey conducted by *Ercilla* in September 1972, the lack of lower-class unanimity is again highlighted. Dr. Allende did not receive, from *lower-class respondents*, even 50 per cent of their hypothetical "votes": 48 to 42 per cent when matched against Frei, 46 per cent when matched against the 1970 candidates. Seventy-five per cent of the *lower class* believed that there was a climate of violence in Chile in 1972; 18 per cent believed the government was to blame for it; 22 per cent believed that both government and opposition were to blame; and 35 per cent thought that the opposition alone was to blame. In other words, 40 per cent saw the government as having full or partial responsibility for creating the climate of violence which other surveys—those conducted by Portes, and by Goldrich *et al.*—had shown to be anathema to them. Only 27 per cent of *lower-class* respondents evaluated the government's performance as "good"; 32 per cent thought it "bad"; 41 per cent fair. And almost as many *lower-class* persons opposed Dr. Allende's proposal to reform the constitution (by instituting a unicameral system) as supported it (41 to 44 per cent).[18]

In sum, the working class was incapable of acting as a strong, united

[16] James Petras, *Politics and Social Forces in Chilean Development* (Berkeley and Los Angeles: University of California Press 1970), 272ff.
[17] Calculations by the authors based on figures from the official *Dirección del Registro Electoral*.
[18] *Ercilla*, September 13, 1972, p. 10.

bulwark of the Allende government for a variety of reasons, including the weakness of its organizations and the plurality of its members' preferences. Neither was there much likelihood of government control over its activities, due to interparty divisions within the UP coalition and the weakness of the parties in the union organizations themselves. The UP government ultimately had to depend upon exhortation and good will, both from its supporters and its opponents in the working class. It was not always forthcoming from either. Let us now look in greater detail at the actual process of the mobilization of the working class, and at its consequences.

Worker Mobilization in Dr. Allende's Chile

1. the goals of the UP

When in November 1970 the UP assumed the reins of government, it did so with a variety of objectives—political, social, and economic, long-term and short-run. Many were mutually reinforcing, others profoundly contradictory. Its overall, relatively cautious, objective was to lay the groundwork for a more pronounced movement toward a Socialist society after the 1976 presidential elections. From the beginning, the UP was plagued by internal differences (particularly the radicalism of the left-wing Socialists as contrasted with the caution of the PC), and the circumstance of its almost accidental, and in part internally unexpected,[19] rise to power with a minimal margin of votes. Still, there was for a time at least general (but again, not specific) agreement on the need to broaden its support among the working class. This support was urgently needed in view of the municipal elections that were to take place in April 1971, the results of which would be interpreted as showing how much of *el pueblo* ("the people") really were behind the government. Specific short-run steps were taken by the UP to achieve "instant mobilization."

Insofar as general policy toward the working class was concerned, there was on the one hand the desire to improve its living standards and increase its share of the national income. The UP believed in this in principle; it also hoped to reap advantages in terms of short-run and long-run increases in political support. In other words, the distribution of economic benefits among the working class was seen in part as a mechanism for mobilizing support. Yet, there were limits to this

[19] It was widely accepted, by members of the UP as well as by its enemies, that detailed plans were far less worked out in 1970 than they had been in 1964—partly because there was less expectation that the election would be won, partly because the parties could agree neither on general principles nor, therefore, on specific plans.

distribution: the profits of the socialized sector (which was expected to be established out of nationalized foreign enterprises and national monopolies) were supposed to be used for investment, i.e., economic development, rather than for consumption. Moreover, since the government expected to maintain a healthy private sector at least temporarily, wage increases could not be big enough to discourage private entrepreneurs either economically or politically. Were the institutions to which the UP had access—its parties and those sectors of the trade union movement in which it was strongly represented—under sufficient control to achieve restrained rather than unlimited distribution? Could a balance be maintained between giving much and giving too much?

The problem was aggravated by a second objective on which, within the UP, there was only agreement in principle, but not on specifics: that of increasing worker participation, both at the level of the firm and in economic planning and policy formulation generally. Dr. Allende had promised to "strengthen popular power and consolidate it . . . by making the unions more powerful with a new awareness, the awareness that they are a fundamental pillar of the government, but that they are not dominated by it, but that, aware, they participate in, support, help, and criticize its action."[20]

The objective of stimulating worker and/or union participation[21] represented a sincere commitment to a doctrinal point. But it was also conceived of as an instrument, hopefully, *both* to mobilize working-class support *and* to make labor "responsible" by eliminating its traditional adversary posture. The hope was both to mobilize, and to control mobilization. Once again the question arises: were the institutional tools available to the UP sufficiently strong to control the mobilization that was about to be fostered? If not, the danger would be, as in the case of indirect mobilization through economic benefits, that attainment of various economic objectives (for instance, in the short run, control of inflation; in the long run, investment) would be impaired, and that political objectives would be threatened at the same time. The middle class would feel particularly alienated by an all-out drive for workers' participation. As the Communist Party realized early, uncontrolled takeovers by workers of privately owned medium-size and small factories were to be particularly feared as a symptom of hypermobilization,

---

[20] Salvador Allende, *Su pensamiento político* (Santiago: Editorial Nacional Quimantu 1972), 98.

[21] The ambiguity was a source of conflict within the UP: the PC wanted the unions to be agents of the workers as a participant; a large faction of the PS wanted to build up participation mechanisms separate from and independent of the established trade unions.

because of their effect on those parts of the middle class that might still be persuaded not to adopt a posture of total opposition to the UP government. In 1970 and early 1971, the middle class was not as committedly anti-UP as it was later to become.

2. THE CUT AS A CONTROL MECHANISM?

The key organization to mediate between the working class and the UP government was the CUT, the Central Labor Federation. Fortunately for the government, it was controlled more by the moderate Communist Party than by the more volatile Socialist Party, insofar as it was "controlled" at all—or, to express our caution more accurately, insofar as control of the CUT mattered at all. For as in most countries, so also in Chile: the central labor organization, whether the TUC in Britain or the AFL-CIO in the United States, is not really in a position to control its constituent unions and their key locals or branches. It is in the latter that the real action takes place. Still, in Luis Figueroa, the experienced general secretary of the CUT, the UP had not just a good friend, but someone from its own inner circle. Figueroa, a moderate and disciplined Communist, became Minister of Labor for a few months in 1972; other officials of the CUT occupied a variety of Cabinet posts during Dr. Allende's presidency—notably Rolando Calderón, more fiery in speech than Figueroa, but not much less moderate in practice.

In the CUT, then, Dr. Allende by and large had substantial support for the policy of controlled mobilization. Even there, of course, the situation was more complex, since opposition sectors of unionized workers—Christian Democrats—were represented in the CUT; moreover, the repeated defense of the government's policy of wage and other restraints would alienate even workers who were politically sympathetic to the UP. In our opinion, at least as important a limitation on the CUT's ability to control mobilization was that the entire process of mobilization is of too great a depth to be switched on and off at will by any agency. It can probably be more easily stimulated than stopped once it is in progress. Even superficial demobilization generally requires severe repression, such as Chile is experiencing now with a right-wing military regime; and as the Soviet Union's workers and peasants experienced from Kronstadt (1921) onward, when Lenin withdrew from the policy of "All power to the Soviets," which was fine for prerevolutionary purposes, but not beyond.

Even the original process of mobilization is not easily controllable: neither the efforts of an official body, nor those of a group of unofficial "agitators" can produce it unless the "mass" is ripe for it; when it is, neither is absolutely necessary, though each no doubt facilitates the process.

3. UNIONIZATION AS AN INDEX OF MOBILIZATION

The Allende years saw the continuation of a trend toward greater working-class unionization that had begun during the presidency of Eduardo Frei (1964–1970). For tactical reasons, majority elements in both the UP and the PDC saw fit to emphasize the differences that distinguished their platforms, their underlying philosophies, and their actual achievements. In particular, the UP was eager to point to evidence which would show that the period after the election of Dr. Allende differed dramatically from that of his Christian Democrat predecessor, and marked a qualitative watershed. Typically, the acceleration in the pace of expropriation of privately owned farms was cited to make this point, as well as structural changes such as the nationalization of banks, the "intervention" of companies, and the creation of a socialized sector.

There is no doubt that some of these deliberate structural changes were unique to the UP government and that the pace of all was accelerated. The somewhat more autonomous evolution of underlying social processes, such as the process of mobilization, is not as clearly delimited by specific electoral dates, and certainly not by the year 1970. In Table 2, we present figures on unionization. This index is particularly relevant when the mobilization of labor is under discussion, as it is in this paper. After a period of decline (1955–1960), followed by very slow growth (1960–1964), a real explosion of union membership took place in the years 1964–1970—i.e., during the presidency of Eduardo Frei. Membership in professional (craft: both blue- and white-collar) unions increased at an annual rate of about 15 per cent; membership in industrial (blue-collar, plant) unions at an annual rate of 6.4 per cent. In the agricultural sector, the growth was phenomenal. Overall, union membership as a percentage of the labor force practically doubled between 1964 and 1970, growing from 10.3 to 19.4 per cent.

We have no particular interest in demonstrating that the rate of expansion slowed down in the two subsequent years, 1971 and 1972 (i.e., the years of the UP regime). For one thing, it inevitably becomes more difficult to organize workers after the easy cases are "picked off." We merely wish to show that mass mobilization—at least as indicated by these figures—took a quantum jump long before the election of September 1970. The earlier growth can be attributed partly to the fact that

Table 2

Number of Unions and Members by Type; Percentage of Increase over Previous Years; and Percentage of Labor Force in Unions, 1955–1972

Year	Professional Unions[a]			Industrial Unions[b]			Agricultural Unions[a]			Total[a]			
	No.	Members	% Increase[c]	No.	Members	% Increase[c]	No.	Members	% Increase[c]	No.	Members	% Increase[c]	% Union Labor Force
1955	1,495	140,373	—	660	162,937	—	22	1,877		2,177	305,192	—	12.1
1960	1,144	108,687	−22.4	608	122,306	−24.9	18	1,424	−24.1	1,770	232,417	−23.9	10.1
1964	1,207	125,929	15.9	632	142,958	16.9	24	1,658	16.4	1,863	270,542	16.4	10.3
1966	1,679	161,363	28.2	990	179,506	25.6	201	10,647	542.2	2,870	350,516	29.6	12.8
% Annual Increase over 1964			14.4			12.8			271.0			14.8	
1970	2,569	239,323	28.1	1,440	197,651	10.1	510	114,112	971.2	4,519	551,086	57.2	19.4
% Annual Increase over 1964			15.0			6.4			1,130.0			17.3	
1972	3,511	282,181	17.9	1,781[c]	213,777[c]	8.2	709	136,527	19.6	6,001	632,485	14.8	22.2
% Annual Increase over 1970			9.0			4.1			9.8			7.9	

[a] From Tables 2-4, Mensaje Presidente Allende Ante Congreso Pleno, May 21, 1973, pp. 793-94.
[b] From Table 5, Mensaje del Presidente Allende Ante El Congreso Pleno, May 21, 1972, p. 861.
[c] Calculated by authors.

there was little difference between the PDC and the UP on the issue of mobilization and participation. The labor code was substantially changed in 1967, but even before that, the old code had been more sympathetically administered by the Frei administration. But our point here is really to argue that mobilization was due to forces for which *neither* the Christian Democrats *nor* the leftist parties of the UP were solely responsible: the growing political awareness of the working class, which was only to some extent caused by the efforts of the parties to develop it as a clientele; the greater level of education among workers; the impact of the mass media; and the rapid growth of the cities because of rural emigration. Laws could slow down or facilitate the process; they could not produce it out of thin air.

Since, as we have seen, the largest single sector of organized labor supported the UP, Dr. Allende's government looked at this form of mobilization in the most favorable light. In Allende's words, "to create more and more unions and link them to the CUT is to strengthen the workers' movement in Chile and thus strengthen the base that sustains this government." But at the same time he presented a qualification: though he wanted the workers' organization to have "the most ample freedom," he hoped it would be accompanied by "the awareness that this government is its government and that, therefore, its critical contribution is an autocriticism."[22] In calling upon the workers to identify their interests with those of the administration, Allende was asking that the workers' increased power be exercised with increased responsibility, i.e., that he be given exactly the support he needed.

4. STRIKES AND "ECONOMISM" AS INDICES OF UNCONTROLLED MOBILIZATION

The strike activity of labor (see Tables 3 and 4) is at least as revealing an indicator of mobilization as labor's degree of unionization. In interpreting strike statistics, we are going to be treading on treacherous ground because beyond a certain level, they may indicate uncontrolled or hypermobilization—a concept that may not be altogether popular.

To keep Tables 3 and 4 short enough to be meaningful, we do not present statistics for each year. 1959 and 1960 are the first two years of the Alessandri administration, corresponding to 1965 and 1966, and to 1971 and 1972, the first two years of the Frei and Allende administrations respectively. Presidential election years (1964 and 1970) are not included because they are divided between different administrations, and are in any case atypical. 1963 and 1969 are included because they

---

[22] *El Mercurio*, May 13, 1973, p. 13.

were the last full years of the Alessandri and Frei presidencies. The middle years of the Alessandri and Frei regimes were omitted for reasons of brevity, and because there are no corresponding years for the Allende presidency.

Concerning the believability of these statistics, it should be noted that Chile has for decades had a reputation for possessing a well-functioning bureaucracy, and a strong state generally. Information on strikes is collected by the national police (*carabineros*), to whose precinct stations employers are legally required to report all work stoppages. (They have considerable self-interest in actually doing so.) The police forward to the Ministry of Labor a standard form about each strike, on which the Ministry bases the official statistics published by the government. In turn, these are the statistics used in the Annual Messages to Congress on which Table 3 is based.

TABLE 3

STRIKES 1959–1972

Year	Col. (1) Number of Strikes	Col. (2) % Increase over previous date, on per-annum basis	Col. (3) Total Number of Workers Involved	Col. (4) % Increase over previous date, on per-annum basis	Col. (5) Total Number of Man-Days Lost	Col. (6) % Increase over previous date, on per-annum basis
1959	204	—	82,188	—	869,728	—
1960	245	20	88,518	8	N.A.	—
1963	416	23	117,084	11	N.A.	—
1965	723	37	182,359	28	N.A.	—
1966	1,073	48	195,435	7	2,015,253	19
1969	977	−3	275,406	13	972,382	−16
1971	2,709	88	302,397	5	1,414,313	23
Number, and as % of total, in public sector*	(332; 12%)		(50,431; 17%)		(132,479; 10%)	
1972	3,289	21	397,142	31	1,654,151	17
Number, and as % of total, in public sector*	(815; 25%)		(135,037; 34%)		(476,965; 29%)	

* Separate subtotals for the public and private sectors were given only in Dr. Allende's presidential messages. If the totals for previous years did not include public sector strikes—and we believe they were included—then this table exaggerates the increase in strike activity between 1971 and 1969. Even then, however, the very high strike activity in 1971 and 1972, and the high and increasing percentage of it taking place in the public sector, are revealing. See text.
Sources: 1959–1969; *Mensaje del Presidente*, May 1970, pp. 366, 368-69; 1971: *Mensaje del Presidente*, May 1972, pp. 853-54; 1972: *Mensaje del Presidente*, May 1973, pp. 788-89.

TABLE 4
SECONDARY STATISTICS ON STRIKES, 1959–1972

Year	Col. (1) Workers per strike[a]	Col. (2) Total number of days per strike[b]	Col. (3) Days per strike per worker[c]
1959	402	4,263	10.6
1960	361	—	—
1963	281	—	—
1965	252	—	—
1966	182	1,878	10.3
1969	281	995	3.5
1971	112	522	4.6
(Public Sector)	(152)	(399)	(2.6)
1972	120	502	4.2
(Public Sector)	(165)	(585)	(3.5)

[a] From Table 3: col. (3) ÷ col. (1).
[b] From Table 3: col. (5) ÷ col. (1).
[c] From Table 4: col. (2) ÷ col. (1).

Since some of the figures in Table 3 may appear puzzling, we calculated some derivative statistics, which are shown in Table 4. It may appear strange that there was a 16 per cent *decrease* per annum in the number of days lost in strikes over the three-year period between 1966 and 1969;[23] and that an increase of 88 per cent *per annum* in the number of strikes occurred between 1969 and 1971, with an increase of only 5 per cent in the number of workers involved (see Table 3). However, the calculations presented in Table 4 bring out that these are not aberrations, but represent consistent trends. Together, the two tables show the following:

(i) A sixteen-fold increase in the number of strikes: from 204 in 1959 to almost 3,300 in 1972; large annual increases (*with the exception of the core years of the Frei period, 1966–1969*): Table 3, col. (2).

(ii) A five-fold increase between 1959 and 1972 in the total number of workers involved: Table 3, col. (3).

(iii) The number of days lost increased also, but at more modest rates— mostly at 10-20 per cent per annum: Table 3, col. (6). Thus, between 1959 and 1972, days lost through strikes did not even double. This more modest growth in the number of days lost was due to two factors:

[23] Year-by-year statistics show a drop to 1.99 million man-days in 1967, but a surge to 3.65 million man-days in 1968 before another drop to .97 million man-days in 1969.

(iv) The number of workers involved *per strike* dropped from 402 workers per strike in 1959 to around 250 in the 1960's, to 110-120 in the
1970's: Table 4, col. (1). This is no doubt another reflection of the
fact that workers in smaller shops were being mobilized. Unionization spread to smaller shops. (Table 2 indicates that the number of
unions grew faster than the number of members; i.e., the new unions
were small ones.) Strikes spread to smaller places of work. The
sluggish growth in "Total Number of Workers Involved," Table
3, cols. (3) and (4), also shows this (with the exception of 1963–
1965 and 1971–1972, when there was a spurt upward).

(v) Strikes seem to have been of shorter duration: 10 days per worker in
1959 and 1966, but steadily below 5 days in later years: Table 4, col.
(3). We believe that this statistic—in the context of other findings—
can be interpreted as indicating a kind of spontaneous irritability,
different from a deliberate long-term strike called by a union in support of its contract demands. By "the context of other findings" we
mean, for example, the fact that the percentage of legal strikes to
total strikes had dropped steadily: from 33 per cent in 1960, 19 per
cent in 1966, and 21 per cent in 1969, to 7 per cent in 1971 and 4 per
cent in 1972. By 1972, 96 per cent of all strikes were formally illegal
—i.e., they did not occur at the end of the legally stipulated mediation and cooling-off period.

For our purposes, the dramatic changes in the period between 1970
and 1973 are of particular interest. The virtual disappearance of legal
strikes between the late sixties and 1971 and 1972 is notable. So is the
31 per cent annual increase in the number of workers involved between 1971 and 1972. But most interesting is the large, and *increasing*,
proportionate role played by strikes in the public sector (Table 3).
Between 1971 and 1972, the ratio of strikes that took place in the public sector increased from 12 to 25 per cent; the number of workers involved went up to 31 per cent; i.e., one out of every three striking
workers was employed in the public sector. The obvious answer—
"yes, but the socialized sector itself increased"—is no answer, because
it assumes that workers in the socialized sector would continue to be
treated as before, and hence act as before. That was not what was being
assumed and hoped for by the UP. Nor did the government give any
indication that it thought strike activity—in the public or the private
sector—was desirable. The cautious but obvious pleasure with which, in
the May 1972 presidential message, a very slight decrease in strike activity in the first three months of 1972 was cited (such tentative evidence had never been used before) indicates how much concern the
intense strike activity of 1971 had occasioned. And 1972 turned out to
be anything but an improvement.

Working-class mobilization as revealed in strike activity—both in quantity and kinds of strikes ("quickies," illegal)—had clearly gotten out of the control of the CUT and the government, both of which showed deep concern. It can properly be labeled uncontrolled, or hypermobilization.

The encouragement of strikes was not government policy, or, at least, not Dr. Allende's. (Individual members of the government may not have been unhappy. Given the chronic divisions in the government, it is not easy to know what "the" government's position was.) But Dr. Allende and the PC realized that any decline in productivity would reflect negatively upon the government's overall performance and would cost it needed support. For example, when a few weeks after Dr. Allende's election, the copper miners in Chuquicamata went on strike for a wage increase of 70 per cent, Dr. Allende berated them as a "labor aristocracy." A year later, he visited Chuquicamata again, and complained bitterly that unauthorized strikes had cost $36 million in 1970 *after* settlement of the earlier strike; and that a further $12 million had been lost by the time he visited in 1971. The CUT, supporter of the UP campaign for greater production and controlled wage increases, also took a leading role in condemning strikes—not just those closely connected to political opposition, such as that of the copper miners in the El Teniente mine in mid-1973, but others as well. For example, the Provincial Council of the Santiago CUT criticized the paralyzation of work in the Volante company when "the people need it most": "This attitude is not compatible with their responsibilities and constitutes an act against the government and the workers as a whole."[24] The CUT's position on such issues drew attacks from both the right and the left; CUT was accused of being a traitor to the workers' interests.

A case could be made that the enormous number of strikes in the private sector, and of man-days lost there, showed increasing worker resistance to private enterprise. Although there is some truth in this interpretation, worker economism appears to be a more satisfactory explanation. Beginning with Karl Marx and Friedrich Engels, continuing with Lenin, and contained in all Marxist writings ever since then, there is the clear recognition that workers, left to themselves (and the workers' own organization, the trade union, left to itself), would not become fully class-conscious, or aware of the need for revolution. Rather, workers and trade unions would fight for piecemeal economic improvements in the condition of specific groups of workers.[25]

Nowhere was this proved more dramatically than in Chile during

[24] *La Nación*, May 17, 1971, p. 15.
[25] See J. A. Banks, *Marxist Sociology in Action* (London: Faber and Faber 1970), chap. 4, pp. 47-55. Footnotes lead to the relevant writings of Marx and Lenin, and to secondary analysts such as Lozovsky and Hammond.

the administration of Dr. Allende. We have already referred to the strikes at Chuquicamata, which were in large part economically motivated. In response to this situation, the President of the CUT declared that because of exaggerated requests for wage increases, the CUT had sent a number of "teachers from its union school" to train copper workers to understand their responsibility to raise production and have their profits go to all of Chile.[26] Dr. Allende himself had earlier criticized excessive economic demands in both the private and public sectors, urging workers not to ask for salaries higher than the possibilities warranted by the profits of their firms.[27] Such comments can be found fairly frequently in the leftist press; for example, Rolando Calderón, Socialist candidate for president of the CUT, admitted that almost all labor conflicts had been resolved at a higher wage level than the CUT-government agreement had specified.[28] Similarly, the plenary of CUT federations listed the limitation of salary increases (as well as of prices) as the first task of the workers.[29]

Dr. Allende himself made perhaps the strongest statements concerning this problem. His "Third Message to the National Congress," of May 21, 1973 (the equivalent of the annual State of the Union Message in the United States), very explicitly addressed itself to the problem of the workers' economic demands. Declaring that redistributive policy had gone beyond the capacity of the economy, the message continued: "The workers must make a decision: they must say whether we continue with an economistic policy whose symbol is El Teniente or if we go toward the sacrifice of having less money for the sake of greater progress and more prosperous development."[30] The reference to El Teniente—Chile's second-largest copper mine—was to the strike which had broken out in mid-April of 1973 and was to last for 75 days. Because of the manner in which their contract on the one hand, and the national annual wage adjustment law on the other, had been written, the miners claimed that they were entitled to a double raise. For political reasons, the PDC later supported the strike, as did various middle-class elements. But the original strike was economic, and when the miners marched to Santiago and occupied the Ministry of Mines in late April 1973, Dr. Allende made the following dramatic declaration: "If the workers do not understand the process of change through which we are living, I'll simply go, and then you'll see the consequences."[31] This discussion of workers in the mines is summarized by

26 *Puro Chile*, December 5, 1971, supplement, p. 20.
27 *El Mercurio*, April 1, 1971, p. 11.   28 *La Nación*, March 1, 1972, p. 6.
29 *La Nación*, October 30, 1972, p. 16.   30 *Ercilla*, May 30, 1973, No. 1976, p. 8.
31 *Latin America*, VII (April 27, 1973), 133.

Petras, who states that "for the workers [nationalization] was seen as a means of substantially improving *their* economic levels—not as a stimulus to national development—although the national development outlook was being promoted by trade union leaders."[32]

Let us cite one further incident which highlighted the "economism" of workers, and the government's growing desperation in the face of it. We use the example because it comes not from the unique, "aristocratic" mining sector, but from the textile industry. This was located substantially in Santiago; it constituted one of the core areas of the newly socialized sector of the Chilean economy; and its workers had suffered more from mistreatment by their employers than the miners had. Here too, President Allende spoke out sharply several times. He took the extraordinary step in January 1973 of making his presidential headquarters for two days in *Sumar* (one of the textile factories around which, later, resistance was planned in case of a coup, since it was considered a UP bastion), in order to attempt to resolve labor problems there once and for all. Allende criticized the very high contract demands continually being made by the plant's workers. He was particularly annoyed by their demand that the amount of payment in kind (270 meters of cloth per year per worker) be increased. For purposes of wage calculations, payments in kind were valued at the low, official price, but the recipients were known to sell it on the black market at several times that price.[33] Minister of Economics Vuskovic had already drawn attention to this widespread practice in mid-1972.[34]

Dr. Allende also criticized the many political meetings that were being held during working hours, and the "contempt" (*desprecio*) that workers showed for all gains in working conditions except higher wages. Workers in *Sumar* had not only failed to increase output, but, according to *Latin America*, they had helped to incur losses equivalent to $1 million.[35] Dr. Allende stated that he had twice thought of resigning: a threat which, as we have seen, he repeated in connection with the El Teniente strike in April 1973. He was quoted as saying that "Neither revolutionary consciousness nor morality exists among the workers."[36] Half a year earlier, the Socialist president of the blue-

---

[32] James Petras, "Chile: Nationalization, Socioeconomic Change, and Popular Participation," in Petras, ed., *Latin America: From Dependence to Revolution* (New York: Wiley 1973), 47.

[33] The government's announcement, a month later, that workers in the socialized sector would no longer be paid in kind ran into strong and vocal opposition. *Ercilla*, February 14, 1973, No. 1961, p. 16.

[34] *Ercilla*, June 14, 1972, No. 1926, p. 15.

[35] *Latin America*, VII (January 26, 1973), 29.

[36] *Ercilla*, January 24, 1973, No. 1958, p. 8.

collar union had admitted that his party had taught workers to be "economistic," and that in order to change this in 1972, "we're letting the workers in on the problems of the plant. If they know how much is spent and produced, they'll know how much they can ask."[37] Given the shortness of time and the galloping inflation (officially admitted to be 163 per cent in 1972), it is understandable that worker restraint and understanding were not forthcoming.

We have no intention of morally condemning the workers' economism. There were certainly plenty of features in the general Chilean context, and especially in UP policy, to make it understandable. To begin with, there was the historical tradition of encouraging economic demands as the best means available to the trade unions for gaining support. The unions' organizational fragmentation also militated against the formulation of moderate and uniform wage increases across different industries; there were no objective standards. The rising inflation that plagued the country from late 1971 onward also made reasonable settlements difficult to achieve.

Just as important were certain aspects of the government's own policy. First, it was clearly inconsistent. For example, the "readjustment of a readjustment" i.e., the double raise which it so vehemently denied to the El Teniente workers, was granted as a matter of course to the Chuquicamata miners, even though their production record was much less impressive than that at El Teniente.[38] There is also an element of sad irony in the fact that one of the UP government's own first acts served to stimulate both the workers' economism and the inflation on which the economism later began to feed in a kind of vicious circle. Soon after taking office, the government decreed a 35 to 40 per cent wage increase while freezing prices. The measure was intended partly as an economic one: to stimulate demand and thereby increase production through the utilization of idle resources, especially unemployed human resources. But as the UP's Minister of Economics, Dr. Pedro Vuskovic, was to declare some fifteen months later, "a central objective of economic policy is to widen political support for the government"[39]—that is, the increase was also intended to augment the UP vote in the upcoming municipal elections of April 1971. Very likely,

[37] *Ercilla*, July 26, 1972, No. 1933, p. 27.

[38] Raul Ampuero, "Politica y sindicatos: la huelga de El Teniente," *Panorama Economico*, No. 279 (August 1973), 2-4.

[39] Pedro Vuskovic, "The Economic Policy of the Popular Unity Government," in J. Ann Zammit, ed., *The Chilean Road to Socialism* (Austin: University of Texas Press 1973), 50.

it did play a part in raising the vote for the UP from 36 to almost 50 per cent. But it not only distorted the economy, it also whetted the workers' appetites for more.

5. THE FAILURE OF WORKER PARTICIPATION AS A FAILURE OF ONE FORM OF CONTROLLED MOBILIZATION

At the very heart of the UP's program was its plan for the establishment of a socialized sector of the economy which was to consist of 90 strategic companies. These firms were to be "the property of all Chileans," with the profits plowed back into investment for economic development. There was never any intention that the workers in the socialized sector were to be the sole or major beneficiaries of nationalization. It was Dr. Allende's policy to bring great changes to their lives in the form of greater participation in economic and social planning at the plant, regional, and national levels. This program, as well as being central to the UP's Socialist vision, was meant to instill a greater sense of responsibility among the workers, and thus encourage productivity and curtail excessive wage demands.[40]

In fact, the socialized sector grew to be much larger than anticipated. By early 1973 it consisted of approximately 250 firms and controlled 80 per cent of industrial production and 50 per cent of GNP.[41] By the middle of 1973, another 250 firms had been taken over. Some of the companies had been sold by their owners (some under greater or lesser *de facto* duress, financial and otherwise); others were "intervened" and "requisitioned" following labor disputes, and production or financial difficulties. In some cases, a reluctant government was presented with a *fait accompli* by workers (or others), who were sometimes led by MIR and left Socialist outsiders. In other words, all kinds of things happened, and no one knows what the proportion of different kinds of takeovers was.

The famous *convenio* (agreement) between the CUT and the government had been signed on December 7, 1970. The first point dealt with the participation of workers, both at the planning level (national, sectoral, regional) and at the level of the enterprise.[42] It was a complicated system of assemblies and committees, in only one of which the plant union as such had a substantial role. Any evaluation of the suc-

[40] Allende (fn. 20), 398.

[41] *The Economist*, February 24, 1973, pp. 14-15.

[42] Central Unica de Trabajadores (CUT), *Depto. de Educación y Cultura: Normas Básicas de Participación de los Trabajadores en la Dirección de las Empresas de las Areas Social y Mixta* (Santiago: *Central Única de Trabajadores* 1972).

cess of this participation program must be tentative at this time,[43] but there was widespread agreement that it did not work well on any level.

Petras's account does not leave one with the impression that enthusiasm for a broad conception of participation (as distinct from an economic one) was widespread.[44] He believes that union leaders and skilled workers had the greatest appreciation for the institutional changes involved. Even on the plant level, relatively few schemes of participation were ever instituted. According to the CUT, no more than 30 per cent of the socialized companies had created participatory committees by the middle of 1972.[45] The estimate of Zimbalist and Stallings is even lower: they consider genuine worker involvement to have taken place in only 35 enterprises.[46] Luis Figueroa, president of the CUT, confessed in mid-1972 that "participation is still weak. Sometimes because the executives or 'intervenors' of the firms of the socialized sector do not understand the importance of allying themselves with the workers. . . . Other times, because the union leaders think that the Councils of Administration have come to supplant their union work."[47] Corroborating this view, Ramón Fernandez, head of the Participation Section of the CUT, declared that participation was "only a pretty word" and that "all of us have some guilt here."[48] He acknowledged that there was no effective worker participation at the level of government planning either. Further, there was general dissatisfaction with the functioning of those systems of participation that had been formed: workers had only an advisory capacity in the management of socialized firms, always being outnumbered by management and the government's representative; and union leaders were prohibited from occupying posts in the participatory structure. Although Dr. Allende gave assurances that "there is no antagonism between the job of the management committee and union leaders,"[49] the existence of these new workers' organizations was bound to lead to a decrease in the power of the unions, especially since the new participation organizations were to take over many of the unions' functions.[50] Instead of the kind of controlled mobil-

---

[43] Several studies have been completed or are in the process of being written about the participation experience. Peter Winn (Princeton); José Luis Rodriguez (Yale); James Wilson (Cornell); and Andy Zimbalist (Harvard) are among those working on manuscripts.

[44] Petras (fn. 30), pp. 9-60, passim.

[45] *Ercilla*, May 24, 1972, No. 1973, p. 13.

[46] Andy Zimbalist and Barbara Stallings, "Showdown in Chile," *Monthly Review*, xxv (October 1973).

[47] *El Siglo*, Supplement, April 9, 1972, pp. 8-9.

[48] *El Siglo*, April 22, 1973, p. 7.   [49] Allende (fn. 20), p. 361.

[50] Manuel Barrera, Complementary material to: "El cambio social en una empresa del APS," mimeo (Institute of Economics, University of Chile, Santiago 1973), 7.

ization that a successful system of worker participation in decision
making might have represented, the UP was increasingly faced with a
form of uncontrolled mobilization which it clearly did not want: a
widespread refusal to obey any kind of institutionalized and previously
legitimate authority, and a rise of "indiscipline."[51]

6. UNCONTROLLED MOBILIZATION: REJECTION OF AUTHORITY AND "BREAK-
DOWN OF DISCIPLINE"

The "breakdown of authority" became a matter of intense concern
during the period 1970–1973; already before then, many professionals
—engineers, doctors, managers—had started to complain that a breakdown of "hierarchy" was occurring. The brain drain among engineers
(which had always been present to some degree) accelerated rapidly
after 1970. It was partly attributed to the fact that their orders were
not carried out in factories, so that their lives became extremely frus-
trating. Accusations—which could be proved by examples, but not by
systematic statistics—were rife that many engineers and managers had
been dismissed after takeovers, not only at the insistence of new gov-
ernment-appointed managers, but of workers. Indeed, there was said
to be a general climate of outright insubordination, hostility, and ag-
gressiveness against educated persons, especially those in authority, in
part explicitly encouraged by extreme left political groups. In late
August 1973, doctors presented a "bill of demands" to the government,
which included a demand that the campaign of *desprestigio* (contempt
against them) be stopped. In early June of 1973, there had been a 48-
hour work stoppage by doctors in Santiago because of "aggression to colleagues and a disregard of authority in the Hospital del Salvador."[52]

But it was said to be in the socialized industrial sector (APS: area of
social property) that workers who had long had to obey the authority of
private employers now went to the opposite extreme. Their "indiscipline" included corruption; stealing; absenteeism; costly carelessness in
the use of machinery, including neglect of maintenance; simply not
working; carrying on vendettas (partly based on political allegiances);
and so forth.[53] Extreme caution, and a total readiness to reverse one's

---

[51] We put this and similar phrases in quotation marks to indicate that they were widely used at the time to describe the process. No value judgment on our part is to be read
into them.

[52] *Ercilla*, June 6-12, 1973, No. 1977.

[53] Dismissal of PDC trade union leaders, activists, and sympathizers was repeatedly
charged—e.g., at the *Sumar* textile plant in September 1971, and after a strike of bank
employees (as part of the "general strike of bosses") in October 1972. The firing of
PDC civil servants from the agrarian reform agency was also an issue. Who exactly
was to blame is not possible to determine: it was a sign of increasing polarization.

view if other evidence appears, is obviously necessary when one accepts this kind of critical description at face value. We do so, temporarily, only because no one—not even government supporters—appeared to be saying anything to the contrary. As early as the beginning of 1971, Allende criticized the high absenteeism in some firms, calling it criminal (*delictual*).[54] In *Chile Hoy*, a left-Socialist weekly, some workers complained of high absenteeism because others had left to sell goods on the black market.[55] At Yarur, Chile's most famous textile plant, absenteeism supposedly rose from 6 to 14 per cent after nationalization, and dropped back to 10 per cent only after a struggle between the union and the factory's Administrative Council had been won by the latter.[56]

In Chuquicamata, the government's attempts to reimpose some discipline triggered one of the major strikes. It involved the suspension of a lower-level supervisor who had walked off the job half an hour early, as a result of which a smelter had been badly damaged (the third such accident in a month).[57] There was, however, a great deal more behind the strike: (1) A party political fight between a Socialist splinter group (not belonging to the UP) and the PC. The new manager was a Communist, and a good engineer, but supposedly abrasive, and without experience in mining. (2) The resignation, because of disgust at the many political appointments, of the respected production manager, who had been appointed by the UP government. (3) Worker protest against inflating the payroll with high-salaried outside personnel who had no productive function (the 'public relations' department had increased three-fold in this nationalized industry). (4) A demand by workers that there be more genuine participation by them in decision making. (5) General demoralization due to technical chaos—a result of the departure not only of U.S., but of Chilean technical personnel, and the shortage of spare parts. (6) Finally, the possibility of C.I.A. influence definitely must be allowed for, but it cannot produce a strike out of the blue.

By mid-1972, the government was considering the imposition of more severe penalties for indiscipline: dismissal, and loss of rights to severance pay and seniority.[58] But a year later, a government report still mentions the same chaotic conditions. Another measure designed to

---

[54] *El Siglo*, April 1, 1971, p. 9.
[55] *Chile Hoy*, August 4-10, 1972, pp. 16-17.
[56] *Ercilla*, December 22, 1971, No. 1901, p. 11.
[57] Norman Gall, "Copper is the Wages of Chile," American Universities Field Staff, West Coast, South America Series, XIX, No. 3 (August 1972), 1-12, pp. 7-10.
[58] *Ercilla*, August 2, 1972, No. 1933, p. 21.

end indiscipline was the enactment of an agreement between CUT and DIRINCO (the state distribution agency) to form Committees of Vigilance in the socialized sector of the economy. These committees, which had been organized much earlier in the private sector, had the function of supervising production and curtailing speculation and the black market. There are no indications that this program was successful.

Without going into root causes, we can offer some suggestions as to why the participation schemes worked out so poorly and why indiscipline was so rampant. The participation program faced a number of obstacles: the untried nature of the system; its Byzantine complexity which inhibited effective organization; a shortage of skilled managerial staff, made more acute by the unexpected size of the socialized sector of the economy; political rivalries within the UP coalition, which led to the appointment of managers on the basis of party quotas instead of competence;[59] and prolonged ideological debates about participation within the UP, and between it and other parties and factions, which had the effect of dividing opinion.[60] Many of the factors responsible for worker indiscipline probably had their sources in more subtle and general social and cultural changes, and are thus more difficult to trace. We refer to the breakdown of old value systems and general patterns of social hierarchy, which can be found in many other modern societies. But whatever combination of the above causes, the participation program neither resulted in, nor was it the consequence of, the kind of "mobilization" helpful to the UP government. And it is this we wish to establish. In addition, the very failure of the participation policy probably led to considerable cynicism and opportunism, with respect both to individual companies and the government program as a whole.

[59] This handicap bedeviled the entire UP regime, especially at the level of cabinet, ministerial, and subministerial appointments. It was known as the *cuoteo* (quota system).

[60] The basic approach to what participation should be, and to the larger issue of how industries were to be administered, was the subject of heated debate between various parties and different ideological groups. (Their perspectives are well summarized by Rodriguez). This debate did not help the system to function at the grassroots level, where the various groups were contending. Thus, the PDC wanted the state to play a small role in running industry, and placed emphasis on worker ownership as well as joint control with management (and private owners). The left feared that worker ownership would lead to converting workers into bourgeois conservatives (as would small ownership in the countryside). There was, moreover, a distinction between the more extreme left, which also did not want the state to have too much of a role (fearing incipient bureaucratization and a failure to mobilize working-class consciousness fully), and the more orthodox PC, which felt that for reasons of rational economic planning, plant autonomy would have to be severely limited.

7. MOBILIZATION AND THE DIVISION OF THE WORKING CLASS: THE STRENGTH-
ENING OF THE ULTRA-LEFT

According to the National Council of the CUT, the working class's
"principal responsibility is to increase its unity, so that united, it can
further the consolidation of the process of change."[61] But in reality,
mobilization led to dissatisfaction with many aspects of the UP's policy,
and to growing support among workers for opposition groups on both
the left and right.

Those who are acquainted with the evolution of Chilean politics
since the mid-1960's are aware of the MIR—the Movement of the Revolutionary Left. Initially mostly limited to students (including sons
and daughters of high party leaders from the PDC and leftward), it
specifically denied the possibility of a bloodless, democratic road to
socialism. Hence, the MIR was skeptical of the entire UP posture, and
especially of the more cautious coalition members. The PC was a particular target of the MIR. By the end of 1971, the Secretary General of
the MIR voiced the belief that the state and the judicial system "play
their historical role, they defend the interests of the bosses against the
workers."[62] Accordingly, at the level of action, the MIR sought to force
the pace by stimulating and organizing *tomas* (takeovers) of both
farms and factories. To enable it to do the latter, and as part of its general policy of mobilizing and radicalizing the working class, it attempted to gain working-class support. Indeed, it soon sponsored its
own trade-union organization, the FTR (Front of Revolutionary
Workers). The degree of its success will partially indicate how revolutionary and radical the working class in Chile was.

The findings are not simple, and cannot be made so. There is no
question about the direction of the statistics of union elections. In a
highly publicized press conference in late May 1972 (the purpose of
which was to warn against disunity *within* the UP over what stance
to take vis-à-vis the MIR), the general secretary of the PC, Luis Cor-
valan, pointed out that in the construction union, the FTR polled
300 votes against 800 for the PC and 6,000 for the PS. At the textile
plant near Concepción where the FTR was founded, it could not gain
even one seat on the executive committee of the plant union. In elections during the Sixth National Congress of the CUT, the MIR received less than 2 per cent of the vote. (This figure has to be treated
with some caution. It took six weeks to count the votes, and the final

[61] *El Siglo*, February 25, 1971, p. 5.   [62] *Punto Final*, November 9, 1971, p. 2.

results were clearly "negotiated" between the major parties, none of which wanted to see the MIR make a strong showing.)

Nevertheless, there were certain ways in which the MIR represented at least the spirit of some groups of workers, and represented it as well as, or better than, the more established trade unions, and especially the CUT. As a result, the CUT was caught between its desire to be loyal to the government, i.e., to restrain itself and go slow, and its need not to appear to be outflanked on the left.

Admittedly, the extent to which even the "foot soldiers," let alone the leadership, in factory takeovers were really workers—as distinct from "young bourgeois adventurers" as the PC called them, or persons living in neighboring slums (*pobladores*)—is a matter of doubt. Not only the Communist Party, but Hugo Blanco, a Peruvian Trotskyist, felt as late as June 1973 that the MIR had little support among urban workers in the establishment of the famous "industrial belts" (*cordones industriales*). His impression was that members of the MIR were young elitists, and were really based on the local community (*comandos comunales*), not on the factory workers.[63] Nevertheless, without at least some working-class support they could not have had even such partial successes as they did in late March and early April 1973 (well before the abortive military coup of June 29), when the MIR announced its intention of organizing a series of takeovers, and did in fact occupy some factories as well as a government distribution center.[64]

Certainly both the CUT, and specifically Dr. Allende, regarded the threat of a parallel organization of workers as a very real one. After the takeovers of March and April 1973, Dr. Allende went on radio and television to ask workers not to take notice of "calls from ultra-left adventurers who want to discredit the government."[65] At the copper mine El Salvador, on July 11, 1973 (the second anniversary of nationalization), Dr. Allende said that "it must be understood that the leadership of the workers is in the hands of the CUT. . . . I am saying plainly that I will not accept powers parallel to and independent of the government of the workers." He went on to say that it is "a mistake for some members of the UP and of other revolutionary sectors outside the UP to stage strikes and occupations for petty reasons . . . something they did not do when they were under reactionary governments." And during the months of July and August 1973—after the abortive *tancazo*,

---

[63] Hugo Blanco and others, in Les Evans, ed., *Disaster in Chile* (New York: Pathfinders Press 1974), 250.

[64] *Latin America*, VII (April 13, 1973), 116.   [65] *Ibid.*

the brief attempt at a coup by an armored batallion—the CUT began to take the threat of a "rival organization" very seriously, and tried hard, but with considerable difficulty, to capture command of the increasingly vigorous *cordones.*

It is our judgment that part of the increased "mobilization"—of workers in the narrow sense, and of the "lower class" in general to a somewhat larger extent—provided force and impetus to ideological currents to the left of a majority of the UP. This ultra-left sector of the working class made Dr. Allende's life very difficult, not only by its economic demands, but even more by permitting the opposition to state with some justification that the government was losing control, and that chaos and civil war were becoming ever more probable.

8. MOBILIZATION AND THE DIVISION OF THE WORKING CLASS: THE STRENGTH-
ENING OF GROUPS TO THE CENTER

Many of the factors that prompted the defection of workers to the left increased worker support for groups to the right of the UP. Both sides, for example, advocated higher wage and salary readjustments. Ironically, the Department of Union Action of the right-wing National Party at one point asked its Political Commission to struggle for a higher wage increase—fifty per cent more than the government was offering. The CUT, it declared, was unwilling to defend the workers' interest.[66] Much the same kind of comment was frequently found in the MIR's newspaper, *El Rebelde.*[67] Hernán Morales, a PDC delegate to the CUT Congress, even remarked that in many areas of debate in the Congress, the Christian Democrats agreed with the FTR and the Revolutionary Communist Party.[68]

After the coup, *Ercilla* made an assertion which remains to be substantiated: that 80 per cent of the union elections in 1973 constituted defeats for the government, and that the General Directorate of Labor had withheld almost a thousand (unspecified) reports concerning new unions—presumably because their leadership was preponderantly anti-government. But in general the results of union elections do seem to show that the UP was losing out to more centrist elements, especially the PDC. For example, according to the left-Socialist *Chile Hoy,* the Christian Democrats did unexpectedly well in the 1972 CUT elections.[69] They are estimated to have obtained between 28 and 35 per cent of the votes cast. Here are examples of some of the last elections

[66] *Tribuna,* December 8, 1971, p. 6.
[67] See, for example, *El Rebelde,* February 8, 1972, p. 4.
[68] *Tercera de la Hora,* December 12, 1971, p. 13.
[69] *Chile Hoy,* No. 1, June 16-22, 1972, p. 8.

before the coup: At the (nationalized) Pacific Steel Company, the PS and PC together obtained 2,049 votes; the opposition 2,638; the FTR and the Revolutionary Communist Party (a splinter) 191 votes; and the Radicals 559. About the same time, the UP lost control in the Chilean Airline, which had previously had a UP majority, with the PDC gaining a 3 to 2 majority on the executive committee. In Chuquicamata, in the white-collar employees' union, the PDC won 3 seats and the PN (National Party) 1, leaving the UP with only a single council member after February 1973. Previously, the UP had held 3 seats, the PDC 2, and the PN none. Among the blue-collar workers, the PDC went up from 1 to 2 in February 1973.

Of greater national importance were the January 1973 elections in the Union of Education Workers, Chile's largest union at the time. The Christian Democrats obtained 35,600 votes out of 73,000; the UP received 36,500. This gave the PDC 16 out of 41 seats on the national executive, where they had held only 3 seats three years earlier. Also of national importance were the elections in the National Federation of Health Workers in which the PDC and two smaller groups won a plurality (5,200 voters out of 13,000, or 40 per cent), partly because the Communists and Socialists went into the election with separate lists, obtaining over 3,000 votes each.

Not only did the Christian Democrats gain support numerically, but their opposition to the UP gradually hardened and became more effective. Partly this was due to what was called the UP's very sectarian policy. For example, in the CUT Congress of 1972, the UP coalition pushed through resolutions pledging unconditional support for the government and condemning the Christian Democrats' proposals for workers' control of plants.[70] Because of these political pronouncements (which were bound to be divisive in a pluralistic context), the National Council of the PDC considered the possibility of withdrawing from the CUT.[71] Similarly, when the CUT condemned the truckers' strike in October 1972, the Christian Democrat union leaders were emphatic in supporting it. The culmination of this process of polarization was probably reached in the miners' strike at El Teniente, which was accompanied by violent confrontations between Christian Democrat workers and UP supporters. Later on, in response to the "industrial cordons" of the left, the PDC workers began to create their own organizations dedicated to mass mobilization.[72]

Symptomatic of this whole process of heightened divisions within

[70] *El Siglo*, December 13, 1971, p. 3.   [71] *La Prensa*, December 12, 1971, p. 5.
[72] *Ercilla*, May 16, 1973, No. 1973, p. 8.

the working class was the progressive loss of control by the CUT. It tried to be as loyal to Dr. Allende as possible and, as a result, left itself open to criticism from both ultra-left and more centrist elements. Most of the key figures of the CUT, especially Luis Figueroa, were loyal to the Allende line. In December 1972, for example, when the MIR-FTR sponsored the occupation of an electronics plant in Arica, in the far north of Chile, the local PC and a CUT delegation attempted to work out a compromise.[73] As we noted earlier, the CUT also entered into agreements with the government over national wage readjustments. But here the loyalists often ran into grass roots (and partly politically motivated) opposition. Throughout late 1972 and early 1973, the "regulars" of the CUT wanted to accept a government wage adjustment proposal which would have given smaller increases to those with higher pay, but several powerful confederations were both against the amount of the increase and the tapered percentage.[74]

Starting in mid-1972, PDC trade union officials had called the CUT nothing but "another party of the government," leaving "the workers defenseless."[75] When the regional CUT of the Province of Santiago (controlled by the PDC) called for a demonstration against price rises in August 1972, the national CUT did not dare take a stand against it.[76] Figueroa's calls for the return of illegally occupied industries and his attacks against leftist adventurism made very little difference.[77] The CUT was also incapable of restraining the militant MIR-controlled *cordones industriales*. Thus, even though the CUT represented the most solid organizational support of the Allende line among workers, its inherent weakness was aggravated by grass-roots pressure and by political assaults from right and left.

In sum, there was no longer any question of a unified and organized working class. The PDC, to the right of the UP, had grown increasingly vigorous. The MIR-FTC, on the extreme left, was capable of drawing upon groups of workers for acts defying Dr. Allende's policy (even though these same workers would not vote for the MIR). In addition, many of the workers were imbued with heightened economic aspirations, aggravated by inflation. With all this, the proportion of workers on whose support the government could count for several crucial issues was apparently diminishing. A general preference on the part of a majority of workers for the UP government was very prob-

[73] *Ercilla*, December 6, 1972, No. 1951, p. 13.
[74] *Ercilla*, March 29, 1973, No. 1967, p. 24.
[75] *Ercilla*, March 22, 1972, No. 1923, p. 13.
[76] *Ercilla*, August 23, 1972, No. 1936, p. 8.
[77] *El Siglo*, July 15, 1973, p. 3.

ably present, since without such a majority, the UP could not have obtained more than 40 per cent of the national vote, as it did in March 1973. The CUT was capable of calling huge demonstrations in support of the government, including demonstrations against striking workers whom it regarded as traitors. No matter how genuine in their own right, however, such acts were offset by continuing wage demands, by absenteeism and low productivity, and by sporadic takeovers of industries. It is on these practical issues that loyalty was not strong enough—as Dr. Allende stated very explicitly on many occasions.

Conclusion: Mobilization as a Double-Edged Sword

Let us attempt to draw some general conclusions concerning the process of mobilization which one might reasonably base on the particular case of Chile.

First, as many Marxists have recognized with their insistence on "objective conditions": the process of consciousness raising (equivalent in many ways to the subjective aspect of mobilization) may be helped or hindered by the deliberate policy of the state or of nonofficial groups and strata; but it is fundamentally a more profound process. Basically, it is not under any one's purposive control, either to start up, or to slow down. Indeed, even astute observers often do not recognize when it is occurring. Most revolutions have taken by surprise even highly intelligent revolutionaries: witness the Russian events of 1905, and Lenin's and Trotsky's astonished reaction to them. Others—like Guevara, who felt sure that objective conditions are always propitious because, in his view, the masses were always miserable and exploited, and therefore always ready to be mobilized—were disappointed when the masses were unwilling to respond to their call to action. Very occasionally, however—as in Chile—the estimate of various interested political elites is partly accurate. For reasons no one really fully understands (though *ex post facto* a convincing list can be drawn up), the Chilean lower classes were, after the election of Eduardo Frei in 1964, even more ready to be actively involved in national life than they always had been. Once the PDC government made it possible for them to do so, they rapidly started joining industrial and agricultural unions. The working class of Chile had never been as "marginal" as those of Peru, Ecuador, and most other Latin American countries. It is highly misleading to use the same terminology to describe their states of consciousness prior to 1965.

In any case, the political elites—the Marxist parties on the one hand, the Christian Democrats on the other—for once gauged accurately that this rising "tide" of consciousness could be "taken at the flood." The gates were opened, not in 1970, but in 1965, by the assumption of power by the PDC. A flood was released and further stimulated, as immediately manifested by rising union membership and a rising rate of strike activity.

But the flood did not lead on to "fortune," because it could not even be rechanneled, let alone contained. Our second point is that mobilization is likely to accentuate—to raise to a more intense level—whatever divisions existed previously in germinal form by way of structural and attitudinal diversity among those to be mobilized. Unity is not likely to result. If there are long-smoldering political divisions within the working class between "moderates" (Chile's Christian Democrats; Germany's Ebert Social Democrats in 1918?), "centrists" (UP; Germany's USPD in 1918?), and ultra-leftists (MIR; Germany's Spartakists?), then these divisions will become exacerbated. A government representing any one of these currents will be caught in the midst of these divisions. If "selfish" (economist) aims are struggling with more long-term ideologically committed ones, then that struggle will become apparent and more pronounced as mobilization proceeds. A government will certainly not benefit from the economism; it might not even benefit from heightened ideology, if that is divided.

Third, mobilization is likely to take quite unanticipated forms. Still, in the Russian Revolution and in the Paris *Commune*, there are historical precedents which should by now enable us to predict to some degree. The rejection of authority and the "indiscipline" (absenteeism, long meetings) are really forms, respectively, of equalitarianism and the kind of festive holiday atmosphere which are part of many revolutionary or semirevolutionary situations. But they can severely hurt an economy already in difficulties—as an economy is apt to be in such situations.

Fourth, what might on the surface appear as useful channels for mobilized energies (new formal structures for participation in decision making) does not seem to work. Quite apart from several basic questions which one might harbor about the meaning of and assumptions behind "participation" even in "normal" times, at times of hypermobilization, participation is likely to take on the characteristics of that very condition. In other words, within the institutions of participation, heightened political and ideological divisions are likely to play themselves out; the struggle between economism and the long-term commitment to a new order is apt to come to the surface; the rejection of authority and of all rules and regulations will manifest itself in the rejection of decisions made by the newly established bodies. Rather than counterbalancing the above nonfunctional aspects of mobilization ("nonfunctional" for a government friendly to "the masses" and hoping to use mobilization to increase its power), these new institutionalized channels for directing mobilized energies are themselves likely to become engulfed in nonfunctional divisions and emerge as ideological battlegrounds, or the means for satisfying "economistic" motives. In any case, it is doubtful that a new institution, with its inevitable problems, can be anything but a negative factor *in the short run* (where it often counts, as it did in Chile).

Fifth, the case of Chile leads us to speculate that governments who feel that they most need mobilized mass support are likely to be most harmed by its "unanticipated" consequences. The governments or extra-official groups most ardently advocating the cause of the "masses and their mobilization" are those whose existing support is inadequate. They therefore hope that the masses, when mobilized, will give a very high proportion of their support to their defenders. The more precarious a government's present balance of power, the more lopsided the support of newly mobilized groups would have to be to really make a difference.

In Chile, the UP—except for one fleeting honeymoon election six months after the presidential election, in which the UP increased its popular support from 36 to 50 per cent—never came close to gaining the support of even half the voters, let alone the kind of solid majority needed by a government that seeks to embark on highly innovative policies. Voting percentages—which count all heads as equal—are probably a naive way to calculate power. In power-currency other than votes, Dr. Allende's coalition was certainly even more impecunious. It therefore badly needed to mobilize new groups whose support would flow wholly toward itself. But if a group such as the UP is substantially short of having the balance of power in its favor, the chances are not great that newly mobilized sectors will be totally unified in support of it. Even if they were, it might not make enough of a difference. In any case, they are unlikely to give the mobilizing group wholehearted support. In the meantime, other sectors—in the case of Chile, the middle classes—are likely to have been alienated by the process of mobilization. The cost of mobilization is certain, its benefits to the mobilizer are dubious. President Frei's Christian Democrats found this to be true in the period 1965-1970; Dr. Allende's UP learned it between 1970 and 1973.

There are other governments which have tried to mobilize unified support, have failed, but have survived nonetheless—often after reversing policy by 180 degrees, and either demobilizing or at least controlling mobilization. The present (1975) military government of Peru (with highly controlled mobilization) is one; so was the Soviet government after 1921—both of them regimes that may be called "left." Both governments survived because they have, or had, plenty of power. But that power is and was quite clearly based on the ability to coerce, in addition to considerable popular support (but probably no more than provided by Dr. Allende's UP). That the Peruvian military should rely on force (as well as substantial popular support) is hardly surprising; that the Bolsheviks maintained themselves in the face of so many enemies, such narrow popular support, and so little coercive power is still something of a mystery—as are all great historical events.

In any case, our central point is that the hope of increasing a government's power through mobilizing previously unmobilized support is in many instances an illusion. New masses are likely to be ambivalent in their support; in any case, the balance of power is probably affected more by the "sub-balance" in the sector "coercion" than in the "subsector" of "mass support." Despite evidence to the contrary, both politicians and academics continue to think that mobilizing the masses is "a good thing," but that it is difficult and in that sense problematic. Historically, mobilization seems to have been more of a hindrance, i.e., a "bad thing" than a help to radical governments, at least after the old centers of power have been weakened with its help. The real problem is then whether "the masses" can be controlled. If the government has enough coercive power to do that (and simultaneously mop up the remnants of its old enemies), it may not need to mobilize the masses in the first place.

The foregoing is probably too flip and facile a generalization, since spontaneous mass action does seem to have been important so often in the early stages of social change, in sweeping away the old system: France in 1789, Mexico in 1910, Russia in 1917, Bolivia in 1952. But that was, indeed, spontaneous action rather than guided mobilization. What the Chilean case seems to show, and other cases do not contradict, is that mass mobilization cannot be channeled in certain highly particular directions (e.g., toward the UP as against the PDC or the MIR). Mass mobilization therefore cannot be expected to change the balance of power in favor of a government which has a precarious hold on it, vis-à-vis other groups which have firm holds on their respective sectors. Spontaneous mass action may help to sweep away various already half-disintegrated power sectors, but that is a very different kind of situation. In Chile, there was some, but not a great deal of mass action of this kind—enough to frighten a fairly powerful bourgeoisie, but not enough to destroy it. And if mass mobilization cannot fulfill the function of helping to sweep away the old order, it probably is more of an obstacle than a help even to governments favorable to the masses. It makes the government's life difficult both directly and, indirectly, by frightening others. The problem then becomes one of gaining and exercising control, and a weak government cannot, by definition, accomplish that.

AGENDA SETTING AND BARGAINING POWER:

The Mexican State versus Transnational Automobile Corporations

By DOUGLAS C. BENNETT and KENNETH E. SHARPE*

I. INTRODUCTION

IN this paper, we will explore the often conflictual bargaining relations between transnational corporations (TNCs) and the host governments of less developed countries (LDCs). Our attention will focus
on the issues of agenda setting and the sources of bargaining power in
a specific case—the conflict that surrounded the creation of the Mexican
automobile industry (1960-1964).[1]

When the administration of Adolfo López Mateos took office in
December 1958, there was no significant automobile industry in Mexico.
All cars sold in Mexico were either imported whole or as CKD (completely knocked-down) kits that needed only to be assembled. The
new government considered the industry to be an important candidate
for import substitution, one that—through the manifold forward and
backward linkages of auto manufacture—could help to reinvigorate a
growth strategy that was showing signs of having exhausted its "easy
stage." When the automobile firms that did exist in Mexico showed
no inclination to increase the scope of their operations, the government
of López Mateos sought to use the state's power to compel the local

* This article was prepared in connection with a research planning activity on the
political economy of the Latin American automobile industry sponsored by the Joint
Committee on Latin American Studies of the American Council of Learned Societies
and the Social Science Research Council. We would like to thank Morris Blachman,
Susan Eckstein, Michael Fleet, Louis Goodman, Rhys Jenkins, Richard Kronish, Ken
Mericle, David Moore, and Miguel Wionczek for useful critical comments on an
earlier draft. Funding from the following foundations made possible the larger research
project of which this paper is a part: The Tinker Foundation, the Social Science
Research Council, the Carnegie Endowment for International Peace, and the Doherty
Foundation.

[1] Much of the data in this paper are drawn from personal interviews with executives
of the automobile industry and with government officials (in Nacional Financiera,
Banco de México, and the Ministries of Finance and of Industry and Commerce) who
were active in the bargaining during period under discussion. The article is concerned
only with automobile policy; truck policy, however, raises similar considerations and
in some cases was regulated in a similar way. A number of the issues discussed here
will be more fully developed in a larger work now in progress.

manufacture of a substantial portion of each vehicle. In view of the size of the Mexican automobile market and the prevailing economies of scale in the industry, the government wanted to limit the domestic industry to very few firms. Because of the intense competition for new markets in the international automobile industry, however, the issue of limiting the number of firms—a matter of the structure of the industry—became a particularly controversial one in the bargaining that ensued between the Mexican Government and the major transnational automobile firms. Other proposals put forward by the Mexican Government—among them certain restrictions on the behavior of the firms that would constitute the industry and on the ownership of these firms —also became issues of contention because the firms believed them to be a threat to their global strategies. Other proposals were not so open to dispute, however. The transnational firms mobilized their power to resist the more uncongenial proposals; on some issues, including the key issue of limiting the number of firms, they succeeded.

In what has become the classic formulation, Charles Kindleberger conceptualized the relationships between transnational firms and the governments of the host countries with regard to direct investment as one of bilateral monopoly: one buyer and one seller of a foreign investment project. "In a typical situation, a company earns more abroad than the minimum it would accept and a country's net social benefits from the company's presence are greater than the minimum *it* would accept . . . with a wide gap between the maximum and minimum demands by the two parties."[2] Thus viewed, the outside limits of acceptability could be located by means of economic theory but the precise terms of the investment would be a function of the relative bargaining strengths of the two parties. Equilibrium analysis must give way to power analysis; economics to political science.

This balance-of-bargaining-power approach has proved to be a useful conceptualization in studies of relations between TNCs and the governments of their host countries,[3] but it is marred by certain recurrent

[2] Charles Kindleberger and Bruce Herrick, *Economic Development* (3d ed., New York: McGraw-Hill 1977), 320.

[3] Among recent literature on this subject, see Theodore H. Moran, "Multinational Corporations and Dependency: A Dialogue for Dependentistas and Non-Dependentistas," *International Organization*, XXXII (Winter 1978), 79-100; Moran, *Multinational Corporations and the Politics of Dependence: Copper in Chile* (Princeton: Princeton University Press 1975); Edith T. Penrose, *The Large International Firm in Developing Countries: The International Petroleum Industry* (London: Allen and Unwin 1968); Raymond Vernon, *Sovereignty at Bay: The Multinational Spread of U.S. Enterprises* (New York: Basic Books 1971), chap. 3; Raymond F. Mikesell, ed., *Foreign Investment in the Petroleum and Mineral Industries: Case Studies of Investor-Host Country Relations* (Baltimore: Johns Hopkins Press 1971), chap. 2. For one of the few case

weaknesses that show its kinship with the pluralist approach to power in American political science. We will focus our attention on two key issues in particular:

(1) Studies utilizing the balance-of-bargaining-power framework have tended to take the *agenda of bargaining* as given. They have concentrated solely on those issues that happen to be topics of conflict and have failed to ask how this agenda was set. Which actors and which interests have been included in the bargaining, and which have been excluded? Why are some issues and not others contested by the parties to the bargaining?

(2) There are weaknesses as well in explaining the *outcomes* of bargaining encounters. Sometimes there is a failure to distinguish between *potential* power and *actual* power, and thus a failure to explore obstacles to the full utilization of potential power. Of equal importance is a tendency to conceptualize potential power as consisting simply in each actor's possession of certain resources. That approach gives little consideration to the relationships or circumstances that may allow a particular attribute to serve as a source of potential power.

II. Agenda Setting

Like the behavioral/pluralist approach to the study of power (to which they perhaps owe unwitting allegiance), studies of bargaining conflicts between TNCs and the LDCs' governments have tended to overlook questions of agenda setting. These studies have accorded consideration solely to overt, "visible" conflicts. They have ignored the question of why some issues and not others became subjects of bargaining and conflict. Bachrach and Baratz's discussion of the "other face of power" first called the attention of political scientists to the questions of agenda setting; they were concerned with the utilization of power to prevent some *issues* from ever forming part of the bargaining agenda.[4] There are other considerations in agenda setting that are equally important, however. Instead of excluding certain issues from the bargaining agenda, some key *actors* may be excluded. As a consequence, their particular concerns and interests may not be articulated unless some other actor has reason to put them forward. In cases where the state is involved in a bargaining situation, it may—for reasons that

studies of a manufacturing industry, see Gary Gereffi, "Drug Firms and Dependency in Mexico: The Case of the Steroid Hormone Industry," *International Organization*, xxxii (Winter 1978), 237-86.

[4] Peter Bachrach and Morton Baratz, "The Two Faces of Power," *American Political Science Review*, Vol. 56 (December 1962), 947-52.

have to do with its social foundations—speak only for certain classes. In Mexico, for example, labor and national entrepreneurs both had interests that were deeply affected by the policy toward the automobile industry. Nevertheless, the bargaining over that policy principally involved only the Mexican Government and the major transnational automobile firms that were based in the United States. The voice of labor was completely excluded, and national entrepreneurs played only a minor role. The exclusion of these actors did not necessarily entail the exclusion of their interests, however: in the bargaining, the Mexican state did articulate some of the interests of the bourgeoisie, though the interests of labor went largely unrepresented.

Noting how and why certain actors (and their interests) are excluded from the bargaining provides one kind of insight into the formation of the bargaining agenda, but there is a further important point to be made about agenda setting. In focusing strictly on overt, visible conflicts—and in taking these issues as the given agenda of bargaining —studies using the balance-of-bargaining-power approach have tended to understate the areas of agreement between TNCs and the LDCs' governments. In studies that concentrate solely on points over which there is conflict, the two actors are often presented as if they were antagonists across the board. The bargaining agenda can be more fully and deeply understood if we attend to areas of agreement (over which there is little or no need to bargain) as well as to areas of disagreement. All the interests of the actors included in the bargaining must be explicated in order to locate points of *conflict* and of *convergence* among them.

In so proceeding, we regard interests as having an objective (or "real") basis. A careful examination of the goals and circumstances of each actor will reveal its fundamental interests. By contrast, the standard procedure of the pluralist approach to power considers interests to be merely subjective: an actor's interests are whatever it says they are, and no further analysis or explication is sought.[5] In basic outline, the interests of our two central actors seem straightforward: the automobile TNCs wanted to maximize broad international earnings, while the Mexican Government sought to promote industrial growth. But there were a number of strategies by which each could have pursued its central goal; thus, subjective considerations entered into the formation of these interests as well. The adoption of particular strategies was not

[5] For a discussion of the concept of "interest" in analyses of power, and a critique of purely subjective conceptions, see Steven Lukes, *Power: A Radical View* (London: Macmillan 1974).

a matter of purely voluntary choice by the actors; rather, it was shaped by the national and international contexts in which the actors found themselves. An examination of the bases of the interests of these actors will not only allow us to locate the points at which these interests converge and conflict (constituting the bargaining agenda), but also to anticipate how changes in the contexts of action prompt changes of strategy and interest.

THE INTERESTS OF TNCS AND THEIR RELATIONS TO THE INTERNATIONAL
AUTOMOBILE INDUSTRY

Two of the central characteristics of the international automobile industry in the late 1950s and early 1960s were its high (and increasing) concentration and the internationalization of competition among the surviving firms.

In the very earliest years of the automobile industry, literally hundreds of firms were producing cars in the United States, Britain, France, Germany, and other industrialized countries. The assembly line and other scale-of-production economies, however, and the substantial degree of risk in the industry, served to promote steadily increasing concentration.[6] In the United States, the number of firms producing automobiles dropped from nine to four in the two decades following World War II. In Europe, a similar process of concentration was taking place; each major producing country tended to have one national firm that competed against a number of smaller foreign (usually American) subsidiaries.[7] The Japanese automobile industry was later in developing, coming to maturity only very late in the 1950s; but here, too, four firms accounted for 82 percent of production by 1961; further concentration was actively promoted by the government. By 1973, the worldwide process of concentration had reached the point where two firms (General Motors and Ford) were responsible for over 40 percent of total automobile sales; the eight largest firms produced about 85 percent.[8]

Changes in the shape of competition among the major automobile producers have been both a cause and a consequence of this increasing concentration. Prior to World War II and extending into the 1950s, firms sought to take advantage of economies of scale through longer

[6] On the role that risk plays in the automobile industry, see Lawrence J. White, *The Automobile Industry Since 1945* (Cambridge: Harvard University Press 1971), 7-9, 44-49.

[7] Rhys Owen Jenkins, *Dependent Industrialization in Latin America: The Automotive Industry in Argentina, Chile and Mexico* (New York: Praeger 1977), 20.

[8] The largest eight, in order, were G.M., Ford, Chrysler, Fiat, Volkswagen, Toyota, Nissan, and Renault. "New Strategies for a World Auto Market," *Business Week*, November 24, 1973, p. 38.

production runs in order to lower costs. Subsequently, non-price forms of competition have predominated. In the United States in particular, annual model changes and the need to supply a full range of models have been important factors in increasing concentration.[9] Until the mid-1950s, furthermore, the major producers enjoyed a well-protected market in their home base and competed internationally only to the extent of exporting assembled vehicles to less developed countries. The American firms, whose home market was not as protected and who had substantial foreign assembly and manufacturing operations (particularly in Europe), constituted a significant exception to this pattern. Since the mid-1950s (i.e., since the return of a buyer's market), however, there has been a substantial interpenetration among the leading producing countries. In Europe, it was facilitated by the E.E.C., while in the United States it manifested itself by the invasion of the market by European and Japanese small cars.

In the developing countries, this internationalization of competition signaled the end of the geographic division of markets among the major producers (the U.S. firms having previously concentrated on Latin America, and the French and British firms on their former colonies, and so forth). The slowdown in growth of the major industrialized markets led first the European firms (spearheaded by Volkswagen) and later the Japanese firms to begin a worldwide export drive. U.S. hegemony in Latin America was threatened, and this area "became a battleground in the competitive struggle within the automobile industry."[10]

As it turned out, the new interest of European and Japanese firms in Latin America coincided with the decision of a number of Latin American governments, including Mexico's, to promote domestic manufacturing of automobiles.

THE STATE'S INTERESTS AND THE MEXICAN POLITICAL ECONOMY

The problem of the interests of the state is particularly difficult conceptually, especially in view of the prevailing tendency (following Weber) to identify the state in terms of means rather than of purposes. A full theory of the state is beyond our scope here, but such a theory would need to view the state as having distinct and discernible interests. These interests can not simply be deduced *a priori* (from the "nature of the capitalist state," for example), but must be explained

---

[9] White (fn. 6). See also J. A. Menge, "Style Change Costs as a Market Weapon," *Quarterly Economic Journal*, Vol. 76 (November 1962), 632-47.

[10] Jenkins (fn. 7), 49.

by the historical manner in which a state comes to rest on particular social class foundations and by the manner in which it institutionalizes solutions to problems in the domestic and international political economy.[11] What, then, were the outlines of the Mexican state's interests?

By 1958, the policy of import substitution was firmly entrenched in Mexico's strategy of economic growth. It had started with the insulation of its domestic market during the Depression and World War II; following the war, a policy apparatus (import licenses, tariffs) was instituted to maintain the protection of the domestic market. Between 1940 and 1960, Mexico's G.N.P. increased at an annual rate of 6.3 percent, with the manufacturing sector (at an average annual growth rate of 7.7 percent), setting the pace.

The particular character of Mexico's strategy of import substitution was conditioned by the changing social foundations of the Mexican regime—especially its attitude toward the domestic private sector, labor, and foreign investment. Despite the strains of social radicalism in the Mexican revolution, primary reliance for investments for economic growth had been placed on the private sector. Lacking a national bourgeoisie that could undertake the necessary entrepreneurial activities, the state deliberately created such a class (one which, as it grew, became increasingly capable of influencing governmental policy).[12] Official policy encouraged private investment in a number of ways: corporate and personal income taxes were kept low; an orthodox monetary policy (*desarrollo establizador*), adopted in 1954, allowed the government to finance its expenditures in an essentially non-inflationary manner through the use of complex reserve requirements and selective credit controls that applied to the private banking system; the state provided long-term, low-interest loans through state investment banks and made investments in infrastructure and basic industries (steel, petroleum refining); and government policies allowed for the emergence of a skewed pattern of income distribution through which an affluent upper middle class of sufficient size spurred import-substituted consumer-goods industries despite low per capita income. Labor peace was maintained politically through the corporatist organization of the ruling Partido Revolucionario Institucional (PRI), the co-optation of labor leaders, and occasional repression. The resulting low wages and relative docility of urban and rural workers helped to encourage con-

[11] For a fuller elaboration, see Bennett and Sharpe, "The State as Banker and as Entrepreneur: The Last Resort Character of the Mexican State's Economic Interventions, 1917–1970," *Comparative Politics*, forthcoming.

[12] For a more detailed discussion, see *ibid.*

tinued high rates of investment.[13] Thus, while the national bourgeoisie
was becoming an increasingly important actor whose interests had to
be taken into account by the state, labor and its interests were usually
excluded; this pattern was to characterize the bargaining in the auto
industry in the early 1960s.

The Mexican state served domestic business interests in another important way: the revolutionary heritage had made economic nationalism a hallmark of government policy for more than fifty years. In
some sectors—natural resources, banking, insurance, transportation,
communications, and so forth—foreign investment was excluded altogether. Such was not the case in manufacturing: import substitution,
particularly as it moved into more sophisticated goods (such as automobiles), required the technology, management capabilities, and marketing skills of transnational corporations. Since 1950, however, the
official emphasis toward foreign investment in manufacturing has increasingly been on Mexicanization. Foreign investment is required to
be associated with a firm the majority of whose capital is Mexican;
this policy allows the participation of TNCs in the economy while
preserving a role for the national bourgeoisie.[14]

THE MEXICAN STATE AND THE AUTO TRANSNATIONALS: CONVERGENCE
AND CONFLICT OF INTEREST

The reliance on private investment, the political control of labor, and
the expanding middle class of consumers proved attractive to foreign
investment, Mexicanization notwithstanding. After the Second World
War, as the policy of import substitution coincided with the expansion-
ary thrust of U.S. transnational corporations, direct foreign investment
in manufacturing increased rapidly—from $32 million to $602 million
between 1940 and 1960. In the automobile industry and other manufacturing, there was a particularly strong convergence of interests between the government's economic policy and the corporate strategies
of the transnational firms.

The government had encouraged the *assembly* of vehicles from im-

[13] Details may be found in Roger D. Hansen, *The Politics of Mexican Development*
(Baltimore: Johns Hopkins Press 1971): Susan Eckstein, *Poverty of Revolution* (Prince-
ton: Princeton University Press 1977); William P. Glade, Jr. and Charles Anderson,
The Political Economy of Mexico (Madison: University of Wisconsin Press 1968).

[14] On Mexican policy toward foreign investment, see Harry K. Wright, *Foreign
Enterprise in Mexico* (Chapel Hill: University of North Carolina Press 1971); and
Douglas Bennett, Morris Blachman, and Kenneth Sharpe, "Mexico and Multinational
Corporations: An Explanation of State Action," in Joseph Grunwald, ed., *Latin Amer-
ica and World Economy: A Changing International Order* (Beverly Hills: Sage Publi-
cations 1978).

ported CKD kits as early as 1925. Ford took advantage of the modest tariff reductions offered and began assembly in 1926; General Motors followed suit in 1937; and a Mexican firm, Fábricas Auto-Mex, started assembling Chryslers in 1938. When import substitution was adopted as a conscious strategy after World War II, import quotas and additional tariff advantages promoted the creation of a number of other assembly operations. There was little conflict of interest here: shipment of parts in CKD kits still allowed the longer production runs (and lower per-unit costs) in the TNCs' home plants which the stiffened international competition required. In auto manufacture, economies of scale are very much lower in assembly operations than they are in the fabrication of motors or in body stamping. In addition, domestic (Mexican) assembly resulted in some economies in transportation costs.[15] When the government's policy moved from a concern with assembly toward an interest in the manufacture of vehicles, however, the convergence of interest between the Mexican state and the transnational automobile firms began to disintegrate.

The policy started to change when the López Mateos Administration came to power in December 1958. The growth "miracle" that had been sustained for nearly twenty years was in serious difficulty. The "easy stage" of import substitution was facing exhaustion: Mexico had already initiated the domestic manufacture of many simple consumer goods, and investments were needed in certain industrial sectors if growth was to continue. The attention of economic policy makers focused on a number of candidates, among them the automobile industry.

The Mexican automobile industry in 1958 consisted of eleven firms that were operating assembly plants. In addition, a small number of assembled vehicles were imported by a few other companies. The Mexican consumer could choose from among 44 makes and 117 models. Ford, General Motors, and Fábricas Auto-Mex dominated the industry; between them, they accounted for three-quarters of the automobiles sold. Ford and G.M. were 100 percent foreign-owned subsidiaries; Fábricas Auto-Mex, long wholly owned by the Azcárraga family, sold one-third of its equity to Chrysler in 1959. The other assembly plants were smaller and wholly Mexican-owned; they operated under licenses from foreign manufacturers.

A number of considerations suggested that the automobile industry be a candidate for the implementation of the new policy. Domestic manufacture of automobiles (as opposed to their mere assembly) would

[15] Jenkins (fn. 7), 39-40.

stimulate a broad array of other industries through backward and forward linkage; it would be expected to further not only an auto-parts industry, but also the sectors that would serve it: machine tools, forgings, paint, glass, steel and aluminum, plastics, and so forth. Automobile manufacturing would thus create a large number of new jobs. There would be savings in foreign exchange: imports of parts and finished vehicles accounted for approximately 11 percent of Mexico's total import bill during the 1950s; foreign ownership of the major firms (with resultant profit remittances) tended to exacerbate this problem. The fact that Argentina and Brazil had already moved to start up their own automobile manufacture set an example, but also constituted a threat; if Mexico did not follow suit, these countries might pressure Mexico to open its markets to their auto exports under the terms of the Latin American Free Trade Area agreements.[16]

The groundwork was done by the Committee for Planning and Development of the Automobile Industry, an interministerial technical body constituted in 1959 and headed by the state's principal development bank, Nacional Financiera (NAFIN). Represented were the Ministry of Finance, the Ministry of Industry and Commerce, and the Bank of Mexico. Final responsibility for formulating and administering the policy rested with the Ministry of Industry and Commerce.

On the basis of considerable staff research and visits to a number of countries (including several that had recently initiated the manufacture of automobiles), but without much consultation with the transnational automobile firms—the bargaining came later—the Committee prepared and approved a report.[17] It constituted the initial policy position of the government's economic *técnicos*.

Because there were a number of these proposals, we will divide them into three types: proposals concerning the *structure* of the industry, proposals concerning the *behavior* or *conduct* of the firms, and proposals concerning the *ownership* of the firms.[18]

---

[16] See the statement of López Mateos's Minister of Industry and Commerce, Raúl Salinas Lozano, in *Comercio Exterior*, August 1964, pp. 547-48; and Salinas Lozano's introduction to Héctor Vázquez Tercero, *Una década de política sobre la industria automotriz* (Mexico, D.F.: Editorial Tecnos 1975), 5-10.

In interviews, a number of officials of the Ministry of Commerce maintained that the balance of payments was not a primary concern (since domestic manufacture would create its own imports for machinery and raw materials). In their view, industrial growth and employment were the principal concerns.

[17] Nacional Financiera, *Elementos para una política de desarrollo de la fabricación de vehículos automotrices en México* (Mexico, D.F.: Nacional Financiera 1960).

[18] The concepts of industry structure and firm behavior are drawn from industrial organization theory: see Joe S. Bain, *Industrial Organization* (New York: Wiley 1959). The presumption underlying the theory is that structure affects firm behavior, and

A. PROPOSALS CONCERNING THE INDUSTRY'S STRUCTURE

1. Limitation of the number of firms in the terminal industry (production of finished vehicles) to three to five firms
2. Limitation of the terminal firms to motor machining and final assembly (other manufacturing to be reserved for a supplier or auto-parts industry)
3. Creation of a central body-stamping plant.

B. PROPOSALS CONCERNING THE FIRMS' BEHAVIOR

1. Production of at least 60 percent of the content of vehicles (measured by direct cost) in Mexico
2. Limitations on the number of acceptable makes and models produced by each firm
3. Limitations on frequency of model changes (freezing of model years)
4. Standardization of certain parts.

C. PROPOSALS CONCERNING THE OWNERSHIP OF FIRMS

1. Mexican majority ownership of firms in the terminal industry
2. Mexican majority ownership of firms in the supplier industry.

These proposals followed from the government's conception of what was required to sustain economic growth, but the transnational automobile firms saw a number of the proposals as threatening their corporate strategies. The bargaining that followed the emergence of this conflict of interests unfolded in two stages. The first stage encompassed the various discussions between the firms and the Ministry of Industry and Commerce prior to the promulgation of the Manufacturing Decree of August 1962, and concerned the terms of the Decree; the second stage consisted in the submission and approval of applications by various firms to manufacture under the terms of the Decree. Issues of ownership and firm behavior were contested in the first stage. Ford, General Motors, and Fábricas Auto-Mex were the major actors: they were the only transnational auto firms who had already invested substantial capital in Mexico; together, they dominated the Mexican market. The number of firms to be admitted—the principal issue of industry structure—was discussed in both stages; consequently, all firms applying for entry (whether U.S.-based or not) participated in the negotiations.

---

behavior in turn leads to performance (the type of contribution that an industry makes to the functioning of an economy) that can be judged against certain standards. I.O. theory, like economic theory more generally, considers ownership to be irrelevant, assuming a rational actor to be directing the firm. A different presumption has underlain the policies of the Mexican Government (among others) toward direct foreign investment: that the nationality of the ownership does make a difference in the firm's behavior, and thus in performance.

The bargaining involved four closely related issues.

(1) *The requirement of 60 percent local content.* The government's interest here was clear: this requirement was to move the Mexican auto industry from *assembly* to *manufacture*, and thus to stimulate further import substitution.

The TNCs, however, were not eager to commence manufacturing operations on this basis. The new investments would be far greater than those already in assembly plants. (The TNCs who merely licensed Mexican-owned assembly operations had yet to commit any capital investment to Mexico.) The Mexican market was still quite small—only 65,000 autos and trucks in 1962; manufacturing in Mexico would mean the surrender of important economies of scale. Finally, there were serious difficulties of supply, since the existing auto-parts industry had been limited mainly to the manufacture of simple replacement parts. The creation of an adequate parts industry would be a substantial undertaking, involving considerations of quality and availability as well as of cost. In some cases, the necessary raw materials were not available at acceptable prices or levels of quality.

Surprisingly, however, the TNCs did *not* take a position in bargaining that was totally set against auto manufacturing in Mexico; the explanation lies in the emergent dynamics of internationalized competition among the firms in the world automobile oligopoly. As Knickerbocker has shown, direct foreign investment in competitive, product-pioneering, manufacturing oligopolies tends to conform to a follow-the-leader pattern of defensive investment. "Rival firms in an industry composed of a few large firms counter one another's moves by making similar moves themselves" as a risk-minimizing strategy.[19] When one firm in the oligopoly makes an investment, other firms defend their positions by making similar investments. In the present case, the Mexican Government (rather than an independent investment decision by one of the firms) triggered the process; as soon as one of the firms agreed (early in the policy-making process, Ford had expressed a willingness to commence manufacturing under the right conditions), the other firms were quick to follow. Eighteen firms submitted applications when the final Decree stipulating automobile manufacturing was promulgated in August 1962.[20] Thus, although it may not have

[19] Frederick T. Knickerbocker, *Oligopolistic Reaction and Multinational Enterprise* (Boston: Harvard University School of Business Administration 1973), 1. Cf. Jenkins (fn. 7), 40-42. For a discussion of oligopolistic reaction in another industry in Mexico, see Gary Gereffi (fn. 3), 271-72.

[20] The same pattern of oligopolistic reaction is to be seen all over Latin America. When Brazil imposed its manufacturing requirements in 1956, 11 firms commenced

been in the interests of the individual firms to commence manufacturing operations in Mexico, they were prepared to do so rather than risk the possibility of that market's being conceded to a competitor.

Consequently, the requirement that, on average, 60 percent of each vehicle be manufactured in Mexico never became an issue of contention in the bargaining between the Mexican state and the transnational automobile firms.[21]

(2) *Limiting the number of firms—the central issue of the industry's structure.* Strictly limiting the number of firms to no more than five was a key provision of the Nacional Financiera Report; it became the most important one in the bargaining. This proposal constituted the Mexican Government's attempt to learn from the mistakes of unrestricted entry of automobile manufacturers in Brazil and Argentina (eleven and twenty-one, respectively). The Mexican market was not expected to exceed a few hundred thousand vehicles annually within the next decade. Allowing the market to become fragmented among many firms, each with a multiplicity of makes and models, would result in overcapitalization and excess capacity in the industry, and would lead to higher consumer prices and thus lower demand. The industry could achieve the significant economies of scale available in automobile manufacture only if the number of firms could be limited.[22]

---

manufacturing operations; when Argentina announced its policy in 1959, 22 firms made the necessary investments; in Chile, 20; in Venezuela, 16; in Peru, 13. Jenkins (fn. 7), 56.

[21] It is worth mentioning that this requirement was made palatable by being considerably lower than the mandatory levels of local content that had been required by Brazil and Argentina a few years earlier, as well as certain attractive tax exemptions. On the latter, see Jenkins (fn. 7), 54-55. Jenkins takes pains to argue, however, that these tax incentives themselves were not responsible for the large number of firms that were willing to commence manufacturing. With regard to the 60 percent of local content, it was the intention of the Mexican policy makers to start at this lower level in order to minimize the inflationary consequences of the transition to domestic manufacture (a low level of inflation being an important goal of the government's policy). With the industry's growth in size and efficiency, a gradual increase to higher levels was expected.

[22] On these economies of scale, see White (fn. 6), 38-53, and Jenkins (fn. 7), 265-71. Even such otherwise staunch defenders of free trade as I.M.D. Little, Tibor Scitovsky, and Maurice Scott advocate the use of investment controls by developing countries in order to limit the number of firms in an industry with significant economies of scale; they single out the automobile industry as an example. *Industry and Trade in Some Developing Countries: A Comparative Study* (London: Oxford University Press 1970), 342.

Another proposal put forward in the Nacional Financiera Report—the establishment of a single, central body-stamping plant—was aimed at the same goal. The plant, to be developed by Altos Hornos, the state's steel firm, would make it possible for all the manufacturers to use the same body stamping presses, with only the stamping dies needing to be changed for each firm. If models were extended for several years each, these dies could be used to nearly full efficiency.

In view of the gains in efficiency, none of the automobile producers opposed such a limitation on the number of firms in principle, though perhaps the American manufacturers were made uncomfortable by a governmental stipulation of this sort. What worried each of them was the prospect that *it* might be one of the excluded ones—a prospect that was of particular concern to the American firms which already had a major stake in the Mexican market. If the Mexican Government were to provide a place for its state-owned auto firm (Diesel Nacional), favor producers of small cars, attempt to diversify the country's sources of foreign investment, and give preference to Mexican-owned firms— all measures that the government had indicated it was inclined to pursue—then a limitation on the number of firms would surely spell exclusion for one or more of the American producers. Consequently, the issue of exclusion became a highly disputed one in the bargaining. In the first stage of the negotiations, the American firms lobbied in order to remove from the Decree any specific limit on the number of firms that would be permitted. In the second stage, a large number of firms took steps to insure that *they* would not be excluded.

(3) *The issues of firm behavior.* Like the proposed limitation on the number of firms, various measures—standardization of parts, freezing of models, limitations on acceptable makes and models—were proposed in the Nacional Financiera Report to insure greater efficiency. Each of them would increase the volume of each part or unit manufactured, and thus allow greater economies of scale. These issues became controversial in the first stage of the bargaining because they threatened the dominant competitive strategies of the U.S. firms. By contrast with European and Japanese companies (whose competition was just becoming a threat to them at home and in Latin America), the U.S. firms favored a strategy of product differentiation based on annual model changes. They also stressed the differences in performance characteristics of their motors; the latter were leading candidates for standardization.

(4) *The issue of ownership.* The proposal by the Nacional Financiera Report that all of the firms be more than 50 percent Mexican-owned reflected the longstanding nationalist orientation of the Mexican state and its desire to encourage and protect Mexican private investment. Furthermore, participation of Mexican investors might help to ensure that the interests of the TNC's subsidiary in Mexico would not be sacrificed to the global rationality of the parent company when the two were in conflict.[23] This issue, too, was negotiated in the first stage

[23] On the sometimes dubious logic of equity participation as a means to control TNC

and came into sharp contention because it threatened a basic operating procedure of two of the American firms—one hundred percent ownership of foreign subsidiaries. Ford and General Motors had adopted a worldwide policy of not entering into joint ventures with foreign nationals; an exception in Mexico might lead to a similar insistence on joint-venture status by other developing countries.

Although technically an issue of industry structure, the proposed restrictions on vertical integration of the terminal firms (limiting them to assembly operations, machining of engine blocks, and any manufacturing operations in which they had been engaged prior to the Decree) were also aimed partly at ownership. Such restrictions would reserve a place for the national bourgeoisie in the manufacture of auto parts,[24] particularly important if the American TNCs prevailed on the issue of ownership. The transnational firms opposed this limitation as well, though with much less vehemence. It would make them dependent on the quality, price, and availability of Mexican-made parts, but it did not threaten their entrenched worldwide competitive strategies. The proposed requirement would limit them to approximately the same array of activities in which they were engaged in the United States (where, because of risk-sharing considerations, a large number of parts are supplied by independent manufacturers).

The interests of the TNCs and the Mexican state conflicted most sharply over the proposals that concerned limiting the number of firms, certain issues of firm behavior (standardization of parts, freezing of models), and ownership restrictions. Consequently, these issues formed the major items on the bargaining agenda. Answering the questions of who prevailed, and why, requires attention to the bases of potential power and to the factors that influence an actor's ability to utilize its potential power fully in a particular contest. We will focus our attention on the issue of limiting the number of firms. Not only was this the point on which the interests of the actors diverged most sharply; it was also the one that would most seriously affect the course of the industry and the success of future governmental regulatory policy.

---

behavior, see Bennett and Sharpe, "Controlling the Multinationals: The Ill Logic of Mexicanization," in Lawrence V. Gould, Jr. and Harry Targ, eds., *Global Dominance and Dependence: Readings in Theory and Research* (Brunswick, Ohio: King's Court Communications, forthcoming).

[24] Restrictions on vertical integration would have two other effects as well: they would encourage economies of scale by avoiding the duplication of parts manufactured in each separate terminal firm, and they would allow better regulation of the requirement of 60 percent local content by making it more difficult for the terminal industry to manipulate percentages through transfer pricing.

III. Bargaining Power

When the Automobile Manufacturing Decree was promulgated in August 1962, it was evident that the bargaining of the U.S. transnationals had succeeded in changing considerably the proposals that had first been put forward in the Nacional Financiera Report.[25] While automobile firms producing for the Mexican market would be required to incorporate at least 60 percent of locally manufactured content in each of their vehicles, and limits were placed on the vertical integration of the firms, the Decree required nothing in the way of Mexicanization of the terminal firms. The other proposals regarding firm behavior had been dropped. Most importantly, the Decree set no explicit limit on the number of firms that would be allowed to operate in Mexico: 10 of the 18 firms that had applied were approved. (See Table.)

What had transpired in the bargaining? What was the relative power of the actors? How and why did they exercise (or not exercise) the potential power at their disposal?

SOURCES OF POTENTIAL POWER

The relative power of actors ought not to be gauged merely from the outcome of a conflict. Such a *post hoc* analysis of power tends to exclude any meaningful analysis of *why* a particular outcome occurred, and forecloses the possibility that one actor had potential power it did not exercise.[26] In the pluralist approach, potential power is generally conceptualized as consisting in the actors' possession of certain *resources*. The following passage from a distinguished work in the balance-of-bargaining-power literature illustrates the approach:

> The foreign investor offers capital, know-how (technological and managerial), some opportunities of commercialization, and, among other possibilities, that of a certain structure of industrial development. The host country offers access to the home market (particularly in the manufacturing sector), access to natural resources (as in extractive industries), and access to special comparative advantages (such as cheap labour).[27]

Variations in these resources may well explain differences in bargaining power. In the Mexican case, the automobile companies had capital,

---

[25] For the full text of the Decree, see *Diario Oficial de la Federación*, August 25, 1962.
[26] For a recent employment of these concepts of potential and actual power in a general approach to international relations, see Robert O. Keohane and Joseph S. Nye, *Power and Interdependence: World Politics in Transition* (Boston: Little, Brown 1977), 11, 53, and passim.
[27] Constantine V. Vaitsos, *Intercounty Income Distribution and Transnational Enterprises* (Oxford: Clarendon Press 1974), 119.

Name of Firm and Date of First Approval	Make	Ownership at Time of First Approval	Subsequent Changes in Status
DIESEL NACIONAL (December 1962)	Renault	100% domestic (Mexican State)	1978: 40% equity sold to Renault
FÁBRICAS AUTO-MEX (December 1962)	Chrysler	33% foreign 67% domestic	1970-1971: Chrysler increased its holdings to 99%; name changed to CHRYSLER DE MÉXICO
FORD MOTOR CO. (December 1962)	Ford	100% foreign	None
GENERAL MOTORS DE MÉXICO (December 1962)	General Motors	100% foreign	None
PROMEXA (December 1962)	Volkswagen	100% domestic	1963: 100% equity sold to Volkswagen A.G.; name changed to VOLKSWAGEN DE MÉXICO
VEHÍCULOS AUTOMO-TORES MEXICANOS (December 1962)	American Motors	100% domestic	1963: 40% equity sold to American Motors; remaining 60% acquired by Mexican state (SOMEX)
IMPULSORA MEXICANA AUTOMOTRIZ (January 1963)	Borgward	100% domestic	1963: name changed to FÁBRICA NACIONAL DE AUTOMÓVILES 1969: ceased operations
REO DE MÉXICO (January 1963)	Toyota	100% domestic	1963: ceased operations
REPRESENTACIONES DELTA (Mid-1963)	D.K.W.	100% domestic	1964: ceased operations
NISSAN MEXICANA (Late 1964)	Datsun	100% foreign	None

technology, and administrative and marketing know-how; the government controlled access to the domestic market, and could (through tax policy, its control of the labor force, and so forth) influence the price of various factors of production. An additional resource that strengthened the hand of the government was its increasing technical expertise, which had been gained by careful study of automobile manufacturing in other countries.[28]

It is not an adequate approach, however, to conceive of potential power simply in terms of the possession of certain resources. What is needed as well is an understanding of how an actor's potential power is shaped by the complex web of relationships—relationships with actors not directly party to the bargaining—in which each actor is enmeshed.[29] The relationships in which we are interested in the present case are conceptualized somewhat differently in world system theory,[30] in dependency theory,[31] and in models of the international power structure and of international organization[32]—to mention a few of the more prominent contemporary analyses. There are important issues separating these approaches, particularly with regard to how asymmetries in global relationships are conceptualized and made subject to empirical analysis. For the purposes of the present investigation, we intend to avoid entering the lists on behalf of any one approach by limiting our attention to the particular set of international and transnational relationships that bear on the case at hand. Most of them have been introduced in Part II (Agenda Setting). We will be especially interested in the relationships among the transnational corporations in the international automobile industry, the relationships of these transnational firms to domestic firms in Mexico, the relationships between the Mexican state and the home governments of the TNCs, the relationships

[28] It is important to note that this resource was different in kind from the other resources since it could not (as the other resources could) be used or withheld as a sanction. It was an infra-resource rather than an instrumental resource; it allowed other resources to be utilized to better advantage. On the notion of infra-resources, see Mary F. Rogers, "Instrumental and Infra-Resources: The Bases of Power," *American Journal of Sociology*, Vol. 79 (May 1974), 1418-33.

[29] This myopia arises partly from the strictly dyadic character of the standard pluralist conception of power ("*A* has power over *B*," etc.). Such an approach abstracts the actors from all other significant relationships in which they are engaged, and thus seeks to locate potential power apart from these other significant relationships.

[30] Immanuel Wallerstein, *The Modern World System* (New York: Academic Press 1974).

[31] See, among others, Theotonio dos Santos, "The Structure of Dependence," *American Economic Review*, Vol. 60 (May 1970), 231-36; Fernando Henrique Cardoso and Enzo Faletto, *Dependency and Development in Latin America* (Berkeley: University of California Press 1979).

[32] On these, see Keohane and Nye (fn. 26), 42-49 and 54-58.

between the Mexican state and certain domestic social classes—especially the bourgeoisie, and the relationships among various ministries and agencies of the Mexican state.

We will argue that the structure of these particular relationships (1) defines what constitutes a power resource, (2) determines when such resources can be employed or withheld, and (3) determines the potential for the entry of new actors into the conflict as allies or as antagonists.

(1) *The structure of relationships defines what constitutes a power resource.* One danger of regarding potential power as consisting simply of the possession of certain resources is the tendency to an easy but dangerously misleading supposition that power resources are "fungible"—that the possession of power resources gives one a generalized capacity which can be employed whenever and wherever one pleases.[33] Power resources are not entirely interchangeable from context to context, or from contest to contest. What serves as a basis of power in one situation may be worthless, perhaps even a liability, in another. This lack of fungibility of power resources is commonly paid due obeisance: what constitutes a power resource depends on the context—on who is trying to get whom to do what; the scope and domain must be specified.[34] Quite obviously, the TNCs' control over automotive technology gave them potential power only in a context where it was *desired* that automotive products be domestically manufactured. But it is not sufficient (though power discussions rarely go further) merely to stipulate the context-dependency of power resources. Rather than delimiting the appropriate context by fiat, we need an analysis that shows how and why certain resources come to serve as bases of power in particular circumstances. Such an analysis will have to feature the specification of relationships of dependency and interdependency in which the

[33] The phrase is from Talcott Parsons, whose suggestion that power be seen on the analogy of money leads to the erroneous supposition of the fungibility of power. See Parsons, "On the Concept of Political Power," in *Sociological Theory and Modern Society* (New York: Free Press 1967). For a corrective, see David Baldwin, "Money and Power," *Journal of Politics*, xxxiii (August 1971), 578-614.

[34] Thus, for example, Robert Dahl: "The domain of an actor's influence consists of the other actors influenced by him. The scope of an actor's influence refers to the matters on which he can influence them. . . . Any statement about influence that does not clearly indicate the domain and scope it refers to verges on being meaningless." Dahl, *Modern Political Analysis* (3d ed.; Englewood Cliffs, N.J.: Prentice-Hall 1976), 33.

For a recent and thorough review of the power literature that pays particular attention to the questions of the fungibility and context dependency of power resources, see David Baldwin, "Power Analysis and World Politics: New Trends versus Old Tendencies," *World Politics*, xxxi (January 1979), 161-94.

actors are enmeshed, and which serve to constitute certain resources as bases of power.

To return to our example, if we say that Mexico's need for automotive technology is what made the TNCs' possession of such technology a basis of power, we need to ask the further question how and why Mexico's need arose; we must not take it for granted. Over several decades, the Mexican state had committed itself to rapid economic growth; its continuation had become a central basis of the regime's legitimacy. Once industrialization of import substitution had been adopted as the growth strategy, it had requisites of its own. When the strategy was threatened with exhaustion in the late 1950s, the state decreed that the automobile sector should commence domestic manufacture. These are important features of the context, but they do not explain why the transnational corporations were needed for technology (and investments). A functional, if not stylish, car of Mexican design was probably not beyond the bounds of feasibility.[35] In order to understand Mexico's need for the TNCs, it is necessary to be aware of the nature of the class structure that had evolved under import substitution, and particularly of the relationship between the Mexican state and the national bourgeoisie. This bourgeoisie had been nurtured for thirty years to pace economic growth; its increasing size and power and its centrality to the growth project made it one of the prime social foundations of the state. Import substitution had been impelled by the burgeoning consumer demand of this national bourgeoisie and of the middle classes (professionals, managers, petite bourgeoisie, and so forth) that had been spawned with it. However, these classes wanted what they had become accustomed to: modern, U.S.-style products. A Mexican car would not have been acceptable. The relationship of the Mexican state to its national bourgeoisie thus demanded that Mexico needed the sort of automobile industry that only the transnational firms could provide.

If the context established Mexico's "need" for the technology of the automobile TNCs, we may then ask how easily the Mexican state could have changed those features of the context that defined the need and thus constituted the technology as a power resource. Clearly, not very easily: fundamental changes in the strategy of economic growth and in the domestic class structure would have been required.[36]

---

[35] It is noteworthy that the state-owned Diesel Nacional S.A. had already begun work on a medium truck of its own design. Some of its components were imported, some were manufactured under license, and a Detroit engineering firm had been consulted; but it was nonetheless a Mexican truck and proved to be a successful venture.

[36] In Keohane and Nye's terminology, Mexico was both "sensitive" and "vulnerable"

(2) *The structure of relationships determines when power resources can be employed or withheld.* Relationships of dependence and interdependence in which the actors are enmeshed affect the choice of their possessions and attributes that may serve as power resources in a particular conflict, but other relationships may serve to limit the actors' freedom to commit or to withhold their resources at will. The structure of relationships defining Mexico's place in the global political economy and the Mexican state's relationship to its domestic class structure decreed the need for a certain kind of automobile industry; the resources of the transnational automobile firms thus became sources of potential power. On the other hand, the pattern of competitive relationships among these transnational automobile firms (in their worldwide competition) served to constrain them from deploying these resources to their own best advantages in bargaining with the Mexican state. More precisely, the follow-the-leader pattern of defensive investment that made the firms so eager to produce for the Mexican market weakened their potential to withhold their participation if conditions and terms were not precisely to their liking. Knickerbocker has called the TNCs' proclivity to defensive investment a "trump card for the LCD": "When one member of the club makes a move, the others pant to follow; and by realizing this, the LDC is in a position to demand a high entrance fee."[37] Since the move to auto manufacture in Mexico coincided with heightened international competition, the potential power of the Mexican state was enhanced as the ability of the TNCs to withhold their resources was weakened. Had the industry been differently organized—had it, for example been characterized by collusion and strategies of mutual forebearance, the Mexican Government would not have had such substantial potential power.

In view of the pattern of competition in the international automobile industry, the Mexican state's control over access to the Mexican market was the most potent power resource available to it in the bargaining, but certain relationships constrained its ability to play this "trump card" to its fullest advantage. Most importantly, in its pursuit of industrial development by way of import substitution, Mexico had come to be dependent upon certain industrialized countries, particularly the United States, for trade and capital inflows. These relationships shaped

---

to this power resource of the TNCs. "Sensitivity involves degrees of responsiveness within a policy framework" or context, and vulnerability refers to the "relative availability and costliness of the alternatives the various actors face." Keohane and Nye (fn. 26), 12-13.

[37] Knickerbocker (fn. 19), 197, 198.

a set of needs for continued flows of trade and capital in a number of
sectors that limited the state's power in the automobile sector: a favorable investment climate had to be maintained if growth was to continue. The Mexican Government was forcefully reminded of this limitation just when the automobile policy was first being formulated.
In 1960–1961, relations with the United States took a turn for the worse
with Mexico's refusal to submit to U.S. pressure to support the trade
sanctions against the Castro regime. The U.S. Government and press
criticized the "left-wing" tendencies of the López Mateos government
—a perception that was reinforced by a variety of new policies toward
foreign investment. Since taking office, the López Mateos Administration had nationalized the electric power industry and implemented
important new policies in the petrochemical and mining sectors, which
were branded as socialist by certain transnational corporations and
conservative Mexican business interests. The effect was felt in a flight
of capital of about $200 million between 1960 and 1961.[38] The Mexican
Government thus had to be cautious in its treatment of the foreign
(especially U.S.) automobile corporations, lest its policy in this sector
threaten the wider growth strategy.

The Mexican state's relationship with its own national bourgeoisie
also limited its ability to play this trump card of market access to
fullest advantage. If some wholly foreign-owned firms were to be approved, it would have been politically disadvantageous not to show a
measure of favoritism to some domestically-owned firms that were also
requesting approval.

(3) *The structure of relationships determines the potential for the
entry of new actors into the conflict as allies or as antagonists.* Having
already established themselves in the Mexican market through their
assembly operations, the three major U.S.-based firms (Ford, General
Motors and Fábricas Auto-Mex) could draw on support from their
consumers and employees, but more importantly from their distributors and from the suppliers of replacement parts and what few parts
were procured in Mexico for original equipment. In bargaining, these
major U.S. firms could (and did) call attention to the disruption that
would attend their exclusion: replacement parts and service would
become hard to find; the value of existing vehicles would decline; their
distributors would be put out of business; and their Mexican employees
would be out of work. The distributors and parts-supply firms made
separate representations of these same points, but they were weak and

[38] Miguel Wionczek, *El Nacionalismo y la Invérsion Extranjera* (Mexico, D.F.:
Siglo XXI Editores 1967), 240-41.

disorganized. It was also impossible to muster a wider alliance between the transnational firms and the national bourgeoisie—for example depicting the attempt to exclude certain TNCs from the market as a general attack on private investment. This strategy had been effective in other cases of LDC-TNC bargaining,[39] but the Mexican state's clear intention to accord its national bourgeoisie special treatment in the automobile industry through the proposals for Mexicanization and for reservation of the supplier industry forestalled such an alliance.

A more formidable set of allies on which the TNCs drew were their home governments. This article is not the place in which to explore the relationships between the transnational automobile firms and their home governments.[40] However, the resources of the latter should no more be taken as given than those of the other central actors in the bargaining. They resided precisely in the ability to influence the trade and capital flows between Mexico and the industrialized countries on which Mexico had become dependent. In order to understand the potential power of these home governments we must, therefore, return to our first two points: the interdependent relationships in which Mexico was enmeshed defined the need for resources over which the home governments had a measure of control, and which thus constituted bases of potential power; and the asymmetric character of these trade and investment (inter-)dependencies meant that the home governments were likely to be more free to commit or withhold those resources than the Mexican Government was to choose whether to do without them.

FROM POTENTIAL POWER TO ACTUAL POWER

How did the two major actors—the TNCs and the Mexican Government—transform (or fail to transform) their potential power into actual power? As Keohane and Nye point out, "political bargaining is the usual means of translating potential into effects, and a lot is often

---

[39] For such an alliance in the bargaining over copper concessions in Chile, see Moran, *Multinational Corporations and the Politics of Dependence: Copper in Chile* (fn. 3), 190-97; for such an alliance in Venezuela in the bargaining over oil concessions, see Franklin Tugwell, *The Politics of Oil in Venezuela* (Stanford: Stanford University Press 1975). For a general discussion of the conditions under which such alliance between TNCs and the national bourgeoisie may form, see Moran in *International Organization* (fn. 3), 93-95.

[40] For one discussion of these relationships that especially concerns European automobile firms, see Louis T. Wells, "Automobiles," in Raymond Vernon, ed., *Big Business and the State* (Cambridge: Harvard University Press 1974). For a discussion that illuminates certain aspects of the relationship of the U.S. and Japanese Governments toward their automobile industries, see William Chandler Duncan, *U.S.-Japan Automobile Diplomacy* (Cambridge: Ballinger Publishing Co. 1973).

lost in translation."[41] Our concern will remain focused on the central issue of industry structure: How did the firms prevail over the Mexican Government's efforts to limit the number of enterprises in the industry?

The mobilization of corporate power. The U.S. firms began early to mobilize their power to influence the terms of the Decree. As the NAFIN committee was preparing its report, Ford was already working on a detailed, two-volume proposal of its own. In frequent discussions with officials of the Ministry of Industry and Commerce (SIC), the firms attempted to use their superior know-how to convince Mexican policy planners of the unreasonableness or impracticality of their proposals. However, on the issues of exclusion and ownership (mandatory Mexicanization would have been tantamount to exclusion of Ford and General Motors), and even on certain questions of the firms' behavior, the government *técnicos* were unmoved.[42] Distributors and parts suppliers also provided little leverage. Instead, a major key to the success of the TNCs was the support they could mobilize from the U.S. Government.

The Minister of Industry and Commerce was informed by the United States Ambassador that the Department of State would look unfavorably on the exclusion of the U.S. firms. Other high officials of the Ministry were told that any such exclusion would be viewed as a "not very friendly act."[43] Precisely *what was said*, however, is not as important as how anything said on this issue by the U.S. Government *would be understood*. Its explicit backing of the interests of these transnational firms meant that automobile policy would be linked with, and would affect, what happened in other spheres of the bilateral relationship, and that sanctions might be employed beyond those strictly under the control of the three firms.[44] In view of the strained relations over Cuba and the recent capital flight, the President, Ministers and other officials of the Mexican Government had to be particularly sensitive to the pronouncements of high corporate executives and U.S. Government officials.

[41] Keohane and Nye (fn. 26), 11. Cf. Moran, *Multinational Corporations and the Politics of Dependence* (fn. 3), 169-215.

[42] It does seem, however, that they did not fully appreciate how much the pattern of oligopolistic competition strengthened their hand, nor how zealously the firms would press their cases in their eagerness to be included.

[43] A well-publicized visit by U.S. Ambassador Thomas Mann to the plant of Fábricas Auto-Mex in August 1961 made it clear that the United States was interested in the treatment of this firm (which was majority Mexican-owned), as well as of Ford and G.M.'s wholly U.S.-owned subsidiaries.

[44] Another case of U.S. Government intervention on behalf of Ford, G.M., and Chrysler over somewhat similar issues is documented in Duncan (fn. 40).

Pressure may also have been forthcoming from the West German Government to ensure that at least one German manufacturer was approved. In any case, the desire of the Ministry of Industry and Commerce to include at least one manufacturer of a small inexpensive car (*auto popular*), their unwillingness to rely wholly on the state-owned Diesel Nacional (Renault) for this purpose, and the Mexican ownership of Promexa (Volkswagen) at the time of approval were probably sufficient to assure the acceptance of Volkswagen as a licensee. (The Mexicans sold out to the German parent company a few months later.)

The acceptance of Nissan's application two years after the legal deadline for approval, however, can only be explained by looking at another relationship between a TNC and its home government.[45] The Japanese Government utilized an additional and unlikely power resource to gain approval for Nissan: cotton.

In 1963, cotton was the single most important source of foreign exchange for Mexico, accounting for earnings of US$196 million—over 20 percent of Mexico's total foreign exchange earnings.[46] In addition, taxes on cotton exports brought in about US$15 million per year.[47] About 70 percent of cotton exports went to Japan, Mexico's most important trade partner after the United States. The balance of trade between the two countries ran strongly in Mexico's favor. In 1962, for example, while Mexico's exports to Japan were valued at US$127.8 million, Mexico's imports from Japan totaled only US$22.6 million. For a number of years, the Japanese Government had been pressuring Mexico to increase its imports; it even offered a loan of US$100 million if there were some improvement in this regard.[48] The Japanese Government was therefore able to use its position as Mexico's major cotton buyer as a lever: it threatened to cut cotton imports if Nissan's application were not approved. The threat worked.

Because of its historical commitment to the national bourgeoisie, the Mexican state's capitulation in approving some wholly foreign-owned firms weakened its ability—and perhaps its resolve—to turn down applications by some firms that were wholly or majority Mexican-owned. State-owned Diesel Nacional (DINA) had been assured of a place in

[45] An application from a wholly Mexican-owned venture to manufacture Datsuns had been turned down during the normal period of application, though the approval of Reo allowed the manufacture of one Japanese make (Toyota). Since Reo failed during the first year, however, no Japanese makes were initially included in the Mexican market.

[46] Lic. Raúl Salinas Lozano, *Memoria de Labores, 1963* (Mexico, D.F.: Secretaria de Industria y Comercio 1963), 136-37.

[47] *Comercio Exterior*, May 1961, p. 287.

[48] *Comercio Exterior*, March 1963, p. 167.

the industry from the beginning. Vehículos Automotores Mexicanos (VAM) was a well-established venture of Sociedad Mexicana de Crédito Industrial, one of the country's largest industrial development banks. Fábricas Auto-Mex's hand was strengthened by its being majority-owned by a wealthy and well-connected Mexican family. In the cases of Impulsora Mexicana Automotriz, Reo, and Representaciones Delta (all private firms, 100 percent Mexican-owned), political favoritism and perhaps bribes rather than technical competence or financial clout were responsible for their being approved when other domestically owned ventures were rejected.

In all, ten firms were approved to manufacture in Mexico, far more than the NAFIN Report had recommended and far more than the size of the Mexican market warranted. When the government realized that it would not prevail in limiting the number of firms, it pinned its hopes on competition to winnow the industry down over the next few years. To some extent, that was a vain hope: the NAFIN Report had correctly predicted that competition would not drive out subsidiaries of the transnational firms, because of the ability of these firms to cross-subsidize their various international operations. Also, steps were taken to protect the national firms (both public and private) from the size and superior resources of the foreign firms. A system of production quotas limited the output of all firms and thus ensured a share of the market for the Mexican firms—thereby further reducing the possibility of elimination through competition.

On some issues, the Mexican Government did succeed in accomplishing its goals. The firms that had been approved would be required to manufacture 60 percent of each vehicle in Mexico. Further, these firms would be limited to the machining of the motor and the final assembly of vehicles. Other manufacturing activities would be reserved for a supplier industry that needed to be created—and the burden would fall squarely on the transnational firms in the terminal industry to assist in this development.[49]

The opposition of the American firms and their allies proved sufficient to have removed from the auto decree the other key requirements concerning product differentiation—freezing of models, standardization of parts, and limits on the number of acceptable makes and models. The question of the exclusion of these firms had been a particularly sharp issue in the bargaining, and when they prevailed on

---

[49] In later bargaining, some of the terminal firms secured approval for more vertical integration. A number of firms now have approval to cast their own engine blocks, Volkswagen is permitted to make its own body stampings, and so forth.

this, they won as well the right to manufacture automobiles in their accustomed manner—with product differentiation and annual model changes.

Organizational constraints on the exercise of state power. The government's proposals for rationalizing the auto industry had been undermined on certain fundamental issues—the number of firms, the ownership of the terminal industry, product differentiation. In view of the potential power of the state, it is important to ask why the state's trump card—the pattern of oligopolistic competition in the automobile industry—was largely un- or under-played.

At first glance, there is a simple and plausible answer: certain characteristics of the structure of dependence—particularly political and economic relations with the United States and Japan—allowed the TNCs to muster the support of their home governments and change the game to one in which Mexico's card was no longer trump. But it is possible that the Mexican state could have acted differently. There were alternative strategies (recognized by at least some high officials at the time) that it might have pursued to take better advantage of its potential power.

In the case of the U.S. firms, a divide-and-rule strategy could have been tried, playing one of them against the other two. Alternatively, the government could have yielded on the question of limiting the number of firms, but insisted that these firms submit to much stiffer regulations on firm behavior, such as limits on product differentiation and on ownership. In the case of Nissan, the state might have responded to the Japanese Government's pressure by negotiating for the entrance of substantial Japanese investment in some other industrial structure, or even by calling its bluff: as some Mexican officials were aware (particularly in the Finance Ministry), Japan could not easily have found suitable alternatives for the long-fibered Mexican cotton needed for its textile industry.

The point is not that these strategies would necessarily have succeeded, but rather that the Mexican state had potential power and alternative courses of action that it did not employ. Why not?

When an actor in a power conflict is a collectivity rather than a single person, there may be organizational constraints on the utilization of potential power. For *internal* reasons, the actor may not be able to draw on all of the potential power that is theoretically available to it. With a complex entity like the state, such internal constraints may stem from a lack of the organizational coordination that is necessary to wield its potential power to full effectiveness. In the case at hand, we must examine the relations among specific agencies and departments and the bureaucratic politics of policy formation inside the Mexican Government.[50] We will confine ourselves to three aspects of internal lack of unity.

1. Not only did the two ministries that were centrally concerned with industrial policy (the very powerful Finance Ministry and the Ministry of Industry and Commerce), fail to coordinate their automobile policy; they were seriously at odds during much of the planning period. Prior to the López Mateos Administration, the Finance Ministry had controlled the two principal policy instruments for industrial planning—tax policy and import tariffs and quotas. Such steps as were taken to encourage greater local content in the automobile industry were the work of the Finance Ministry's capable Department of Financial Studies. When the Ministry of Industry and Commerce was reorganized in 1959, it was given control (among other measures to strengthen it) over import tariffs and quotas; questions of automobile policy became principally its concern. The Finance Ministry resisted the diminution of its control over import policy, however, and the conflict between the two ministries became quite sharp, at times requiring presidential mediation. The Director of the Department of Financial Studies (who had been in his post a number of years, and had considerable experience with the automobile industry) supported a much stronger automobile policy along the lines of the original NAFIN Report. Had there been effective coordination between these two ministries, Industry and Commerce would have had powerful support for taking a tougher line. However, Industry and Commerce proceeded alone, using import controls as its only tool. (Tax policy toward the industry was not negotiated until after the 1962 Decree, and the Finance Ministry flatly refused to grant the firms any fiscal incentives.) The making and implementing of automobile policy became a means by which Industry and Commerce established a sphere of autonomy, but the cost was a diminution of the state's effective power.[51]

[50] Cf. the discussion of divisions within the Mexican state as weakening its bargaining position vis-à-vis foreign drug companies, in Gereffi (fn. 3), 279-84. Organizational constraints *within* the TNCs themselves, while beyond the scope of this paper, are also important to a full analysis of the transformation of potential into actual power. See Gereffi, *ibid.* For a broad general discussion, see also Alfred D. Chandler, Jr., *Strategy and Structure: Chapters in the History of the American Industrial Enterprise* (Cambridge: M.I.T. Press 1962).

[51] Parallel to this lack of coordination was the failure of Industry and Commerce to make use of the state's own automobile firm, Diesel Nacional, nominal control over

2. There were also serious divisions inside the Ministry of Industry and Commerce. The Director and Sub-Director of Industries had been deeply involved in the technical studies that preceded the bargaining. Like their counterparts in the Department of Financial Studies with whom they had developed close informal relationships (the antagonism was chiefly at the Ministerial level), they believed that a much stronger policy could be successfully carried forward. Their superiors, however, the Secretary and the Assistant Secretary, felt that moderation, and compromise with the companies, was necessary. It is difficult to know for certain why these top officials were reluctant to take a tougher position, but interviews with officials in and out of the Ministry indicate that there were several factors. For one, there was a difference of goals. While there was broad agreement in the Ministry that limiting the number of firms was important, these top officials also placed a high priority on diversification of the sources of foreign investment; hence, they were inclined to look favorably on the applications of, for example, Promexa (Volkswagen) and Nissan.

Moreover, the political situation of the Secretary and Assistant Secretary made it somewhat difficult for them to assume a tougher position in the face of corporate pressure. In the Mexican political system, the change of President every six years brings with it changes in all major policy-making posts. Although a person is unlikely to retain the same position, many move to new positions of importance.[52] Cabinet Secretaries are typically the strongest candidates for selection as the next President. Among other factors, a politician's future will depend on the immediate political consequences of his decisions in the previous sexennium—the friends and enemies he has made, the controversies in which he has been involved. Thus, the incentive to pursue risk-minimizing strategies and to judge policies narrowly in terms of their short-run political consequences is strong. Since the deleterious effects of admitting too many firms to the industry would not be felt immediately, only an unusual person would have risked a full-scale confrontation with Ford, General Motors and the U.S. Government, or with the Japanese Government—unless he had the support of the President.

---

which lay with yet a third ministry, National Properties. DINA could have been a valuable source of technical and financial information about automobile manufacturing; it could have been allotted a place in the industry which would have made it a tool of industrial policy (a competitive check on the other firms). DINA's earlier troubles, however, hardly inspired confidence.

[52] Peter Smith, "Does Mexico Have a Power Elite?" in Richard S. Weinert and José Luis Reyna, eds., *Authoritarianism in Mexico* (Philadelphia: ISHI Publications 1977).

Finally, there was a close connection between the Ford Company and the Ministry of Industry and Commerce. It was not simply a personal relationship between the manager of Ford de México and the Minister: from the very beginning of the López Mateos Administration, Ford had openly supported the Ministry's goal of moving toward the manufacturing of automobiles. In 1960, following a strategy he had recently employed in Argentina, Ford's manager put his staff to work on a lengthy feasibility report and an accompanying proposal of what Ford itself would be willing to do in Mexico. He reckoned—quite rightly—that such early cooperation would give Ford an inside track on approval and policy input that would result in a policy that the company would find amenable. How much Ford's influence was responsible for the divisions within the Ministry of Industry and Commerce, and how much it was made possible by divisions already there, is difficult to determine.

3. Because of the centralization of power in the hands of a Mexican President, it is possible that his explicit direction and firm support could have forged the inter- and intra-Ministerial unity necessary to act more forcefully in putting forward a stronger automobile policy. Indeed, interviews show that a lack of direction left key officials on their own (and thus made it rational for them to pursue risk-mini-mizing strategies), and that specific directives to "ease up" on the transnational firms, and to give favorable consideration to applications from certain Mexican-owned firms, filtered down from the President himself at crucial points in the bargaining. In the context of the Mexican political system, only resolute guidance from the President could have fended off the pressures that were being brought to bear, and this guidance was not forthcoming.

IV. Conclusion

The bargaining conflict between the Mexican state and the transnational automobile corporations between 1960 and 1964 was only the first round of what has proved to be an ongoing struggle. There have been a number of new negotiations, the most important of which took place in 1968–1969 and again in 1976–1977; but the initial round was the most decisive encounter because it set the terms for all subsequent bargaining.

Studies of bargaining power in natural resource industries have shown that the power of the state is lowest at the time of initial bargaining because of uncertainties about the amount, quality, and costs of extraction of the natural resources. Once the large initial investments have been made, however, the balance of power swings dramatically in favor of the state: the uncertainties are reduced and the fixed investments are "hostage" to the LDC.[53]

In a high-technology, consumer-goods manufacturing sector such as the automobile industry, the situation is often reversed. Access to the domestic market is the state's principal basis of bargaining power, and can be used most effectively at the point of initial investment. After that, the firms are entrenched in the host country through their relationships with suppliers, distributors, labor, and consumers. Because such manufacturing enterprises are integrated into the local economy to a far higher degree than resource extractors, they establish relationships within the host country which significantly enhance their bargaining power, both by reinforcing the host country's needs for their kind of production and products and by being able to mobilize domestic allies. And so long as the industry is dependent upon external sources of technology, the possibility of nationalization by the host country is not a credible threat.

Other things being equal, then, the balance of bargaining power in such a manufacturing industry may with time shift toward the transnational firms rather than toward the LDC. The first bargaining encounter between the Mexican state and the automobile TNCs was therefore of paramount importance: here, the structure of the industry was first laid down; the state never again had the power to restructure the industry, and each subsequent renegotiation of policy occurred within the bounds set down in the first bargaining encounter. Both the problems and the alternative possibilities are defined within this structure.

The theoretical approach taken in this paper could be employed in the analysis of these subsequent bargaining encounters in the Mexican automobile industry, as well as in the analysis of bargaining between TNCs and the governments of other less developed countries, and in other industries. We have been concerned with two central issues: agenda setting and bargaining power.

Agenda setting. Understanding the bargaining agenda requires a knowledge of the actors (or interests) that obtain access to the bargaining arena and of those that are excluded. The character of Mexico's political institutions explains not only the exclusion of labor from the

---

[53] On this argument, see Moran, *Multinational Corporations and the Politics of Dependence* (fn. 3), 157-62.

bargaining table, but also the promotion of certain interests of the national bourgeoisie by the Mexican state (despite the rather small role played by Mexican entrepreneurs in the bargaining). Once it is clear which actors and interests are to be included, the points of conflict and of convergence of interest among the major actors must be analyzed. It should not be supposed that the interests of TNCs and LDC governments conflict across the board: the points of convergence of interests simply do not become bargaining issues. In the case of Mexico after World War II, a strategy of import substitution laid the basis for substantial convergence of interests among the government and TNCs in a range of manufacturing industries. The convergence of interests in the automobile industry—given its worldwide dynamics of competition—went no further than assembly operations, however. The exercise of state power was necessary to induce the auto firms to commence domestic manufacture. The state's requirement for local content was not the most controversial proposal, however, because it merely propelled the firms further along a competitive trajectory on which they were already engaged worldwide. But other proposals—a strict limitation on the number of firms, ownership restrictions, and constraints on product differentiation—did become major points of conflict in the bargaining: they threatened the established competitive strategies of the firms in the industry (particularly of the U.S.-based firms, which were the most active in the bargaining because of their prior penetration of the market).

Bargaining power. The potential power available to each actor to settle the contested issues cannot be understood as consisting simply of its possession of certain resources. Whether a resource can serve as a source of potential power depends on the context—particularly on the structure of domestic and international relationships in which each actor is enmeshed. Such relationships help in defining which resources can serve as bases of potential power. It was, for example, the relationship between the Mexican state and certain domestic classes that established Mexico's "need" for a domestic automobile industry and thus allowed the TNCs' control of automobile technology to serve as their power resource. Such relationships also determine when power resources can be employed or withheld, as demonstrated in the pattern of competitive relationships in the world's automobile oligopoly that made each of the firms eager to gain access to the Mexican market. Finally, such relationships define the potential for the entry of new actors into the conflict as allies—as shown by the firms' mobilization of domestic suppliers and distributors and of their home governments.

Potential power must be carefully distinguished from actual power: an actor may have sources of power upon which it does not draw effectively. In this conflict, the TNCs drew more effectively upon their potential power than did the Mexican state. The potential power that accrued to the Mexican state from the pattern of oligopolistic competition in the world's automobile industry was an advantage which it did not utilize fully. In order to understand the reasons, we must realize that the host government is not a single unified entity. Conflicts within and especially between various agencies, and the lack of central direction from the President weakened the Mexican state's ability to draw fully upon its potential power.

PATRIMONIALISM AND MILITARY
RULE IN INDONESIA

By HAROLD CROUCH*

INSTABILITY has been a striking characteristic of Third-World politics. Since gaining independence, most Third-World states have experienced sudden and drastic changes in government, brought about by mass demonstrations, riots, rebellions, and coups. Relatively soft "democratic" governments have proved particularly vulnerable, but many of the more authoritarian regimes that replaced them have been equally incapable of maintaining their hold on power. However, not all Third-World states are politically unstable. Some, such as Saudi Arabia and Nepal, have managed to isolate themselves to a large extent from the modernizing process that affects most of the Third World and have preserved traditional political institutions which continue to be regarded as legitimate by most of the populace. Others, more exposed to Western penetration, underwent periods of considerable social upheaval and political instability, but have since instituted governments that were able to restore order and seem capable of maintaining stability in the future.

A prominent feature of some of the authoritarian regimes that have succeeded in maintaining political stability is the persistence of traditional features that seem to be inherited from the polities of the pre-colonial past. The process of modernization—economic, social, cultural, and political—has of course brought about fundamental changes in traditional societies—changes that cannot be reversed. But it is widely recognized that the modern features of developing societies have not always replaced traditional elements, and indeed, that traditional modes of thought and behavior have often continued to influence the workings of apparently modern institutions. Although no contemporary state conforms fully to the contours of the states of the past, certain key features of traditional systems seem to have persisted and now constitute central elements of the political process in some of the Third-World states that have succeeded in establishing apparently stable institutions. In seeking to explain the character and stability of these systems, some political scientists have turned to the Weberian

* This article is based on a paper presented to the Seventh Conference of the International Association of Historians of Asia, held in Bangkok in August 1977. I am grateful to Herbert Feith for his comments and suggestions.

concept of "patrimonialism," and have used the term "neo-patrimonialism" to describe modern states exhibiting patrimonial characteristics.[1]

Most traditional polities had patrimonial features. In a patrimonial state, the ruler's power depended on his capacity to win and retain the loyalty of key sections of the political elite. Lacking sufficient coercive capacity to enforce acceptance of his rule, the ruler sought to win voluntary allegiance by satisfying the aspirations—especially the material interests—of his supporters through the distribution of fiefs and benefices in exchange for tribute and loyalty. The government was able to rule in the interests of the elite without taking much account of the interests of the masses because the latter were poor, socially backward, politically passive, and kept in check by the regime's military forces. Politics thus took the form of a struggle within the elite itself, among rival factions and cliques that were concerned principally with gaining influence with the ruler who determined the distribution of the rewards of office. The ruler was able to maintain his authority by preserving the balance among the competing cliques. As long as the masses remained politically quiescent, and rivalries within the elite were contained so that they did not threaten its basic unity of interest, the patrimonial system could continue indefinitely.

The environment in which patrimonial characteristics have persisted, however, has been very different from the one in which they originally appeared. Modernization has brought new challenges that threaten the capacity of governments to meet demands and maintain stability. Economic change has produced new social groupings and classes with distinctive political interests, while the political quiescence of the masses has been undermined and modern political organization has enabled leaders to mobilize support on a wide scale. On the other hand, the capacity of governments to meet demands and deal with threats to their position has also grown, in part through the increasing sophistication of the means of coercion. As the problems of containing conflict and instability become more serious, the patrimonial distribution of largesse and the balancing of rival elite interests may prove insufficient for keeping the new Third-World regimes in power.

Indonesia provides an example of a society that has undergone considerable economic, social, and political change, but still exhibits important traditional features in its political system. During the phases

---

[1] See Guenther Roth, "Personal Rulership, Patrimonialism, and Empire-Building in the New States," *World Politics*, xx (January 1968), 194-206; S. N. Eisenstadt, *Traditional Patrimonialism and Modern Neo-Patrimonialism* (Beverly Hills and London: Sage Publications 1973).

of both "Guided Democracy" and "New Order," many features of the political system seemed to hark back to the patrimonial politics of earlier, precolonial Javanese empires.

THE PERIOD OF GUIDED DEMOCRACY

The re-emergence of traditional features in the politics of Guided Democracy, which replaced the parliamentary system in 1959, has been pointed out by several scholars.[2] At the apex of the Guided Democracy system stood President Sukarno, who "assumed lifetime tenure, an impressive array of titles, and a style of life that included the entourage, regalia and rituals customarily maintained by traditional Javanese monarchs."[3] The traditional sultan's possession of the *wahyu* (divine endorsement) was demonstrated to the masses by the splendor of his palace, the lavishness of his court, and the grandeur of his ceremonies; Sukarno's ritualistic rallies, commemorations, and celebrations, together with the splendid monuments and edifices which he built in the capital, were also meant to indicate to the masses that the *wahyu* was still with him.

The struggle to influence the President that was waged by the leaders of the army, the Communist Party (PKI), and other parties and groups paralleled the factionalism and intrigue that had marked the politics of the traditional courts. As in the past, the ruler was not in a position to employ coercion on a wide scale against discontented sections of the elite; his aim therefore was to maintain balance by bestowing his favors evenly among the contending factions, particularly through the distribution of opportunities for personal profit. As a result, the President's preoccupation with balancing rival factions overshadowed activities directed toward the achievement of modern goals such as economic development and the creation of an effective administrative apparatus.

However, there were key differences between the patrimonial sultanates of the past and Sukarno's Guided Democracy. Although many of the rural masses were still traditional in outlook and politically inert, a substantial section, especially in Java, had been attracted to the PKI,

[2] See Clifford Geertz, *Islam Observed: Religious Development in Morocco and Indonesia* (New Haven: Yale University Press 1968); Ann Ruth Willner, "The Neotraditional Accommodation to Political Independence: The Case of Indonesia," in Lucian W. Pye, ed., *Cases in Comparative Politics: Asia* (Boston: Little, Brown 1970), 242-306; Benedict R. O'G. Anderson, "The Idea of Power in Javanese Culture," in Claire Holt, ed., *Culture and Politics in Indonesia* (Ithaca: Cornell University Press 1972), 1-69.

[3] Willner (fn. 2), 249.

which vigorously championed the interests of the rural poor. During the 1950s, the PKI succeeded in mobilizing the support of part of the peasantry; during the 1960s, it launched a campaign of "unilateral action" in which communist-led poor peasants occupied the land of their better-off neighbors. At the same time, the PKI attracted urban supporters by sponsoring nationalist agitation and spearheading attacks on Dutch, British, and American property. By 1964, the PKI had become President Sukarno's most important source of mass support. It served as the major element with which he was able to balance the power of the army.[4]

The Indonesian army had, since its formation in 1945 at the beginning of the revolution against the Dutch, always been politically oriented. After parliamentary democracy collapsed when it proved unable to deal with an incipient rebellion in the Outer Islands in 1957, martial law was introduced—enabling the army to expand its role into the fields of politics, administration, and the economy. Army officers were appointed to the cabinet, occupied high positions in the bureaucracy, and became regional governors. The army's "territorial" organization was strengthened with the stationing of military units in cities, towns, and townships throughout the nation. As the PKI established itself as the army's main rival for the succession, the army leaders took steps to block its expansion and to meet its challenge.[5] At the same time, the growth of the PKI's strength stirred the party's civilian opponents to defend themselves; both the Muslim and nationalist parties mobilized their supporters against the PKI in the rural areas.

Like the sultans in the patrimonial states of the past, Sukarno sought to keep the courtiers jostling among themselves for his favors in order not to become overly dependent on any one of them. But, unlike the sultan's officials in the patrimonial courts, Sukarno's courtiers were backed by modern organizations whose members confronted each other throughout the nation. While Sukarno succeeded in playing off

[4] See Rex Mortimer, *Indonesian Communism Under Sukarno* (Ithaca: Cornell University Press 1974).

[5] On the development of the army's political role, see Guy J. Pauker, "The Role of the Military in Indonesia," in John J. Johnson, ed., *The Role of the Military in Underdeveloped Countries* (Princeton: Princeton University Press 1962), 185-230; Daniel S. Lev, "The Political Role of the Army in Indonesia," *Pacific Affairs*, xxxvi (Winter 1963-64), 349-64; Ruth McVey, "The Post-Revolutionary Transformation of the Indonesian Army," Part I, *Indonesia*, No. 11 (April 1971), 131-76, and Part II, *Indonesia*, No. 13 (April 1972), 147-81; Ulf Sundhaussen, "The Political Orientation and Political Involvement of the Indonesian Officer Corps, 1945-1966," Ph.D. diss. (Monash University 1971).

factions against each other in Jakarta, he had no way of effecting a reconciliation between the interests and organizations that they represented in the nation. In 1965, an attempted coup against the army leadership by dissident colonels who were backed by PKI leaders provided the opening for the army to move against its rival. In the massacre that followed, some half-million supporters of the PKI lost their lives. Patrimonial ritual and the distribution of fiefdoms had proved insufficient to hold together a polity that was sharply divided between competing interests organized on a national scale. As long as the system survived, it had *seemed* patrimonial; but its disintegration demonstrated that the patrimonial structure had been resting on non-patrimonial foundations.

The Period of the New Order

Guided Democracy deviated from the stable patrimonial model in that its elite was sharply divided along ideological lines, and the masses were partially mobilized. The rise of the PKI meant that political competition could not be centered purely on a struggle over the allocation of appointments and opportunities for material benefit within the elite, but involved basically contrasting conceptions of the social and political order. The PKI's successful mobilization of mass support—especially during the latter phase of Guided Democracy— forced its rivals also to mobilize their supporters. As a result, the intra-elite struggle for power became enmeshed with political competition among the masses; conflicts between opposing sections of the elite could no longer be settled by means of political shifts, maneuvers, and compromises executed by the sultan in the capital, but involved apparently irreconcilable interests throughout the nation. The army's accession to power and repression of its opponents, however, helped to restore conditions favorable to patrimonialism. By eliminating communists, left-wing nationalists, and Sukarnoists, army leaders achieved harmony among the elite. At the same time, they rejected claims to a major role by Muslim leaders who had sided with the military in 1965. The post-coup massacres were followed by steps to emasculate the remaining political parties and depoliticize the masses.

1. DEPOLITICIZATION

The first step toward depoliticization was a result of the massacres that followed the attempted coup of October 1, 1965. Some two hundred thousand PKI supporters were arrested at that time; another three hundred thousand were arrested during the years that followed. The elimination of the PKI not only removed the most important source of mass mobilization that had arisen before 1965, but served as a terrifying warning to those who might have been inclined to seek mass support for radical causes during the period of the New Order.

Following the dismissal of President Sukarno in 1967, the army's leaders moved against the remaining political parties, purging them of dissidents and forcing them to accept leaders whom the new government regarded as amenable. When general elections were held in 1971, the government-sponsored Joint Secretariat of Functional Groups (*Golkar*) won 63 percent of the votes, while the other parties, with the exception of the conservative Muslim *Nahdatul Ulama*, suffered severe defeats. Although it lacked a party organization at the local level, the *Golkar* was backed by the government's civilian and military apparatus; many voters were subjected to blatant military pressure during the campaign.[6] After the elections, the government severely restricted the activities of the parties in the rural areas. In the 1977 elections, the *Golkar* scored another overwhelming victory; the Muslim opposition won almost 30 percent of the votes, however.

More than a decade of military domination led to a substantial depoliticization of the masses. The army's repressive measures resulted in the political parties' losing much of their potential for mobilizing mass protests against the government, although they had not been made completely prostrate. The enforced political isolation of the masses under the New Order was a factor favorable to the emergence of a new patrimonial system.

2. ELITE POLITICS

The emasculation of the political parties and depoliticization of the masses meant that patrimonial politics again largely took the form of a struggle for influence within the elite. But, unlike the ideological diversity of the elite during the period of Guided Democracy, the consolidation of the army's power produced a more or less uniform political outlook. The elite of the New Order was dominated by army officers and the Western-educated technocrats who helped them formulate economic policy. The government now gave top priority to its program of economic development based on the inflow of foreign capital in the form of both private investment and government aid.

After 1966, General Suharto gradually tightened his hold on the

[6] See Kenneth E. Ward, *The 1971 Election in Indonesia: An East Java Case Study* (Melbourne: Centre of Southeast Asian Studies, Monash University 1974).

armed forces. The expansion of his authority was backed by his growing capacity to use coercion against resisting groups; but the main
means was through the distribution of patronage. In full control of
the government administration, he was able to reward loyal supporters
and win over dissident and potentially dissident officers with appointments to civilian posts that offered prospects of material gain. Other
officers were encouraged to go into business, with a promise of help
from the administration whenever they needed licenses, credit, or
contracts. Control over the machinery of patronage was thus the key
factor that enabled Suharto to win and maintain the support of the
armed forces for his leadership.

The involvement of military men in civil administration and business
was not new. In the patrimonial atmosphere of Guided Democracy,
army officers—like most other officials—had used their public positions
to further their private interests. Military involvement in the economy
had become well established as the army leaders sought to supplement
budget allocations, and strengthen their independence from the government, by raising their own operating expenses through military-
sponsored businesses and the siphoning of funds from state enterprises
managed by army officers. At the same time, many officers became involved in private business activities. Under the New Order, army-
sponsored businesses continued to flourish as the military kept on
supplementing its allocations from the government budget by means
of independently raised funds. Once they were in control of the government administration, army officers increasingly used their influence
to secure licenses, contracts, credit, and other amenities for enterprises
with which they were privately associated; the business activities of
officers' wives, brothers, and cousins expanded. Most enterprises with
which military officers were associated were in fact managed by Indonesian Chinese whose commercial skills the generals usually lacked;
following the inrush of foreign capital in the late 1960s, foreign investment usually took the form of joint ventures in which the Indonesian
partner was a Chinese-managed enterprise backed by the military.[7]

The domination of the economy by these enterprises which were able
to secure favored treatment from military officials in the administration
led to accusations of corruption from some civilian quarters. But most
members of the military elite regarded the use of their official powers
to provide amenities for colleagues, relatives, and friends, or in exchange for commissions, as normal practice. As Anderson has pointed

---

[7] For documentation, see Harold Crouch, *The Army and Politics in Indonesia*
(Ithaca: Cornell University Press 1978), chap. 11.

out, in the traditional precolonial states of Java, "payment of officials (was) essentially in the form of specified benefices allotted by the ruler for the period of tenure of each particular office."[8] Like appointments in patrimonial states, the appointment of a military officer to a potentially lucrative civilian post was regarded as a reward for past loyalty; he was expected to make the most of his opportunity. The use of an official position for self-enrichment was thus not regarded as corruption, although "excessive" profiteering giving rise to disruption of the economy or public protests—like excessive exactions by patrimonial officials in the past—was to be avoided.

The complete domination of the government by the army, and the subjugation of other organizations such as the political parties, meant that the most important political competition took place within the military elite. The basic contours of the system were accepted by all groups. Although Suharto's leadership was not challenged, sharp rivalries continued between individuals and factions whose influence depended on their ability to win the confidence of the President and their fellow-generals rather than on their ability to mobilize support outside the elite. Thus, the struggle was essentially over the distribution of appointments and the accompanying opportunities for profit. Suharto rewarded his key supporters handsomely, but he was careful not to antagonize unnecessarily those who had lost in the inter-group struggles: many losers were also compensated with appointments and opportunities. In this way, Suharto presided over a system of balancing vested interests: the business opportunities enjoyed by his closest supporters were complemented by favors to former or potential dissidents, so that all had an interest in the continuation of the system. Suharto's capacity to keep the system functioning smoothly was greatly facilitated by the rapid expansion of the economy which took place under his rule. A constantly expanding resource base due to the influx of foreign capital and oil funds made it possible for him to reward and buy off a growing circle of beneficiaries, with the result that the stability of the regime was maintained.

The New Order thus bore a strong resemblance to the patrimonial model. Political competition among the elite did not involve policy, but power and the distribution of spoils. Meanwhile, the masses in the urban slums and rural areas were increasingly isolated from politics. The patrimonial distribution of perquisites within the elite and the

[8] Anderson (fn. 2), 33.

enforced depoliticization of the masses enabled the New Order to attain a level of stability never before achieved since independence.

THE FUTURE OF PATRIMONIALISM

A system that is essentially patrimonial can maintain itself only as long as two conditions are fulfilled. First, the elite must be ideologically homogeneous, so that the struggle for power centers on the allocation of private material benefits rather than on alternative political programs. But the New Order government's dependence on economic growth seems to require an administrative system based on the bureaucratic values of predictability, regularity, order, and rationality—in contrast to patrimonial favoritism and arbitrariness. As a result, basic conflicts over policy and the nature of the regime are becoming increasingly important. Second, the masses must continue to be passive and isolated from the political process. However, there are doubts as to the long-term effectiveness of the Indonesian regime's efforts to depoliticize and isolate the masses. It is therefore likely that the stability of the New Order government will be increasingly challenged, forcing it to turn much more to straightforward repression in order to deal not only with opposition from the masses, but also from within the elite.

I. THE TREND TOWARD REGULARIZATION

After 1966, the army's leadership was convinced that in the long run the viability of the regime would depend on an expanding pool of available resources, not only for patrimonial distribution within the elite, but also for the pre-emption of potential opposition from outside. In contrast to traditional patrimonial states, which acquired funds largely through the exploitation of the peasantry and through wholesale trade, the New Order has depended on a rapidly expanding modern economy financed by foreign aid, foreign investment, and rising oil prices. In the early stages, a patrimonial political structure need not be an obstacle to capitalist economic development. By placing themselves as clients under the protection and patronage of powerful members of the ruler's court, industrialists can acquire the security and predictability they need. But as a modern economy grows and becomes increasingly complex, industrialists require more than informal understandings with officials to assure them of the safety of their investments

—particularly as the increase in the number of business enterprises provides opportunities and incentives for officials to play their clients off against one another.

Discussing traditional patrimonial states of the past, Max Weber argued that their very patrimonial character inhibited the development of "production-oriented capitalism":

> The patrimonial state offers the whole realm of the ruler's discretion as a hunting ground for accumulating wealth. Wherever traditional or stereotyped prescription does not impose strict limitations, patrimonialism gives free rein to the enrichment of the ruler himself, the court officials, favorites, governors, mandarins, tax collectors, influence peddlers, and the great merchants and financiers who function as tax farmers, purveyors and creditors. The ruler's favor and disfavor, grants and confiscations, continually create new wealth and destroy it again.[9]

On the other hand,

> Industrial capitalism must be able to count on the continuity, trustworthiness and objectivity of the legal order, and on the rational, predictable functioning of legal and administrative agencies. Otherwise those guarantees of predictability are absent that are indispensable for the large industrial enterprise.[10]

According to Weber, the confidence of industrial investors can best be assured through the consistent application of rules rather than through private arrangements with particular officials. Trade, which is not so dependent on long-term predictability, quite often flourishes in patrimonial states under the sponsorship of rulers and officials.

The predictability that Weber believed to be necessary for modern economic development was almost entirely lacking during the period of Guided Democracy. Political struggles within the elite prevented the formulation and implementation of rational and coherent economic policies; resources were diverted to the President's "prestige projects" and to military campaigns against the Dutch in West Irian and the British in Malaysia. Dutch, British, and American enterprises were taken over by nationalist and communist agitators and placed formally under government control; in effect, they were in the hands of military and other officials who managed them as private fiefdoms. Inflation turned into hyperinflation, and budgetary controls over government expenditure lost their meaning as budget *deficits* alone exceeded total revenues. Meanwhile, administrative efficiency declined

[9] Max Weber, *Economy and Society: An Outline of Interpretive Sociology*, III, edited by Guenther Roth and Claus Wittich (New York: Bedminster Press 1968), 1099.
[10] *Ibid.*, 1095.

as competing government agencies claimed jurisdiction in overlapping fields; real salaries of civil servants fell, forcing officials to indulge in corruption or to seek extra incomes. As the PKI grew in strength, it was not surprising that investment in industry almost halted, since neither foreign nor domestic businessmen were willing to risk capital in projects that did not bear immediate fruit.[11] On the other hand, huge profits were to be made in trade by those with political connections. A circle of "palace millionaires" arose whose business success was largely due to the patronage of the President and the ministers with responsibility for economic affairs.

Although in the early years of the New Order the political struggle of the period of Guided Democracy had been settled in the army's favor, rational economic policy making was still obstructed, and important obstacles to technocratic management of the economy remained. Powerful vested interests stood to lose much from the vigorous enforcement of strict priorities through orderly administrative procedures.

The army leadership, however, realized that the loyalty of the army as well as the support of the middle class could be retained only if the government succeeded in promoting rapid economic growth. Since these officers were largely ignorant of the technicalities of economic policy making, they turned to a group of Western-educated economists —the "technocrats"—to formulate policies to control inflation, restore balance in foreign trade, and create conditions favorable for foreign and domestic investment. The efforts of the technocrats to restore order and regularity in the economy, however, met with strong opposition from many senior military officers whose power and private incomes depended on their ability to bypass formal rules and regulations. Thus, the oil corporation, *Pertamina*, lay outside the purview of the technocrats; their influence on the operations of the state's rice trading agency, *Bulog*, was also very limited. Although the technocrats had formal authority to examine foreign investment proposals, many investments took the form of joint ventures in which the Indonesian partner was an influential military figure. As a result, technocratic criteria were often ignored. Nevertheless, there were signs that the influence of the technocrats was growing during the 1970s, as the modern sector of the economy expanded and foreign investors demanded more stable and predictable conditions. The growth of the technocrats' power was further aided by the spectacular failures of several military-dominated

[11] See J.A.C. Mackie, *Problems of the Indonesian Inflation* (Ithaca: Modern Indonesia Project, Cornell University 1967).

agencies, most notably *Bulog* in 1973 and *Pertamina* in 1975. However, the technocrats are still far from exercising control over the economy.[12]

In Europe, the main pressure toward regularization and bureaucratization had come from the rising class of capitalist entrepreneurs. But in Indonesia this class is still weak, and the main impetus comes from sections of the army that are concerned about the long-term legitimacy of military rule. Not all officers became millionaires, and many field officers were worried that open and excessive profiteering by members of the military elite in association with foreigners and domestic-Chinese businessmen would not only hinder economic development, but bring the regime into public disrepute. It would thus increase the problems faced by the officers who were directly responsible for the maintenance of order and stability. Officers of a more "professional" orientation usually did not in principle disapprove of the involvement of military personnel in business activities, but were anxious to strengthen the regime's legitimacy by restraining excessive profiteering and the blatant use of public authority to further private interests. Rivalry within the army came to a head following signs of rising civilian discontent in the latter part of 1973. A serious riot in Bandung was followed by agitation by students and Muslims, and culminated in another, much bigger, riot in Jakarta during the visit of Japanese Prime Minister Tanaka in January 1974. Reform-minded officers and other dissidents apparently sought to exploit public discontent in order to force the President to dismiss some of his closest colleagues and replace them with more bureaucratically oriented "professional" officers. Although this move failed, many of the reform-minded officers continued to exert influence. Their increasing strength was a major factor leading to the dismissal of the head of *Pertamina*, General Ibnu Sutowo, in 1976, and to the tension in Jakarta during the months preceding the re-election of President Suharto in March 1978.

It seems likely that the trend toward regularization will continue. The growing size and complexity of the modern sector of the economy can be expected to require greater bureaucratization of economic management in order to guarantee stable and predictable conditions on which investors can base their calculations. At the same time, the restraint of blatantly excessive profiteering and corruption would strengthen the regime's legitimacy, especially in the eyes of the growing urban middle class. Moreover, within the army itself, the older generation of officers who took part in the guerilla war against the

[12] For a detailed discussion of the relations between the military and the technocrats, see Crouch (fn. 7), 318-30.

Dutch is gradually being replaced by academy-trained officers recruited since independence; this change will also tend to strengthen the hand of the military "technocrats." The professional and technocratic elements in the army do not seek a drastic overhaul of the regime; they want to preserve it through regularization.

These pressures, however, are not strong enough to lead to the establishment of a Weberian legal-rational order in the immediate future. Regularization and bureaucratization will run counter to the interests of many powerful military figures. Still, the regime is dependent on economic development for the resources it needs to preempt both military and civilian opposition. Greater emphasis on technocratic policies is therefore imperative. But this trend is likely to give rise to increasing political conflict within the military elite.

2. THE PASSIVITY OF THE MASSES?

A key condition for patrimonial stability is the political passivity of the non-elite. Under the New Order, considerable progress has been made toward depoliticizing the masses, but the taste for politics is not dead. The depoliticization program has been imposed on a people who, during the twenty years after the end of World War II, experienced the revolution against the Dutch, intense political competition under parliamentary democracy, mass mobilization under Guided Democracy, and the rise and decimation of a powerful Communist Party. While many, no doubt, welcomed the opportunity provided by the New Order to escape from the ubiquitous political struggle of the recent past, there are now signs of growing resentment which could conceivably give rise to renewed political activity in the future.

The urban middle class has been the major non-elite beneficiary of the New Order's economic policies. During the period of Guided Democracy, this class suffered from hyperinflation, the unavailability of imported consumer goods, declining real salaries for civil servants, and lack of employment opportunities in the private sector. However, the rapid economic expansion promoted by the Suharto government has resulted in a transformation of living standards for the middle class. Inflation has been brought under control; consumer goods are being imported; civil-service salaries have risen sharply during the 1970s; and numerous well-paid employment opportunities with foreign firms have opened up. Despite their lack of political influence, many in the professional and white-collar strata have found the New Order to be a material improvement over the old.

However, there are several groups within the middle class that have shown signs of disappointment and frustration. One group that has not benefited much from the New Order is the small class of indigenous entrepreneurs who in the past looked to the political parties to protect their interests, and who lack military patrons and access to Chinese capital. Indigenous businesses have generally suffered in the face of competition from modern, capital-intensive plants established by foreign companies in association with military partners. Many of the former, especially in the textile industry, have been forced to close down. Another middle-class group that is disillusioned with the regime consists of intellectuals, journalists, former party activists, and students who have been alienated by the military elite's monopoly of power, corruption, identification with foreign business interests, and—in some circles at least—its failure to improve the conditions of the poor. Dissident members of the middle class represent an important danger to the regime because they have the potential to mobilize the urban masses against the government. That the urban poor are susceptible to antigovernment appeals was demonstrated most forcefully in the Bandung and Jakarta riots of 1973 and 1974, and the drop, to less than 40 percent, in the *Golkar*'s vote in Jakarta in the 1977 elections.

Indeed, the elections of 1971 and 1977 showed that, despite the victories won by the government-sponsored *Golkar*, significantly large numbers of citizens were prepared to risk incurring the government's wrath by voting for other parties. In particular, the strong performance of the Muslim party in 1977 proved that politically, Islam was still a force to be reckoned with. In the long run, the success of the depoliticization drive will depend on the reaction of the urban and rural masses to the government's apparent inability to bring about an improvement in their condition. In rural areas, the better-off class of peasants has benefited from the "Green Revolution," improved irrigation and rural roads, and better marketing facilities. But the prospect for the majority of the peasantry is bleak—especially in Java, where at least two-thirds of rural families do not have access to enough land to meet their daily needs. The population of Java is expected to rise from 76 million in 1971 to 146 million in the year 2000; according to the calculations of the Minister for Research, Professor Sumitro, the population density throughout the island will then reach 1,105 per square kilometer—a density greater than that of any West European city today.[13] With the work force expanding by 1.4 million annually, land-

[13] Sumitro Djojohadikusumo, *Indonesia Dalam Perkembangan Dunia* [Indonesia in World Development] (Jakarta: Lembaga Penelitian, Pendidikan dan Penerangan Ekonomi dan Sosial 1976), 163.

lessness will obviously increase, while the government has little chance of providing sufficient employment in the non-agricultural sector. At the beginning of the 1970s, only 850,000, or 2.2 percent of the work force, were employed in medium- and large-scale manufacturing; the huge influx of foreign capital since 1967 had provided employment for only an additional 175,000 by 1976.[14] Even if the government's programs for family planning and transmigration from Java to the Outer Islands meet with more success than they have hitherto, their impact on the overall situation is likely to be marginal.

Increasingly severe poverty, of course, does not necessarily lead to outbreaks of political activity by the masses. Indeed, the opposite is often true as the poor are forced to devote all their attention to meeting their daily needs, and become more dependent on better-off patrons for work and for aid in emergencies. However, in rural Java there have been signs that the traditional bonds holding society together have weakened as agriculture has become more commercialized. The Green Revolution and the rehabilitation of the rural infrastructure have bene-fited primarily the better-off peasants. New crop varieties have led to the use of less labor-intensive harvesting methods; many landowners are finding it more profitable to hire outside contractors for harvesting rather than to continue traditional labor-sharing practices in the village.[15] In a society which in the past was not marked by an extremely wide gap between rich and poor, the prospect of growing class conflict cannot be dismissed as economic development gives rise to sharp polar-ization. Still, it remains an open question whether such disaffection can be effectively mobilized and channelled by political forces organ-ized against the government.

3. INCREASING REPRESSION

The trend toward greater regularization of bureaucratic procedures in the interest of promoting economic development implies increasing conflict within the military leadership and decreasing scope for the government to consolidate its position through the patrimonial dis-tribution of material benefits within the elite. At the same time, in-creased restiveness and resistance by the non-elite are likely to create conditions favorable for periodic challenges to the regime. Under these circumstances, the patrimonial purchasing of political support within

[14] Peter McCawley and Christopher Manning, "Survey of Recent Developments," *Bulletin of Indonesian Economic Studies*, xii (November 1976), 37.

[15] See William L. Collier, Gunawan Wiradi, and Soentoro, "Recent Changes in Rice Harvesting Methods," *Bulletin of Indonesian Economic Studies*, ix (July 1973), 36-45.

the elite may be increasingly accompanied by much more direct repression in order to maintain political stability.

During the period of Guided Democracy, the repressive apparatus of the state was used relatively sparingly as a means of maintaining the authority of the regime. President Sukarno, playing not only the role of charismatic leader but also that of patrimonial sultan, sought to keep rival segments of the elite in balance by allocating power, resources, and prestige among them. Although the President and the army each had their own internal security apparatus, neither was strong enough to take severely repressive measures against the other's supporters. In the early years of Guided Democracy, several dozen opponents of the President, together with participants in various regional rebellions, were detained; in the later phase, a communist and leftist campaign against right-wing politicians and officials resulted in a few arrests and dismissals and the banning of several organizations. Under the protection of the army, most critics of the President and the PKI not only escaped arrest, but kept their official positions. On the other hand, several moves by army officers against the PKI were foiled by the President, since his own power depended in large part on communist support.

The New Order government has been more repressive than its predecessor. The old balance of power was upset in the wake of the coup attempt of 1965, which left the army, as the dominant political force, free to use coercion against its enemies. Following the massacre, several hundred thousand supporters of the PKI were imprisoned, tens of thousands for more than a decade; a smaller number of non-communist dissidents was detained at various times for shorter periods. Nevertheless, while the persecution of PKI supporters was carried out in a thoroughgoing manner, the repression of non-communist opponents of the regime was often erratic, partly because many of them enjoyed the covert encouragement and protection of dissatisfied groups of army officers. The patrimonial struggle for power within the military elite thus gave relatively wide scope to civilian dissidents. Further, especially at the local level, the operations of military security bodies—like the administration of justice in patrimonial states—depended much on the personal disposition of individual officers. Some prisoners with influential family connections were released quickly; others sometimes got out of jail after the payment of bribes.

It seems likely, however, that the New Order government will turn more to direct repression—not only to deal with mass discontent, but also in response to increasing conflict within the elite. Whereas patrimonial-style rivalry over the spoils of office can usually be kept within bounds through the distribution of "consolation prizes" to defeated contenders, the emerging conflict within the Indonesian armed forces has ideological overtones involving contrasting perceptions of the goals of the government. As a consequence, compromise becomes more difficult to achieve, and direct repression will seem necessary in order to deal with the defeated factions. In particular, the growing influence of the academy-trained, professional generation of officers at the expense of the older, revolutionary generation seems likely to lead to new attitudes on the part of the military leadership. Apart from their orientation toward regularization and bureaucratization in the administration of the economy, the younger officers may be more disposed toward a disciplined and consistent approach to issues of security, including the repression of political dissent.

CONCLUSION

The short-term stability of both the Guided Democracy and the New Order regimes in Indonesia can be explained partly in terms of the persistence of strong patrimonial characteristics that existed alongside the nonpatrimonial features arising from modernization. In the case of the Guided Democracy system, sharp ideological and organizational divisions in the elite, together with substantial political mass-mobilization, eventually undermined the stability that had been created partly through patrimonial means. During the early period of the New Order, ideological and organizational conflict within the elite all but disappeared, and the masses were increasingly isolated from politics; but the dependence of the regime on economic development resulted in increasing emphasis on greater regularity, bureaucratization, and rationality, eventually bringing reform-minded officers into conflict with generals holding patrimonial-style fiefdoms. In the long run, the regime—whether still essentially patrimonial or already partially bureaucratic—may well be faced with large-scale outbreaks of mass opposition which would almost certainly become linked with intra-elite conflict. Such circumstances would force the government to give greater emphasis to straightforward repression and less to the patrimonial buying-off of dissidents in its efforts to maintain stability. It seems, therefore, that Indonesia's apparently patrimonial political structures have been built on nonpatrimonial foundations, with the result that patrimonial-style stability is not likely to endure.

WHY AFRICA'S WEAK STATES PERSIST:
The Empirical and the Juridical in Statehood

By ROBERT H. JACKSON and CARL G. ROSBERG*

INTRODUCTION

BLACK Africa's forty-odd states are among the weakest in the world. State institutions and organizations are less developed in the sub-Saharan region than almost anywhere else; political instability (as indicated by coups, plots, internal wars, and similar forms of violence) has been prevalent in the two-and-a-half decades during which the region gained independence from colonial rule. Most of the national governments exercise only tenuous control over the people, organizations, and activities within their territorial jurisdictions. In almost all of these countries, the populations are divided along ethnic lines; in some, there has been a threat of political disorder stemming from such divisions; in a few, disorder has deteriorated into civil warfare. Some governments have periodically ceased to control substantial segments of their country's territory and population. For example, there have been times when Angola, Chad, Ethiopia, Nigeria, Sudan, Uganda, and Zaire have ceased to be "states" in the empirical sense—that is, their central governments lost control of important areas in their jurisdiction during struggles with rival political organizations.

In spite of the weakness of their national governments, none of the Black African states have been destroyed or even significantly changed. No country has disintegrated into smaller jurisdictions or been absorbed into a larger one against the wishes of its legitimate government and as a result of violence or the threat of violence. No territories or people—or even a segment of them—have been taken over by another country. No African state has been divided as a result of internal warfare. In other words, the serious empirical weaknesses and vulnerabilities of some African states have not led to enforced jurisdictional change.

* We gratefully acknowledge the comments of Leonard Binder, Alan C. Cairns, David Gordon, Ernst B. Haas, F. John Ravenhill, and George von der Muhll on an earlier version of this paper, which was delivered at the 1981 Annual Meeting of the American Political Science Association in New York City.

Why not? How can the persistence of Africa's weak states be explained? In order to answer the latter question, we must enquire into contemporary African political history as well as into the empirical and juridical components of statehood. An investigation of this question has implications not only for our understanding of African states and perhaps other Third World states, but also of statehood and contemporary international society.

THE CONCEPT OF STATEHOOD

Many political scientists employ a concept of the state that is influenced by Max Weber's famous definition: a corporate group that has compulsory jurisdiction, exercises continuous organization, and claims a monopoly of force over a territory and its population, including "all action taking place in the area of its jurisdiction."[1] As Weber emphasized, his definition is one of "means" and not "ends," and the distinctive means for him are force.[2] A definition of the state primarily in terms of means rather than ends—particularly the means of force—emphasizes the empirical rather than the juridical, the *de facto* rather than the *de jure*, attributes of statehood. This emphasis is undoubtedly an important element in the appeal of Weber's sociology of the state to political scientists. To be sure, Weber does not overlook the juridical aspects of statehood. However, he does not explore what many students of international law consider to be the true character of territorial jurisdiction: the reality that such jurisdiction is an international legal condition rather than some kind of sociological given.

By Weber's definition, the basic test of the existence of a state is whether or not its national government can lay claim to a monopoly of force in the territory under its jurisdiction. If some external or internal organization can effectively challenge a national government and carve out an area of monopolistic control for itself, it thereby acquires the essential characteristic of statehood. According to Weber's *de facto* terms of statehood, two concurrent monopolies of force cannot exist over one territory and population. In situations where one of several rival groups—that is, claimant states—is unable to establish permanent control over a contested territory, Weber would maintain that it is more appropriate to speak of "statelessness."

By Weber's definition, a few of Africa's governments would not qualify as states—at least not all of the time—because they cannot

[1] Weber, *The Theory of Social and Economic Organization*, ed. by Talcott Parsons (New York: Free Press, 1964), 156.
[2] *Ibid.*, 155.

always effectively claim to have a monopoly of force throughout their territorial jurisdictions. In some countries, rivals to the national government have been able to establish an effective monopoly of force over significant territories and populations for extended periods—for example, Biafra in Nigeria and Katanga in the Congo (now Zaire). In other countries—such as Chad and Uganda—some of the territories have not been under the continuous control of one permanent political organization, and a condition of anarchy has existed. Furthermore, the governments of many Black African countries do not effectively control all of the important public activities within their jurisdictions; in some, government is perilously uncertain, so that important laws and regulations cannot be enforced with confidence and are not always complied with. If the persistence of a state were primarily the result of empirical statehood, some sub-Saharan African countries would clearly not qualify as states some of the time. Yet it is evident that all of them persist as members of the international society of states; it is also evident that none of the claimant governments that have on occasion exercised *de facto* control over large territories and populations within the jurisdictions of existing states have yet succeeded in creating new states in these areas.

Definitions that give priority to the juridical rather than the empirical attributes of statehood are employed by international legal scholars and institutionally oriented international theorists. One such definition—which shares a number of characteristics with Weber's, but gives them a different emphasis—is that of Ian Brownlie, a British legal scholar. Following the Montevideo Convention on Rights and Duties of States, Brownlie describes the state as a legal person, recognized by international law, with the following attributes: (a) a defined territory, (b) a permanent population, (c) an effective government, and (d) independence, or the right "to enter into relations with other states."[3]

If the assumption of juridical statehood as a sociological given is a shortcoming of Weber's definition, a limitation of Brownlie's is the tendency to postulate that the empirical attributes of statehood—i.e., a permanent population and effective government—are as definite as the juridical attributes; they are not. What does it mean to say that a state consists, *inter alia*, of a permanent population and an effective government? Our research reveals that within sub-Saharan African states, these empirical properties have been highly variable, while the juridical components have been constant. Kenya's population has been more

[3] Brownlie, *Principles of Public International Law*, 3d ed. (Oxford: Clarendon Press, 1979), 73-76.

"permanent" and its goverment more "effective" than Uganda's; yet both states have survived as sovereign jurisdictions. Moreover, an exclusively legal approach cannot adequately deal with the empirical properties of statehood: "Once a state has been established, extensive civil strife or the breakdown of order through foreign invasion or natural disasters are not considered to affect personality."[4] In the formulation of concepts, empirical properties can be determined only by investigation, not by definition.[5] Although Brownlie recognizes the need to incorporate empirical criteria into a "working legal definition of statehood,"[6] he acknowledges (as do other scholars) that there is considerable difficulty in employing these criteria without specifying them concretely. Nonetheless, his definition enables us to undertake an analysis of the empirical as well as the juridical aspects of statehood—that is, a sociological-legal analysis.

Political scientists do not need to be convinced of the limitations of an exclusively legalistic approach to the state, which is usually summed up as "legal-formalism": an undue emphasis on abstract rules, leading to the neglect of concrete behavior and the social conditions that support or undermine legal rules.[7] What is more difficult is to convince a generation of political scientists whose theories and models were formulated in reaction to legal, institutional, and philosophical studies of the state, of the limitations of an exclusively sociological conception of statehood. However, if one assumes that the state is essentially an empirical phenomenon—as was suggested not only by Weber but also by David Easton in a systems approach that has been very influential—one cannot explain why some states manage to persist when important empirical conditions of statehood are absent, or are present only in a very qualified manner.[8] In sum, one cannot explain the persistence of some "states" by using a concept of the state that does not give sufficient attention to the juridical properties of statehood.

The Empirical State in Black Africa

Weber's and Brownlie's definitons of statehood provide a useful point of departure for examining empirical and juridical statehood in con-

[4] *Ibid.*, 75.

[5] See Giovanni Sartori, "Guidelines for Concept Analysis," in Sartori, ed., *Social Science Concepts: A Systematic Analysis* (forthcoming).

[6] Brownlie (fn. 3), 75.

[7] See Harry Eckstein's brilliant critique, "On the 'Science' of the State," in "The State," *Daedalus*, Vol. 108 (Fall 1979), 1-20.

[8] Easton avoids the concept of the "state" in favor of that of the "political system"; see *The Political System: An Inquiry into the State of Political Science* (New York: Knopf, 1953), 90-124.

temporary Black Africa. (Juridical statehood is discussed in the following section.) We shall begin with Brownlie's definition, which is more explicit and current. As we noted above, Brownlie specifies two empirical attributes of the state: "a permanent population [which] is intended to be used in association with that of territory, and connotes a stable community," and an "effective government, with centralized administrative and legislative organs."[9]

Before we can apply Brownlie's empirical attributes to our analysis, we must clarify them. First, what exactly do we understand by "a stable community" and its crucial empirical component, "a permanent population"? In attempting to define these terms in the context of contemporary Africa, we find that political sociology may be of considerably more help than law. In political sociology, societies are seen as integrated or disunited, culturally homogeneous or fragmented—resting on common norms and values or not. If we take "a stable community" to signify an integrated political community resting on a common culture, we must conclude that few contemporary Black African states can be said to possess this attribute. The populations of many Black African countries are divided internally among several—and often many—distinctive ethnic entities by differences of language, religion, race, region of residence, and so forth. Moreover, these ethnic cleavages can reinforce each other, thus aggravating the differences. In Sudan, for example, the racial division between Arabs and Africans is reinforced by geography, religion, and language; it has resulted in bitter conflicts over the control of the state. Furthermore, many ethnic entities are divided by international boundaries, with members residing in two or more countries; however, the social and political boundaries between these ethnic entities may well be more significant in terms of public attitudes and behavior than are the boundaries between the countries. As a result, political tensions and conflicts arising from ethnic divisions can seriously affect national political stability and the capacity of governments to control their territories.

From our discussion, it appears that few African states can qualify as stable communities. Where ethnic divisions have been politicized, the result has been serious civil conflict. Thus, ethnic divisions have been a major factor contributing to extreme disorder or civil war in the following countries: Sudan (1956-1972); Rwanda (1959-1964); Zaire (1960-1965; 1977-1978); Ethiopia (1962-1982); Zanzibar (1964); Burundi (1966-1972); Chad (1966-1982); Uganda (1966; 1978-1982); Nigeria (1967-1970); and Angola (1975-1982). In other countries, ethnic divisions have

[9] Brownlie (fn. 3), 75.

been sufficiently threatening to prompt governments to control political participation severely out of fear that they would otherwise jeopardize their command of the state.[10] Recent African politics have been characterized by the opposition of most African governments to competitive party systems, their preference for political monopoly generally, their lack of sympathy for federalism, and their attack on political liberties (among other things). All of these can be explained at least in part by the governments' fear of politicized ethnicity. Efforts by African governments to emphasize the "nation" and "nationalism" at the expense of the "ethnos"—efforts that are evident elsewhere in the Third World as well—indicate their concern about the instability of their political communities and the threat posed by that instability not only to individual governments, but to statehood itself.[11]

Second, by "an effective government" Brownlie means exactly what Weber means by "compulsory jurisdiction": centralized administrative and legislative organs.[12] Such a definition is somewhat Eurocentric because it identifies governing not only with administering, but also with legislating. In contemporary Africa, governments do not necessarily govern by legislation; personal rulers often operate in an arbitrary and autocratic manner by means of commands, edicts, decrees, and so forth.[13] To make this empirical attribute more universal, let us redefine it as a centralized government with the capacity to exercise control over a state's territory and the people residing in it. By "exercise control" we mean the ability to pronounce, implement, and enforce commands, laws, policies, and regulations.

The capacity to exercise control raises the question of means. Analytically, the means of government can be considered in terms of the domestic authority or right to govern (legitimacy) on the one hand, and the power or ability to govern on the other. In Michael Oakeshott's terms, the modern state consists, among other things, of both an "office of authority" and "an apparatus of power"; the two are analytically different and should not be confused.[14] For example, governmental

[10] See Nelson Kasfir, *The Shrinking Political Arena: Participation and Ethnicity in African Politics, with a Case Study of Uganda* (Berkeley, Los Angeles, London: University of California Press, 1976).

[11] See Clifford Geertz, "The Judging of Nations: Some Comments on the Assessment of Regimes in the New States," *European Journal of Sociology*, XVIII (No. 2, 1977), 249-52.

[12] Brownlie (fn. 3), 75; Weber (fn. 1), 156.

[13] See Robert H. Jackson and Carl G. Rosberg, *Personal Rule in Black Africa: Prince, Autocrat, Prophet, Tyrant* (Berkeley, Los Angeles, London: University of California Press, 1982).

[14] See Michael Oakeshott, "The Vocabulary of a Modern European State," *Political Studies*, XXIII (June and September, 1977), 319-41, 409-14.

administration usually involves the (delegated) authority to issue regulations *and* the power to enforce them. A government may possess legitimacy, but have little in the way of an effective apparatus of power; or it may have an imposing power apparatus, but little legitimacy in the eyes of its citizens. Other combinations are also possible.[15]

In our judgment, the capacity of Africa's governments to exercise control hinges upon three factors: domestic authority, the apparatus of power, and economic circumstances. First, political authority in Africa (and in other parts of the Third World as well) tends to be personal rather than institutional. Geertz has commented:

> Fifteen years ago, scholarly writings on the New States... were full of discussions of parties, parliaments, and elections. A great deal seemed to turn on whether these institutions were viable in the Third World and what adjustments in them... might prove necessary to make them so. Today, nothing in those writings seems more *passé*, relic of a different time.[16]

Constitutional and institutional offices that are independent of the personal authority of rulers have not taken root in most Black African countries. Instead, the state and state offices are dominated by ambitious individuals, both civilian and military. Post-independence rulers of Africa and Asia, Geertz writes, "are autocrats, and it is as autocrats, and not as preludes to liberalism (or, for that matter, to totalitarianism), that they, and the governments they dominate, must be judged and understood."[17] Wherever African governments have exercised substantial control, strong personal rulers have been firmly in the saddle. This has been the case in regimes that are primarily autocratic—such as Félix Houphouët-Boigny's Ivory Coast, H. Kamazu Banda's Malawi, Omar Bongo's Gabon, Ahmadou Ahidjo's Cameroon, and Gnassingbé Eyadéma's Togo. It has also been the case where regimes are primarily oligarchic—such as Léopold Sédar Senghor's Senegal, Jomo Kenyatta's Kenya, and Gaafar Mohamed Numeiri's Sudan—and where they are primarily ideological—such as Julius Nyerere's Tanzania and Sékou Touré's Guinea (which exhibits features of despotism as well). Where African governments have not exercised control, it has often been because no personal leader has taken firm command; alternatively, it has been as a result of excessively arbitrary and abusive personal rule, as

[15] The legitimacy of a government in the eyes of its citizens must be distinguished from its legitimacy in the eyes of other states; it is international legitimacy that is significant in the juridical attribute of statehood. A government may be legitimate internationally but illegitimate domestically, or *vice versa*. An instance of the former is Uganda during the last years of Idi Amin's regime; of the latter, the Soviet Union in its early years.

[16] Geertz (fn. 11), 252.   [17] *Ibid.*, 253.

was the case in Uganda under Idi Amin. In the most unstable African regimes, the military has repeatedly intervened in politics—as in Benin from 1960 to 1972 and in Chad from 1975 to 1982.

Related to the problem of institutional weakness in African states is the disaffection of important elites from the government. The frequency of military coups is perhaps the best indication of elite alienation and disloyalty. Between 1958 and the summer of 1981, more than 41 successful coups had taken place in 22 countries of Black Africa; in addition, there had been many unsuccessful ones.[18] Gutteridge has noted that, "by 1966, military intervention in politics in Africa had become endemic. . . . Even the smallest armies [had] carried out successful coups."[19] There is little doubt that the internal opponent most feared by African rulers—both military and civilian—is the military. Indeed, military rulers have themselves been the victims of military coups—for instance, Yakubu Gowon of Nigeria, and Ignatius Kutu Acheampong and Frederick Akuffo of Ghana in the 1970s. It should be noted that, although Africa's military formations are called "armies" and their members wear uniforms and display other symbols of state authority, they cannot be assumed to be loyal to the government. A military career is sometimes a promising avenue for political advancement; soldiers in Black Africa have become not only government officials, but also rulers of their countries.

Second, the apparatus of power in African governments—the agents and agencies that implement and enforce government laws, edicts, decrees, orders, and the like—can in general be considered "underdeveloped" in regard both to their stock of resources and to the deployment of these resources. In proportion to their territories and populations, African governments typically have a smaller stock of finances, personnel, and materiel than Asian or Western governments, and their staffs are less experienced and reliable. As a result, the concept of governmental administration as a policy instrument bears less relation to reality. Governmental incapacity is exacerbated by overly ambitious plans and policies that are prepared on the assumption that underdevelopment is a problem of economy and society, but not of government. In fact, it

[18] There is a wealth of literature on military intervention in Africa. Two outstanding accounts are Samuel Decalo, *Coups and Army Rule in Africa: Studies in Military Style* (New Haven: Yale University Press, 1976), and Claude E. Welch, Jr., ed., *Soldier and State in Africa: A Comparative Analysis of Military Intervention and Political Change* (Evanston, Ill.: Northwestern University Press, 1970). Both have excellent bibliographies.

[19] William Gutteridge, "Introduction," in Richard Booth, "The Armed Forces of African States, 1970," *Adelphi Papers*, No. 67 (London: International Institute for Strategic Studies, 1970), 4.

is also African governments that are underdeveloped, and in most countries they are very far from being an instrument of development.[20] The modern "administrative state" image of government is of questionable applicability in many parts of the world, but Black African governments are even less likely than others to be rational agencies.

Undoubtedly the biggest problem of both civilian and military administrations in Africa is the questionable reliability of staffs. In a famous phrase, Gunnar Myrdal characterized the governments of South Asia as "soft states."[21] The term can be applied equally to many governments in Black Africa which must operate amidst corruption and disorder. The problem of inefficient staff has rarely been as candidly exposed as in a 1977 report by Julius Nyerere on socialist progress in Tanzania. He noted that ministries were overspending in disregard of severe budgetary restraints; the Rural Development Bank was issuing loans that were not being repaid; state enterprises were operating far below capacity—sometimes at less than 50 percent; "management" was preoccupied with privilege and displayed little enterprise; and "workers" were slack, incompetent, and undisciplined.[22]

Of course, there is considerable variation in the administrative capacity of African governments, and Tanzania is by no means the country most seriously affected by an inefficient state apparatus. While the comparative effectiveness of the Ivory Coast, Kenya (at least under Kenyatta), and Malawi is striking, Benin, Congo-Brazzaville, Mali, Togo, and Upper Volta are infamous for their swollen bureaucracies and administrative lethargy. Once relatively efficient Ghana and Uganda are examples of marked deterioration, the origins of which are perhaps more political than economic and relate to a failure to establish an effective and responsible ruling class. One of the worst cases of administrative decay is Zaire, where the state's resources have been plundered and regulations abused by government officials at all levels. President Mobutu Sese Seko has identified abuses such as the case of army officers who divert for "their own personal profit the supplies intended for

[20] Jon R. Moris, "The Transferability of Western Management Concepts and Programs, An East African Perspective," in Lawrence D. Stifel, James S. Coleman, and Joseph E. Black, eds., *Education and Training for Public Sector Management in Developing Countries* (Special Report from the Rockefeller Foundation, March 1977), 73-83. For Ghana, see Robert M. Price, *Society and Bureaucracy in Contemporary Ghana* (Berkeley and Los Angeles: University of California Press, 1975); for Kenya, Goran Hyden, Robert Jackson, and John Okumu, eds., *Development Administration: The Kenya Experience* (Nairobi: Oxford University Press, 1970).

[21] Myrdal, *Asian Drama: An Inquiry into the Poverty of Nations* (New York: Twentieth Century Fund, 1968).

[22] Nyerere, *The Arusha Declaration Ten Years After* (Dar es Salaam: Government Printer, 1977), esp. chap. 3: "Our Mistakes and Failures," 27-48.

frontline soldiers"; the refusal of rural development officials to leave their air-conditioned offices in Kinshasa; and the "misuse of judicial machinery for revenging private disputes, . . . selective justice depending upon one's status and wealth."[23] So extreme is the corruption that observers have had to invent new phrases to describe it; Zaire has been referred to as "an extortionist culture" in which corruption is a "structural fact" and bribery assumes the form of "economic mugging."[24] It has been estimated that as much as 60 percent of the annual national budget is misappropriated by the governing elite.

As we have noted, the inefficiency of African governments extends to the military as well as the civilian organs of the state. As in the case of civilian maladministration, military ineffectiveness stems from sociopolitical as well as technical-material factors; the size and firepower of the armed forces can also play a role. Typically, military forces in African countries are small in relation to the size or population of a state; however, they are considerably larger than the colonial armies they replaced. Over the past two decades, the size of African armies has increased (primarily for purposes of internal security), and their equipment has been upgraded. As early as 1970, Gutteridge commented that "there is no doubting a general upward trend in the numbers of men under arms in regular forces";[25] there have been no significant developments since 1970 to suggest any change in what appears to be military "growth without development."

In practice, most African armies are less like military organizations and more like political establishments: they are infected by corruption, factionalism, and patterns of authority based not only on rank, role, or function, but also on personal and ethnic loyalties. The ability of African armies to deal with internal conflicts is dubious. Despite overwhelming superiority in men and equipment, the Nigerian Federal Army had great difficulty in defeating the forces of Biafra in the late 1960s; according to Gutteridge, "there were times when the Federal Army seemed to have lost the will to win."[26] Moreover, the state's apparatus of power may be not only aided and supported by the solicited intervention of a foreign power in the form of troops, military equipment, advisers, and so forth, but such intervention can be essential to the survival of a regime. In a number of French-speaking countries,

---

[23] Independence Day Speech of President Mobutu Sese Seko, July 1, 1977, typescript, translated from the French by James S. Coleman.

[24] See *West Africa*, No. 3255 (December 3, 1979), 2224; and Ghislain C. Kabwit, "Zaire: The Roots of the Continuing Crisis," *Journal of Modern African Studies*, XVII (No. 3, 1979), 397-98.

[25] Gutteridge (fn. 19), 1.   [26] *Ibid.*, 3.

a French military presence has enhanced the power of the African government; in Angola and Ethiopia, Cuban soldiers and Soviet arms and advisers have made a decisive difference to the power and survival of incumbent African regimes in their conflicts with both internal and external powers. The lethargy of African armies has sometimes been acutely embarrassing. When Zaire's copper-rich Shaba Province (formerly Katanga) was invaded by Katangan forces from neighboring Angola in 1977 and again in 1978, President Mobutu's army proved incapable of stopping them; Mobutu had to call upon friendly powers (Morocco, Belgium, France, and the United States) to save his regime.

Third, governmental incapacity in Black Africa is affected by economic circumstances, which are exacerbated by the small size of the skilled work force. African economies are among the poorest and weakest in the world: in 1978, 22 of them had a per capita GNP below $250; throughout the 1970s, the Black African countries had the lowest worldwide rates of growth. Of the world's poorest countries—those with per capita incomes below $330—the 28 that were African had the lowest projected growth rates for the 1980s. In many of these countries, absolute poverty is increasing as birthrates continue to exceed economic growth rates.[27]

Many African countries are highly dependent on a few primary exports for their foreign exchange earnings. They are therefore vulnerable to uncontrollable fluctuations in world commodity prices and, in the case of agricultural commodites, unpredictable changes in weather conditions and harvest returns. The countries without petroleum resources have had to face dramatically increased prices for oil imports, resulting in very severe balance-of-payments problems. In some countries, more than 50 percent of scarce foreign exchange had to be used to pay for imported oil. Moreover, 27 countries had a shortfall in their production of food crops—principally maize—in 1980; they were therefore forced to import food, which resulted in a further drain of scarce foreign exchange. (South Africa became an important supplier of food to Angola, Kenya, Malawi, Mozambique, Zaire, and Zambia, among others). Lacking industrial and manufacturing sectors of any significance and being highly dependent upon imports, most African countries are caught between the certainty of their demand for foreign goods and the uncertainty of their ability to earn the foreign exchange to pay for them. In many (if not most) of these countries, inflated and consumption-oriented government administrations—whose members

[27] *Africa Contemporary Record*, 1979-80, p. C 109.

enjoy a standard of living far in excess of the national average—weigh down the already overburdened and sluggish economies; in many, the economy is simply exploited to support the political class. The hope that intelligent government planning might effect a substantial economic transformation has long since faded.

It is evident that the term "empirical state" can only be used selectively to describe many states in Black Africa today. With some notable exceptions—for example, Kenya and the Ivory Coast—it seems accurate to characterize Africa's states as empirically weak or underdeveloped. If we adopted a narrow empirical criterion of statehood—such as Weber's monopoly of force—we would have to conclude that some African countries were not states, and that statehood in others has periodically been in doubt. In 1981, the governments of Angola, Chad, Ethiopia, and Uganda could not claim a monopoly of force within their jurisdictions. Furthermore, these countries and some others—for example, Nigeria, Sudan, and Zaire—have exhibited *de facto* statelessness in the past, and there are reasons to believe that they might do so again. Yet it is unlikely that any of their jurisdictions will be altered without the consent of their governments. Jurisdictional change by consent has happened, however. In 1981, The Gambia was forced to call upon neighboring Senegal for troops to put down an armed rebellion by a substantial segment of its own field force under the leadership of leftist militants. The episode undermined the security of the Gambian government to such an extent that it consented to a form of association with Senegal which resulted in a new confederation: Senegambia.

THE JURIDICAL STATE IN BLACK AFRICA

Before we investigate the significance of the juridical state in Black Africa, let us emphasize that "juridical statehood" is not only a normative but essentially an international attribute. The juridical state is both a creature and a component of the international society of states, and its properties can only be defined in international terms. At this point, it is important to clarify what is meant by "international society."[28] It is a society composed solely of states and the international organizations formed by states; it excludes not only individuals and private groups, but also political organizations that are not states or are

[28] The concept of "international society" is explored in Martin Wight, *Power Politics*, ed. by Hedley Bull and Carsten Holbraad (London: Royal Institute of International Affairs, 1978), 105-12. Also see Hedley Bull, *The Anarchical Society: A Study of Order in World Politics* (London: Macmillan, 1977), 24-52; and Alan James, "International Society," *British Journal of International Studies*, IV (July 1978), 91-106.

not composed of states. The doctrine of "states' rights"—that is, sovereignty—is the central principle of international society. It often comes into conflict with the doctrine of international human rights, but international society does not promote the welfare of individuals and private groups within a country or transnational groups among countries; nor does it protect individuals or private groups from their governments.[29] Rather, international society provides legal protection for member states from any powers, internal and external, that seek to intervene in, invade, encroach upon, or otherwise assault their sovereignty.[30] A secondary but increasingly important goal—one that is linked to the emergence of Third World states—is to promote the welfare and development of member states.

According to Brownlie, the juridical attributes of statehood are "territory" and "independence" (as recognized by the international community). In international law, a demarcated territory is the equivalent of the "property" of a government—national real estate, including offshore waters and airspace; international boundaries are the mutually acknowledged but entirely artificial lines where one government's property rights end and another's begin. Determinate and recognized frontiers are therefore a basic institution of the state system and an essential legal attribute of any state. A government recognized as having political independence is legally the equal of other independent governments, and is not only the highest authority within its territorial jurisdiction but is under no higher authority.[31] It has the right to enter into relations with other states and to belong to the international society of states.

A political system may possess some or all of the empirical qualifications of statehood, but without the juridical attributes of territory and independence it is not a state. Furthermore, these attributes—which constitute territorial jurisdiction—serve as a test of a government's claim to be a state; there is no empirical test. For example, the Transkei, Bophuthatswana, Venda, and Ciskei—black "homelands" in South Af-

[29] In considering the issue of human rights in Africa, the O.A.U.'s Assembly of Heads of States stressed the equal importance of "peoples' rights," and recently recommended that an "African Charter on Human and Peoples' Rights" be drafted. Peoples' rights are the rights of a sovereign people and can only be claimed and exercised by state governments. See *Africa Contemporary Record*, 1979-80, p. C 21.

[30] Bull argues that the primary historical goal of international society has been to preserve the society of states itself; but it is difficult to see how this can be accomplished in the long run without first guaranteeing the sovereignty of member states. See *The Anarchical Society* (fn. 28), 17.

[31] This is essentially the Austinian concept of "sovereignty." See John Austin, *The Province of Jurisprudence Determined*, ed. by H.L.A. Hart (London: Weidenfeld and Nicolson, 1954).

rica—are as much empirical states as some other territories in Africa, but they lack statehood because they are not recognized by any state except South Africa and enjoy none of the rights of membership in international society. Since they are creatures wholly of South Africa's apartheid regime, their political survival is probably tied to the survival of apartheid. On the other hand, the former British territory of Lesotho, which is also an enclave within South Africa, but was never ruled by Pretoria and has gained its independence from Britain, is a recognized state and exercises full rights of membership in international society, which are not likely to be threatened in this way precisely because it is independent.

The juridical state in Black Africa is a novel and arbitrary political unit; the territorial boundaries, legal identities, and often even the names of states are contrivances of colonial rule. Only rarely did a colonial territory reflect the shape and identity of a preexisting African sociopolitical boundary, as in the cases of the British Protectorate of Zanzibar (formerly a sultanate) and the High Commission Territories of Swaziland and Basutoland (Lesotho), which had been African kingdoms. (Under British rule, the *internal* administrative boundaries of a colony were often drawn to conform with indigenous borders where these could be determined.) During the European colonization of Africa in the late 19th century, international society was conceived as a "European association, to which non-European states could be admitted only if and when they met a standard of civilization laid down by the Europeans."[32] With the exceptions of Ethiopia and Liberia, which escaped colonialism and were treated as states, Black African political systems did not qualify as states, but were regarded as the objects of a justified colonialism.

At independence (beginning in the late 1950s), there were therefore very few traditional African states to whom sovereignty could revert.[33] Consequently, there was little choice but to establish independence in terms of the colonial entities;[34] in most cases, a colony simply became a state with its territorial frontiers unchanged. Most attempts to create larger political units—usually conceived as federations—failed, as hap-

[32] Bull (fn. 28), 34.

[33] For an argument that at least in some cases "independence" was a "reversion" to sovereignty, see Charles H. Alexandrowicz, "New and Original States: The Issue of Reversion to Sovereignty," *International Affairs*, XLVII (July 1969), 465-80. For an opposing view, see Martin Wight, *Systems of States*, ed. by Hedley Bull (Leicester: Leicester University Press, 1977), 16-28.

[34] French West Africa rather than its constituent units—Senegal, Mali, Upper Volta, Ivory Coast, etc.—could have been one state had Africans been able to agree to it; Nigeria could have been more than one.

pened in the cases of the Mali Federation and the Central African Federation.[35] Kwame Nkrumah's vision of a United States of Africa received virtually no support from his counterparts in the newly independent states. Instead, the Organization of African Unity (O.A.U.), formed in May 1963, fully acknowledged and legitimated the colonial frontiers and the principle of state sovereignty within them. As President Modibo Keita of Mali put it: although the colonial system divided Africa, "it permitted nations to be born. . . . African unity . . . requires full respect for the frontiers we have inherited from the colonial system."[36]

It is a paradox of African independence that it awakened both national and ethnic political awareness. In almost every Black African country there are ethnic groups that desire to redraw international boundaries in order to form independent states. Self-determination, which accelerated after World War I and reached its peak in the years after World War II with the independence of numerous colonies, came to a halt in Black Africa at the inherited (colonial) frontiers. The movement, which is still alive sociologically among millions of Africans and within many ethnic communities, is unlikely to make further political-legal progress. The opposition of existing African states and of international society has reinforced the legitimacy of the inherited frontiers and undermined that of the traditional cultural borders. One of the exceptions to ethnic Balkanization has been Somali irredentism in Ethiopia and Kenya, which has sought the creation of a greater Somalia defined by cultural rather than colonial boundaries. But so far, Somali irrendentism—as well as Biafran nationalism, Katangan separatism, and Eritrean secessionism—has failed to win international legitimacy. When the claims of Somali cultural nationalists were debated at the founding meeting of the O.A.U. in 1963, the argument advanced by the Kenyan delegation represented the view of the vast majority of African governments: "If they [the Somalis] do not want to live with us in Kenya, they are perfectly free to leave us and our territory. . . . This is the only way they can legally exercise their right of self-determination."[37] When the Kingdom of Buganda—an administrative region within the colony

[35] At the time of independence in 1960, British-governed Somaliland joined the Italian-administered trust territory to form the Somali Democratic Republic. In October 1961, the Federal Republic of Cameroon came into being, composed of East Cameroon (formerly a French Trust Territory) and West Cameroon (part of a former British Trust Territory). Independent Tanganyika joined with Zanzibar to form the United Republic of Tanzania in April 1964.

[36] Quoted in Robert C. Good, "Changing Patterns of African International Relations," *American Political Science Review*, Vol. 58 (September 1964), 632.

[37] Quoted in Ali A. Mazrui, *Towards a Pax Africana: A Study of Ideology and Ambition* (Chicago and London: University of Chicago Press, 1967), 12.

of Uganda and a traditional African state—declared itself independent in 1960 after realizing that the British authorities were going to give independence to Uganda, no other state recognized the declaration. Buganda failed to achieve juridical statehood; it remained a region— albeit a troublesome one—of the new Ugandan state, which became independent in 1962.

African decolonization—like decolonization elsewhere—demonstrated that it is impossible to have rational empirical qualifications for statehood. Many colonies became states although the viability of their economic bases and their developmental potentiality were questionable. Some of the new states had minuscule populations and/or territories: Cape Verde, the Comoros Islands, Djibouti, Equatorial Guinea, Gabon, The Gambia, Sao Tome and Principe, the Seychelles, and Swaziland. Empirically these entities are really microstates, but juridically they are full-fledged states.[38] Their independence reveals the assumption of the contemporary international community that even countries of very questionable viability and capacities can be preserved by a benevolent international society. In other words, international society has become a global "democracy" based on the principle of legal equality of members. Even the most profound socioeconomic inadequacies of some countries are not considered to be a barrier to their membership: all former colonies and dependencies have the right to belong if they wish. The existence of a large number of weak states poses one of the foremost international problems of our time: their protection and preservation, not to mention development. The survival of states is not a new issue; indeed, it is the historical problem of international relations, which has served to define traditional international theory as "the theory of survival."[39] What is new is the enlarged scope, added dimensions, and greater complexity and delicacy of the problem in contemporary international society.

INTERNATIONAL SOCIETY AND THE AFRICAN STATE

The juridical attributes of statehood can only be conferred upon governments by the international community. The Transkei is not a state because South Africa alone does not have the right to confer statehood, whereas Lesotho is a state because the international com-

[38] According to the United Nations, in 1978 there were 13 African countries (8 on the continent and 5 island countries) with a population of less than one million. Nine of these had populations of 600,000 or fewer. See *Africa Contemporary Record*, 1979-80, p. C 107.

[39] Martin Wight, "Why is there no International Theory?" in Herbert Butterfield and Martin Wight, eds., *Diplomatic Investigations* (London: George Allen & Unwin, 1966), 33.

munity accepted—indeed encouraged—British decolonization in Africa. Even though a state's jurisdictions and boundaries often appear to be "natural" phenomena and sometimes correspond with natural land forms, they are political artifacts upheld by the international community. Among other things, the international society of states was formed to support the doctrine of states' or sovereigns' rights as a cornerstone of international order. Basically, it involves mutual rights and obligations—for example, the right of a country to exist and not to have its jurisdiction violated, and its duty not to violate the rights of others.

In this section we offer an explanation as to why the existing pattern of juridical statehood has been maintained in Africa. The most important conditions that have contributed to this phenomenon appear to be: the ideology of Pan-Africanism; the vulnerability of all states in the region and the insecurity of statesmen; the support of the larger international society, including particularly its institutions and associations; and the reluctance, to date, of non-African powers to intervene in the affairs of African states without having been invited to do so by their governments. We will briefly discuss each of these conditions.

First, unlike any other continent except Australia, "Africa" is a political idea as well as a geographical fact with a distinctive ideology: African nationalism. This ideology emerged largely as a result of the universal African experience of colonial domination. European colonialism and its practices fostered the reactive ideology of African nationalism, which was directed at political independence and the freedom of the continent from European rule. Colonialism was the experience of Africans not only as individuals or as members of subordinated communities, or even as members of particular colonies; it was also their experience as Africans—a common political experience. As long as any country on the continent remains dominated by non-Africans, Pan-Africanism means the liberation of the continent in the name of African "freedom." Almost without exception, the Pan-Africanists came to realize that freedom could in practice only be achieved within the existing framework of the colonial territories that the Europeans had established. The European colonies were the only political vehicles that could give expression to African nationalism; as a consequence, these artificial jurisdictions acquired a vital legitimacy in the eyes of most knowledgeable Africans. Politicians in particular have maintained that, whatever the size, shape, population, and resources of these jurisdictions, they have a right to exist because they are the embodiment of the African political revolution. The only practical way of realizing the goal of African freedom was through the independence of the colonial territories. By this process, the successor states were made legitimate—not one, or several, or many individually, but all equally. Moreover, it is consistent with the ideology of Pan-Africanism that until Namibia—and perhaps even South Africa—are free, "Africa" is not yet free.

Therefore, however arbitrary and alien in origin the inherited state jurisdictions might have been—and however far removed from traditional African values—they have been endowed with legitimacy. The ideology of Pan-Africanism that has gained historical expression in this way is a fundamental bulwark within Africa against the violation of existing, inherited state jurisdictions. At the same time, Pan-Africanism disposed the new African statesmen to associate in a common continental body whose rules would legitimize existing jurisdictions and specify any international actions that would be considered illegitimate. As a result, the principles of the O.A.U., as set down in Article III of its Charter, affirm: the sovereign equality of member states; non-interference; respect for sovereignty; peaceful settlement of disputes; and the illegitimacy of subversion.[40] In sum, the ideology of Pan-Africanism has been expressed in the acceptance of the inherited colonial jurisdictions and the international legitimacy of all of the existing African states.[41]

Second, there is a common interest in the support of international rules and institutions and state jurisdictions in the African region that derives from the common vulnerability of states and the insecurity of statesmen. This approach would appear to be a variant of Hobbes's explanation of why rational individuals would prefer subordination to Leviathan as against freedom in the state of nature: general insecurity. "Since many are vulnerable to external incitement for secession it was obvious to most of the O.A.U. Members that a reciprocal respect for boundaries, and abstention from demands for their immediate revision, would be to their general advantage."[42] In order to survive, weak African governments had to be assured of the recognition and respect for their sovereignty by neighboring states, as well as any other states in a position to undermine their authority and control. Regional vulnerability and the general apprehension of externally promoted interference and subversion have disposed African governments to collaborate in maintaining their jurisdictions.

From a balance-of-power perspective, it might be objected that, in

[40] Zdenek Cervenka, *The Organization of African Unity and its Charter* (New York and Washington: Praeger, 1969), 232-33.
[41] Martin Wight defined "international legitimacy" as "the *collective* judgement of international society about rightful membership in the family of nations." See his *Systems of States* (fn. 33), 153 (emphasis added).
[42] Cervenka (fn. 40), 93.

actual fact, the roughly equal powerlessness of African governments is what upholds state jurisdictions by making violation very difficult and therefore unlikely. But military weakness did not prevent the Tanzanian army from invading Uganda and overthrowing Amin's tyranny, and it did not prevent the Katangan rebels from invading Shaba province in Zaire on two separate occasions. To the contrary, the civil and military weakness of most African governments disposes them to fear international subversion by neighboring states and others who may support their internal enemies. Consequently, it is weakness that induces all of them to support the rules and practices of the O.A.U. which are intended to uphold existing state jurisdictions. African international society—specifically the O.A.U.—is intended to provide international political goods that guarantee the survival, security, identity, and integrity of African states, which the majority of African states cannot provide individually.

The O.A.U. is less an "organization" with its own agents, agencies, and resources than it is an "association" with its own rules: a club of statesmen who are obligated to subscribe to a small number of rules and practices of regional conduct, and to which every state except South Africa belongs. It is evident from the rules of Article III that the O.A.U. is very much a traditional association of states. But the O.A.U.'s effectiveness, like that of other successful international associations, probably owes less to its formal procedures than to its internal political processes. According to a leading student of the association, its main source of strength is the way in which it fosters the peaceful settlement of disputes.[43] Conflict resolution has often taken place outside the Commission of Mediation, Conciliation, and Arbitration—which was specifically set up for the purpose. Most statesmen involved in disputes have resorted to mediation or conciliation by the O.A.U. Chairman, who is elected annually by the members, or by another respected member who is not involved in the disputes. The success of the O.A.U. is indicated by the fact that the majority of the numerous disputes among its members have been contained through its internal political process. Its only significant failures to date have been the wars in the Horn of Africa prompted by Somalia's attempts to claim border territories in Ethiopia and Kenya (challenging the inherited boundaries as well as a fundamental principle of the O.A.U.) and the Uganda-Tanzania war of 1978-1979, which resulted in the overthrow of Idi Amin's tyranny.[44]

[43] Zdenek Cervenka, *The Unfinished Quest for Unity: Africa and the OAU* (New York: Africana Publishing Co., 1977), 65.

[44] As of March 1982, it was unclear whether the war between Morocco and the Polisario over the former Spanish Sahara could be considered a failure for the O.A.U., since it was

Third, the African states all became independent at a time when international society was highly organized and integrated. Its elaborate framework of international associations of both a worldwide and a regional or functional kind includes bodies that are important for African states: the United Nations (and its numerous specialized agencies that deal in whole or in part with Africa), the Commonwealth, Francophonie, the Lomé Convention of the European Economic Community (EEC), and so forth. Membership in such associations is an acknowledgement of the existence of the member states and of their international rights and duties, including the right not to be interfered with. Their membership in international society acknowledges the legitimacy and supports the independence of African states. Indeed, the states' rights that derive from membership in the United Nations and other bodies are commonly used by African governments—sometimes with considerable skill and success—to secure both material and nonmaterial benefits from the international system.

International society is a conservative order. Any international actor that seeks to interfere by force or any other illegitimate means in the affairs of a member state is almost certain to be confronted by a condemnation of its actions by most other states. The only interventions that are acceptable under present international rules and practices are those to which the legitimate government of the target country has consented. Imposed or unsolicited interference is difficult to justify; in Africa, the attempts by Katangan rebels, Biafran secessionists, Eritrean separatists, and Somalian and Morrocan irredentists to alter existing jurisdictions by force have to date not only been roundly condemned, but successfully resisted. Moreover, external powers that have been in a position to assist African claimant or expansionist states in their attempts at forced jurisdictional change have usually been loath to do so. For example, in 1977 the U.S.S.R. switched its military support from Somalia to Ethiopia when the Somalis seized Ethiopian territory by force. The Ethiopian army did not invade Somalia after it had expulsed the Somali forces from Ethiopia's Ogaden region (with major Cuban as well as Soviet assistance). When external powers have intervened in Africa, they have usually respected existing state jurisdictions: most such interventions were in response to solicitations by African governments or revolutionary movements fighting against colonial or white minority regimes.

The rare interventions in independent African states that were not

uncertain whether the Sahrawi Democratic Republic (SADR) was as yet a legal member of the organization. See "The OAU's Sahara Crisis," *West Africa*, March 8, 1982, p. 639.

solicited by a sovereign government, and thus did not respect existing state jurisdicitons, can—with two exceptions involving France—be explained by the intervening power's status as an international outcast. In southern Africa, there have been numerous armed intrusions by the South African army into Angola to destroy, harass, or contain forces of the South West Africa People's Organization (SWAPO), and at least one dramatic raid into Mozambique to punish or destroy anti-apartheid movements in their sanctuaries. They can be accounted for by Pretoria's outcast status and preoccupation with political survival. The military interventions by the Rhodesian armed forces into Zambia and Mozambique toward the end of the Rhodesian conflict can be understood in similar terms, as can the 1970 raid by Portuguese soldiers and African collaborators on Conakry, the capital of independent Guinea. The only interventions that cannot be explained in this way were made by France: in Gabon (1964) to restore a regime that had been overthrown, and in the Central African Republic (1979) to overthrow a government and impose a new regime. In the first case, France had entered into an international agreement to protect the M'Ba government; in the second, it appears that other African states had given their tacit consent to the action, and may even have solicited it.

Conclusion

We have argued that juridical statehood is more important than empirical statehood in accounting for the persistence of states in Black Africa. International organizations have served as "post-imperial ordering devices" for the new African states,[45] in effect freezing them in their inherited colonial jurisdictions and blocking any post-independence movements toward self-determination. So far, they have successfully outlawed force as a method of producing new states in Africa.

Membership in the international society provides an opportunity—denied to Black Africa under colonialism—to both influence and take advantage of international rules and ideologies concerning what is desirable and undesirable in the relations of states. The impact of Third World states on those rules and ideologies is likely to increase as the new statesmen learn how to take advantage of international democracy. They have already been successful in influencing the creation of some new ideologies. For example, the efforts of the Third World have led

[45] Peter Lyon, "New States and International Order," in Alan James, ed., *The Bases of International Order: Essays in Honour of C.A.W. Manning* (London: Oxford University Press, 1973), 47.

to the formation of the North-South dialogue which would legitimate an international theory of morality based on assumptions of social justice that have heretofore been largely confined to internal politics.[46] The states of the South—supported by some Northern statesmen—have asserted a moral claim on the actions and resources of the North; international society is not only being subjected to demands for peace, order, and security, but for international social justice as well. This radical new development in international relations is associated with the emergence of the Third World. If it succeeds, a revolutionary change in international morality will have been brought about.

The global international society whose most important institutions have been established or expanded since the end of World War II has been generally successful in supporting the new state jurisdictions of independent Africa; thus, the survival of Africa's existing states is largely an international achievement. Still, international effects on empirical statehood are ambiguous. International society has legitimated and fostered the transfer of goods, services, technology, skills, and the like from rich to poor countries with the intention of contributing to the development of the latter. But there are definite limits to what international society can contribute to the further development of the capabilities of African states. A society of states that exists chiefly in order to maintain the existing state system and the independence and survival of its members cannot regulate the internal affairs of members without the consent of their governments. It is therefore limited in its ability to determine that the resources transferred to the new states are effectively and properly used. In spite of a strong desire to do so, there is no way to guarantee such transfers against the wishes of a sovereign government without interfering in its internal affairs. Consequently, the enforcement of state jurisdictions may be at odds with the effort to develop the empirical state in Africa and elsewhere in the Third World. By enforcing juridical statehood, international society is in some cases also sustaining and perpetuating incompetent and corrupt governments. Perhaps the best example in sub-Saharan Africa is the international support that has gone into ensuring the survival of the corrupt government of Zaire. If this relationship is not an uncommon one, we must conclude that international society is at least partly responsible for perpetuating the underdevelopment of the empirical state in Africa by

---

[46] Independent Commission on International Development Issues, *North-South, a Programme for Survival* (Cambridge: MIT Press, 1980); Roger Hansen, *Beyond the North-South Stalemate* (New York: McGraw-Hill, 1979); Robert L. Rothstein, *Global Bargaining: UNCTAD and the Quest for a New Economic Order* (Princeton: Princeton University Press), 1979.

providing resources to incompetent or corrupt governments without being permitted to ensure that these resources are effectively and properly used.

State-building theories which assume that empirical statehood is more fundamental than juridical statehood, and that the internal is prior to the international in state formation and survival, are at odds with contemporary African experience. To study Black Africa's states from the internal perspective of political sociology is to assume that the state-building process here is basically the same as it was in Europe (where the political sociology of the modern state largely developed). In Europe, empirical statehood preceded juridical statehood or was concurrent with it,[47] and the formation of modern states preceded (and later accompanied) the emergence of a state system. European statesmen created jurisdictions over the course of several centuries in Machiavellian fashion—by dominating internal rivals and competing with external rivals—until the international system had attained its present-day jurisdictions.[48] However, as Tilly points out: "The later the state-making experience . . . the less likely . . . internal processes . . . are to provide an adequate explanation of the formation, survival or growth of a state."[49] In Black Africa (and, by implication, in other regions of the Third World), external factors are more likely than internal factors to provide an adequate explanation of the formation and persistence of states. State jurisdictions and international society, which once were consequences of the success and survival of states, today are more likely to be conditions.

Arnold Wolfers pointed out that in the Anglo-American conceptualization of the international system versus the nation-state, the most persistent image has been one of international discord versus internal order and civility.[50] In contemporary Black Africa, an image of international accord and civility and internal disorder and violence would be more accurate. At the level of international society, a framework of

---

[47] Charles H. McIlwain has noted that "Independence *de facto* was ultimately translated into a sovereignty *de jure*." Quoted by John H. Herz, "Rise and Demise of the Territorial State," in Heinz Lubasz, ed., *The Development of the Modern State* (New York: Macmillan, 1964), 133.

[48] See Wight (fn. 28), chaps. 1 and 2.

[49] Charles Tilly, ed., *The Formation of National States in Western Europe* (Princeton: Princeton University Press, 1975), 46. Unfortunately, Tilly tends to neglect the international dimension of European state making. For two excellent essays on this topic, see Martin Wight, "The Origins of Our States-System: Geographical Limits," and "The Origins of Our States-System: Chronological Limits" (fn. 33, 110-52).

[50] "Political Theory and International Relations," in Wolfers, *Discord and Collaboration: Essays on International Politics* (Baltimore and London: The Johns Hopkins University Press, 1965), 239-40.

rules and conventions governing the relations of the states in the region has been founded and sustained for almost two decades. But far less institutionalization and political order has been evident during this period at the level of national society: many African countries have been experiencing internal political violence and some internal warfare. Insofar as our theoretical images follow rather than precede concrete historical change, it is evident that the recent national and international history of Black Africa challenges more than it supports some of the major postulates of international relations theory.

Books Written Under the Auspices of
CENTER OF INTERNATIONAL STUDIES
PRINCETON UNIVERSITY
1952-85

Gabriel A. Almond, *The Appeals of Communism* (Princeton University Press 1954)

William W. Kaufmann, ed., *Military Policy and National Security* (Princeton University Press 1956)

Klaus Knorr, *The War Potential of Nations* (Princeton University Press 1956)

Lucian W. Pye, *Guerrilla Communism in Malaya* (Princeton University Press 1956)

Charles De Visscher, *Theory and Reality in Public International Law*, trans. by P. E. Corbett (Princeton University Press 1957; rev. ed. 1968)

Bernard C. Cohen, *The Political Process and Foreign Policy: The Making of the Japanese Peace Settlement* (Princeton University Press 1957)

Myron Weiner, *Party Politics in India: The Development of a Multi-Party System* (Princeton University Press 1957)

Percy E. Corbett, *Law in Diplomacy* (Princeton University Press 1959)

Rolf Sannwald and Jacques Stohler, *Economic Integration: Theoretical Assumptions and Consequences of European Unification*, trans. by Herman Karreman (Princeton University Press 1959)

Klaus Knorr, ed., *NATO and American Security* (Princeton University Press 1959)

Gabriel A. Almond and James S. Coleman, eds., *The Politics of the Developing Areas* (Princeton University Press 1960)

Herman Kahn, *On Thermonuclear War* (Princeton University Press 1960)

Sidney Verba, *Small Groups and Political Behavior: A Study of Leadership* (Princeton University Press 1961)

Robert J. C. Butow, *Tojo and the Coming of the War* (Princeton University Press 1961)

Glenn H. Snyder, *Deterrence and Defense: Toward a Theory of National Security* (Princeton University Press 1961)

Klaus Knorr and Sidney Verba, eds., *The International System: Theoretical Essays* (Princeton University Press 1961)

Peter Paret and John W. Shy, *Guerrillas in the 1960's* (Praeger 1962)

George Modelski, *A Theory of Foreign Policy* (Praeger 1962)

Klaus Knorr and Thornton Read, eds., *Limited Strategic War* (Praeger 1963)

Frederick S. Dunn, *Peace-Making and the Settlement with Japan* (Princeton University Press 1963)

Arthur L. Burns and Nina Heathcote, *Peace-Keeping by United Nations Forces* (Praeger 1963)

Richard A. Falk, *Law, Morality, and War in the Contemporary World* (Praeger 1963)

James N. Rosenau, *National Leadership and Foreign Policy: A Case Study in the Mobilization of Public Support* (Princeton University Press 1963)

Gabriel A. Almond and Sidney Verba, *The Civic Culture: Political Attitudes and Democracy in Five Nations* (Princeton University Press 1963)

Bernard C. Cohen, *The Press and Foreign Policy* (Princeton University Press 1963)

Richard L. Sklar, *Nigerian Political Parties: Power in an Emergent African Nation* (Princeton University Press 1963)

Peter Paret, *French Revolutionary Warfare from Indochina to Algeria: The Analysis of a Political and Military Doctrine* (Praeger 1964)

Harry Eckstein, ed., *Internal War: Problems and Approaches* (Free Press 1964)

Cyril E. Black and Thomas P. Thornton, eds., *Communism and Revolution: The Strategic Uses of Political Violence* (Princeton University Press 1964)

Miriam Camps, *Britain and the European Community 1955-1963* (Princeton University Press 1964)

Thomas P. Thornton, ed., *The Third World in Soviet Perspective: Studies by Soviet Writers on the Developing Areas* (Princeton University Press 1964)

James N. Rosenau, ed., *International Aspects of Civil Strife* (Princeton University Press 1964)

Sidney I. Ploss, *Conflict and Decision-Making in Soviet Russia: A Case Study of Agricultural Policy, 1953-1963* (Princeton University Press 1965)

Richard A. Falk and Richard J. Barnet, eds., *Security in Disarmament* (Princeton University Press 1965)

Karl von Vorys, *Political Development in Pakistan* (Princeton University Press 1965)

Harold and Margaret Sprout, *The Ecological Perspective on Human Affairs, With Special Reference to International Politics* (Princeton University Press 1965)

Klaus Knorr, *On the Uses of Military Power in the Nuclear Age* (Princeton University Press 1966)

Harry Eckstein, *Division and Cohesion in Democracy: A Study of Norway* (Princeton University Press 1966)

Cyril E. Black, *The Dynamics of Modernization: A Study in Comparative History* (Harper and Row 1966)

Peter Kunstadter, ed., *Southeast Asian Tribes, Minorities, and Nations* (Princeton University Press 1967)

E. Victor Wolfenstein, *The Revolutionary Personality: Lenin, Trotsky, Gandhi* (Princeton University Press 1967)

Leon Gordenker, *The UN Secretary-General and the Maintenance of Peace* (Columbia University Press 1967)

Oran R. Young, *The Intermediaries: Third Parties in International Crises* (Princeton University Press 1967)

James N. Rosenau, ed., *Domestic Sources of Foreign Policy* (Free Press 1967)

Richard F. Hamilton, *Affluence and the French Worker in the Fourth Republic* (Princeton University Press 1967)

Linda B. Miller, *World Order and Local Disorder: The United Nations and Internal Conflicts* (Princeton University Press 1967)

Henry Bienen, *Tanzania: Party Transformation and Economic Development* (Princeton University Press 1967)

Wolfram F. Hanrieder, *West German Foreign Policy, 1949-1963: International Pressures and Domestic Response* (Stanford University Press 1967)

Richard H. Ullman, *Britain and the Russian Civil War: November 1918-February 1920* (Princeton University Press 1968)

Robert Gilpin, *France in the Age of the Scientific State* (Princeton University Press 1968)

William B. Bader, *The United States and the Spread of Nuclear Weapons* (Pegasus 1968)

Richard A. Falk, *Legal Order in a Violent World* (Princeton University Press 1968)

Cyril E. Black, Richard A. Falk, Klaus Knorr and Oran R. Young, *Neutralization and World Politics* (Princeton University Press 1968)

Oran R. Young, *The Politics of Force: Bargaining During International Crises* (Princeton University Press 1969)

Klaus Knorr and James N. Rosenau, eds., *Contending Approaches to International Politics* (Princeton University Press 1969)

James N. Rosenau, ed., *Linkage Politics: Essays on the Convergence of National and International Systems* (Free Press 1969)

John T. McAlister, Jr., *Viet Nam: The Origins of Revolution* (Knopf 1969)

Jean Edward Smith, *Germany Beyond the Wall: People, Politics and Prosperity* (Little, Brown 1969)

James Barros, *Betrayal from Within: Joseph Avenol, Secretary-General of the League of Nations, 1933-1940* (Yale University Press 1969)

Charles Hermann, *Crises in Foreign Policy: A Simulation Analysis* (Bobbs-Merrill 1969)

Robert C. Tucker, *The Marxian Revolutionary Idea: Essays on Marxist Thought and Its Impact on Radical Movements* (W. W. Norton 1969)

Harvey Waterman, *Political Change in Contemporary France: The Politics of an Industrial Democracy* (Charles E. Merrill 1969)

Cyril E. Black and Richard A. Falk, eds., *The Future of the International Legal Order*. Vol. I: *Trends and Patterns* (Princeton University Press 1969)

Ted Robert Gurr, *Why Men Rebel* (Princeton University Press 1969)

C. Sylvester Whitaker, *The Politics of Tradition: Continuity and Change in Northern Nigeria 1946-1966* (Princeton University Press 1970)

Richard A. Falk, *The Status of Law in International Society* (Princeton University Press 1970)

John T. McAlister, Jr. and Paul Mus, *The Vietnamese and Their Revolution* (Harper & Row 1970)

Klaus Knorr, *Military Power and Potential* (D. C. Heath 1970)

Cyril E. Black and Richard A. Falk, eds., *The Future of the International Legal Order*. Vol. II: *Wealth and Resources* (Princeton University Press 1970)

Leon Gordenker, ed., *The United Nations in International Politics* (Princeton University Press 1971)

Cyril E. Black and Richard A. Falk, eds., *The Future of the International Legal Order*. Vol. III: *Conflict Management* (Princeton University Press 1971)

Francine R. Frankel, *India's Green Revolution: Economic Gains and Political Costs* (Princeton University Press 1971)

Harold and Margaret Sprout, *Toward a Politics of the Planet Earth* (Van Nostrand Reinhold Co. 1971)

Cyril E. Black and Richard A. Falk, eds., *The Future of the International Legal Order*. Vol. IV: *The Structure of the International Environment* (Princeton University Press 1972)

Gerald Garvey, *Energy, Ecology, Economy* (W. W. Norton 1972)

Richard H. Ullman, *The Anglo-Soviet Accord* (Princeton University Press 1973)

Klaus Knorr, *Power and Wealth: The Political Economy of International Power* (Basic Books 1973)

Anton Bebler, *Military Rule in Africa: Dahomey, Ghana, Sierra Leone, and Mali* (Praeger Publishers 1973)

Robert C. Tucker, *Stalin as Revolutionary 1879-1929: A Study in History and Personality* (W. W. Norton 1973)

Edward L. Morse, *Foreign Policy and Interdependence in Gaullist France* (Princeton University Press 1973)

Henry Bienen, *Kenya: The Politics of Participation and Control* (Princeton University Press 1974)

Gregory J. Massell, *The Surrogate Proletariat: Moslem Women and Revolutionary Strategies in Soviet Central Asia, 1919-1929* (Princeton University Press 1974)

James N. Rosenau, *Citizenship Between Elections: An Inquiry Into The Mobilizable American* (Free Press 1974)

Ervin Laszlo, *A Strategy for the Future: The Systems Approach to World Order* (George Braziller 1974)

R. J. Vincent, *Nonintervention and International Order* (Princeton University Press 1974)

Jan H. Kalicki, *The Pattern of Sino-American Crises: Political-Military Interactions in the 1950s* (Cambridge University Press 1975)

Klaus Knorr, *The Power of Nations: The Political Economy of International Relations* (Basic Books, Inc. 1975)

James P. Sewell, *UNESCO and World Politics: Engaging in International Relations* (Princeton University Press 1975)

Richard A. Falk, *A Global Approach to National Policy* (Harvard University Press 1975)

Harry Eckstein and Ted Robert Gurr, *Patterns of Authority: A Structural Basis for Political Inquiry* (John Wiley & Sons 1975)

Cyril E. Black, Marius B. Jansen, Herbert S. Levine, Marion J. Levy, Jr., Henry Rosovsky, Gilbert Rozman, Henry D. Smith, II, and S. Frederick Starr, *The Modernization of Japan and Russia* (Free Press 1975)

Leon Gordenker, *International Aid and National Decisions: Development Programs in Malawi, Tanzania, and Zambia* (Princeton University Press 1976)

Carl von Clausewitz, *On War*, edited and translated by Michael Howard and Peter Paret (Princeton University Press 1976)

Gerald Garvey and Lou Ann Garvey, *International Resource Flows* (D. C. Heath 1977)

Walter F. Murphy and Joseph Tanenhaus, *Comparative Constitutional Law: Cases and Commentaries* (St. Martin's Press 1977)

Gerald Garvey, *Nuclear Power and Social Planning: The City of the Second Sun* (D. C. Heath 1977)

Richard E. Bissell, *Apartheid and International Organizations* (Westview Press 1977)

David P. Forsythe, *Humanitarian Politics: The International Committee of the Red Cross* (Johns Hopkins University Press 1977)

Paul E. Sigmund, *The Overthrow of Allende and the Politics of Chile, 1964-1976* (University of Pittsburgh Press 1977)

Henry S. Bienen, *Armies and Parties in Africa* (Holmes and Meier 1978)

Harold and Margaret Sprout, *The Context of Environmental Politics: Unfinished Business for America's Third Century* (University Press of Kentucky 1978)

Samuel S. Kim, *China, The United Nations, and World Order* (Princeton University Press 1979)

S. Basheer Ahmed, *Nuclear Fuel and Energy* (D.C. Heath 1979)

Robert C. Johansen, *The National Interest and the Human Interest: An Analysis of U.S. Foreign Policy* (Princeton University Press 1980)

Richard A. Falk and Samuel S. Kim, eds., *The War System: An Interdisciplinary Approach* (Westview Press 1980).

James H. Billington, *Fire in the Minds of Men: Origins of the Revolutionary Faith* (Basic Books 1980)

Bennett Ramberg, *Destruction of Nuclear Energy Facilities in War: The Problem and the Implications* (D. C. Heath 1980)

Gregory T. Kruglak, *The Politics of United States Decision-Making in United Nations Specialized Agencies: The Case of the International Labor Organization* (University Press of America 1980)

W. P. Davison and Leon Gordenker, eds., *Resolving Nationality Conflicts: The Role of Public Opinion Research* (Praeger Publishers 1980)

James C. Hsiung and Samuel S. Kim, eds., *China in the Global Community* (Praeger Publishers 1980)

Douglas Kinnard, *The Secretary of Defense* (University Press of Kentucky 1980)

Richard Falk, *Human Rights and State Sovereignty* (Holmes & Meier 1981)

James H. Mittelman, *Underdevelopment and the Transition to Socialism: Mozambique and Tanzania* (Academic Press 1981)

Gilbert Rozman, ed., *The Modernization of China* (The Free Press 1981)

Robert C. Tucker, *Politics as Leadership.* The Paul Anthony Brick Lectures. Eleventh Series (University of Missouri Press 1981)

Robert Gilpin, *War and Change in World Politics* (Cambridge University Press 1981)

Nicholas G. Onuf, ed., *Law-Making in the Global Community* (Carolina Academic Press 1982)

Ali E. Hillal Dessouki, ed., *Islamic Resurgence in the Arab World* (Praeger Publishers 1981)

Richard Falk, *The End of World Order* (Holmes & Meier 1983)

Klaus Knorr, ed., *Power, Strategy, and Security* (Princeton University Press 1983)

Finn Laursen, *Superpower at Sea* (Praeger 1983)

Samuel S. Kim, *The Quest for a Just World Order* (Westview Press 1984)

Gerald Garvey, *Strategy and the Defense Dilemma* (D.C. Heath 1984)

Peter R. Baehr and Leon Gordenker, *The United Nations: Reality and Ideal* (Praeger Publishers 1984)

Joseph M. Grieco, *Between Dependency and Autonomy: India's Experience with the International Computer Industry* (University of California Press 1984)

Jan Hallenberg, *Foreign Policy Change: United States Foreign Policy Toward the Soviet Union and the People's Republic of China, 1961-1980* (University of Stockholm 1984)

Michael Krepon, *Strategic Stalemate: Nuclear Weapons and Arms control in American Politics* (New York: St. Martin's Press 1984)

Gilbert Rozman, *A Mirror for Socialism: Soviet Criticisms of China* (Princeton University Press 1985)

Henry Bienen, *Political Conflict and Economic Change in Nigeria* (London: Frank Cass 1985)

Library of Congress Cataloging-in-Publication Data

The State and development in the third world.

(World politics reader)
"Essays collected . . . were published in World politics between 1976 and 1984"—Introd.
Includes bibliographies.
1. Developing countries—Politics and government. 2. Political stability—Developing
countries. 3. Developing countries—Economic policy.
I. Kohli, Atul. II. World politics. III. Series.
JF60.S69 1986   320.9172′4   86-5045
ISBN 0-691-07699-5
ISBN 0-691-02245-3 (pbk.)